2

WESTMINSTER ABBEY.

HISTORY

OF

ENGLISH LITERATURE

BY

REUBEN POST HALLECK, M.A. (YALE)

17145

NEW YORK ·:· CINCINNATI ·:· CHICAGO

AMERICAN BOOK COMPANY

PREFACE

In the following pages the author aims to furnish a concise and interesting text-book of the history and development of English literature from the earliest times to the present. Especial attention is paid to literary movements, to the essential qualities which differentiate one period from another, and to showing the animating spirit of each age. It is more important to understand the relation of the age of Pope to that of Wordsworth than to know these two writers merely as individuals. It is better for the student to catch the general drift of literary thought than to study a large number of comparatively unimportant authors and to ignore the law of the survival of the fittest. The majority of people never have time for the study of any but the masters. Such people need a guide to tell them what to select from each age, just as much as travelers in England require a guidebook to indicate the most interesting places.

The writer has made no attempt to minimize the study of authors as individuals. One of the features of this work consists in devoting a special section to summing up the general characteristics of each of the greatest individual authors. The theory that it is wise to teach the general before the special is now happily going out of fashion. But the moment we know two authors we ought to begin to compare them, to note their likeness and their difference. For the cultivation of the thinking powers, the study of the development of English literature may be made as serviceable as mathematics. The individuality and general characteristics of one author present themselves in sharpest outline only in comparison with those of another author. For instance, Spenser's subjective cast of mind will impress the student more forcibly when contrasted with Chaucer's objective method of regarding the world (see pp. 130–132).

During a long period of teaching English literature and of superintending the instruction of others in that branch, the author has repeatedly found that pupils who have not had consecutive instruction in the history of English literature have the most vague ideas of its development and of the relation of its parts. Various masterpieces seem like unconnected islands in an unexplored ocean. There is no way of making these masterpieces seem otherwise except by teaching the history and development of the literature of which they form a part. Mental association is based primarily on contiguity. Ideas must be grasped by the mind at the same time before they can be known to be related. It is difficult for young minds to knit into one fabric ideas which are presented at considerable intervals and under associations so different as occur in the study of various masterpieces.

In so far as the limits of his space would allow, the author has endeavored to justify his criticisms by quotations that show the characteristics attributed to authors. Since it is the object of this work to enable students to read English literature for themselves more intelligently, there have been indicated at the end of each chapter definite *Required Readings* from the works of the authors discussed. To guard against discouraging students, the writer has tried to call for no more than they may be

expected to read as they study this work. There have also been added questions which, it is hoped, will stimulate pupils to do some original thinking and to make a comparison of different ages and representative authors.

The optional list of *Works for Consultation and Further Study* has been prepared to guide those who wish to make a more extended study of certain periods and authors. A *Supplementary List of Minor Authors and their Chief Works* is given on pp. 485–491 for the purpose of aiding those who wish to read the best work of minor authors, as well as for the purpose of serving for convenient reference.

On account of the extent of the field to be covered, the treatment of American literature is left to works dealing especially with that branch.

The pronunciation of difficult names is indicated sufficiently in the index.

The student should refer to the *Literary Map of England*, pp. 8, 9, to familiarize himself with the location of the birthplaces and homes of eminent authors. Whenever he reads of the Quantock Hills or of the Lake District, of the *Exeter Book* or of Stoke Poges churchyard, he ought immediately to turn to the map to find the place indicated.

While the writer owes much to the great masters of criticism, he has written this work only after long and careful original study of the authors under discussion. From one source he has received such valuable assistance as to demand emphatic mention. During three years of the time in which this work has been in preparation, he has had the constant assistance of his wife, a critical student of English literature. To her is due the entire treatment of certain authors in periods that she has made the subject of special study.

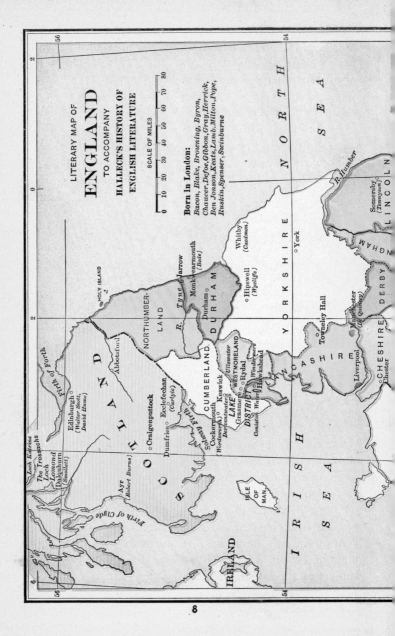

LITERARY MAP OF

ENGLAND

TO ACCOMPANY

HALLECK'S HISTORY OF
ENGLISH LITERATURE

SCALE OF MILES

0 10 20 30 40 50 60 70 80

Born in London:

Bacon, Blake, Browning, Byron,
Chaucer, Defoe, Gibbon, Gray, Herrick,
Ben Jonson, Keats, Lamb, Milton, Pope,
Ruskin, Spenser, Swinburne

NORTH SEA

IRISH SEA

IRELAND

ISLE OF MAN

SCOTLAND

Loch Katrine
The Trosachs
Loch Lomond
Dalquhurn
(*Smollett*)

Ayr
(*Robert Burns*)

Firth of Clyde

Firth of Forth

Edinburgh
(*Walter Scott,*
David Hume)

Abbotsford

Craigenputtock

Ecclefechan
(*Carlyle*)

Dumfries

Solway Firth

HOLY ISLAND

NORTHUMBER-
LAND

R. Tyne

Jarrow

Monkwearmouth
(*Bede*)

DURHAM

Durham

Cockermouth
(*Wordsworth*)

Derwentwater

Keswick

CUMBERLAND

Grasmere

Rydal

LAKE
DISTRICT

WESTMORELAND

Ulleswater

Windermere

Coniston Water

Hawkshead

Hipswell
(*Wycliffe*)

Whitby
(*Caedmon*)

York

YORKSHIRE

LANCASHIRE

Towneley Hall

Liverpool

Manchester
(*De Quincey*)

CHESHIRE

Chester

DERBY

NGHAM

LINCOLN

Somersby
(*Tennyson*)

R. Humber

8

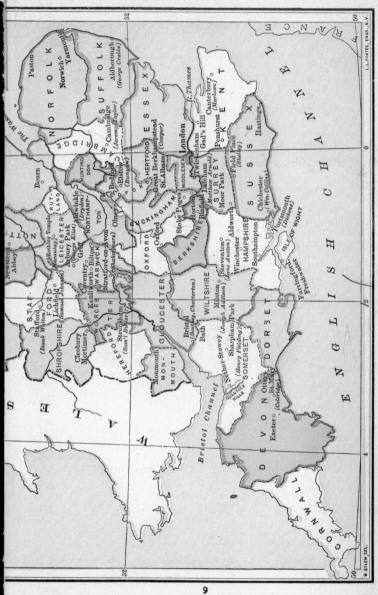

CONTENTS

HISTORY OF ENGLISH LITERATURE

CHAPTER I

FROM 449 A.D. TO THE NORMAN CONQUEST, 1066

The Subject Matter. — The history of English literature is a record of the best thoughts that have been expressed in the English language. Literature appeals especially to the imagination and the emotions. Literature aims not so much to state a fact after the manner of a text-book on science as to start imaginative activity and to appeal to the emotions. When Macbeth says of the dead King : —

> " After life's fitful fever he sleeps well,"

our feelings are touched and the door is opened for imaginative activity, as we wonder why life is called a fitful fever and try to realize the mystery of that long and restful sleep. True literature calls for such activity.

If we would broaden ourselves and increase our capacity for appreciating the manifold sides of the life of the spirit, we must become familiar with the thoughts and ideals of those who have given us our inspiring literature. For nearly fifteen hundred years the Anglo-Saxon race has been producing the greatest of all literatures. The most boastful of other nations make no claim to having a Shakespeare on the list of their immortals.

The Home and Migrations of the Anglo-Saxon Race. — Just as there was a time when no Anglo-Saxon foot had touched the shores of America, so there was a period when the ancestors of the English lived far away from the British Isles, and were rightly looked upon as foreigners there. For nearly four hundred years prior to the coming of the English, Britain had been a Roman province.   In 410 A.D. the Romans withdrew their legions from Britain to protect Rome herself against swarms of Teutonic invaders. About 449 a band of Teutons, called Jutes, left Denmark, landed on the Isle of Thanet (northeastern part of Kent), and began the conquest of Britain.   Warriors from the tribes of the Angles and the Saxons soon followed, and drove westward the original inhabitants, the Britons or Welsh, *i.e.* foreigners, as the Teutons styled the natives.

Before the invasion of Britain, the Teutons inhabited the central part of Europe as far south as the Rhine, a tract which in a large measure coincides with modern Germany.   The Jutes, Angles, and Saxons were different tribes of Teutons.   These ancestors of the English dwelt in Denmark and in the lands extending southward along the North Sea.

The Angles, an important Teutonic tribe, furnished the name for the new home, which was called Angle-land, afterward shortened into England.   The language spoken by these tribes is generally called Anglo-Saxon or Saxon.

The Training of the Race. — The climate is a potent factor in determining the vigor and characteristics of a race. Nature had reared the Teuton like a wise but not indulgent parent.   By every method known to her, she endeavored to render him fit to colonize and sway the world. Summer paid him but a brief visit.   His companions were the frost, the fluttering snowflake, the stinging hail.   For music, instead of the soft notes of a shepherd's pipe under blue Italian or Grecian skies, he listened to the north wind whistling among the bare branches, or to the roar of an angry northern sea upon the bleak coast.

The feeble could not withstand the rigor of such a climate in the absence of the comforts of civilization. Only the strongest in each generation survived; and these transmitted to their children increasing vigor. Warfare was incessant, not only with nature but also with the surrounding tribes. Nature kept the Teuton in such a school until he seemed fit to colonize the world, and to produce a literature which would appeal to humanity in every age.

The Early Teutonic Religion. — Our ancestors were heathen for some time after they came to England. Their principal deity was Woden, the All-father, from whom Wednesday is named. Thunor, the invincible god of thunder, has also given his name to a day of the week. In the old Norse mythology, to which the old Teutonic religions are closely allied, heaven was called Valhal. Woden's daughters were called Valkyries, and it was their mission to ride their cloudlike steeds over earthly battlefields, to note the bravest warriors, and to conduct to Valhal such as were selected to fall. Death while courageously fighting on the battlefield made the hero sure of being taken to Valhal to become Woden's guest. There at the table of the gods, the warrior ate of the flesh of the magic boar, drank from a river of ale, and indulged to his heart's content in the sword game. This old Norse religion was instinct with a gloomy fatalism. Upon Valhal and the throng of heroes whom Woden summoned to help him fight his foes, could be seen a ravenlike shadow, growing ever larger and threatening to wrap all in lasting darkness. Loki, the spirit of evil, was fated to break his chains, and he, with the life-destroying giants of the frost, would devour the very gods.

We cannot say exactly how much of this belief was held by our ancestors in England. They certainly worshiped some gods of the same names and were imbued with the same fatalism. In *Beowulf* there is allusion to Wyrd (fate), and the web of destiny is mentioned in several old poems.

Somber Cast of the Teutonic Mind. — The early religious beliefs of the Teuton received their gloomy coloring from the rigor of nature's forces, from the frost giants with whom he battled. The winter twilight fell upon him in his northern home about three o'clock in the afternoon. During the long evenings he would often think how the world had promised him much and given him little, and the gloom of this life would cast its shadow upon the next. Even in summer days, his leaden sky was often obscured with rain clouds driven by the restless winds. In wintry nights the hours would drag wearily as he listened to the hail or heard the half-human moaning of the fir trees.

We must remember this cast of the Teutonic mind in order to understand its literature. We find Shakespeare likening life to a fitful fever, and considering the gloomy problem of existence in the person of Hamlet. We listen to Gray, singing that everything we prize "awaits alike the inevitable hour"; to Burns, comparing pleasure to a snowflake falling in the river; to Poe, singing the melancholy song of the *Raven;* to Tennyson, sighing: —

> " He will not hear the north wind rave,
> Nor, moaning, household shelter crave
> From winter rains that beat his grave." [1]

The Anglo-Saxon Language. — Our oldest English liter-

[1] *The Two Voices.*

ature is written in the language spoken by the Angles and the Saxons. This at first sight looks like a strange tongue to one conversant with modern English only; but the language that we employ to-day has the framework, the bone and sinew, of the earlier tongue. Modern English is no more unlike Anglo-Saxon than a bearded man is unlike his former childish self. A few examples will show the likeness and the difference. "The noble queen" would in Anglo-Saxon be *sēo æðele cwēn;* "the noble queen's," *ðære æðelan cwēne. Sēo* is the nominative feminine singular, *ðære* the genitive, of the definite article. The adjective and the noun also change their forms with the varying cases. In its inflections Anglo-Saxon resembles its sister language, the modern German.

After the first feeling of strangeness has passed away, it is easy to recognize many of the old words. Take, for instance, this from *Beowulf:* —

> ". . . ðy hē ðone fēond ofercwōm,
> gehnægde helle gāst."

Here are eight words, apparently strange, but even a novice soon recognizes five of them: *hē, fēond* (fiend), *ofercwōm* (overcame), *helle* (hell), *gāst* (ghost). The word *ðone,* strange as it looks, is merely the article "the."

> . . . therefore he overcame the fiend,
> Subdued the ghost of hell.

Let us take from the same poem another passage, containing the famous simile: —

> ". . . lēoht inne stōd,
> efne swā of hefene hādre scīneð
> rodores candel."

Of these eleven words, seven may be recognized: *lēoht*

(light), *inne* (in), *stōd* (stood), *of*, *hefene* (heaven), *scīneð* (shineth), *candel* (candle).

> . . . a light stood within,
> Even so from heaven serenely shineth
> The firmament's candle.

Some object to using the term "Anglo-Saxon," and insist on substituting "Old English," because it might otherwise be thought that modern English is a different language and not merely a growth. They might with equal justice claim that "grown boy" should be used in place of a new term "man," to emphasize the fact that the boy, who has grown into a man, is still the same person.

Earliest Anglo-Saxon Literature. — As in the case of the Greeks and Romans, poetry afforded the first outlet for the feelings of the Teutonic race. The first productions were handed down by memory. Poetry is easily memorized and naturally lends itself to singing and musical accompaniment. Under such circumstances, even prose would speedily fall into metrical form. In addition to these reasons, poetry is the most suitable vehicle of expression for the emotions. Unlike modern writers, the ancients seldom undertook to make literature unless they felt so deeply that silence was impossible.

The Form of Anglo-Saxon Poetry. — Each line is divided into two parts by a major pause. Because each of these parts was often printed as a complete line in old texts, *Beowulf* has sometimes been called a poem of 6368 lines, although it has but 3184.

A striking characteristic of Anglo-Saxon poetry is consonantal alliteration, that is, the repetition of the same consonant at the beginning of words in the same line : —

> "Grendel gongan; Godes yrre bær."
> Grendel going   ; God's anger bare.

The usual type of Anglo-Saxon poetry has two alliterations in the first half of the line and one in the second. The lines vary considerably in the number of syllables. The line from *Beowulf* quoted just above has nine syllables. The following line from the same poem has eleven: —

> " Flota   fāmig-heals,   fugle   gelīcost."
> The floater foamy-necked, to a fowl most like.

This line, also from *Beowulf*, has eight syllables : —

> " Nīpende niht,   and norðan   wind."
> Noisome night, and northern wind.

Vowel alliteration is less common. Where this is employed, the vowels are generally different, as is shown in the principal words of the following line : —

> " On ēad,   on æht,   on eorcan   stān."
> On wealth, on goods, on precious stone.

End rhyme is uncommon, but we must beware of thinking that there is no rhythm, for that is a pronounced characteristic. Anglo-Saxon verse was intended to be sung, and hence a fixed number of beats was necessary. There are normally four accents in each line, two in the first half and two in the second. In the first half, the two alliterative syllables are accented ; in the second, besides the alliterative syllable, the word corresponding to the most important idea is accented. It should also be observed that alliteration seldom falls on any but the most important words.

The Manuscripts that have handed down Anglo-Saxon Literature. — The earliest Anglo-Saxon poetry was transmitted by the memories of men. Finally, with the slow growth of learning, a few acquired the art of writing, and transcribed on parchment a small portion of the current songs. The introduction of Christianity ushered in prose translations and a few original compositions, which were taken down on parchment and kept in the monasteries.

The study of Anglo-Saxon literature is comparatively recent, for its treasures have not been long accessible. Its most famous poem, *Beowulf*, was not discovered until the close of the eighteenth century. In 1822 Dr. Blume, a German professor of law, happened to find in a monastery at Vercelli, Italy, a large volume of Anglo-Saxon manuscript, containing a number of fine poems and twenty-two sermons. This is now known as the *Vercelli Book*. No one knows how it happened to reach Italy. Another large

EXETER CATHEDRAL

parchment volume of poems and miscellany was deposited by Bishop Leofric at the cathedral of Exeter in Devonshire, about 1050 A.D. This collection is now called the *Exeter Book*, and it is still one of the prized treasures of that cathedral.

Many valuable manuscripts were destroyed at the dissolution of the monasteries in the time of Henry VIII., between 1535 and 1540. John Bale, a contemporary writer, says that "those who purchased the monasteries reserved the books, some to scour their candlesticks, some to rub their boots, some they sold to the grocers and soap-sellers, and some they sent over sea to the bookbinders, not in small numbers, but at times whole ships full, to the wondering of foreign nations." Part of the valuable Anglo-Saxon poem *Waldhere* was discovered in 1860 on leaves of parchment which had been used in binding another book.

The Anglo-Saxon Scop and Gleeman.—Our earliest poetry was made current and kept fresh in memory by the singers. The kings and nobles often attached to them a *scop*, or maker of verses. When the warriors, after some victorious battle, were feasting at their long tables, the banquet was not complete without the songs of the *scop*. While the warriors ate the flesh of boar and deer, and warmed their blood with horns of foaming ale, the *scop*, standing where the blaze from a pile of logs disclosed to him the grizzly features of the men, sang his most stirring songs, often accompanying them with the music of a rude harp. As the feasters roused his enthusiasm with their applause, he would sometimes indulge in an outburst of eloquent extempore song. Not infrequently the imagination of some king or noble would be fired, and he would sing of his own great deeds.

We read in *Beowulf* that in Hrothgar's famous hall

> " . . . ðær wæs hearpan swēg,
> swutol sang scopes."

> . . . there was sound of harp,
> Loud the singing of the scop.

In addition to the *scop*, who was more or less permanently attached to the royal court or hall of noble, there was a craft of gleemen who roved from hall to hall. In the song of *Widsiŏ* we catch a glimpse of the life of a gleeman: —

> " Swā scriŏende gesceapum hweorfaŏ
> glēomen gumena geond grunda fela."

> Thus roving, with shapéd songs there wander
> The gleemen of the people through many lands.

The *scop* was an originator of poetry, the gleeman more often a mere repeater, although this distinction in the use of the terms was not observed in later times.

The Songs of Scop and Gleeman. — The subject matter of these songs was suggested by the most common experiences of the time. These were with war, the sea, and death.

The oldest Anglo-Saxon song known is called *Widsiŏ* or the *Far Traveler*, and it has been preserved in the *Exeter Book*. This song was probably composed in the older Angle-land on the continent, and brought to England in the memories of the singers. The poem is an account of the wanderings of a gleeman over a great part of Europe. Such a song will mean little to us unless we can imaginatively represent the circumstances under which it was sung, the long hall with its tables of feasting, drinking warriors, the firelight throwing weird shadows among the smoky rafters. The imagination of the warriors would be roused as similar experiences of their own were suggested by these lines in Widsiŏ's song: —

> " Ful oft of ŏām hēape hwīnende flēag
> giellende gār on grome ŏēode."

> Full oft from that host hissing flew
> The whistling spear on the fierce folk.

The gleeman ends this song with two thoughts characteristic of the poets of the Saxon race. He shows his love
for noble deeds, and he next thinks of the shortness of life,
as he sings: —

> "In mortal court his deeds are not unsung,
>   Such as a noble man will show to men,
>   Till all doth flit away, both life and light."

A greater *scop*, looking at life through Saxon eyes,
sings : —
> "We are such stuff
>   As dreams are made on; and our little life
>   Is rounded with a sleep." [1]

Another old song, also found in the *Exeter Book*, is the
Seafarer. We must imagine the *scop* recalling vivid experiences to our early ancestors with this song of the sea : —

> " Hail flew in hard showers,
>   And nothing I heard
>   But the wrath of the waters,
>   The icy-cold way ;
>   At times the swan's song ;
>   In the scream of the gannet
>   I sought for my joy,
>   In the moan of the sea whelp
>   For laughter of men,
>   In the song of the sea-mew
>   For drinking of mead." [2]

To show that love of the sea yet remains one of the
characteristics of English poetry, we may quote by way of
comparison a song sung more than a thousand years later,
in Victoria's reign : —

[1] Shakespeare: *The Tempest*, Act IV., scene 1.
[2] Morley's translation, *English Writers*, Vol. II., p. 21.

> " The wind is as iron that rings,
>   The foam heads loosen and flee;
>   It swells and welters and swings,
>   The pulse of the tide of the sea.
>
> " Let the wind shake our flag like a feather,
>   Like the plumes of the foam of the sea !
>   .   .   .   .
>   In the teeth of the hard glad weather,
>   In the blown wet face of the sea." [1]

Another song from the *Exeter Book* is called *The Fortunes of Men*. It gives vivid pictures of certain phases of life among the Anglo-Saxons. The notes of the harp must have sounded sad, as the *scop* sang : —

> " One shall sharp hunger slay;
>   One shall the storms beat down;
>   One be destroyed by darts,
>   One die in war.
>   One shall live losing
>   The light of his eyes,
>   Feel blindly with fingers;
>   And one lame of foot,
>   With sinew-wound wearily
>   Wasteth away,
>   Musing and mourning,
>   With death in his mind.
>   .   .   .   .
>   One shall die by the dagger,
>   In wrath, drenched with ale,
>   Wild through wine, on the mead bench,
>   Too swift with his words;
>   Too lightly his life
>   Shall the wretched one lose." [2]

The songs that we have noted are only a small fraction of *scopic* poetry, but they will, together with *Beowulf*, the greatest of them all, give a fair idea of this type of verse.

[1] Swinburne's *A Song in Time of Order*.
[2] Morley's *English Writers*, Vol. II., pp. 33, 34.

BEOWULF

Evolution of the Poem. — The greatest monument of Anglo-Saxon poetry is called *Beowulf*, from the name of its hero. It is the oldest epic poem of the Teutonic race. *Beowulf* was probably a long time in process of evolution. Many different *scops* added new episodes to the song, altering it by expansion or contraction under the influence of the inspiration of the hour and the circumstances of place and time. Finally, some monk or monks edited the poem, changing it in various ways, endeavoring especially to introduce into it Christian opinions.

Time and Place of Composition. — Critics are divided about the time and place of the composition of *Beowulf*. It is possible that some of the songs which enter into its framework were sung by the *scop* on the continent before any of our ancestors came to England; that is, before 449 A.D. With regard to the form in which we now have the poem, Ten Brink is probably right in saying that it dates from about the beginning of the eighth century. The places mentioned in the poem seem to indicate the correctness of the following statement from Stopford Brooke : "The scenery then is laid on the coast of the North Sea and the Kattegat, the first act of the poem among the Danes in Seeland, the second among the Geats in South Sweden."

The student who wishes to enter into the spirit of the poem will do well to familiarize himself with the position of these coasts, and with a description of their natural features in winter as well as in summer. Heine says of the sea which Beowulf sailed : —

"Before me rolleth a waste of water . . . and above me go rolling the storm clouds, the formless dark gray daughters of air, which from the sea in cloudy buckets scoop up the water, ever wearied lifting and lifting, and then pour it again in the sea, a mournful, wearisome business. Over the sea, flat on his face, lies the monstrous, terrible North Wind, sighing and sinking his voice as in secret, like an old grumbler; for once in good humor, unto the ocean he talks, and he tells her wonderful stories."

The Subject Matter. — This poem of 3184 lines describes the deeds of the Teutonic hero Beowulf. Hrothgar, the King of the Danes, built a magnificent mead hall to which he gave the name of Heorot.[1] While the Danes were eating and drinking their fill in this famous hall, Grendel, a monster half-human, came from the moor, burst in upon them, mangled thirty warriors, and then rushed off into the darkness. For twelve years this monster harried the warriors whenever they feasted in the hall, until the bravest were afraid to enter it. When Beowulf heard of this, he sailed with his warriors to Heorot, and persuaded the Danes to feast with him in the hall. After they had fallen asleep there, Grendel burst in the door, seized a warrior, and devoured him in a few mouthfuls. Then he grasped Beowulf. The hero, disdaining to use a sword against the dire monster, grappled with him, and together they wrestled up and down the hall. In their mad contest they overturned the tables and made the vast hall tremble as if it were in the throes of an earthquake.

Finally Beowulf, with a grip like that of thirty men, tore away the arm and shoulder of the monster, who rushed out to the marshes to die. The next night a banquet was given in fateful Heorot in honor of the hero. After the

---

[1] The student will do well to note in his atlas the location which authorities have assigned to this hall. Thomas Arnold says: "The view of Sarrazin and Danish scholars that the site of Hrothgar's mansion must be placed in close proximity to that of Leire, near the head of the Röskilde Fiord in Zealand [Seeland] is now generally accepted."

feast, the warriors slept in the hall, but Beowulf went to the palace. He had been gone but a short time, when in rushed Grendel's mother to avenge the death of her son. She seized a warrior, the king's dearest friend, and carried him away. In the morning the king said to Beowulf : —

"My trusty friend Æschere is dead. . . . The cruel hag has wreaked on him her vengeance. The country folk said there were two of them, one the semblance of a woman ; the other, the specter of a man. Their haunt is in the remote land, in the crags of the wolf, the wind-beaten cliffs, and untrodden bogs, where the dismal stream plunges into the drear abyss of an awful lake, overhung with a dark and grizzly wood rooted down to the water's edge, where a lurid flame plays nightly on the surface of the flood — and there lives not the man who knows its depth ! So dreadful is the place that the hunted stag, hard driven by the hounds, will rather die on the bank than find a shelter there. A place of terror ! When the wind rises, the waves mingle hurly-burly with the clouds, the air is stifling and rumbles with thunder. To thee alone we look for relief." [1]

This selection shows why the poetry of wild nature was largely a growth of later times. Ignorance peopled unknown places with monsters. Weird scenery, which might to-day move the pen of the poet, was then looked upon as the dwelling place of evil spirits. The very mists took the shape of a Grendel stalking over the moor.

Beowulf followed the bloody trail of Grendel's mother to the terrible flood. Undaunted by the dragons and serpents that made their home within the depths, he grasped a sword and plunged beneath the waves. After sinking what seemed to him a day's space, he saw Grendel's mother, who came forward to meet him. She dragged him into her dwelling, where there was no water, and the fight began. The issue was for a time doubtful,

[1] Earle's translation.

but at last Beowulf ran her through with a gigantic sword, and she fell dead upon the floor of her dwelling. A little distance away, he saw the dead body of Grendel. The hero cut off the heads of the monster and his mother and hastened away to Hrothgar's court. After receiving much praise and many presents, Beowulf sailed homeward with his warriors, where he ruled as king for fifty years.

The closing part of the poem tells how one of Beowulf's subjects stole some of the treasure which a firedrake had for three hundred years been guarding in a cavern. The enraged monster with his fiery breath laid waste the land. Beowulf sought the dragon in his cavern and after a terrible fight slew the monster, but was himself mortally wounded, and died after seeing in the cavern the heaps of treasure which he had won for his people.

So passed away the hero of the earliest epic poem of any branch of the Teutonic race. *Beowulf* affords valuable insight into the characteristics of that age. We are given the events of an entire day in the life of our forefathers. In *Beowulf* we look upon the scenery with which they were familiar; we are brought face to face with their hopes and fears, their ideas of duty, their manner of regarding life, and the way they took their exit from it.

THE CÆDMONIAN CYCLE

Cædmon. — In 597 A.D. St. Augustine began to teach the Christian religion to the Anglo-Saxons. The results of this teaching were shown in the subsequent literature. In what is known as Cædmon's *Paraphrase*, the next great Anglo-Saxon epic, there is no decrease in the warlike spirit. Instead of Grendel we have Satan as the archenemy against whom the battle rages.

Cædmon, who died in 680, was until middle life a lay-
man attached to the monastery at Whitby, on the northeast coast of Yorkshire.   Since the *Paraphrase* has been

RUINS OF WHITBY ABBEY

attributed to Cædmon on the authority of the Saxon historian Bede, born 673, we shall quote Bede himself on
the subject, from his famous *Ecclesiastical History* : —

   " Cædmon, having lived in a secular habit until he was well advanced
in years, had never learned anything of versifying; for which reason,
being sometimes at entertainments, where it was agreed for the sake
of mirth that all present should sing in their turns, when he saw the
instrument come toward him, he rose up from table and returned home.

   " Having done so at a certain time, and gone out of the house where
the entertainment was, to the stable, where he had to take care of the
horses that night, he there composed himself to rest at the proper
time ; a person appeared to him in his sleep, and, saluting him by his
name, said, ' Cædmon, sing some song to me.'   He answered, ' I cannot sing ; for that was the reason why I left the entertainment, and
retired to this place, because I could not sing.'   The other who talked

to him replied, 'However, you shall sing.' 'What shall I sing?' re-joined he. 'Sing the beginning of created beings,' said the other. Hereupon he presently began to sing verses to the praise of God.''

Cædmon remembered the poetry which he had composed in his dreams and he repeated it in the morning to the inmates of the monastery. They concluded that the gift of song was divinely given and had him enter the monastery and devote his time to poetry.

Of Cædmon's work Bede says : —

"He sang the creation of the world, the origin of man, and all the history of Genesis : and made many verses on the departure of the children of Israel out of Egypt, and their entering into the land of promise, with many other histories from Holy Writ ; the incarnation, passion, resurrection of our Lord, and his ascension into heaven ; the coming of the Holy Ghost, and the preaching of the Apostles ; also the terror of future judgment, the horror of the pains of hell, and the delights of heaven."

The Authorship and Subject Matter of the Cædmonian Cycle. — The first edition of the *Paraphrase* was published in 1655 by Junius, an acquaintance of Milton. Junius attributed the entire *Paraphrase* to Cædmon, on the authority of the above quotations from Bede.

The *Paraphrase* is really composed of three separate poems : the *Genesis*, the *Exodus*, and the *Daniel;* and these are probably the works of different writers. Critics are not agreed whether any of these poems in their present form can be ascribed to Cædmon. The *Genesis* shows too much difference in its parts to be produced by one author, but some portions of this poem may be Cædmon's own work. The *Genesis*, like Milton's *Paradise Lost,* has for its subject matter the fall of man and its consequences. The *Exodus*, the work of an unknown writer, is a poem of much originality on the escape of the Children of Israel from Egypt, their passage through the Red Sea, and the destruction of Pharaoh's host. The *Daniel*, an uninteresting poem of 765 lines, paraphrases portions of the book of *Daniel*, relating to Nebuchadnezzar's dreams, the fiery furnace, and Belshazzar's feast.

Characteristics of the Poetry. — No matter who wrote the *Paraphrase*, we have the poetry, a fact which critics too often overlook. Though the narrative sometimes closely follows the Biblical account in *Genesis*, *Exodus*, and *Daniel*, there are frequent unfettered outbursts of the imagination. The *Exodus* rings with the warlike notes of the victorious Teutonic race.

The *Genesis* possesses special interest for the student, since many of its strong passages show a marked likeness to certain parts of Milton's *Paradise Lost* (p. 202). Some critics have concluded that Milton must have been familiar with the Cædmonian *Genesis*. It will be instructive to note the parallelism between the following passages from the two poems. The earlier poem pictures the home of the fallen angels as a place of

> " . . . eternal night and sulphur pains,
> Fulness of fire, dread cold, reek, and red flames."

It is further described as a land

> " That was without light and full of flame." [1]

With this description we may compare these lines from Milton : —

> " A dungeon horrible, on all sides round,
> As one great furnace flamed ; yet from those flames
> No light ; but rather darkness visible.
> . . . a fiery deluge, fed
> With ever burning sulphur unconsumed." [2]

[1] Morley's translation.   [2] *Paradise Lost*, Book I., lines 61–69.

The older poet sings with forceful simplicity : —

> "Then comes, at dawn, the east wind, keen with frost."

Milton writes : —

> ". . . the parching air
> Burns frore, and cold performs the effect of fire."[1]

In the *Genesis*, Satan's description of his new home is as strong as in the *Paradise Lost :* —

> ". . . Above, below,
> Here is vast fire, and never have I seen
> More loathly landscape ; never fade the flames,
> Hot over Hell."

Here is the parallel passage from Milton : —

> "Seest thou yon dreary plain, forlorn and wild,
> The seat of desolation, void of light,
> Save what the glimmering of these livid flames
> Casts pale and dreadful?"[2]

When Satan rises on his wings to cross the flaming vault, the *Genesis* gives in one line an idea which Milton expands into two and a half : —

> "Swang ðæt fȳr on twā   fēondes cræfte."
> Struck the fire asunder with fiendish craft.

> ". . . on each hand the flames,
> Driven backward, slope their pointing spires, and, roll'd
> In billows, leave i' th' midst a horrid vale."[3]

It is not certain that Milton ever knew of the existence of the Cædmonian *Genesis ;* for he was blind three years before it was published. But whether he knew of it or not, it is a striking fact that the temper of the Teutonic mind during a thousand years should have changed so

---

[1] *Paradise Lost*, II., 594.   [2] *Ibid.*, I., 180–183.   [3] *Ibid.*, I., 222–224.

little toward the choice and treatment of the subject of an epic, and that the first great poem known to have been written on English soil should in so many points have anticipated the greatest epic of the English race.

THE CYNEWULF CYCLE

Cynewulf's Work. — Cynewulf is the only great Anglo-Saxon poet who affixed his name to certain poems and thus settled their authorship. We know nothing of his life except what we infer from his poetry. He was born near the middle of the eighth century, and it is not unlikely that he passed part of his youth as a thane of some noble. It is improbable that he was a wandering gleeman. He became a man of wide learning, well skilled in "word-craft." Such learning could then hardly have been acquired outside of some monastery whither he may have retired. He shows a poet's love for the beauty of the sun and the moon (*heofon-condelle*), æthelings among the constellations, for the dew and the rain, for the strife of the waves (*holm-ðræce*), for the steeds of the sea (*sund-hengestas*), and for the "all-green" (*eal-grēne*) earth.

The *Christ*, the *Elene*, the *Juliana*, and the *Fates of the Apostles* contain his runes, which prove that he is the author of these poems. The *Christ* is a poem on the Savior's Nativity, Ascension, and Judgment of the world at the last day. No other Anglo-Saxon poet better represents the essence and spirit of Christianity. The description of the Last Judgment is specially powerful and dramatic : —

"Lo ! the fire blast, flaming far, fierce and hungry as a sword,
  Whelms the world withal ! "[1]

[1] Brooke's translation.

Cynewulf closes the poem with a picture of a happy
land. This conception would never have occurred to a
poet of the warlike Saxon race before the introduction
of Christianity.

> ". . . Hunger is not there nor thirst,
> Sleep nor heavy sickness, nor the scorching of the Sun,
> Neither cold nor care."

Elene, the story of the finding of the Cross, is a strong
dramatic poem. It tells how Constantine, frightened at
the number of his foes, falls asleep and dreams of seeing
the Cross with the inscription: " With this shalt thou
conquer." He then has a cross made and borne at the
head of his army, which is victorious. Seized by a desire
to recover the true Cross, he sends his mother, Elene,
with a large force to the Holy Land. The story proceeds in a dramatic way to the finding of three crosses far
beneath the surface of the earth. In order to ascertain
which is the Holy Rood, a dead man is brought in contact
with the first cross, but the watchers see no sign of its
power. The second is tried with like result, but when he
touches the third, he is immediately restored to life.

The *Juliana* also has dramatic elements. Juliana is a
beautiful maiden, whom her father tries to compel to
marry a persecutor of the Christians. She refuses and
is thrown into prison, where a being in the guise of an
angel appears and bids her worship her lover's pagan
gods. She prays, and her prayer compels her visitor to
assume his proper fiendish shape and gives her complete
power over him. The story of his discomfiture and the
task to which she subjects him, introduces an element of
humor. The action then proceeds to her martyrdom.

Andreas and Phœnix. — Cynewulf is probably the author
of *Andreas*, an unsigned poem of special excellence and

dramatic power. The poem describes Andrew's voyage to Mermedonia to deliver St. Matthew. The Savior in disguise is the pilot. The dialogue between him and Andrew is specially fine. The saint has all the admiration of a Viking for his unknown Pilot, who stands at the helm in a gale and manages the vessel as he would a thought.

Cynewulf is also the probable author of the *Phœnix*, which is in part an adaptation of an old Latin poem. The *Phœnix* is the only Saxon poem which gives us the rich scenery of the South, in place of the stern northern landscape. He thus describes the land where this fabulous bird dwells : —

> " Calm and fair this glorious field, flashes there the sunny grove ;
> Happy is the holt of trees, never withers fruitage there.
> Bright are there the blossoms. . . .
> In that home the hating foe houses not at all,
> . . . .
> Neither sleep nor sadness, nor the sick man's weary bed,
> Nor the winter-whirling snow. . . .
> . . . but the liquid streamlets,
> Wonderfully beautiful, from their wells upspringing,
> Softly lap the land with their lovely floods." [1]

GENERAL CHARACTERISTICS OF ANGLO-SAXON POETRY

Martial Spirit. — The love of war is very marked in Anglo-Saxon poetry. This characteristic might have been expected in the songs of a race that had withstood the well-nigh all-conquering arm of the vast Roman Empire.

Our study of *Beowulf* has already shown the intensity of the martial spirit in heathen times. These lines from

---

[1] Brooke's translation.

the *Fight at Finnsburg*, dating from about the same time
as *Beowulf*, have only the flash of the sword to lighten
their gloom. They introduce the raven, for whom the
Saxon felt it his duty to provide food on the battlefield : —

> " . . . hræfen wandrode
> sweart and sealo-brūn ; swurd-lēoma stōd
> swylce eal Finns-buruh fȳrenu wǣre."

> . . . the raven wandered
> Swart and sallow-brown ; the sword-flash stood
> As if all Finnsburg were afire.

The love of war is almost as marked in the Christian
poetry. There are vivid pictures of battle against the
heathen and the enemies of God. A selection from one
of the poems of the Cædmonian Cycle will show this : —

> " Helmeted men went from the holy burgh,
> At the first reddening of dawn, to fight :
> Loud stormed the din of shields.
> For that rejoiced the lank wolf in the wood,
> And the black raven, slaughter-greedy bird."[1]

The poems often describe battle as if it was an enjoyable game. They mention the " play of the spear " and
speak of " putting to sleep with the sword," as if the din
of war was in their ears a slumber melody.

One of the latest of Anglo-Saxon poems, *The Battle of
Brunanburh*, 937, is a famous example of war poetry. We
quote a few lines from Tennyson's excellent translation : —

> " Grimly with swords that were sharp from the grindstone,
> Fiercely we hack'd at the flyers before us.
>
> Five young kings put asleep by the sword-stroke.
> Seven strong earls of the army of Anlaf
> Fell on the war-field, numberless numbers.

[1] Morley's translation.

> " Slender reason had
> He to be glad of
> The clash of the war glaive,
> .   .   .   .   .
> The wielding of weapons —
> The play that they play'd with
> The children of Edward."

Love of the Sea. — The Anglo-Saxon fondness for the sea has been noted, together with the fact that this characteristic has been transmitted to more recent English poetry. Our forefathers rank among the best seamen that the world has ever known. Had they not loved to dare an unknown sea, English literature might not have existed, and the sun might never have risen on any English flag.

The *scop* sings thus of Beowulf's adventure on the North Sea : —

> " Swoln were the surges, of storms 'twas the coldest,
> Dark grew the night, and northern the wind,
> Rattling and roaring, rough were the billows." [1]

In the *Seafarer*, the *scop* also sings : —

> " My mind now is set,
> My heart's thought, on wide waters,
> The home of the whale ;
> It wanders away
> Beyond limits of land.
> .   .   .   .   .   .
> And stirs the mind's longing
> To travel the way that is trackless." [2]

In the *Andreas*, the poet speaks of the ship in one of the most charming of Saxon similes : —

> "Foaming Ocean beats our steed : full of speed this boat is ;
> Fares along foam-throated, flieth on the wave,
> Likest to a bird." [3]

---

[1] Brooke's translation.   [2] Morley's translation.   [3] Brooke's translation.

Some of the most striking Saxon epithets are applied to the sea. We may instance such a compound as *ār-ge-bland* (*ār*, "oar"; *blendan*, "to blend"), which conveys the idea of the companionship of the oar with the sea. From this compound modern poets have borrowed their "oar-disturbéd sea," "oaréd sea," "oar-blending sea," and "oar-wedded sea." The Anglo-Saxon poets call the sun rising or setting in the sea the *mere-candel*. In *Beowulf*, *mere-strǣta*, "sea-streets," are spoken of as if they were the easily traversed avenues of a town.

Figures of Rhetoric. — A special characteristic of Anglo-Saxon poetry is the rarity of similes. In Homer they are frequent, but Anglo-Saxon verse is too abrupt and rapid in the succession of images to employ the expanded simile. The long poem of *Beowulf* contains only five similes, and these are of the shorter kind. Two of them, the comparison of the light in Grendel's dwelling to the beams of the sun, and of a vessel to a flying bird, have been given in the original Anglo-Saxon on pp. 15, 17. Other similes compare the light from Grendel's eyes to a flame, and the nails on his fingers to steel, while the most complete simile says that the sword, when bathed in the monster's poisonous blood, melted like ice.

On the other hand, this poetry uses many direct and forcible metaphors, such as "wave-ropes" for ice, the "whale-road" or "swan-road" for the sea, the "foamy-necked floater" for a ship, the "war-adder" for an arrow, the "bone-house" for body. The sword is said to sing a war song, the slain to be put to sleep with the sword, the sun to be a candle, the flood to boil. War is appropriately called the sword-game.

Parallelisms. — The repetition of the same ideas in slightly differing form, known as parallelism, is frequent.

The author wished to make certain ideas emphatic, and he repeated them with varying phraseology. The first sight of land is important to the sailor, and hence the poet used four different terms for the shore that met Beowulf's eyes on his voyage to Hrothgar : *land, brimclifu, beorgas, sǽ-nǽssas* (land, sea-cliffs, mountains, promontories).

This passage from the *Phœnix* shows how repetition emphasizes the absence of disagreeable things : —

> "... there may neither snow nor rain,
>   Nor the furious air of frost, nor the flare of fire,
>   Nor the headlong squall of hail, nor the hoar frost's fall,
>   Nor the burning of the sun, nor the bitter cold,
>   Nor the weather over-warm, nor the winter shower,
>   Do their wrong to any wight." [1]

The general absence of cold is here made emphatic by mentioning special cold things: "snow," "frost," "hail," "hoar frost," "bitter cold," "winter shower." The absence of heat is emphasized in the same way.

Saxon contrasted with Celtic Imagery. — A critic rightly says : "The gay wit of the Celt would pour into the song of a few minutes more phrases of ornament than are to be found in the whole poem of *Beowulf*." In three lines of an old Celtic death song, we find three similes : —

> " Black as the raven was his brow ;
>   Sharp as a razor was his spear ;
>   White as lime was his skin."

We look in Anglo-Saxon poetry in vain for a touch like this : —

> " Sweetly a bird sang on a pear tree above the head of Guenn before they covered him with a turf." [2]

----

[1] Brooke's translation.   [2] *Llywarch's Lament for his Son Gwenn.*

If the Saxon repeats, the Celt exaggerates : —

" More yellow was her head than the flower of the broom, and her skin was whiter than the foam of the wave, and fairer were her hands and fingers than the blossoms of the wood anemone amidst the spray of the meadow fountain." [1]

Sometimes, as in the foregoing passage, the Celtic exaggeration is pleasing, but it is often ridiculous, as in the account of the fight between the white-horned and brown bulls. We are told that the "sky was darkened by the turf thrown up by their feet and by the foam from their mouths. The province rang with their roar and the inhabitants hid in caves or climbed the hills." We might expect from this the story of the Kilkenny cats.

In order to produce a poet able to write both *A Midsummer Night's Dream* and *Hamlet*, the Celtic imagination must blend with the Anglo-Saxon seriousness. As we shall see, this was accomplished by the Norman conquest.

ANGLO-SAXON PROSE

When and where written. — We have seen that poetry normally precedes prose. The principal part of Anglo-Saxon poetry had been produced before much prose was written. The most productive poetic period was between 650 and 825. Near the close of the eighth century, the Danes began their plundering expeditions into England. By 800 they had destroyed the great northern monasteries, like the one at Whitby, where Cædmon is said to have composed the first religious song. The home of poetry was in the north of England, and these Danish inroads almost completely silenced the singers. What prose there

---

[1] Guest's *Mabinogion*, p. 219.

was in the north was principally in Latin. On the other hand, the Saxon prose was produced chiefly in the south of England. The most glorious period of Anglo-Saxon prose was during Alfred's reign, 871–901.

Bede. — This writer (673–735) has slight claims to be considered in a history of English literature, for all of his extant work is in Latin. He is said to have translated the *Gospel of St. John* into Saxon, but the translation is lost. He wrote in Latin on a vast range of subjects, from the *Scriptures* to natural science, and from grammar to history. He has given a list of thirty-seven works of which he is the author. His most important work is the *Ecclesiastical History*, which is really a history of England from Julius Cæsar's invasion to 731. The quotation from Bede's work relative to Cædmon (p. 27) shows that Bede could relate things simply and well. He passed a great part of his life at the monastery of Jarrow on the Tyne.

Alfred. — A king of England was its greatest Anglo-Saxon prose writer. Alfred, who reigned from 871 to 901, is rightly surnamed the Great from every point of view. Although the most of his works are called translations from the Latin, he has yet left the stamp of his own originality and sterling sense upon them all. He desired to give his people text-books on all important subjects, and he shrank from no labor in accomplishing his purpose. He consulted all accessible authorities and made alterations and additions to suit his plan.

He prepared a text-book of geography in this way. He found a Latin work by Orosius, who was a Spanish Christian of the fifth century. Here was a mass of material, much of which was unsuited to Alfred's purposes, and so he omitted, changed, and added. He interviewed travelers from the far North and inserted some original matter.

These additions are the best material in the book, and they are not uninteresting reading now. The work is known as Alfred's *Orosius*.

There was extreme necessity for these text-books, since none existed in the native tongue. He translated Pope Gregory's *Pastoral Rule* in order to show the clergy how to teach and care for their flocks. Alfred's own words at the beginning of the volume show how great was the need for such work as he was doing. Speaking of the clergy, he says : —

> "There were very few on this side Humber who would know how to render their services in English, or so much as translate an epistle out of Latin into English; and I ween that not many would be on the other side Humber. So few of them were there, that I cannot think of so much as a single one, south of Thames, when I took to the realm."[1]

Alfred produced a work on moral philosophy by altering and amending Boëthius's *De Consolatione Philosophiæ*. Boëthius was a Roman, who was thrown into prison and wrongfully executed about 525 A.D. This work teaches that a wise Power rules the world, that a fuller knowledge of untoward events would reveal their wisdom, and that temporal things are of slight worth in comparison with eternal welfare.

A text-book of English history was made by translating portions of Bede's *Ecclesiastical History* from the original Latin.

The Anglo-Saxon Chronicle. — This is the first history of any branch of the Teutonic people in their own tongue. The *Chronicle* has come down to us in several different texts, according as it was compiled or copied at different monasteries. The *Chronicle* was probably begun in

[1] Earle's translation.

Alfred's reign. The entries relating to earlier events were copied from Bede's *Ecclesiastical History* and from other Latin authorities. The *Chronicle* contains chiefly those events which each year impressed the clerical compilers as the most important in the history of the nation. This work is a fountain head to which writers of the history of those times must turn.

A few extracts (translated) will show its character: —

A.D. 449. "This year . . . Hengist and Horsa, invited by Vortigern, King of Britons, landed in Britain, on the shore which is called Wappidsfleet; at first in aid of the Britons, but afterwards they fought against them."

806. "This year the moon was eclipsed on the Kalends of September; and Eardulf, King of the Northumbrians, was driven from his kingdom; and Eanbert, Bishop of Hexham, died."

Sometimes the narrative is extremely vivid. Those who know the difficulty of describing anything impressively in a few words will realize the excellence of this portraiture of William the Conqueror: —

1087. "If any would know what manner of man King William was, the glory that he obtained, and of how many lands he was lord; then will we describe him as we have known him. . . . He was mild to those good men who loved God, but severe beyond measure to those who withstood his will. . . . So also was he a very stern and a wrathful man, so that none durst do anything against his will, and he kept in prison those earls who acted against his pleasure. He removed bishops from their sees, and abbots from their offices, and he imprisoned thanes, and at length he spared not his own brother, Odo. . . . Amongst other things, the good order that William established is not to be forgotten; it was such that any man, who was himself aught, might travel over the kingdom with a bosom-full of gold, unmolested; and no man durst kill another. . . . He made large forests for the deer, and enacted laws therewith, so that whoever killed a hart or a hind should be blinded . . . and he loved the tall stags as if he were their father."

The *Chronicle* continues until 1154, when its last entry was made to record the death of King Stephen.

SUMMARY

The most flourishing period of Anglo-Saxon poetry was between 650 and 825 A.D. It was produced for the most part in the north of England, which was overrun by the Danes about 800. These marauders destroyed many of the monasteries and silenced the voices of the singers.

Among the poems of this age, we may emphasize : (1) the shorter *scopic* pieces, of which the *Far Traveler*, *The Seafarer*, *The Fortunes of Men*, and *The Battle of Brunanburh* are important examples; (2) *Beowulf*, the greatest Anglo-Saxon epic poem, which was probably composed on the continent and brought to England in the memories of the singers; (3) the *Cædmonian Cycle* of scriptural paraphrases, some of which have Miltonic qualities; and (4) the *Cynewulf Cycle*, which shows the most variety and lyrical excellence.

The subject matter of the poetry is principally war, the sea, and religion. The martial spirit and love of the sea, thus early shown, are typical of the nation that has raised her flag in every clime. The chief qualities of the poetry are earnestness, somberness, the consciousness of the approach of the "inevitable hour," and strength rather than delicacy or melody. Parallelisms and strong metaphorical expressions abound.

Anglo-Saxon prose was written chiefly in the southern part of England. The golden period of prose coincides with Alfred's reign, 871–901, and he is the greatest prose writer. His translations of Latin text-books for his people contain excellent additions by him. The *Anglo-Saxon*

Chronicle is an important record of contemporaneous events for the historian. There are also the *Homilies* and *Colloquium* of Ælfric, a tenth century prose writer; but the prose as a whole is far inferior to the poetry.

Anglo-Saxon should be studied not only because it is the foundation of the language in which Shakespeare wrote, but also for its own intrinsic merits. We can point to few other literatures which owe less to outside influences, or which at a like stage in the development of the race possessed as much power. A literature which could accomplish so much under such unfavorable conditions might justly have awakened great expectations.

REQUIRED READINGS FOR CHAPTER I

HISTORICAL

In connection with the progress of literature, students should obtain for themselves a general idea of contemporary historical events from the pages specified in any of the following named works: —

Gardiner's *Student's History of England*, pp. 1–96; Green's *Short History of the English People*, Chap. I.; Underwood-Guest's *A Handbook of English History*, pp. 35–129; Guerber's *Story of the English*, pp. 31–76; Robertson's *Making of the English Nation*, pp. 7–78 (*Oxford Manuals of English History*); Traill's *Social England*, Vol. I, pp. 116–230.

LITERARY

The student who is not familiar with the original Anglo-Saxon should read the translations specified below: —

Scopic Poetry.[1] — *Widsið* or the *Far Traveler*, translated in Morley's *English Writers*, Vol. II., pp. 1–11.

---

[1] In his *Education of the Central Nervous System*, Chaps. VII.–X., the author has endeavored to give some special directions for securing definite ideas in the study of poetry.

The Seafarer, translated in Morley, II., 21–26, or in Morley's *Illustrations of English Religion*, pp. 13–15, or in Brooke's *English Literature from the Beginning to the Norman Conquest*, pp. 311, 312, or in Brooke's *History of Early English Literature*, pp. 362, 363.

The Fortunes of Men, translated in Morley's *English Writers*, II., pp. 32–37, or in Morley's *Shorter English Poems*, pp. 8–11.

Battle of Brunanburh, Tennyson's translation.

What light do these poems throw on (*a*) the life of the *scop* ? (*b*) the subject matter of his songs? (*c*) the life and ideals of the Anglo-Saxons?

Beowulf. — This important poem should be read entire in one of the following translations : Earle's *The Deeds of Beowulf, Done into Modern Prose* (Clarendon Press) ; Lumsden's *Beowulf, an Old English Poem, Translated into Modern Rhymes ;* Morris and Wyatt's *The Tale of Beowulf ;* Hall's *Beowulf, Translated into Modern Metres* (Student's edition, paper, 30 cents). Morley's *English Writers*, I., 278–310, and Brooke's *History of Early English Literature*, pp. 26–73, contain translations of many of the best parts of *Beowulf*.

How does the sea figure in the action of the poem? Name as many epithets as possible applied to the sea. How does nature figure in the poem? What difference is there in the treatment of nature in the poetry of to-day? What glimpses are given of the life of women? Describe the three funerals in *Beowulf*. Is there any analogy between the conflict of natural forces in the Norseland and Beowulf's fight with Grendel? In what ways does the poem show the ideals of our forefathers? Does the poem teach any ethical lesson?

The Cædmonian Cycle. — This has been translated by Thorpe, but the translation is out of print. The student may find some of the strongest passages in Morley's *English Writers*, II., 81–101, or in Morley's *Illustrations of English Religion*, pp. 5–9, or in Brooke's *History of Early English Literature*, pp. 290–340.

Compare these selections with the first book of *Paradise Lost*, and note any likeness in imagery and thought. Did the introduction of Christianity alter the character of the Saxon mind, or merely change the direction of its energies? Quote passages from the *Cædmonian Cycle* to prove your conclusion. Compare this *Cycle* with *Beowulf*.

The Cynewulf Cycle. — Many fine selections are translated in Morley's *English Writers*, II., 206–241 ; in Brooke's *History of Early English Literature*, pp. 371–443 ; in Brooke's *English Literature from the Beginning to the Norman Conquest*, pp. 163–202 ; and in the *Exeter Book*, translated by Israel Gollancz for the Early English Text Society.

What new qualities are added to Anglo-Saxon poetry in this *Cycle?* What old qualities are retained? Does the poetry seem more modern in any respect? Why is the *Phœnix* (Brooke's *History of Early English Literature*, pp. 428–430; Gollancz's *Exeter Book*, Part I., pp. 201–241) remarkable?

General Questions on Anglo-Saxon Poetry. — What most striking passages (*a*) in *Beowulf*, (*b*) elsewhere, show the Saxon love of war and of the sea?

Instance the most striking parallelisms found in your readings. Give a list of vivid metaphors. What conspicuous differences do you find between Anglo-Saxon and old Celtic literature? (Morley's *English Writers*, I., 165–239, gives a sufficient number of selections from old Celtic literature to enable the student to answer this question. See also this volume, p. 37.) What excellences and defects seem to you most pronounced in Anglo-Saxon verse?

Prose. — The *Anglo-Saxon Chronicle* and Bede's *Ecclesiastical History* are both translated in one volume of Bohn's *Antiquarian Library*. The most interesting part of Bede for the student of literature is the chapter relating to Cædmon (Chap. XXIV., pp. 217–220).

In the *Chronicle*, read the entries for the years 871, 878, 897, 975, 1087, and 1137. What is there of interest in these selections? Why is the *Chronicle* specially valuable for the historian?

The qualities of Alfred's prose may be seen in the passages translated in Brooke's *English Literature from the Beginning to the Norman Conquest*, pp. 221–241, and in Earle's *Anglo-Saxon Literature*, pp. 186–206. A translation of Alfred's *Orosius* entire is given in Pauli's *Life of Alfred* (Bohn's *Antiquarian Library*). The most interesting part of *Orosius* is the original matter describing the voyages of Ohthere and Wulfstan, pp. 249–255.

What guided all Alfred's efforts in literature? What qualities are most manifest in his prose? Why is Anglo-Saxon poetry so vastly superior to the prose?

WORKS FOR CONSULTATION AND FURTHER STUDY

(OPTIONAL)

Ramsay's *The Foundations of England.*
Freeman's *Old English History.*
Turner's *History of the Anglo-Saxons.*

Grant Allen's *Anglo-Saxon England*.

Green's *History of the English People*.

Green's *Making of England*.

Green's *Conquest of England*.

Ten Brink's *Early English Literature*, Vol. I., pp. 1–115.

Brooke's *History of Early English Literature to the Accession of King Alfred*, 500 pp., contains many metrical translations of specimens of the best Anglo-Saxon poetry.

Brooke's *English Literature from the Beginning to the Norman Conquest*, 338 pp.

Earle's *Anglo-Saxon Literature*.

Morley's *English Writers*, Vols. I. and II., contains translations of many fine passages in Anglo-Saxon literature.

Azarias's *The Development of English Literature*.

Taine's *English Literature*, Book I., Chap. I.

Jusserand's *Literary History of the English People from the Origins to the Renaissance*, pp. 3–93.

Arnold's *Notes on Beowulf*.

The Exeter Book, edited and translated by Gollancz.

Gurteen's *The Epic of the Fall of Man: A Comparative Study of Cædmon, Dante, and Milton*.

Bosworth and Waring's *Anglo-Saxon Gospels*.

Bede's *Ecclesiastical History of England, and The Anglo-Saxon Chronicle*, 1 vol., translated by Giles in Bohn's *Antiquarian Library*.

Bohn's *Six Old English Chronicles*.

Mabinogion (a collection of Welsh fairy tales and romances), translated by Lady Charlotte Guest.

Sidney Lanier's *The Boy's Mabinogion*.

Cook's *The Christ of Cynewulf*. (The *Introduction* of 97 pages gives a valuable account of the life and writings of Cynewulf.)

CHAPTER II

The Norman Conquest. — The overthrow of the Saxon rule in England by William the Conqueror in 1066 was an event of vast importance to English literature. The Normans (Norsemen or Northmen), as they were called, a term which shows their northern extraction, were originally of the same blood as the English race. They settled in France in the ninth century, married French wives, and adopted the French language. In 1066 their leader, Duke William, crossed the English Channel with an army, won the battle of Hastings, and became King of England.

Characteristics of the Normans. — The intermixture of Teutonic and French blood had given to the Normans the best qualities of both races. The Norman was nimble-witted, highly imaginative, and full of northern energy. The Saxon possessed dogged perseverance, good common sense, if he had long enough to think, and but little imagination. Some one has well said that the union of Norman with Saxon was like joining the swift spirit of the eagle to the strong body of the ox, or, again, that the Saxon furnished the dough, and the Norman the yeast. Had it not been for the blending of these necessary qualities in one race, English literature could not have become the first in the world. We see the characteristics of both the Teuton and the Norman in Shake-

47

speare's greatest plays. A pure Saxon could not have turned from Hamlet's soliloquy to write : —

> "Where the bee sucks, there suck I."[1]

Changes Wrought in the Language

The Emergence of Modern English. — The productions of English authors during the three centuries after the Norman Conquest are of more philological than literary interest. The student should note the principal changes in the language because the relation between literature and its medium of expression is specially intimate. A great literature demands a rich vocabulary capable of expressing delicate shades of difference in thought and feeling. A musician may possess the highest type of ability, but if he is compelled to perform on a defective instrument, his music will show the shortcomings of its vehicle of expression. The period of growth of a literature and its language cannot be neglected by one who wishes a broad comprehension of the literary masterpieces alone.

Modern English literature did not suddenly make its appearance like the fabled roses which sprang full-blown wherever the feet of Venus touched the soil. The language in which Chaucer and Shakespeare wrote was formed in a conflict in which no quarter was given or asked. Two great languages, the Saxon and the French, struggled for the mastery. The contest terminated with the survival of the fittest expressions from each. In the same ranks beside the Saxon words "mother" and "home," stand the French "duty" and "family."

[1] *The Tempest*, V., I.

The student will the more intelligently comprehend the great change in his mother tongue if he looks at the transformation as an evolutionary process. Zoölogy shows that when animal organs become unnecessary, they tend to atrophy and to pass into the rudimentary stage or disappear entirely, and that those organs best adapted to further the welfare of the animal have developed. The reason why other branches of the Teutonic language have not developed so far as English is because their environment was not so favorable, since both French and Latin exercised comparatively small influence in their growth.

Three Languages used in England. — For three hundred years after the Norman Conquest, three languages were widely used in England. The Normans introduced French, which was the language of the court and the aristocracy. William the Conqueror brought over many Norman priests, who used Latin almost exclusively in their service. The influence of this book Latin is generally underestimated by those who do not appreciate the power of the church. The Domesday survey shows that in 1085 the church, with her dependents, held more than one third of some counties.

In addition to the Latin and the French (which was itself principally of Latin origin), there was, thirdly, the Anglo-Saxon, to which the middle and the lower classes of the English stubbornly adhered.

The Loss of Inflections. — Anglo-Saxon was a language with changing endings, like modern German. If a Saxon wished to say "good gifts," he had to have the proper case endings for both the adjective and the noun, and his expression would have been *gōde giefa*. For "the good gifts," he would have inflected "the" and made the

case ending of "good" different from what it was when
"good" was not preceded by an article, and he would
have said, *ðā gōdan giefa*.

The Norman Conquest helped to lop off these endings,
which German has never entirely lost. We no longer
decline articles or ordinary adjectives. Instead of having our attention taken up with thinking of the proper
endings, the mental powers are left free to attend to the
thought rather than to the vehicle of its expression.
With the exception of a few nouns like *ox*, *oxen*, or *mouse*,
mice, the sole inflection of nouns is the addition of *'s, s*, or
es for the possessive and the plural. Our pronouns are
still declined, and mistakes are frequent in their use.

It should be emphasized that Anglo-Saxon had already
begun to lose some of its inflections before the Conquest,
and that the coming of the Normans merely hastened a
development which would, to a considerable degree, have
ultimately taken place without their influence. Even
with this influence, the dropping of inflections was not
the work of a year, but of several centuries.

Change in Gender. — Before any one could speak Anglo-
Saxon correctly, he had first to learn the fanciful genders
that were attached to nouns : "trousers" was feminine,
"childhood" masculine, "child" neuter. The Norman
Conquest helped to give the natural genders to objects.
The German still retains these fanciful genders. A critic
thus illustrates the use of genders in that language : "A
German gentleman writes a masculine letter of feminine
love to a neuter young lady with a feminine pen and
feminine ink on masculine sheets of neuter paper, and
incloses it in a masculine envelope with a feminine address
to his darling, though neuter, Gretchen. He has a masculine head, a feminine hand, and a neuter heart."

Prefixes, Suffixes, and Self-explaining Compounds. — The Norman Conquest was instrumental in causing the English tongue to lose much of its power of using prefixes. A prefix joined to a well-known word changes its meaning and renders the coining of a new term unnecessary. The Anglo-Saxons, by the use of prefixes, formed ten compounds from their verb *flōwan*, "to flow." Of these, only one survives in our "overflow." From *sittan*, "to sit," thirteen compounds were thus formed, but every one has perished. A larger percentage of suffixes was retained, and we still have many words like "wholesomeness," "child-hood," "sing-er."

The power of forming self-explaining compounds was largely lost. The Saxon compounded the words for "tree" and "worker," and said *trēow-wyrhta*, "tree-wright," but we now make use of the single word "carpenter." We have replaced the Saxon *bōc-crǽft*, "book-art," by "literature"; *ǽfen-glōm*, "evening-gloom," by "twilight"; *mere-swīn*, "sea-swine," by "porpoise"; *ēag-wrǽc*, "eye-rack," by "pain in the eye"; *leornung-cild*, "learning-child," by "pupil." The title of an old work, *Ayen-bite of In-wit*, "Again-bite of In-wit," was translated into "Remorse of Conscience." *Grund-weall* and *word-hord* were displaced by "foundation" and "vocabulary." The German language still retains this power and calls a glove a "hand-shoe," a thimble a "finger-hat," and rolls up such clumsy compound expressions as *Unabhängigkeitserklärung*.

We might lament this loss more if we did not remember that Shakespeare found our language ample for his needs, and that a considerable number of the old compounds still survive, as *home-stead*, *man-hood*, *in-sight*, *break-fast*, *house-hold*, *horse-back*, *ship-man*, and *sea-shore*.

Introduction of New Words and Loss of Old Ones. — Since the Normans were for some time the governing race, while many of the Saxons occupied comparatively menial positions, numerous French words indicative of rank, power, science, luxury, and fashion were introduced. Many titles were derived from a French source. English thus obtained words like "sovereign," "royalty," "duke," "marquis," "mayor," and "clerk." Many terms of government are from the French, for instance, "parliament," "peers," "commons." The language of law abounds in French terms, like "damage," "trespass," "circuit," "judge," "jury," "verdict," "sentence," "counsel," "prisoner." Many words used in war, architecture, and medicine also have a French origin. Examples are "fort," "arch," "mason," "surgery." In fact, we find words from the French in almost every field. "Uncle" and "cousin," "rabbit" and "falcon," "trot" and "stable," "money" and "soldier," "reason" and "virtue," "Bible" and "preach," are instances in point.

French words often displaced Saxon ones. Thus, the Saxon *Hælend*, the Healer, gave way to the French *Savior*, *wanhope* and *wonstead* were displaced by *despair* and *residence*. Sometimes the Saxon stubbornly kept its place beside the French term. The English language is thus especially rich in synonyms, or rather in slightly differentiated forms of expression capable of denoting the exact shade of thought and feeling. The following words are instances:

SAXON:	FRENCH:	SAXON:	FRENCH:
body,	corpse,	green,	verdant,
folk,	people,	food,	nourishment,
swine,	pork,	wrangle,	contend,
calf,	veal,	fatherly,	paternal,
worth,	value,	workman,	laborer.

English was enriched not only by those expressions gained from the daily speech of the Normans, but also by words which were added from literary Latin. Thus, we have the Saxon "ask," the Norman-French "inquire" and "question," and the Latin "interrogate." "Bold," "impudent," "audacious;" "bright," "cheerful," "animated;" "earnings," "wages," "remuneration;" "short," "brief," "concise," are other examples of words, largely synonymous, from the Saxon, the Norman-French, and the Latin, respectively.

The Changes Slowly Accomplished. — For over a hundred years after the Conquest, but few French words found their way into current English use. This is shown by the fact that the *Brut,* a poem of 32,250 lines, translated from a French original into English about 1205, has not more than a hundred words of Norman-French origin.

At first the Normans despised the tongue of the conquered Saxons, but, as time progressed, the two races intermarried, and the children would be certain to learn some Saxon words from their mothers or nurses. On the other hand, many well-to-do Saxons, like parents in later times, would have their children taught French because it was considered aristocratic.

Until 1204 the nobles were going back and forth to Normandy to estates held there, and it was necessary for the nobles to speak French. In 1204 King John lost Normandy, and in the next reign both English and French kings decreed that no subject of the one should hold land in the territory of the other. This narrowing of the attention of English subjects down to England, was a foundation stone in building up the supremacy of the English tongue.

In 1338 the Hundred Years' War between France and England began. In Edward the Third's reign (1327–1377), it was demonstrated that one Englishman could whip six Frenchmen, and the language of a hostile and partly conquered race naturally began to occupy a less high position. In 1362 Parliament enacted that English should thereafter be used in law-courts, "because the laws, customs, and statutes of this realm, be not commonly known in the same realm, for that they be pleaded, shewed, and judged in the French tongue, which is much unknown in the said realm."

The Fallow Period. — Sometimes a language increases its strength during a period of rest from literary production, just as land acquires new vigor from lying fallow. If the Norman Conquest reduced the Saxon language "almost to a peasant's dialect" and kept it for more than two centuries in that position, even this condition gave additional power to the resulting tongue. Like Antæus, who gained sevenfold strength every time that he was thrown to the earth by his adversary, this "peasant's dialect" was strong because it developed in the soil of actual life. That tongue voiced no affectations. It was the language of common sense and of the heart, and their vocabulary contained not a single insincere or high-flown expression.

The qualities developed by contact with earnest life were necessary requisites in a language with which Shakespeare was to speak to the common heart of humanity, and with which Scotland's plowman poet was to charm the peasant's cot and the palace of the lord. In some of Shakespeare's greatest plays, we shall find that eighty-nine per cent of the words used are those which the Saxon found sufficient to voice his hopes, fears, loves, and woes.

The authorized translation of the *Gospels* employs over ninety per cent of words of Anglo-Saxon origin.

The Superiority of the Composite Tongue. — While we insist on the truth that Anglo-Saxon gained much of its wonderful directness and power from standing in such close relations to earnest life, it is necessary to remember that many words of Latin origin did, by an apprenticeship at the fireside, in the field, the workshop, and the laboratory, equally fit themselves for taking their place in the language. Such words from Latin roots as "faith," "pray," "joke," "vein," "beast," "poor," "nurse," "flower," "taste," "state," and "fool" remain in our vocabulary because they were used in everyday life.

Pure Anglo-Saxon was a forcible language, but it lacked the wealth of expression and the flexibility necessary to respond to the most delicate touches of the master musicians who were to come. When Shakespeare has Lear say of Cordelia : —

> "Her voice was ever soft,
> Gentle, and low ; an excellent thing in woman,"

we find that ten of the thirteen words are Saxon, but the other three of Romance (French) origin are as necessary as is a small amount of tin added to copper to make bronze. Two of these three words express varying shades of quality. When Macbeth asks : —

> "Will all great Neptune's ocean wash this blood
> Clean from my hand? No, this my hand will rather
> The multitudinous seas incarnadine,
> Making the green one red,"

the Saxon again preponderates, but "multitudinous" seems in one sonorous word to include all the countless waves of the seas of every clime, and "incarnadine" to intensify, far more than "redden," the idea of the penetration and the magnitude of the stain. This line as a whole, coming between two lines of pure Saxon, adds not only variety but also sublimity.

Lounsbury well says: "There result, indeed, from the union of the foreign and native elements, a wealth of phraseology and a many-sidedness in English, which give it in these respects a superiority over any other modern cultivated tongue. German is strictly a pure Teutonic speech, but no native speaker of it claims for it any superiority over the English as an instrument of expression, while many are willing to concede its inferiority."

It is true that the bone, sinew, and framework of this composite tongue remain Saxon, but it is also true that the English beloved by Chaucer, Shakespeare, and Milton was something more than bone and sinew. That English was a creature of flesh and blood as well. With all her sinewy strength, she possessed rare beauty, grace, and perfection of rounded form.

LITERATURE OF THE TRANSITION PERIOD, FROM THE NORMAN CONQUEST TO CHAUCER'S DEATH

A Literature of Dialects. — During this period and even until printing had helped to render the language stable, not only was English undergoing a transition, but the language in one part of the country was often difficult to be understood by those living in another part. Even in the fifteenth century, Caxton, the first English printer, was sometimes puzzled to know which dialect to place in permanent type. In one of his *Prefaces* he says that a man went into a house at some distance from his native

place and "axyd after eggys," but the good wife replied
that she "coude speke no frenshe." She had mistaken
his English dialect for French. He found an interpreter
who told her that the man wanted "eyren." She then
brought him eggs.

All works of the period treated in this chapter were
written in a dialect. In such a small country as England,
this fact had the effect of lessening the circulation of
books and the number of readers. There were three principal dialects : the Northern, spoken north of the river
Humber; the Midland, from the Humber to the Thames;
and the Southern from the Thames to the English Channel. It was the Midland dialect which the genius of
Chaucer helped to raise from its provincial rank to become
the national language of England.

A Latin Chronicler. — One chronicler, Geoffrey of Monmouth, although he wrote in Latin, must receive some
attention because of his vast influence on English poetry.
He probably acquired his last name from being arch-
deacon of Monmouth. He was appointed Bishop of St.
Asaph in 1152 and died about 1154. Unlike the majority
of the monkish chroniclers, he possessed a vivid imagination, which he used in his so-called *History of the Kings of
Britain*.

Geoffrey pretended to have found an old manuscript
which related the deeds of all British kings from Brutus,
the mythical founder of the kingdom of Britain, and the
great-grandson of Æneas, to Cæsar. Geoffrey wrote an
account of all British kings down to Cadwallo in 689 with
as much minuteness and gravity as Swift employed in
the *Voyage to Lilliput* (p. 242). Other chroniclers declared
that Geoffrey lied saucily and shamelessly, but his book
became extremely popular. The monks could not then

comprehend that the world's greatest literary works were to be products of the imagination.

In Geoffrey of Monmouth's *History of the Kings of Britain* we are given vivid pictures of King Lear and his daughters, of Cymbeline, of King Arthur and his Knights, of Guinevere and the rest of that company whom later poets have immortalized. It is probable that Geoffrey was not particular whether he obtained his materials from old chroniclers, Welsh bards, floating tradition, or from his own imagination. His book left its impress on the historical imagination of the Middle Ages. Had it not been for Geoffrey's *History*, the dramas of *King Lear* and *Cymbeline* might never have been suggested to Shakespeare.

Layamon's Brut. — About 1155 a Frenchman named Wace translated into his own language Geoffrey of Monmouth's work. This translation fell into the hands of Layamon, a priest living in Worcestershire, and he proceeded to render the poem, with additions of his own, into the Southern English dialect. Wace's *Brut* has 15,300 lines; Layamon's, 32,250. As the matter which Layamon added is the best in the poem, he is, in so far, an original author of much imaginative power. He is certainly the greatest poet between the Conquest and Chaucer's time.

A selection from the *Brut* will give the student an opportunity of comparing this transition English with the language in its modern form : —

" And Ich wulle varan to Avalun :	And I will fare to Avalon,
To vairest alre maidene,	To the fairest of all maidens,
To Argante ðere quene,	To Argante the queen,
Alven swiðe sceone ;	Elf surpassing fair ;
And heo scal mine wunden	And she shall my wounds
Makien alle isunde,	Make all sound,
Al hal me makien	All hale me make
Mid halweige drenchen.	With healing draughts.

And seoðe Ich cumen wulle
To mine kineriche
And wunien mid Brutten
Mid muchelere wunne."

And afterwards I will come
To my kingdom
And dwell with Britons
With much joy.

With this, compare the following lines from Tennyson's *The Passing of Arthur :* —

> ". . . I am going a long way
> To the island-valley of Avilion,
> Where falls not hail, or rain, or any snow,
> Nor ever wind blows loudly ; but it lies
> Deep-meadow'd, happy, fair with orchard lawns
> And bowery hollows crown'd with summer sea,
> Where I will heal me of my grievous wound.
> . . . .
> He passes to be King among the dead,
> And after healing of his grievous wound
> He comes again."

Layamon employed less alliteration than is found in Anglo-Saxon poetry. He also used an occasional rhyme, but the accent and rhythm of his verse are more Saxon than modern. When reading Tennyson's *Idylls of the King*, we must not forget that Layamon was the first poet to celebrate in English King Arthur's deeds. The *Brut* shows little trace of French influences, and not more than a hundred French words can be found in it.

Orm's Ormulum. — A monk named Orm wrote in the Midland dialect a metrical paraphrase of those parts of the *Gospels* used in the church on each service day throughout the year. After the paraphrase comes his metrical explanation and application of the Scripture. He says : —

> " Þiss boc iss nemmnedd Orrmulum
> Forrði ðatt Ormm itt wrohhte."

> This book is named Ormulum
> For that Orm it wrote.

There was no fixed spelling at this time. Orm generally doubled the consonant after a short vowel, and he insisted that any one who copied his work should be careful to do the same. We shall find on counting the syllables in the two lines quoted from him that the first line has eight; the second, seven. This scheme is followed with great precision throughout the poem, which employs neither rhyme nor regular alliteration. Orm used even fewer French words than Layamon. The date of the *Ormulum* is probably somewhere between 1200 and 1215.

The Ancren Riwle. — About 1225 appeared the most notable prose work in the native tongue since the time of Alfred, if we except the *Anglo-Saxon Chronicle*. Three young ladies had secluded themselves from the world in Dorsetshire, and they wished rules for guidance in their seclusion. An unknown author, to oblige them, wrote the *Ancren Riwle* (Rule of Anchoresses). This book lays down rules for their future conduct in all the affairs of life, and it also offers much religious consolation.

The following selection shows some of the curious rules for the guidance of the nuns, and furnishes a specimen of the Southern dialect of transitional English prose in the early part of the thirteenth century : —

"ȝe, mine leoue sustren,	Ye, my beloved sisters,
ne schulen habben no best	shall have no beast
bute kat one. . . . ȝe schulen	but one cat. . . . Ye shall
beon i-dodded four siðen	be cropped four times
iðe ȝere, uorto lihten ower	in the year for to lighten your
heaued. . . Of idelnesse awakeneð	head. . . . Of idleness ariseth
muchel flesshes fondunge. . . .	much temptation of the flesh. . . .
Iren ðet lið stille gedereð	Iron that lieth still soon gathereth
sone rust."	rust.

The keynote of the work is the renunciation of self. Few productions of modern literature contain finer pictures of the Divine love and sympathy. Across the fierce storm clouds of theology, which continued to sweep the heavens for hundreds of years, the pages of the *Ancren Riwle* reflect the rainbow hues of the Galilean's compassion for laboring and heavy-laden humanity. The following simile affords an instance of this quality in the work : —

"Ðe sixte kunfort is ðet ure Louerd, hwon he iðoleð ðet we beoð itented, he plaieð mid us, ase ðe moder mid hire ȝunge deorlinge; vlihð from him, and hut hire, and let hit sitten one, and loken ȝeorne abuten, and cleopien Dame! dame! and weopen one hwule; and ðeonne mid ispredde ermes leapeð lauhwinde vorð, and cluppeð and cusseð and wipeð his eien. Riht so ure Louerd let us one iwurðen oðer hwules, and wiðdraweð his grace and his kunfort, ðet we ne ivindeð swetnesse in none ðinge ðet we wel doð, ne savur of heorte; and ðauh, iðet ilke point ne luveð he us ure leove veder never ðe lesce, auh he deð hit for muchel luve ðet he haveð to us."

The sixth comfort is that our Lord, when he suffers that we be tempted, he plays with us, as the mother with her young darling; she flees from it, and hides herself, and lets it sit alone and look anxiously about and cry "Dame! dame!" and weep awhile; and then with outspread arms leaps laughing forth and clasps and kisses it and wipes its eyes. Exactly so our Lord leaves us alone once in a while and withdraws his grace and his comfort, that we find sweetness in nothing that we do well, no relish of heart; and notwithstanding, at the same time, he, our dear Father, loves us nevertheless, but he does it for the great love that he has for us.

Professor Sweet calls the *Ancren Riwle* " one of the most perfect models of simple, natural, eloquent prose in our language." The work occupies a prominent place in the development of the English language. A philologist says : " If it be true, as some tell us, that the mingling of the Teutonic and Romance in our tongue makes a happy marriage, we see in the author of the *Ancren Riwle* the man that first gave out the bans." Among the words of French origin found in it, we may instance :

"dainty," "cruelty," "vestments," "comfort," "journey," "mercer."

Lyrical Poetry. — About the year 1250 an unknown author wrote in the Southern dialect a fine poem entitled *The Owl and the Nightingale*. A nightingale is singing upon a blossoming bough, when she spies an owl sitting upon a dead tree, with ivy trailing around the trunk. The sight of the lugubrious bird stops the nightingale's song, and she calls to the owl to take her uncanny self away. The owl defends herself and points out her own excellent qualities. The nightingale then sings a beautiful song to put the hooting owl to shame.

A debate on the respective merits of each bird follows. In the course of the poem, the nightingale gives her spring song, which shows that even then the poets were beginning to appreciate the beauties of nature. It should be noticed that the song employs the modern end rhyme : —

> "Ðe blostme ginneð springe and sprede
> Beoðe ine treo and ek on mede ;
> Ðe lilie mid hire faire wlite
> Welcumeð me, ðat ðu hit wite,
> Bit me mid hire faire bleo
> Ðat ich schulle to hire fleo ;
> Ðe rose also mid hire rude,
> Ðat cumeð ut of ðe ðorne wude,
> Bit me ðat ich shulle singe
> Vor hire luve one skentinge."

A free translation of this would be : —

> The blossom begins to spring and to spread
> Both in the tree and in the mead ;
> The lily with her form so fair
> Doth welcome me, you are aware,
> With winsome face doth bid that I
> On airy wings should to her fly ;

The rose also with the blush of morn,
That cometh from a bush of thorn,
Now asks of me that I shall sing
For her own love one charming thing.

Another lyric, of uncertain date, likewise shows a study of nature : —

"Sumer is i-cumen in
    Lhude sing cuccu
    Groweth sed and bloweth med
    And springeth the wde nu.
    Sing cuccu, cuccu."

Summer is a-coming in,
Loud sing cuckoo,
Groweth seed and bloometh mead,
And springeth the wood now.
Sing cuckoo, cuckoo.

Robert Manning of Brunne. — We have now come to fourteenth century literature, which begins to wear a more modern aspect. Robert Manning, generally known as Robert of Brunne, because he was born at Brunne, now called Bourn, in Lincolnshire, adapted from a Norman-French original a work entitled *Handlyng Synne* (*Manual of Sins*). This book, written in the Midland dialect in 1303, discourses of the Seven Deadly Sins and the best ways of living a godly life.

A careful inspection of the following selection from the *Handlyng Synne* will show that, aside from the spelling, the English is essentially modern. Most persons will be able to understand all but a few words. He was the first English writer to use the modern order of words. The end rhyme is also modern. A beggar, seeing a beast laden with bread at the house of a rich man, asks for food. The poem says of the rich man : —

"He stouped down to seke a stone,
    But, as hap was, than fonde he
        none.
For the stone he toke a lofe,
And at the pore man hyt drofe.

He stooped down to seek a stone,
But, as chance was, then found he
    none.
For the stone he took a loaf,
And at the poor man it drove.

The pore man hente hyt up belyue,	The poor man caught it up quickly,
And was thereof ful ferly blythe,	And was thereof full strangely glad,
To hys felaws fast he ran	To his fellows fast he ran
With the lofe, thys pore man."	With the loaf, this poor man.

Oliphant says: "Strange it is that Dante should have been compiling his *Inferno*, which settled the course of Italian literature forever, in the selfsame years that Robert of Brunne was compiling the earliest pattern of well-formed New English. . . . Almost every one of the Teutonic changes in idiom, distinguishing the New English from the Old, the speech of Queen Victoria from the speech of Hengist, is to be found in Manning's work. We have had few Teutonic changes since his day, a fact which marks the influence he has had upon our tongue. . . . Robert of Brunne, the Patriarch of the New English, fairly well foreshadowed the proportion of outlandish gear that was to be the common rule in our land after his time. He has six French words out of fifty; a little later Chaucer was to have eight French words out of fifty; this is the proportion in Shakespeare's comic parts; and it is also the proportion in the everyday talk of our own time."

Mandeville's Travels. — Sir John Mandeville, who is popularly considered the author of a very entertaining work of travels, states that he was born in St. Albans in 1300, that he left England in 1322, and traveled in the East for thirty-four years. His *Travels* relates what he saw and heard in his wanderings through Ethiopia, Persia, Tartary, India, and Cathay. What he tells on his own authority, he vouches for as true, but what he relates as hearsay, he leaves to the reader's judgment for belief.

There is a difference of opinion among scholars in regard to whether any such traveler as Mandeville existed. Parts of the work attributed to him have been proved to be a compilation from the writings of other travelers. A French critic says wittily : " He first lost his character as a truthful writer; then out of the three versions of his book, French, English, and Latin, two were withdrawn from him, leaving him only the first. Existence has now been taken from him, and he is left with nothing at all." But no matter who the author was, the book exists. More manuscripts of it survive than of any other work except the *Scriptures*. It is the most entertaining volume of English prose that we have before 1360. The sentences are simple and direct, and they describe things vividly : —

"In Ethiope ben many dyverse folk : and Ethiope is clept[1] Cusis. In that contree ben folk, that han but o foot : and thei gon so fast, that it is marvaylle : and the foot is so large, that it schadewethe alle the body a;en[2] the Sonne whanne thei wole[3] lye and reste hem."[4]

Mandeville also tells of a bird that used to amuse itself by flying away with an elephant in its talons. In the land of Prester John was a valley where Mandeville says he saw devils jumping about as thick as grasshoppers. Stories like these make the work as interesting as *Gulliver's Travels*.

The so-called Mandeville's *Travels* was one of the few works which the unlearned of that age could understand and enjoy. Its consequent popularity was so great as to bring a large number of French words into familiar use. The native "againbought" is, however, used instead of the foreign "redeemed."

John Wycliffe.— Wycliffe (1324–1384) was born at Hipswell, near Richmond, in the northern part of Yorkshire. He became a doctor of divinity and a master of one of the colleges at Oxford. Afterward he was installed vicar

[1] called. [2] against. [3] will. [4] them.

JOHN WYCLIFFE

of Lutterworth in Leicestershire, where he died. In history he is principally known as the first great figure in the English Reformation, preceding the others by more than a century. In literature he is best known for the first complete translation of the *Bible*, — a work that exerted great influence on English prose. All the translation was not made by him personally, but all was done under his direction. The translation of the most of the *New Testament* is thought to be his own special work. He is the most important prose writer of the fourteenth century. His prose had an influence as wide as the circulation of the *Bible*. The fact that it was forced to circulate in manuscript, because printing had not then been invented, limited his readers, but his translation was, nevertheless, read by many. He wrote argumentative religious pamphlets to help the cause of the Reformation, and they are excellent specimens of energetic fourteenth century prose.

Of his place in literature, Ten Brink says: "Wycliffe's literary importance lies in the fact that he extended the domain of English prose and enhanced its powers of expression. He accustomed it to terse reasoning, and perfected it as an instrument for expressing rigorous logical thought and argument; he brought it into the service of great ideas and questions of the day, and made it the medium of polemics and satire. And above all, he raised it to the dignity of the national language of the *Bible*."

The following is a specimen verse of Wycliffe's translation. We may note that the strong old English word "againrising" had not then been displaced by the Latin "resurrection."

"Jhesu seith to hir, I am agenrisyng and lyf; he that bileueth in me, he, if he schal be deed, schall lyue."

Piers Plowman. — About 1362 a poem was written by a man most commonly known as William Langland. He was probably born at Cleobury Mortimer in Shropshire about 1332, and was educated as a cleric, but he never became a fully ordained priest, although he seems to have performed certain offices in connection with the church, such as singing at funerals. We know scarcely anything of his life, except what we learn indirectly from his *Piers Plowman*.

This poem opens on a pleasant May morning amid rural scenery. The poet falls asleep by the side of a brook and

dreams.   In his dream he has a vision of the world passing before his eyes, like a drama.   The poem tells what he
saw.   Its opening lines are : —

> "In a *s*omer *s*eson · whan *s*oft was the *s*onne
> I *sh*ope [1] me in *sh*roudes [2] · as I a *sh*epe [3] were,
> In *h*abite as an *h*eremite [4] · un*h*oly of workes
> *W*ent *w*yde in þis *w*orld · *w*ondres to here
> Ac on a *M*ay *m*ornynge · on *M*aluerne hulles [5]
> Me by*f*el a *f*erly [6] · of *f*airy me thouȝte
> I *w*as *w*ery for*w*andred [7] ·· and *w*ent me to reste
> Under a *b*rode *b*ank · *b*i a *b*ornes [8] side,
> And as I *l*ay and *l*ened [9] · and *l*oked in þe wateres
> I *s*lombred in a *s*lepyng · it *s*weyved [10] so merye."

The language of *Piers Plowman* is a mixture of the
Southern and the Midland dialects.   It should be noticed
that the poem employs the old Anglo-Saxon alliterative
meter.   There is no end rhyme.   *Piers Plowman* is the
last great poem written in this way.

The actors in this poem are largely allegorical.   Abstractions are personified.   Prominent characters are
Conscience, Lady Meed or Bribery, Reason, Truth,
Gluttony, Hunger, and the Seven Deadly Sins.   In some
respects, the poem is not unlike the *Pilgrim's Progress*
(p. 226), for the battle in passing from this life to the next
is well described in both ; but there are more humor, satire,
and descriptions of common life in Langland.   Piers is at
first a simple plowman, who offers to guide men to truth.
He is finally identified with the Savior.

Throughout the poem, the writer displays all the old
Saxon earnestness.   His hatred of hypocrisy is manifest
on every page.   His sadness, because what is, is not what

---

[1] arrayed.   [2] garments.   [3] shepherd.   [4] hermit.   [5] hills.   [6] wonder.
[7] tired out with wandering.   [8] brook.   [9] reclined.   [10] sounded.

ought to be, makes itself constantly felt. He cannot reconcile the contradiction between the real and the ideal. In attacking the hypocrisy of the clergy and preaching the excellency of a life of good deeds, in showing how men ought to progress in the sphere of action from doing well to doing better and doing best, — " Do-well, Do-bet, Do-best," — he was one of those who helped to lay the foundations of the Reformation.

In order to have a well-rounded conception of the life of the fourteenth century, Langland must be read as well as Chaucer. Langland was the poet of the lower, Chaucer of the upper, classes. Langland's verse gives valuable pictures of the life of the common people and shows them working

> " To kepe kyne in þe field, þe corne fro þe bestes,
> Diken [1] or deluen [2] or dyngen [3] vppon sheues,[4]
> Or helpe make mortar or bere mukke a-felde."

Although Langland was the poet of the common people, he used almost as many words of French derivation as the more aristocratic Chaucer. This fact shows how thoroughly the French element had become incorporated in the speech of all classes. Langland revised his great poem twice, and he has left three texts which differ considerably, although the general tenor of all is the same.

John Gower. — Gower, a very learned poet, was born about 1325 and died in 1408. He did not know that the Midland dialect would become the language of all England. Gower was, therefore, undecided in what language to write, and so he tried each of the three languages used in England. His first principal work, the *Speculum Meditantis*, was written in French; his second, the *Vox Clamantis*, in Latin; his third, the *Confessio Amantis*, in English.

---

[1] to make dykes or ditches.   [2] to dig.   [3] to thrash (ding).   [4] sheaves.

The *Confessio Amantis* (*Confession of a Lover*) is a long poem, in the nature of a dialogue between a lover and his confessor, wherein the things tending to further or hinder love are discussed. But the poem is principally a collection of tales about love. With the exception of a very few tales, the *Confessio Amantis* is rightly noted for its dullness.

JOHN GOWER

The *Confessio Amantis* contains one hundred and twelve short tales, of which not more than three are interesting. The story of *Knight Florent* is his best. The Knight has forfeited his life. He will not be spared unless he correctly answers the riddle: "What do women most desire?" He promises to marry any woman who will tell him. An ugly old hag gives him the right answer, "mastery in love." A knight must keep his word, and so he marries her. After the ceremony she becomes a young and beautiful woman.

GEOFFREY CHAUCER, 1340 ?-1400

Life. — Chaucer was born in London about 1340. His father and grandfather were vintners, who belonged to the upper class of merchants. Our first knowledge of Geoffrey Chaucer is obtained from the household accounts of the Princess Elizabeth, daughter-in-law of Edward III. Chaucer, then in his teens, was a page in her family. An entry shows that she bought him a fine suit of clothes, including a pair of red and black breeches. Such evidence points to the fact that he was early accustomed to

GEOFFREY CHAUCER

associating with the nobility, and enables us to understand why the subject matter of his poetry should differ from Langland's.

In 1359 Chaucer accompanied the English army to France and was taken prisoner. Edward III. thought enough of the youth to pay for his ransom a sum equivalent to-day to about $1200. After his return he was made valet of the King's chamber. The duties of that office "consisted in making the royal bed, holding torches, and carrying messages." Later, Chaucer became a squire.

In 1370 he was sent to the continent on a diplomatic mission. He seems to have succeeded so well that during the next ten years he was repeatedly abroad in the royal service, and he visited Italy twice. He may thus have met the Italian poet Petrarch. These journeys inspired Chaucer with a desire to study Italian literature, a literature that had just been enriched by the pens of Dante and Boccaccio.

We must next note that Chaucer's life was not that of a poetic dreamer, but of a stirring business man. For more than twelve years he was controller of customs for London. This office necessitated assessing duties on wools, skins, wines, candles, etc. Only a part of this work could be performed by deputy. He was later clerk of the King's works, and while on his way to oversee the repairs on a building, Chaucer was twice robbed. His repeated selection for foreign and diplomatic business shows that he was considered sagacious as well as trustworthy. Had he not kept in close touch with life, he could never have become such a great poet. In this connection we may remark that England's second greatest writer, Milton, spent his prime in attending to affairs of state. Chaucer's busy life did not keep him from attaining third place on the list of England's poets.

There are many passages of autobiographical interest in his poems. People noticed that he was a student of books as well as of men, as these lines from the *Hous of Fame* show : —

> " For whan thy labour doon al is,
> And hast y-maad thy rekeninges,
> Instede of rest and newe thinges,
> Thou gost hoom to thy hous anoon,
> And, also domb as any stoon,
> Thou sittest at another boke,
> Til fully daswed [1] is thy loke,
> And livest thus as an hermyte." [2]

[1] dazed.   [2] hermit.

A passage from the *Legende of Good Women* emphasizes another side of his life. He had a sympathetic appreciation for nature as well as for men and books : —

> " . . . whan that the month of May
> Is comen, and that I here the foules[1] singe,
> And that the floures ginnen[2] for to springe
> Farwel my boke and my devocioun ! "

Chaucer was pensioned by three kings : Edward III., Richard II., and Henry IV. Before the reign of Henry IV., Chaucer's pensions were either not always regularly paid, or they were insufficient for certain emergencies, for he complained of poverty in his old age. The pension of Henry IV. in 1399 was ample, and in that year Chaucer leased a house in the garden of a chapel at Westminster for as many of fifty-three years as he should live. He had occasion to use this house but ten months.

One day, looking wistfully back upon the joys of youth, he wrote : —

> "And on the ground, which is my modres[3] gate,
> I knokke with my staf, bothe erly and late,
> And seye,[4] 'Leve[5] moder, leet me in!'"[6]

In 1400 the mother heard his call, and he was laid at rest in the Poets' Corner in Westminster Abbey.

Chaucer's Earlier Poems. — Before Chaucer was forty, he had probably not written more than one seventh of the 35,000 lines which, in round numbers, he left at his death. Before forty he had not done his greatest work, for he was hampered by too close an adherence to Latin and French models. His *Dethe of Blaunche the Duchesse*, the wife of Edward III.'s son, John of Gaunt, shows the influence of Ovid and of the French school.

---

[1] birds. [2] begin. [3] mother's. [4] say. [5] dear. [6] *Pardoner's Tale.*

In his next period, Chaucer studied Italian models, and gradually acquired that skill which enabled him to produce the masterpieces of his third period. The influence of Boccaccio and, sometimes, of Dante is noticeable in the principal poems of the second period, — the *Troilus and Criseyde*, *Parlement of Foules*, *Hous of Fame*, and *Legende of Good Women*. The *Troilus and Criseyde* is a tale of love that was not true. The *Parlement of Foules* is an allegorical poem, in which birds are represented as assembling to decide to which of three suitors shall be awarded a beautiful female eagle. This eagle represents Anne of Bohemia, and the successful suitor is typical of King Richard II. Lines like the following from this poem show what a loving observer of nature Chaucer was : —

> "The sparow, Venus sone, and the nightingale
> That clepeth [1] forth the fresshe leves newe ;
> The swalow mordrer of the flyës [2] smale,
> That maken hony of floures fresshe of hewe ;
> The wedded turtel, with his herte trewe,
> The pecok, with his aungels fethres brighte."

The pleasing fancy of the song of the nightingale awaking the buds from their sleep has not been surpassed by later poets of nature.

The *Hous of Fame* is an unfinished poem, descriptive of a vision of a vast palace of ice on which the names of the famous are carved to await the melting rays of the sun. The *Legende of Good Women* is a series of stories of those who, like Alcestis, were willing to give up everything for love. In *A Dream of Fair Women* Tennyson says : —

> "' The Legend of Good Women,' long ago
> Sung by the morning-star of song, who made
> His music heard below ;

1 calleth.   2 bees.

Dan Chaucer, the first warbler, whose sweet breath
Preluded those melodious bursts that fill
The spacious times of great Elizabeth
With sounds that echo still."

In this series of poems Chaucer learned how to rely less and less on an Italian crutch. He next took his immortal ride to Canterbury on an English Pegasus.

CANTERBURY CATHEDRAL

The Canterbury Tales

General Plan. — The majority of the world has always been more interested in stories than in any other form of literature. Chaucer probably did not realize that he had such positive genius for telling tales in verse that the next five hundred years would fail to produce his superior in that branch of English literature, but he knew that he enjoyed telling such tales.

All that Chaucer needed was some framework into which he could fit the stories that occurred to him, and make them something more than mere stray tales, which might soon be forgotten. The great contemporary Italian story teller, Boccaccio, conceived the idea of representing some of the nobility of Florence as fleeing from the plague, and telling in their retirement the tales which he used in his *Decameron*. It is doubtful, however, if Chaucer ever knew of the existence of the *Decameron*.

In 1170 Thomas à Becket, Archbishop of Canterbury, was murdered at the altar. He was considered both a martyr and a saint, and his body was placed in a splendid mausoleum at the Cathedral. It was said that miracles were worked at his tomb, that the sick were cured, and that the worldly affairs of those who knelt at his shrine prospered. It became the fashion for all sorts and conditions of men to go on pilgrimages to his tomb. As robbers infested the highways, the pilgrims usually waited at some inn until there was a sufficient band to resist attack. In time the journey came to be looked on as a holiday which relieved the monotony of everyday life. About 1385 Chaucer probably went on such a pilgrimage. To furnish amusement, as the pilgrims cantered along, some of them may have told stories. The idea occurred to Chaucer to write a collection of such tales as the various pilgrims might have been supposed to tell on their journey. The result was the *Canterbury Tales*.

Characters in the Tales. — Chaucer's plan is superior to Boccaccio's, for only the nobility figure as story tellers in the *Decameron*. The Canterbury pilgrims represent all ranks of English life, from the knight to the sailor.

The *Prologue* to the *Tales* places these characters before us almost as distinctly as they would appear in real life. At the Tabard Inn in Southwark, just across

From an old print.

TABARD INN

the Thames from London, we see that merry band of pilgrims on a fragrant April day. We look first upon a manly figure who strikes us as being every inch a knight. His cassock shows the marks of his coat of mail.

> "At mortal batailles hadde he been fiftene.
> . . . .
> And of his port as meke as is a mayde.
> He never yet no vileinye ne sayde
> In al his lyf, unto no maner wight.
> He was a verray parfit, gentil knyght."

His son, the Squire, next catches our attention. We notice his curly locks, his garments embroidered with gay flowers, and the graceful way in which he rides his horse. By his side is his servant the Yeoman, "clad in cote and hood of grene," with a sheaf of arrows at his belt. We may even note his cropped head and his horn suspended from a green belt. We next catch sight of a Nun's gracefully pleated wimple, shapely nose, small mouth, "eyen greye as glas," well-made cloak, coral beads, and brooch of gold. She is attended by a second Nun and three Priests. The Monk is a striking figure : —

> "His heed was balled, that shoon as any glas,
> And eek his face as he hadde been anoint.
> He was a lord ful fat and in good point."

There follow the Friar with twinkling eyes, "the beste beggere in his hous," the Merchant with his forked beard, the Clerk (scholar) of Oxford in his threadbare garments, the Sergeant-at-Law, the Franklyn (country gentleman), Haberdasher, Carpenter, Weaver, Dyer, Tapycer (tapestry maker), Cook, Shipman, Physician, Wife of Bath, Parish Priest, Plowman, Miller, Manciple (purchaser of provisions), Reeve (bailiff of a farm), Summoner (official of an ecclesiastical court), and Pardoner. These characters, exclusive of Baily (the host of the Tabard) and Chaucer himself, are alluded to in the *Prologue* to the *Tales* as

> "Wel nyne and twenty in a companye,
> Of sondry folk, by aventure y-falle
> In felawshipe, and pilgrims were they alle,
> That toward Caunterbury wolden ryde."

The completeness of the picture of fourteenth century English life in the *Canterbury Tales* makes them absolutely necessary reading for the historian as well as for the student of literature. We have, for instance, a better idea of fourteenth century seamen after reading about

Chaucer's Shipman, who knew all the havens on the western coast of the continent and every creek in Britain and Spain. We see him with his brown face as he steals wine from the casks in his cargo, and we again catch a glimpse of him as he turns pirate, when a good opportunity offers, and makes his captives walk the plank. We are given an interesting picture of a Pardoner pretending that pigs' bones are the bones of saints. The finest character in the company is that of the Parish Priest, who attends to his flock like a good Samaritan:—

> "Cristes lore, and his apostles twelve,
> He taughte, but first he folwed it him-selve."

Certainly no one who has ever read the *Prologue* to the *Tales* will question Chaucer's right to be considered a great *original* poet, no matter how much he may have owed to foreign teachers.

The Tales. — Harry Baily, the keeper of the Tabard Inn, accompanied the Pilgrims, and he proposed that each member of the party should tell four tales, two going and two returning. The one who told the best story was to have a supper at the expense of the rest. The plan thus outlined was not fully executed by Chaucer, for the collection contains but twenty-four tales, all but two of which are in verse.

The *Knightes Tale*, which is the first, is also the best. It is a very interesting story of love and chivalry. Two young Theban noblemen, Palamon and Arcite, sworn friends, are prisoners of war at Athens. Looking through the windows of their dungeon, they see walking in the garden the beautiful sister of the Queen. Each one swears that he will have the Princess. Arcite is finally pardoned on condition that he will leave Athens and

never return, on penalty of death.   He soon finds that he
loves the Princess Emily so that he would prefer to be in
the Athenian prison where he could see her.   Reduced
almost to a skeleton, he disguises himself, goes to Athens,
and becomes a servant in the house of King Theseus.
Finally Palamon escapes from prison, and by chance over-
hears Arcite moaning half aloud his lover's woes.   The
two men promptly fight and are caught in the act by the
King, who orders them killed.   The Princess intercedes
for them, and the King directs them to return in a year,
each one with a hundred of the bravest knights that he
can find.   Each shall lead his forces in a mortal battle in
the lists, and the Princess shall be awarded to the one who
is the victor.

On the morning of the fight, Palamon goes before dawn
to the temple of Venus and prays that, since this is
a case of love, she will hear his prayer, and grant him
Emily.   The goddess promises that his prayer shall be
answered.   Arcite at the same time steals to the temple
of Mars and beseeches the god to grant him the victory,
since this is a case of war.   The martial deity promises
the victory to Arcite.

The descriptions of the temples, and the remainder of
the story, should be read by the student in the original.
Although Boccaccio's *Teseide* furnished the general plot
for the *Knightes Tale*, Chaucer's story is, as Skeat says,
"to all intents, a truly original poem."

The other pilgrims tell stories in keeping with their pro-
fessions and characters.   Perhaps the next best tale is the
merry story of *Chanticleer and the Fox*.   This is related
by the Nun's Priest.   The Clerk of Oxford tells the pathetic tale of *Patient Griselda*, and the Nun relates a
touching story of a little martyr.

General Characteristics of Chaucer's Work and its Effect upon the Language

Chief Qualities. — I. His descriptions are unusually clear-cut and vivid. For instance, he says of the Friar : —

> "His eyen twinkled in his heed aright,
> As doon the sterres in the frosty night."

Our eyes and ears distinctly perceive the jolly Monk, as he canters along : —

> "And, whan he rood, men might his brydel here
> Ginglen in a whistling wind as clere,
> And eek as loude as dooth the chapel-belle."

II. Chaucer's kindly, sympathetic humor is especially characteristic. We can see him looking with twinkling eyes at the Miller, "tolling thrice"; at the Pardoner, showing a piece of the sail from St. Peter's ship, or the pigs' bones in place of those of a saint; at the Squire, keeping the nightingale company; at the Doctor, prescribing by the rules of astrology. The Nun feels a touch of his humor : —

> "Ful wel she song the service divyne,
> Entuned in hir nose ful semely."

Of the lawyer, he says : —

> "No-wher so bisy a man as he ther nas,
> And yet he semed bisier than he was."

Sometimes Chaucer's humor is so delicate as to be lost on those who are not quick-witted. Lowell instances the case of the Friar, who, "before setting himself softly down, drives away the cat," and adds what is true only of those who have acute understanding : "We know, without need of more words, that he has chosen the snuggest corner."

III. Although Chaucer's humor and excellence in lighter vein are such marked characteristics, we must not forget his serious qualities, for he has the Saxon seriousness as well as the Norman airiness. As he looked over the struggling world, he said with sympathetic heart: —

> "Infinite been the sorwes and the téres
>   Of olde folk, and folk of tendre yeres." [1]

In like vein, we have : —

> "This world nis but a thurghfare ful of wo,
>   And we ben pilgrimes, passinge to and fro ;
>   Deeth is an ende of every worldly sore." [1]

> "Her nis non hoom, her nis but wildernesse.
>   Forthe, pylgrime, forthe! forthe, beste out of thi stal!
>   Knowe thi contree, look up, thank God of al!" [2]

His humor is often a graceful cloak for his serious philosophy of existence. The humor in the *Prologue* does not impair its worth to the student of fourteenth century life.

IV. The largeness of his view of human nature is remarkable. Some poets paint one type of men accurately and distort all the rest, either intentionally or unintentionally. Chaucer impartially portrays the highest and the lowest, the honest man and the hypocrite. The pictures of the roguish Friar and the self-denying Parish Priest, the Oxford Scholar and the Miller, the Physician and the Shipman, are painted with equal fidelity to life. In the breadth and kindliness of his view of life, Chaucer is a worthy predecessor of Shakespeare. Dryden's verdict on Chaucer's poetry is : "Here is God's plenty."

V. His love of nature is noteworthy for that early age. The quotations on pp. 73, 74, show this characteristic. Such

---

[1] *Knightes Tale.*   [2] *Truth: Balade de bon Conseyl.*

lines as these manifest something more than a desire for rhetorical effect in speaking of nature's phenomena: —

> "Now welcom somer, with thy sonne softe
> That hast this wintres weders over-shake,
> And driven awey the longe nightes blake [1]!"[2]

His affection for the daisy has for five hundred years caused many other people to look with fonder eyes upon that flower.

VI. He stands in the front rank of those who have attempted to tell stories in melodious verse. Lowell justly says: "One of the world's three or four great story tellers, he was also one of the best versifiers that ever made English trip and sing with a gayety that seems careless, but where every foot beats time to the tune of the thought."

What Chaucer did for the English Language. — Before Chaucer's works, English was, as we have seen, a language of dialects. He wrote in the Midland dialect, and aided in making that the language of England. Lounsbury says of Chaucer's influence: "No really national language could exist until a literature had been created which would be admired and studied by all who could read, and taken as a model by all who could write. It was only a man of genius that could lift up one of these dialects into a preëminence over the rest, or could ever give to the scattered forces existing in any one of them the unity and vigor of life. This was the work that Chaucer did." For this reason he deserves to be called our first modern English poet. At first sight, his works look far harder to read than they really are, because the spelling has changed so much since Chaucer's day.

---

[1] black.   [2] *The Parlement of Foules.*

Summary

The period from the Norman Conquest to the death of Chaucer contains one, and only one, of the world's great authors, — Geoffrey Chaucer. But the time is important because it gave to England a new language of greater flexibility and power. The old inflections, formative prefixes, and capacity of making self-explaining compounds were for the most part lost. For more than two hundred years after the Norman Conquest, Saxon was the language of the hearth and the field, not of literature and amusement. No language was ever more closely linked to earnest life and feeling. No affectation of speech survived that period of trial, but the Saxon preserved for us those words which caused his heart to throb with warmest feeling, words like "mother," "home," "hearth," "birth," "death," and "love." Such a genuine language of the heart enabled Shakespeare to speak more effectively to the ear of all time.

To supply the places of lost words and to express those new ideas which came with the broader experiences of an emancipated, progressive nation, many new words were adopted from the French and the Latin. When the time for literature came, Chaucer found ready for his pen the strongest, sincerest, and most flexible language that ever expressed a poet's thought.

In tracing the development of English literature, we have noted (1) Geoffrey of Monmouth's (Latin) *History of the Kings of Britain*, and Layamon's *Brut*, with their stories of Lear, Cymbeline, and King Arthur; (2) the *Ormulum*, a metrical paraphrase of those parts of the *Gospels* used in church service; (3) the *Ancren Riwle*, remarkable for its natural eloquent prose and its noble ethics, as well as for showing the development of the language; (4) the lyrical poetry, beginning to be redolent of the odor of the blossom and resonant with the song of the bird; (5) the *Handlyng Synne*, in which we stand on the threshold of modern English; (6) Mandeville's *Travels*, with its entertaining stories; (7) Wycliffe's monumental translation of the *Bible;* (8) Langland's *Piers Plowman*, with its pictures of homely life and its intense desire for higher ideals; (9) Gower's *Confessio Amantis*, a dull collection of tales about love; and (10) Chaucer's poetry, which stands in the front rank for the number of vivid pictures of contemporary life, for humor, love of nature, melody, and capacity for story telling.

In brief, the 334 years following the Norman Conquest are remarkable (*a*) for the development of English into the greatest of the world's languages, (*b*) for the rising of the Reformation spirit and for the translation of the *Bible*, and (*c*) for the emergence of modern English in one of the world's poetic masterpieces, the *Canterbury Tales* of Chaucer. His line, —

"The lyf so short, the craft so long to lerne," [1]

shows that English poetry could still look at life through Saxon eyes.

REQUIRED READINGS FOR CHAPTER II

HISTORICAL

Gardiner,[2] pp. 89–288; Green, Chaps. II., III., IV., V.; Underwood-Guest, pp. 130–311; Guerber, pp. 76–173; Robertson, pp. 79–108; Hutton's *King and Baronage*, pp. 8–112 (*Oxford Manuals of English History*); Oman's *England and the Hundred Years' War*

[1] *The Parlement of Foules.*
[2] For full titles of histories see list at end of Chap. I.

(same series), pp. 7-96; Freeman's *William the Conqueror* (200 pp., 50 cents); Traill, I., 231-491, 11., 1-276.

LITERARY [1]

Lounsbury's *History of the English Language*, pp. 48-160, gives a good account of the linguistic changes following the Norman Conquest.

Mandeville's *Travels* may be read in modernized form in Cassell's *National Library*, No. 10, edited by Morley (paper, 10 cents). Read the last page of the *Prologue* and pp. 168-177, or substitute the selections to be found in Craik's *English Prose Selections*, Vol. I., pp. 22-26. It will be instructive to compare as products of the story teller's art these *Travels* with *Gulliver's Travels*.

Selections from Wycliffe's *Bible* are given in No. 107 of Maynard, Merrill & Co.'s *English Classics* (12 cents). Compare the words and forms of expression in Wycliffe's translation with those of our *Authorized Version*.

Morris and Skeat's *Specimens of Early English*, Part II., gives in their original form, with notes and glossary, selections from Mandeville's *Travels*, Wycliffe's *Translation of the Gospel of Mark*, Langland's *Piers the Plowman*, Gower's *Confessio Amantis*. Good selections from Langland and Gower, with modernized spelling, may be found in Ward's *English Poets*, Vol. I., pp. 96-101 and 107-113.

Chaucer. — His finest production is the *Prologue* (*Eclectic English Classics*, American Book Co., *Prologue and Knightes Tale*, 25 cents; Ward's *English Poets*, I., 46-56), which should be read and re-read. The student should be able to give a clear-cut description of each one of the leading pilgrims and to answer definitely the following questions : —

How has the *Prologue* added to our knowledge of life in the fourteenth century? Give examples of Chaucer's vivid pictures. What specimens of his humor does the *Prologue* contain? Do any of Chaucer's lines in the *Prologue* show that the Reformation spirit was in the air, or did Wycliffe and Langland alone among contemporary authors afford evidence of this spirit? Compare the subject matter of Chaucer's verse with Langland's. What qualities in Chaucer save him from the charge of cynicism when he alludes to human faults? Does

[1] Every school library should own Ward's *English Poets*, 4 vols., $4, and Craik's *English Prose Selections*, 5 vols., $5.50.

the *Prologue* attempt to portray any of the nobler sides of human nature? Is the *Prologue* mainly or entirely concerned with the personality of the pilgrims? Has Chaucer any philosophy of life? Are there any references to the delights of nature? Note any passages that show special powers of melody and mastery over verse. Does the poem reveal anything of Chaucer's personality?

The student who has the time at this point should also read one or two of Chaucer's delightful tales, *e.g.*, *The Knightes Tale* and *The Nonne Preestes Tale*. These two, together with the *Prologue*, may be found in Morris's Clarendon Press edition (70 cents) and in Corson's *Selections from Chaucer's Canterbury Tales* (90 cents). Outside of the drama, does English literature contain any other story teller in verse who can be classed with Chaucer?

WORKS FOR CONSULTATION AND FURTHER STUDY

(OPTIONAL)

Ramsay's *The Foundations of England*.

Ten Brink's *Early English Literature*, Vol. I., pp. 119–367 ; Vol. II., pp. 3-206.

Morley's *English Writers*, Vols. III., IV., V.

Jusserand's *Literary History of the English People, from the Origins to the Renaissance*, pp. 97–438.

Courthope's *History of English Poetry*, Vol. I.

Lounsbury's *History of the English Language*.

Champney's *History of English*.

Morris's *Specimens of Early English*, Part I., contains selections from the *Ormulum*, Layamon's *Brut*, the *Ancren Riwle*, and *The Owl and the Nightingale*. Part II. contains specimens of the lyrics, the *Handlyng Synne* of Robert Manning of Brunne, Mandeville's *Travels*, Langland's *Piers the Plowman*, Wycliffe's *Translation of St. Mark*, Gower's *Confessio Amantis*, and Chaucer's *Canterbury Tales*, with *Notes* and *Glossary*.

Sweet's *First Middle English Primer* contains extracts from the *Ancren Riwle* and the *Ormulum*.

Jusserand's *Piers Plowman*.

Skeat's text of *Piers the Plowman*, with *Glossary* and *Notes*.

Bosworth and Waring's edition of the *Gospels* contains the Gothic and the Anglo-Saxon text, together with the translations by Wycliffe and Tyndale (p. 98).

Skeat's *Complete Works of Geoffrey Chaucer*, 6 vols., is the best edition. Skeat's *Student's Edition* of same, 1 vol., has the same text.

Chaucer's *Canterbury Tales Annotated and Accented, with Illustrations of English Life in Chaucer's Time*, by John Saunders.

Pollard's *Primer of Chaucer*.

Lounsbury's *Studies in Chaucer*, 3 vols.

Ward's *Life of Chaucer*, in *English Men of Letters* Series.

Lowell's *My Study Windows* contains one of the best essays ever written on Chaucer.

Minto's *Characteristics of English Poets*, pp. 1–58 (Chaucer, Langland, Gower).

Morley's *Early English Romances*.

Ellis's *Specimens of Early English Metrical Romances*.

Jusserand's *English Wayfaring Life in the Fourteenth Century*.

Cutts's *Scenes and Characters of the Middle Ages*.

Jessop's *The Coming of the Friars*.

Cutts's *Parish Priests and their People in the Middle Ages in England*.

CHAPTER III

Reasons for Comparative Lack of Progress of Fifteenth Century Literature. — It might be expected that the fifteenth century would show the effect of Chaucer's quickening influence and produce a literature of surpassing interest. Let us inquire why the reverse is the case.

I. No genius like Chaucer was born; or, if there was such a potential genius, his talents were diverted into channels other than those of literature.

II. There was not so much freedom of thought in the fifteenth as in the fourteenth century. Wycliffe could write his polemical tracts then, and translate and interpret the *Bible*, but his followers could not in the next century. In 1401 the first Englishman was burned at the stake because of individual opinions on religious matters. From this time the expenses of burning heretics are sometimes found in the regular accounts of cities and boroughs. Literature should be the full expression of a nation's thought and feeling, and such literature did not flourish again until Elizabethan days ushered in more freedom.

III. Chivalry, the moving spirit of the preceding age, was changing. This fact necessitated the growth of some new ideal. The increasing use of gunpowder gradually put an end to the superiority of the knight. The great castles began to decline, and people mingled more familiarly with one another. There was no longer so vast a gulf between the rich and the poor. The poor man with his firearm was a match for a horse and a rider. The rise of the common people was soon to have a marked influence on literature. From their ranks was to come an audience that would appreciate and support Shakespeare.

IV. The studies of the Schoolmen had helped to undermine literature and make it repellent. " Schoolmen " is merely a term for those who pursued the studies of the schools or universities. Many of these studies finally became little more than juggling with words or forming smoke wreaths of abstractions. The scholars took nothing for their subject and talked about it at great length. Some of their subjects were : whether all children in a state of innocence are masculine; whether God ever knows more things than he is aware of ; whether one angel can occupy at the same time precisely the same space as another angel ; whether God can make a yardstick without two ends. Science brings new facts into being, but these wordy gymnastics accomplished nothing. Taine says: " Three centuries of labor at the bottom of this black moat added not one idea to the human mind."

V. The Wars of the Roses, or the struggle of the houses of Lancaster and York for the throne, broke out in 1455 and lasted for thirty years. During this time many of the nobles were killed. The effects of this civil war in depressing literature have been overestimated. The times of Richard II. were unsettled, and yet Chaucer wrote then. However, some who might have become writers may have had their energies diverted in another direction by the war.

Malory's Morte d'Arthur. — The greatest prose work of the fifteenth century was completed in 1470 by a man who styles himself Sir Thomas Malory, Knight. We know nothing of the author's life, but he has left as a monument a great prose epic of the deeds of King Arthur and his Knights of the Round Table. From the various French legends concerning King Arthur, Malory selected his materials and fashioned them into the completest Arthuriad that we possess. While his work cannot be called original, he displayed rare artistic power in arranging, abridging, and selecting the various parts from different French works.

Malory's prose is remarkably simple and direct. Even in the impressive scene where Sir Bedivere throws the dying King Arthur's sword into the sea, the language tells the story simply and shows no straining after effect : —

"And then he threw the sword as far into the water as he might, and there came an arm and a hand above the water, and met it and caught it, and so shook it thrice and brandished. And then vanished away the hand with the sword in the water. . . . 'Now put me into the barge,' said the King; and so he did softly. And there received him three queens with great mourning, and so they set him down, and in one of their laps King Arthur laid his head, and then that queen said, 'Ah, dear brother, why have ye tarried so long from me?'"

After the dusky barge has borne Arthur away from mortal sight, Malory writes : " Here in this world he changed his life." A century before, Chaucer had with equal simplicity voiced the Saxon faith : —

"His spiryt chaungede hous."[1]

Sometimes this prose narrative, in its condensation and expression of feeling, shows something of the poetic spirit. When the damsel on the white palfrey sees that her knightly lover has been killed, she cries : —

[1] *Knightes Tale.*

"'O Balin ! two bodies hast thou slain and one heart, and two hearts in one body, and two souls thou hast lost.' And therewith she took the sword from her love that lay dead, and as she took it, she fell to the ground in a swoon."

Malory's work, rather than Layamon's *Brut*, has been the storehouse to which later poets have turned. Many nineteenth century poets are indebted to Malory. Tennyson's *Idylls of the King*, Matthew Arnold's *Death of Tristram*, Swinburne's *Tristram of Lyonesse*, and William Morris's *Defence of Guinevere* were inspired by the *Morte d'Arthur*. Few other English prose works have had more influence on the poetry of the Victorian age.

Scottish Poetry. — The best poetry of the fifteenth century was written in the Northern dialect, that spoken north of the river Humber. This language was just as much English as the Midland tongue in which Chaucer wrote. Not until the sixteenth century was this dialect called Scotch.

This poetry is remarkable for showing in that early age a genuine love of nature. Changes are not rung on some typical landscape, copied from an Italian versifier. The northern poet had his eye fixed on the scenery and the sky of Scotland. About the middle of the century, Robert Henryson, a teacher in Dunfermline, wrote : —

> "The northin wind had purifyit the air
> And sched the misty cloudis fra the sky." [1]

This may lack the magic of Shelley's rhythm (p. 364), but the feeling for nature is as genuine as in the latter poet's lines : —

> "For after the rain, when with never a stain
> The pavilion of heaven is bare." [2]

---

[1] *Testament of Cresseid.*   [2] *The Cloud.*

William Dunbar, the greatest poet of this group, who lived in the last half of the fifteenth century, was a loving student of the nature which greeted him in his northland. No Italian poet, as he wandered beside a brook, would have thought of a simile like this : —

> "The stonés clear as stars in frosty night."[1]

Dunbar takes us with him on a fresh spring morning, where

> "Enamelled was the field with all coloúrs,
> The pearly droppés shook in silver showers,"[1]

where we can hear the matin song of the birds hopping among the buds, while

> "Up rose the lark, the heaven's minstrel fine."[1]

Both Dunbar and Gawain Douglas (1474?–1522), the son of a Scotch nobleman, had keen eyes for all coloring in sky, leaf, and flower. In one line Dunbar calls our attention to these varied patches of color in a Scotch garden : "purple, azure, gold, and gulés [red]." In the verses of Douglas we see the purple streaks of the morning, the bluish-gray, blood-rèd, fawn-yellow, golden, and freckled red and white flowers, and

> "Some watery-hued, as the blue wavy sea."[2]

Outside the pages of Shakespeare, we shall for the next two hundred years look in vain for such a genuine love of scenery and natural phenomena as we can find in fifteenth century Scottish poetry. These poets obtained many of their images of nature at first hand, a quality rare in any age.

[1] *The Golden Targe.*   [2] *Prologue to Æneid*, Book XII.

"Songs for Man or Woman, of All Sizes." — When Shakespeare shows us Autolycus offering such songs at a rustic festival,[1] the great poet emphasizes the fondness for the ballad which had for a long time been developing a taste for poetry. While it is difficult to assign exact dates to the composition of many ballads, we know that they flourished in the fifteenth century. They were then as much prized as the novel is now, and, like it, they had a story to tell. The verse was often halting, but it succeeded in conveying to the hearer tales of love, adventure, and the supernatural. These ballads were sometimes tinged with pathos, but there was an energy in the rude lines which made the heart beat faster and often stirred the listeners to find in a dance an outlet for their emotions. Even now, with all the poetry of centuries from which to choose, it is refreshing to turn to a Robin Hood ballad and look upon the greensward, hear the rustle of the leaves in Nottingham forest, and follow the adventures of the hero. We read the opening lines : —

> " There are twelve months in all the year,
>   As I hear many say,
> But the merriest month in all the year
>   Is the merry month of May.
>
> " Now Robin Hood is to Nottingham gone,
>   With a link a down, and a day,
> And there he met a silly old woman
>   Was weeping on the way."

Of our own accord we finish the ballad to see if Robin Hood rescued her sons, who were condemned to death for shooting the fallow deer. The ballad of the *Nut-Brown Maid* has some touches which are almost Shakespearean.

[1] *The Winter's Tale*, IV., 4.

Some of the carols of the fifteenth century give a fore-taste of Elizabethan song. One carol on the birth of the Christ-child, beginning: " I syng a of a mayden," contains stanzas like these, which show artistic workmanship, imaginative power, and, above all, rare lyrical beauty : —

> " He cam also stylle
>> to his moderes bowr,
> As dew in Aprille
>> that fallyt on the flour.

> " He cam also stylle
>> ther his moder lay,
> As dew in Aprille
>> that fallyt on the spray." [1]

We saw that the English tongue during its period of exclusion from the Norman court gained strength from coming in such close contact with life. Although the higher types of poetry were for the most part wanting during the fifteenth century, yet the ballads multiplied and sang their songs to the ear of life. Critics may say that the rude stanzas seldom soar far from the ground, but we are again reminded of the invincible strength of Antæus so long as he kept close to his mother earth. English poetry is so great because it has not withdrawn from life, because it was nurtured in such a cradle.

When Shakespeare wrote his plays, he found an audi-ence to understand and to appreciate them. Not only those who occupied the boxes, but also those who stood in the pit, listened intelligently to his dramatic stories. The ballad had played its part in teaching the humblest home to love poetry. These rude fireside songs were no mean factors in preparing the nation to welcome Shake-speare.

[1] Wright's *Songs and Carols of the Fifteenth Century*, **p. 30.**

The Renaissance. — The causes leading to the revival of learning, usually called the Renaissance, constitute the chief glories of the fifteenth century and the first part of the sixteenth. We must remember that the Renaissance was a necessary factor in giving us Shakespeare in the next century. Before the buds and the flowers start forth in the spring, the warm sun has shone and the showers have fallen for some time. They apparently produce no result for a long while, but finally the soft green leaves will clothe the barren trees and the meadows be dotted with fragrant flowers. The revival of learning stands in the same relation to Elizabethan literature as the sun and showers to vegetation.

There were several prominent causes helping to usher in the Renaissance : —

I. The art of printing multiplied books and made their wisdom accessible to a larger number. About 1477 William Caxton printed the first book in England. In the intellectual growth of a nation, it would be difficult to overestimate the importance of printing. When the same forms of speech and idioms circulated among all, an important step was taken in permanently fixing the language. Among a large number of books, Caxton printed the *Canterbury Tales*, and thus gave Chaucer's genius and language wider influence. When we speak of English books before this time, it should be remembered that they were laboriously copied on parchment, and that the copies were consequently few and costly.

II. The capture of Constantinople by the Turks in 1453 was a factor in hastening the influence of Grecian literature on western Christendom. Constantinople, the capital of the Eastern Roman Empire, was the headquarters of Grecian learning. Because of the remoteness of this capital, English literature had not been greatly influenced by Greece. When Constantinople fell, many of her scholars went to Italy, taking with them precious Grecian manuscripts. As Englishmen often visited Italy, they soon began to study Grecian masterpieces, and to fall under the spell of Homer and the Athenian dramatists.

III. Science was gradually developing. Men were asking the why and the wherefore of all things, even of those beliefs grounded on faith. Copernicus was thinking out the true movements of the solar system, and showing that the universe does not revolve around this world as a center. Men began to demonstrate that the world is round and can be circumnavigated. New colleges were established at both Cambridge and Oxford.

IV. The discovery of the New World fired the imaginations of men and made the most wonderful dreams seem capable of realization. It is hard for us to-day, with little undiscovered territory except near the Poles, to appreciate the effect that the finding of a new world would have upon the imaginations and the ambitions of men.

William Tyndale, 1490?–1536. — The Reformation was another mighty influence, working side by side with all the other forces to effect a lasting change in English history and literature. In the early part of the sixteenth century, Martin Luther was electrifying Germany with his demands for church reformation. In order to decide which religious party was in the right, there arose a desire for more knowledge of the *Scriptures*. The language had changed much since Wycliffe's translation of the *Bible*, and, besides, that was accessible only in manuscript. William Tyndale was a clergyman who had been educated at both Oxford and Cambridge. He was an excellent linguist and he conceived the idea of giving the English people the *Bible* in

their own tongue.   He found that he could not translate
and print it with safety in England, and so he went to the
continent, where with the help of friends he turned the
Bible into English and had it printed.   He was forced to
move frequently from place to place, and he was finally
betrayed in his hiding place near Brussels.   After eighteen
months' imprisonment without pen or books, he was stran-
gled and his body was burned at the stake.

Of his translation, Brooke says : " It was this *Bible*
which, revised by Coverdale, and edited and re-edited as

Cromwell's Bible, 1539, and again as *Cranmer's Bible*, 1540, was set up in every parish church in England. It got north into Scotland and made the Lowland English more like the London English. It passed over into the Protestant settlements in Ireland. After its revival in 1611 it went with the Puritan Fathers to New England and fixed the standard of English in America. Many millions of people now speak the English of Tyndale's Bible, and there is no other book which has had, through the *Authorized Version*, so great an influence on the style of English literature and the standard of English prose."

The following verses from Tyndale's version will show its simplicity and directness and how much the translation in present use owes to this: —

"Jesus sayde unto her, Thy brother shall ryse agayne.

"Martha sayde unto hym, I knowe wele, he shall ryse agayne in the resurreccion att the last daye.

"Jesus sayde unto her, I am the resurreccion and lyfe; whosoever beleveth on me, ye, though he were deed, yet shall he lyve."

Italian Influence : Wyatt and Surrey. — During the reign of Henry VIII. (1509–1547), the influence of Italian poetry made itself distinctly felt. The roots of Elizabethan poetry were watered by many fountains, one of the chief of which flowed from Italian soil. To Sir Thomas Wyatt (1503–1542) and to the Earl of Surrey (1517–1547) belongs the credit of introducing from Italian sources new influences which helped to remodel English poetry and give it a distinctly modern cast.

These poets were the first to introduce the sonnet, which Shakespeare, Milton, and Wordsworth employed with such power in after times. Blank verse was first used in England by the Earl of Surrey, who translated a portion of

Virgil's *Æneid* into that measure. When Shakespeare took up his pen, he found that vehicle of poetic expression ready for his use.

Wyatt and Surrey adopted Italian subject matter as well as form. They introduced the poetry of the amourists, that is, verse which tells of the woes and joys of a lover. We find Shakespeare in his *Sonnets* turning to this subject, which he made as broad and deep as life. In 1557, the year before Elizabeth's accession, the poems of Wyatt and Surrey appeared in Tottel's *Miscellany*, one of the earliest printed collections of modern English poetry.

Summary

While the period between the death of Chaucer and the accession of Elizabeth did not furnish to English literature a single great name, the nation was preparing for Elizabethan times. The influences of the Renaissance and the Reformation were at work. The invention of printing began to make it possible for the best literature to be given to the cottage and the palace. The passing of the knight and the rise of the common people helped to knit the entire nation together and to extend the influences of the revival of learning and the religious awakening.

The most important prose works are Sir Thomas Malory's *Morte d'Arthur*, a masterly retelling of the Arthurian legends, and Tyndale's translation of the *Bible*. The best poetry was written in Scotland, and this poetry anticipates in some measure that love of nature which is a dominant characteristic of the last part of the eighteenth century. The age is noted for its ballads, which aided in developing among high and low a liking for poetry. At the close of the period, we find Italian influences at work.

REQUIRED READINGS FOR CHAPTER III

HISTORICAL

Gardiner,[1] pp. 289–427; Green, Chap. VI.; Underwood-Guest, pp. 312–426; Guerber, pp. 174–232; Oman's *England and the Hundred Years' War*, pp. 96–159; Powers's *England and the Reformation*, pp. 7–87; Traill, II., 276–574, III., 1–303.

LITERARY

Malory. — Craik's *English Prose Selections*, Vol. I, pp. 72–74, and the *Camelot Series* edition of Malory's *History of King Arthur*, pp. 311–313, contain the part relating to the death (or passing) of Arthur. This should be compared with Tennyson's *The Passing of Arthur*. Are the finest thoughts in the poem original with Tennyson?

Early Scottish Poetry. — Selections from fifteenth century Scottish poetry, showing an early appreciation of the phenomena of nature, may be found in Ward's *English Poets*, Vol. I., pp. 139, 151, 152, 164, and 165, and in Fitzgibbon's *Early English Poetry* (*Canterbury Poets* Series, 40 cents), pp. 81–85, and 121.

What shows that the references to nature are not merely conventional? The student should be on the alert to notice the next appearance of poetry which shows a genuine love for nature.

Ballads. — The student will find in Ward, I., p. 210, the ballad of *Sir Patrick Spens*; p. 224, *The Twa Corbies*; and, p. 239, *Robin Hood Rescuing the Widow's Three Sons*. The teacher should read to the class parts of *The Nut-Brown Maid* (Fitzgibbon's *Early English Poetry*, pp. 155–167).

What qualities in the ballad caused it to take such a hold on the people? Did it have any educating power?

Tyndale. — The student who has access to Bosworth and Waring's *Gospels*, containing the Anglo-Saxon, Wycliffe, and Tyndale versions, will find it profitable to compare these with the version now in use, and to observe how much current English speech owes to these early translations of the *Gospels*. A specimen of Tyndale's prose is given in Craik's *English Prose Selections*, I., 185–187.

Wyatt and Surrey. — A characteristic love sonnet by Wyatt may be

[1] For complete titles see list at end of Chap. I.

found on p. 251 of Vol. I. of Ward's *English Poets*, and two by Surrey on p. 257. A specimen of the first English blank verse, employed by Surrey in translating Virgil's *Æneid*, is given on pp. 233, 234, of Fitzgibbon's *Early English Poetry*.

Why are these poets called amourists? What contributions did they make to the form of English verse? What foreign influence did they help to usher in?

WORKS FOR CONSULTATION AND FURTHER STUDY

(Optional)

Morley's *English Writers*, Vols. VI. and VII.

Ten Brink's *English Literature*, Vol. II., Wycliffe to Renaissance, pp. 209–234.

Jusserand's *Literary History of the English People from the Origins to the Renaissance*, pp. 503–525.

Gosse's *History of Modern English Literature*, pp. 33–72.

Minto's *Characteristics of English Poets*, pp. 69–130.

Saintsbury's *Short History of English Literature*, pp. 157–218.

Fitzgibbon's *Early English Poetry* (*Canterbury Poets* Series) *Introduction* and pp. 30–234.

Ward's *English Poets*, Vol. I., pp. 114–262.

Craik's *English Prose Selections*, Vol. I., pp. 50–234.

Malory's *Le Morte d'Arthur*, edited by Sommer, with Essay on Malory's Prose by Andrew Lang.

Dictionary of National Biography, articles, *Malory, Caxton, Henryson, Gawain Douglas, Dunbar, Tyndale, Wyatt*, and *Surrey*.

Veitch's *The Feeling for Nature in Scottish Poetry*.

McLaughlin's *Mediæval Life and Literature*.

Child's *English and Scottish Popular Ballads*.

Percy's *Reliques of Ancient English Poetry*.

Gummere's *Old English Ballads*.

Hazlitt's *Early Popular Poetry of England*.

Songs and Carols of the Fifteenth Century, edited by Warton.

Carols and Poems, edited by Bullen.

The *Paston Letters* (1422–1509), 3 vols., edited by Gairdner.

Denton's *England in the Fifteenth Century* (excellent).

Green's *Town Life in the Fifteenth Century*.

CHAPTER IV

THE LITERATURE OF THE AGE OF ELIZABETH

The High-water Mark of the World's Poetry. — The poetry of the Elizabethan age has never been equaled at any other time in the history of the world. It has been well said that one might become a person of broad culture from the study of only two works: the one, the *Bible*; the other, the writings of the greatest of the Elizabethans. Since Shakespeare's day, there have been many improvements in science, but no writer of later times has equaled him. The highest compliment that we can pay to the literature of any other age is to say that it has Elizabethan characteristics.

Unlike other countries, England felt the strong influences from the Renaissance and the Reformation at one and the same time. When the attractions of the sun and moon unite to draw the tides in one direction, they reach their highest point. At no other time have two forces like the Renaissance and the Reformation combined to stimulate the human mind. The Elizabethan imagination took at the flood the tide raised by these mighty forces, and that tide bore the English drama on to a Shakespearean fortune.

We must proceed to note specifically the causes which conspired to produce such a glorious literature in the reign of Elizabeth. We shall seek them in the expansion of both the New and the Old World, in the greater freedom of thought, in the democratic and patriotic spirit, in the desire born of fuller knowledge to live a life as varied and as complete as possible, and in the awakening of the imagination to grasp life's newly suggested and un-fathomed possibilities, and to express them in poetry of sufficient fullness and depth to include all human aspiration.

The Effect of the Exploration of the New World. — A New World had been previously discovered, but many of its wonders had not been explored until Elizabethan times. In the wonderful land beyond the sea, there seemed to be everything necessary to usher in that Utopian age for which men had so long sighed. There were precious stones and gold in quantities that promised wealth and enjoyment for all. There was the fabled Fountain of Youth that would drive away the pains and decrepitude of old age and enable all again to enjoy the promised en-chantments of the new Utopia. At home things might be prosaic, slow of movement, and obtained only by such wearying toil as to preclude enjoyment of them when secured. But this would not be the case in the fairy-land of the New World.

There was the absolute proof sufficient to satisfy the most skeptical that the New World was a wonderful land of plenty. When Shakespeare was in his teens, Sir Francis Drake, the first Englishman to circumnavigate the world, returned from his voyage. Besides what he kept for himself, he placed in the Tower for the use of the Queen twenty tons of silver bullion, huge blocks of gold, and many pearls, emeralds, and other precious stones. The New World was a land of sufficient promise to spur the ambition and quicken the imagination of the Eliza-bethans. Even their third-rate poets could write : —

"Xanthus shall run liquid gold for thee to wash thy hands;
  And if thou like to tend thy flock and not from them to fly,
  Their fleeces shall be curléd gold to please their master's eye." [1]

The Expansion of the Old World. — When we emphasize the influence of the wonders of the New World upon the imagination, we are in danger of forgetting that the Old World was expanding more than the New. Never before had traveling been so popular. Englishmen went to Italy, felt the spell of her literature and art, and came home to spread Italian influence. A contemporary writer on education speaks of "the enchantments of Circe, brought out of Italy" to mold the thought and manners of English youth. Every time England felt a new stimulus from the literature of another great nation, she was receiving advantages from the expansion of the Old World.

The powerful example of Queen Elizabeth aroused in the English people a desire to learn the best things from every nation. Although Italian influence was in the ascendency during the sixteenth century, other literatures were studied. A quotation from Roger Ascham's *Scholemaster*, a distinguished educational work (published in 1570), will show what languages were on the fashionable list. He had been the Queen's tutor, and he says: —

"Yea, I beleue, that beside her perfit readines, in Latin, Italian, French, and Spanish, she readeth here now at Windsore more Greeke euery day, than some Prebendarie of this Chirch doth read Latin in a whole weeke."

We thus see that learning was no longer confined to the church, that even the laity might be more energetic students than churchmen, that the royal example welcomed learning from every land, and that Elizabethan England

[1] Peele: *The Arraignment of Paris*, II., I.

anticipated the age of Victoria in teaching Greek to women.

Nothing contributed to this expansion of the Old World more than the newly acquired freedom of thought, and we must now consider the influence of this factor.

Freedom of Thought and its Results. — In the reign of Elizabeth's father, Catholics and Protestants alike had been put to death for exercising freedom of thought. Under her immediate predecessor on the throne many fagot fires had been lighted in England to punish those whose opinions were considered heretical. In the next century the Puritan reformers would tolerate only that kind of thought pleasing to themselves. Although there was some persecution of Catholics and Dissenters in Elizabeth's time, yet she allowed comparatively great freedom of opinion and action, and English thought reaped a wonderful harvest during her reign.

The Puritans were even then beginning to display their narrowness, but the Queen would not permit them to stifle thought. Had they been given the power to exercise the same censorship which was allowed them in the next century, the greatest of all dramas would have been throttled in its cradle. During the time of Puritan ascendency in the next century, the theaters were torn down.

Thought that is not free is like a bird in a cage. There may be glorious meadows, leafy groves, and murmuring streams with flower-fringed banks, but the caged bird cannot gladden its eye with these, sing its song in the grove, or bathe in the stream. Once open the door of the cage, and the world seems a different one to the bird. Many causes, among which the Reformation was the chief one, had conspired to open the cage, and Elizabeth would not permit the door to be closed.

The Rise of the Middle Class and the Mingling of Different Elements. — Improvement in seamanship, in the art of building vessels, and in the manner of life, which demanded more comforts, caused a vast increase in commerce and trade, and this naturally led to the rise of the middle class. The nobility were no longer the sole leaders in England's rapid progress. The men chosen by Elizabeth to manage affairs of state were not selected merely on account of their titles. Many of her great ministers and councilors were said to have sprung from the earth, and no reign could boast of wiser ones.

When any one moves in an exclusive set or coterie, his opinions are generally narrow. Such a one usually despises others because he does not understand them. Those who are careful not to mingle with others outside of what is termed "our set" are not leaders in human advancement. Different elements of society look at life from different points of view. Difference of opinion has always been a powerful spur to human progress. We can understand others only from sympathetic association with them.

In speaking of the various elements of Elizabethan society, an English critic says : " But these materials, and to a very large extent the members of the upper classes already described, were intermingled and shaken together in a manner quite unknown to-day. At present, society moves in sharply separated groups, while even the individuals of these groups keep very much to themselves. The same people meet each other at the same places and times ; and they do not, as a rule, meet other people of different classes. Then, life was led much more in common and much more in the open air."

When we study Shakespeare, we shall find that he paints

almost every phase of human nature with unerring touch. It is well that he was born in an age when the mingling of different classes was common, so that it was easier for him to become the poet of all humanity. The audience that stood in the pit or sat in the boxes to witness the performance of his plays, comprised not only lords and wealthy merchants, but also weavers, sailors, and country folk.

The mingling of the different classes took place with less friction, because of the spirit of patriotism in the air. When Englishmen, high and low alike, aided in destroying the Spanish Armada and in maintaining England's freedom, all felt that they had a common share in her greatness.

This mingling was further aided by the attempts of the Elizabethans to try many different pursuits. Men thus escaped the social restrictions of modern over-specialized life.

The Many-sidedness of Life. — The revival of learning and the opportunity which the sea constantly afforded for making discoveries and gaining wealth, infused into almost all classes a desire for more knowledge, a longing to find out those secrets which had before been hidden.

We may instance Sir Walter Raleigh to show how many sides to his nature an Elizabethan could develop. He was a courtier, a warden of the tin mines, a vice-admiral, a captain of the guard, a colonizer, a country gentleman managing a vast Irish estate, a pirate, and a writer. Sir Philip Sidney, who died at the age of thirty-two, was an envoy to a foreign court, a writer of romances, an officer in the army, a poet, and a courtier. Even such an idealist as the poet Edmund Spenser was an active servant of the crown in Irish affairs. It became an ambition to have as many different experiences as possible, to search for that variety which youth and a youthful age always crave. This characteristic enabled the Elizabethans to speak to all mankind out of the fullness of this varied experience, and proved an important factor in enriching the literature of the age with such marvelous variety.

The Fullness of Elizabethan Literature. — For the first time in the world, nearly every type of humanity then found adequate recognition and expression. That age gave lasting utterance to almost every feeling which any human soul has ever known. Nothing was suppressed, neither the imaginative longing of youth nor the disappointment of old age. We see the white soul of a Cordelia and the black one of an Iago, a man in the grasp of ambition, like Macbeth, and after it has passed, like Lear, the imaginative Hamlet and the dull gravediggers, the servant and the master, the beggar and the prince. We see how the same man behaves on the crest of Fortune's wave and when overwhelmed by adverse storms. For the first time the shepherd's crook was given an equal rank beside the scepter.

No one has ever complained because his inmost thoughts could not find expression in Elizabethan literature. When we have feelings which we regard as peculiarly our own, we shall often be surprised, as we read the literature of the Elizabethans, to find that they have preceded us in traversing that land of feeling which we were on the point of claiming as the first discoverers.

An Age of Imagination and Enthusiasm. — The world in every direction seemed to offer untold possibilities. A nation which felt its youth in every vein was fired with new hopes, new ambitions, new ideals. The imagination is the only power with which we can grasp the unseen and the ideal. There was never a time in the history of the world when the imagination was more exercised and stimulated. It grew by what it fed on until it attained first Spenserian and then Shakespearean greatness. The stage on which the Elizabethan imagination acted was built by the extension of two worlds, the physical and the mental, the land beyond the western wave and the empire of increasing knowledge, which promised· to unlock the secrets of wind and tide, of plant and metal, of disease and remedy, of sun and star and Milky Way, and finally, perhaps, of life and love, of death and the immortal spirit world.

No literature demands sympathetic interpretation from the point of view of the spirit of the age more than the Elizabethan. When we read Marlowe's *Tamburlaine*, we may unsympathetically declare it a mass of exaggeration and bombast. If we can make our own the imagination and youthful feeling of that time, and remember that a world expanding in every direction promised almost everything, we shall catch something of young Marlowe's enthusiasm and modify our former judgment. If we cannot do this, there is much of Elizabethan literature that we can never read aright.

We shall come later to an age of cold, juiceless reason, but now the imagination sat on the throne beside the reason. Imagination can tinge the leaden clouds of any age with all the colors of the dawn. Taine says: "I can well believe that things had no more beauty then than now; but I am sure that men found them more beautiful." Let us remember that this added beauty was due to the working of the imagination.

Even the poets who rank low in that age could write : —

> "To joy her love, I'll build a kingly bower,
> Seated in hearing of a hundred streams," [1]

and speak without effort

> "Of moss that sleeps with sound the waters make." [1]

As indicative of the intensity of youthful feeling, another poet, meaning every syllable he uttered, says : —

> "I live and love, what would you more?
> As never lover lived before." [2]

A great Elizabethan, trying to define beauty, begins thus : —

> "If all the pens that ever poets held
> Had fed the feeling of their masters' thoughts." [3]

The faults of Elizabethan literature sprang from this very exuberance of imagination and youthful feeling. In connection with the praiseworthy qualities of spontaneity and enthusiasm, manifested in connection with a vivid imagination, we find in much of the literature exaggeration, lack of pruning, and lack of artistic finish. Even Shakespeare has some of these faults, but in his case they are mostly concealed by the brilliancy of his genius.

A Nest of Singing Birds.— To make a careful study of Elizabethan literature would require more than a lifetime. We must guard against thinking that, after we have studied Shakespeare, Spenser, Marlowe, Ben Jonson, and Bacon, we have finished the greater part of Elizabethan literature. It has been aptly said that the

---

[1] Peele : *David and Bethsabe*, I., 1.
[2] Gascoigne : *A Strange Passion of a Lover*.
[3] Marlowe : *Tamburlaine*, V., 1.

writers of the age were a nest of singing birds.   Many of
them occasionally burst into songs of marvelous sweetness.
It is the purpose of this book to describe only the greatest
works.   To show that there were other singers, we need
merely give a few stray snatches of song from some of
the minor poets.

> "Love in my bosom, like a bee,
>   Doth suck his sweet;
> Now with his wings he plays with me,
>   Now with his feet." — LODGE.

> "Weep not, my wanton, smile upon my knee,
> When thou art old, there's grief enough for thee." — GREENE.

> "There is One
> That wakes above, whose eye no sleep can bind." —CHAPMAN.

> "I shall have one hand in heaven
> To write my happiness in leaves of stars." — DEKKER.

> "For see! the dapple gray coursers of the morn
> Beat up the light with their bright silver hoofs
> And chase it through the sky." — MARSTON.

> "Not that fair hair with which the wanton winds
> Delight to play and love to make it curl,
> Wherein the nightingales would build their nests,
> And make sweet bowers in every golden tress
> To sing their lover every night asleep." — PEELE.

Even a nameless poet could say to his dead children : —

> "But you are playing in the angels' laps
> And will not look at me."

Symonds truly says: "Shakespeare stands alone and
has no second; but without the multifarious excellence

of Jonson, Webster, Heywood, Beaumont, Fletcher, Ford, Massinger, and a score whom it would be tedious to enumerate, the student would have to regard Shakespeare as an inexplicable prodigy, instead of as the central sun of a luminous sidereal system."

A Dramatic Age. — As we sum up the characteristics of the Elizabethan age, we can hardly fail to note that it was a time of action in every direction. The exploration of the new physical world and the unknown seas called for action. To master the new world of knowledge, which the Renaissance had disclosed, demanded the exercise of youthful activities to their full, if the power which such knowledge promised was to be acquired and enjoyed before the curtain of life fell. The Reformation gave new activities to thought, which, leaving its cage, revelled in the new freedom.

The unwonted activities of the time of Elizabeth demanded a form of literature that would give them adequate expression. Only the drama or the novel could have afforded full expression to that age of action. There were several reasons why the novel was not chosen. In the first place, prose, the necessary vehicle of expression for the novel, had not reached so high a stage of development as poetry. The most finished prose could hardly have successfully competed with Elizabethan poetry in expressing the harmonies and the discords of life. Certain dramatists used prose, but Shakespeare's genius taught him to employ poetry and to resort to prose only occasionally as an alloy. It is in their poetry that we behold the Elizabethans

" Affecting thoughts co-equal with the clouds."[1]

[1] Marlowe: *Tamburlaine*, I., 2.

In the second place, although Shakespeare's time produced some popular novels (see p. 276), yet they had not reached the same stage of development as the drama. The literature of both Greece and Rome furnished dramatic models. The English nation had been undergoing an apprenticeship with both Miracle plays and Moralities and had consequently become accustomed to dramatic expression. Even the highly developed nineteenth century novel would not have satisfied the Elizabethans. They would not have enjoyed the analytic vein of Thackeray and George Eliot, nor would they have cared much for either the minute dissection of emotion or for the analysis of motive, so common in modern novels. In largeness of view, boldness of touch, and hearty humor, Scott is perhaps the only great master of English prose fiction who would have appealed strongly to the Elizabethans, but they would have missed in him the height and depth and breadth, the sympathy, the mystery, and the universality, which characterize Shakespeare's dramas.

Thirdly, although the novel was in later times a powerful factor in dethroning the drama, even the nineteenth century novel could not have brought all life to a focus in so small a compass as the drama. Unlike it, the novel could not have displayed such

"Infinite riches in a little room."[1]

The Elizabethans demanded a form of literature that would present to them life in all its variety and rapidity of movement. Only the drama could satisfy such demands. Even the apprentices, who could not read a

[1] Marlowe: *The Jew of Malta*, I., 1.

line of the novels of Lodge or Greene or Nash, could for a penny walk into the pit of the Globe Theater and see all classes of humanity, from King Richard III. to the gravediggers, act the play of life itself upon the stage.

For these reasons, the responsibility of presenting Elizabethan ideals embodied in action fell upon the drama. Accordingly, we need not be surprised to find that all the greatest poets of that master age, with the single exception of Spenser, were dramatists. Much of the literature of subsequent times is sicklied o'er with the pale cast of thought without action, but everything that obtained the greatest currency in that age was obliged to bear the dramatic stamp. The highest types of imagination and thought have always been embodied in action. The literature of the age of Elizabeth furnishes such types in the greatest state of perfection yet attained.

LITERATURE OF THE FIRST PART OF ELIZABETH'S REIGN

Productions of the First Twenty Years. — The first twenty years of the Elizabethan age passed without the appearance of any literary work of the highest rank. Writers were, however, trying a wide range of subjects. Books were written in prose on subjects as dissimilar as martyrs and education, history and travels. Greek and Latin classics were translated into English to serve as stimulating models.

Poetic activity was even more marked. Almost every important event gave rise to a ballad. The poets tried lyrical verse of well-nigh endless variety. There appeared in 1576 a collection of miscellaneous songs, known as *Paradise of Dainty Devices*. This very title shows what the poets were attempting. They were pluming their wings for longer flights in every clime of human experience. In every direction the nation was attempting and learning on a larger scale than at any preceding time.

Only one poet in the first half of the reign, Thomas Sackville (1536–1608), towers sufficiently high above the others to receive individual attention. He helped to produce the first Elizabethan tragedy in blank verse (see p. 142).

In 1563 he wrote the *Induction* and *Complaint of Buckingham*, which appeared in a narrative collection of poetry by various writers, under the general title of *Mirror for Magistrates*. These poems relate the haps and mishaps of the illustrious dead, and the way their spirits view this mortal life.

THOMAS SACKVILLE

These lines from the *Induction* describe a part of the journey to the land of spirits. Sorrow says : —

> "I shall thee guide first to the grisly lake,
> And thence unto the blissful place of rest,
> Where thou shalt see, and hear the plaint they make
> That whilom here bare swing among the best.
>   .   .   .   .
> Thence come we to the horrour and the hell,
> The large great kingdoms, and the dreadful reign
> Of Pluto in his throne where he did dwell,
> The wide waste places, and the hugy plain,
> The wailings, shrieks, and sundry sorts of pain,
> The sighs, the sobs, the deep and deadly groan :
> Earth, air, and all, resounding plaint and moan."

These lines, notwithstanding their lack of ornament, have a directness, poetic certainty, and firmness of grasp that we miss in the productions of the preceding hundred and fifty years.

LITERATURE OF THE SECOND PART OF ELIZABETH'S REIGN

I. THE PROSE

Lyly, Sidney, Hooker. — The year 1579 ushered in the second and more productive part of Elizabeth's reign. The prose is far inferior to the poetry ; in fact, Bacon's is the only Elizabethan prose which is much read to-day. The imaginative spirit of the age was more favorable to the production of poetry than of prose, and the drama afforded a poetical outlet more popular with all classes than prose.

John Lyly (1554?–1606) published in 1579 a peculiar prose work entitled, *Euphues, The Anatomy of Wit*, which has given a new critical term to our vocabulary. We apply the term "Euphuism" to any stilted, antithetical style, which pays more attention to the manner of expressing a thought than to its worth. Lyly's prose work shows an excessive use of antithesis, of far-fetched similes, and of obscure learning. This quotation is typical : —

"Achilles spear could as well heal as hurt, the scorpion though he sting, yet he stints the pain, though the herb *Nerius* poison the sheep, yet is a remedy to man against poison. . . . There is great difference between the standing puddle and the running stream, yet both water : great odds between the adamant and the pomice, yet both stones, a great distinction to be put between *vitrum* and the crystal, yet both glass : great contrariety between Lais and Lucretia, yet both women."

We may also notice conscious art in this, a desire to vary the diction and to avoid the repetition of the same

word for the same idea.   To find four different terms for
the same idea: "difference," "odds," "distinction," and
"contrariety," involves considerable painstaking.   In the
course of time, attention, centered on both the form and
the thought, produced a good prose style.   Lyly was one
of the pioneers on the formal side.

Sir Philip Sidney (1554–1586) wrote a romance, entitled
Arcadia, for his sister, the Countess of Pembroke.   The
style is poetic throughout 'and the characters in the
romance move in a partial Utopia, which is called Arcadia.   Certain passages like the following, because of
their exuberant fancy, read as if they had been written
by a Celt (see p. 38): —

> " Her breath is more sweet than a gentle southwest wind, which
> comes creeping over flowery fields and shadowed waters in the extreme
> heat of summer; and yet is nothing compared to the honey-flowing
> speech that breath doth carry."

To Sidney belongs the credit of having written the first
meritorious essay on criticism in the English language,
The Apologie for Poetrie.   This defends the poetic art,
and shows how necessary such exercise of the imagination
is to take us away from the cold, hard facts of life.

Richard Hooker (1554?–1600), an Episcopal clergyman,
wrote a theological work, *The Laws of Ecclesiastical Polity*.
This is a defense of the doctrines of the Church of England,
and the theologians of that Church yet refer to him as
one of their authorities.   Hooker's is one of the greatest
English prose works written before 1600.   Its chief excellences are (1) positive dignity of style, (2) freedom from
the excessive antithesis and conceits of Lyly, and (3)
from the over-profuse poetic ornamentation of much of
Sidney's work.   (4) It often expresses profound thought

in a richly musical succession of syllables. On the other hand, the work has striking faults. The sentences are often formed after a Latin model. They are long and involved, and the verb is frequently placed last. For these reasons, one soon wearies if he reads consecutively much of Hooker.

Fr Bacon

FRANCIS BACON, 1561-1626

Life. — A study of Bacon takes us beyond the limits
of the reign of Elizabeth, but not beyond the continued
influences of that reign. Francis Bacon, the son of Sir
Nicholas Bacon, Lord Keeper of the Great Seal under
Elizabeth, was born in London and grew up under the
influences of the court. We must remember the influences
which helped to fashion him in his boyhood days, in order
to understand some of his actions in later life. He early
acquired a taste for many luxuries, and these necessitated

his getting much money. Those with whom he early associated and who unconsciously molded him were not very scrupulous about the way in which they secured the favor of the court or the means which they took to outstrip an adversary. These unfortunate influences were intensified when, at the age of sixteen, he was sent with the English ambassador to Paris, where the youth remained for two and a half years, studying statecraft and diplomacy.

When Bacon was nineteen, his father died. The son, being without money, returned from Paris and became a lawyer. His uncle, Lord Burleigh, was one of Elizabeth's ministers. To him Bacon appealed for some lucrative position at the court. In a letter to his uncle, Bacon says: "I confess I have as vast contemplative ends as I have moderate civil ends; for I have taken all knowledge to be my province." This shows that he wished leisure for study and writing. Such an intention should be especially noted because it manifests the Elizabethan desire to master the entire world of the New Learning. Instead of helping his nephew, Lord Burleigh seems to have done all in his power to thwart him.

Bacon entered Parliament in 1584 and distinguished himself as a speaker. Ben Jonson, the dramatist, says of him: "There happened in my time, one noble speaker who was full of gravity in his speaking. No man ever spoke more neatly, more presly, more weightily, or suffered less emptiness, less idleness, in what he uttered. His hearers could not cough or look aside from him without loss. The fear of every man that heard him was lest he should make an end." This speaking was valuable training for Bacon in writing the pithy sentences of his *Essays*. A man who uses the long, involved sentences of Hooker can never become a speaker to whom people will listen. The habit of directness and simplicity, which Bacon formed in his speaking, remained with him through life.

After James I. came to the throne in 1603, Bacon's rise was rapid. He ascended step by step, until he became Lord High Chancellor of England. He was accused in 1621 of having received bribes as a judge. This was no new thing in English jurisprudence. It had long been customary for judges to accept presents. Bacon's love for luxuries was so great that he had probably received, or allowed his subordinates to receive, presents from rival contestants. Some complained when the decision went against them, but there is no complaint on record that his decisions were unjust. Bacon himself said that he was pleased to receive presents, but that they made no difference with his decisions. He was tried, found guilty, fined £40,000, and sentenced to be imprisoned in the Tower during the King's pleasure. After a few days the King released him, remitted the fine, and gave him an annual pension of £1200.

Bacon passed the remaining five years of his life in retirement, studying and writing. His interest in observing natural objects and experimenting with them was the cause of his death. He was riding in a snowstorm when it occurred to him to experiment with snow as a preservative agent. He stopped at a house, procured a fowl, and stuffed it with snow. He caught cold while doing this, was improperly cared for, and soon died.

The Essays. — The first ten of his *Essays*, his most popular work, appeared in the year 1597. At the time of his death, he had increased them to fifty-eight. They deal with a wide range of subjects, from *Studies* and *Nobility*, on the one hand, to *Marriage and Single Life* and

Gardens, on the other. The great critic Hallam says : " It would be somewhat derogatory to a man of the slightest claim to polite letters, were he unacquainted with the *Essays* of Bacon. It is, indeed, little worth while to read this or any other book for reputation's sake ; but very few in our language so well repay the pains, or afford more nourishment to the thoughts."

The following sentence from the essay *Of Studies* will show some of the characteristics of his way of presenting thought : —

"Reading maketh a full man, conference a ready man, and writing an exact man ; and, therefore, if a man write little, he had need have a great memory ; if he confer little, he had need have a present wit ; and if he read little, he had need have much cunning to seem to know that he doth not."

We may notice here (1) clearness, (2) conciseness, (3) breadth of thought and observation.

A shrewd Scotchman says : " It may be said that to men wishing to rise in the world by politic management of their fellow-men, Bacon's *Essays* are the best handbook hitherto published." In justification of this criticism, we need only quote from the essay *Of Negotiations :* —

"It is generally better to deal by speech than by letter. Letters are good, when a man would draw an answer by letter back again, or when it may serve for a man's justification afterwards to produce his own letter, or where it may be danger to be interrupted or heard by pieces. To deal in person is good, when a man's face breedeth regard, as commonly with inferiors, or in tender cases, where a man's eye upon the countenance of him with whom he speaketh may give him a direction how far to go, and generally, when a man will reserve to himself liberty either to disavow or to expound."

Scientific and Miscellaneous Works. — *The Advancement of Learning* is another of Bacon's great works. The title aptly expresses the purpose of the book. He insists on the necessity of close observation of nature and of making experiments with various forms of matter. He decries the habit of spinning things out of one's inner consciousness, without patiently studying the outside world to see whether the facts justify the conclusions. In other words, he insists on induction. Bacon was not the father of the inductive principle, as is sometimes wrongly stated, for prehistoric man was compelled to make inductions before he could advance one step from barbarism.

Bacon had so little faith in the enduring qualities of the English language, that he wrote the most of his philosophical works in Latin. He planned a Latin work in six parts, to cover the whole field of the philosophy of natural science. The most famous of the parts completed is the *Novum Organum*, which deals with certain methods for searching after definite truth, and shows how to avoid some ever-present tendencies toward error.

Bacon wrote an excellent *History of the Reign of Henry VII.*, which is standard to this day. He also wrote *The New Atlantis*, which may be termed a Baconian Utopia, or study of an ideal commonwealth.

General Characteristics. — In Bacon's sentences we may often find remarkable condensation of thought in few words. One does not have to search for two grains of wheat hid in two bushels of chaff. A modern essayist has taken seven pages to express, or rather to obscure, the ideas in these three lines from Bacon : —

" Men of age object too much, consult too long, adventure too little, repent too soon, and seldom drive business home to the full period, but content themselves with a mediocrity of success." [1]

[1] *Of Youth and Age.*

His work abounds in illustrations, analogies, and striking imagery ; but, unlike the great Elizabethan poets, he appeals more to cold intellect than to the feelings. We are pleased with his intellectual ingenuity in comparing a man who is courteous to foreigners, not to an island cut off from other lands, but to a continent joined to them ; or in likening the Schoolmen to spiders, spinning such stuff as webs are made of " out of no great quantity of matter."

He resembles the Elizabethans in preferring magnificent to commonplace images.   It has been often noticed that if he essays to write of buildings in general, he prefers to describe palaces.   His knowledge of the intellectual side of human nature is specially remarkable, but, unlike Shakespeare, Bacon never drops his plummet into the emotional depths of the soul.

II. The Poetry

EDMUND SPENSER, 1552-1599

Life and Minor Poems. — Since Chaucer's day there had been no poet of the first rank in England.   In the last year of the reign of Edward VI., was born Edmund Spenser, who takes rank only slightly below Chaucer in the list of English poets.   Spenser was six years old when Elizabeth became queen.

His parents were poor, but fortunately there were generous men in Elizabethan times as now, men who found their chief pleasure, not in their own selfish gratification, but in making others happy.   Such a man assisted Spenser in going to Cambridge.   His benefactor was wise enough not to make this assistance sufficient to support Spenser without additional effort.   His patron realized

that the student's will and capacity for depending on himself would have been weakened thereby. We know that Spenser was a sizar at Cambridge; that is, one of those students who, to quote Macaulay, "had to perform some menial services. They swept the court; they carried up the dinner to the fellows' table, and changed the plate and poured out the ale of the rulers of society." We further know that Spenser was handicapped by ill health during a

part of his course, for we find entrances of allowances paid
" Spenser *ægrotanti*."

After leaving Cambridge he went to the north of England, probably in the capacity of tutor.   While there, he
fell in love with a young woman whom he calls Rosalind.
This event colored his after life.   Although she refused
him, she had penetration enough to see in what his greatness consisted, and her opinion spurred him to develop
his abilities as a poet.   He was in his twenties when he fell
in love with Rosalind, and he remained single until he was
forty-two, when he married an Irish maiden named Elizabeth.   In honor of that event, he composed the *Epithala-
mion*, the noblest marriage song in any literature.   So strong
are early impressions that even in its lines he seems to be
thinking of Rosalind and fancying that she is his bride.

After returning from the north, he spent some time with
Sir Philip Sidney, who helped fashion Spenser's ideals of
a chivalrous gentleman.   Sidney's influence is seen in
Spenser's greatest work, the *Faerie Queene*.   Sir Walter
Raleigh was another friend who left his imprint on
Spenser.

In 1579 Spenser published the *Shepherd's Calendar*.
This is a pastoral poem, consisting of twelve different
parts, one part being assigned to each of the twelve
months.   This poem occupies an inferior position beside
his greatest work ; but, considering the time, the *Shepherd's Calendar* is a remarkable production, and it shows
that its author had genius.

In 1580 he was appointed secretary to Lord Gray, Lord
Lieutenant of Ireland.   In one capacity or another, in the
service of the crown, Spenser passed in Ireland almost the
entire remaining eighteen years of his life.   In 1591 he
received in the south of Ireland a grant of three thousand

acres, a part of the estate of a rebellious Irish earl. Sir Walter Raleigh was also given forty-two thousand acres near Spenser. Ireland was then in a state of continuous turmoil. In such a country Spenser lived and wrote his *Faerie Queene*. Of course, this environment powerfully affected the character of that poem. It has been said that to read a contemporary's account of " Raleigh's adventures with the Irish chieftains, his challenges and single combats, his escapes at fords and woods, is like reading bits of the *Faerie Queene* in prose."

From an old print.

RUINS OF KILCOLMAN CASTLE (SPENSER'S HOME IN IRELAND)

In 1598 Spenser's castle was set on fire by the Irish. He and his family barely escaped with their lives. He crossed to England, and died the next year, according to some accounts, in want. He was buried, at the expense of Lord Essex, in Westminster Abbey, near Chaucer.

The Faerie Queene. — In 1590 Spenser published the first three books of the *Faerie Queene*. The original plan was to have the poem contain twelve books, like Virgil's *Æneid*, but only six were published. If more were written, they have been lost.

The poem is an allegory with the avowed moral purpose of fashioning "a gentleman or noble person in vertuous and gentle discipline." Spenser says : " I labour to pour-traict in Arthure, before he was King, the image of a brave knight, perfected in the twelve private morall vertues, as Aristotle hath devised." Twelve Knights personifying twelve Virtues were to fight with their opposing Vices, and the twelve books were to tell the story of the conflict. The Knights set out from the court of Gloriana, the Faerie Queene, in search of their enemies, and meet with divers adventures and enchantments.

The hero of the tale is Arthur, who has figured so much in English song and legend. Spenser makes him typical of all the Virtues taken together. The first book, which is really a complete poem by itself, and which is generally admitted to be the finest, contains an account of the adventures of the Red Cross Knight, who represents Holiness. Other books tell of the warfare of the Knights who typify Temperance, Chastity, Friendship, Justice, and Courtesy.

The poem begins thus : —

> " A gentle Knight was pricking [1] on the plaine,
>   Ycladd in mightie armes and silver shielde,
>   Wherein old dints of deepe woundes did remaine,
>   The cruell markes of many' a bloody fielde ;
>   Yet armes till that time did he never wield.

> . . . .

[1] riding.

" And on his brest a bloodie Crosse he bore,
   The deare remembrance of his dying Lord,
   For whose sweete sake that glorious badge he wore.

.   .   .   .

" Upon a great adventure he was bond,
   That greatest Gloriana to him gave,
   That greatest glorious Queene of Faerie lond."

The entire poem really typifies the aspirations of the human soul for something nobler and better than can be gained without effort.   In Spenser's imaginative mind, these aspirations became real persons who set out to win laurels in a fairyland, lighted with the soft light of the moon, and presided over by the good genius that loves to uplift struggling and weary souls.

The allegory certainly becomes confused.   A critic well says : " We can hardly lose our way in it, for there is no way to lose."   We are not called on to understand the intricacies of the allegory, but to read between the lines, catch the noble moral lesson, and drink to our fill at the fountain of beauty and melody.

Spenser a Subjective Poet. — The subjective cast of Spenser's mind next demands attention.   We feel that his is an ideal world, one that does not exist outside of the imagination.   In order to understand the difference between subjective and objective, let us compare Chaucer with Spenser.   No one can really be said to study literature without constantly bringing in the principle of comparison.   We must notice the likeness and the difference between literary productions, or the faint impression which they make upon our minds will soon pass away.

Chaucer is objective ; that is, he identifies himself with things that have a real existence in the outside world.   For instance, when he says : —

" The bisy larke, messager of daye,
  Saluteth in hir song the morwe graye,
  And fyry Phebus ryseth up so brighte
  That al the orient laugheth of the lighte,
  And with hise stremes dryeth in the greves
  The silver dropes, hangynge on the leves," [1]

our attention is here drawn to the song of an actual lark,
to the beauty of the morning light, to the sunbeams dancing on the dewdrops, which sparkle on the green leaves.
There is nothing here which a sympathetic observer of
nature might not notice and regard without a thought of
self. In like manner we find ourselves looking at the
shiny bald head of Chaucer's Monk, at the lean horse
and threadbare clothes of the Student of Oxford, at the
brown complexion of the Shipman, at the enormous hat
and large figure of the Wife of Bath, at the red face of
the Summoner, at the hair of the Pardoner "yelow as
wex." These are not mere figments of the imagination.
We feel that they are either realities or that they could
have existed.

While the adventures in the Irish wars undoubtedly
gave the original suggestions for many of the contests
between good and evil in the *Faerie Queene*, Spenser intentionally idealized these knightly struggles to uphold the
right and placed them in fairyland. This great poem is
the work of a mind that loved to elaborate purely subjective images. The pictures were not painted from gazing at
the outside world. We feel that they are mostly creations
of the imagination, and that few of them could exist in a
real world. The passages in the next section show this.
There is no bower in the bottom of the sea, " built of hollow
billowes heaped hye," and no lion ever follows a lost maiden

[1] *Knightes Tale.*

to protect her. We feel that the principal part of Shakespeare's world could have existed in reality as well as in imagination. Spenser was never able to reach this highest type of art.

The world, however, needs poets to create images of a higher type of beauty than this life can offer. These images react on our material lives and cast them in a nobler mold. Spenser's belief that the subjective has power to fashion the objective is expressed in two of the finest lines that he ever wrote : —

> "For of the soule the bodie forme doth take;
> For soule is forme, and doth the bodie make."[1]

Chief Characteristics of Spenser's Poetry. — We can say of Spenser's verse that it stands in the front rank for (1) melody, (2) love of the beautiful, and (3) nobility of the ideals presented. His poetry also (4) shows a preference for the subjective world, (5) exerts a remarkable influence over other poets, and (6) displays a peculiar liking for obsolete forms of expression.

Spenser's melody is noteworthy. If we read aloud correctly such lines as these, we can scarcely fail to be impressed with their harmonious flow : —

> "A teme of Dolphins raunged in aray
> Drew the smooth charett of sad Cymoent:
> They were all taught by Triton to obay
> To the long raynes at her commaundement:
> As swifte as swallowes on the waves they went.

> "Upon great Neptune's neck they softly swim,
> And to her watry chamber swiftly carry him.
> Deepe in the bottome of the sea her bowre
> Is built of hollow billowes heaped hye."[2]

---

[1] *An Hymne in Honour of Beautie.*   [2] *Faerie Queene*, Book III., Canto 4.

The following lines will show Spenser's love for beauty, and at the same time indicate the nobility of some of his ideal characters. He is describing Lady Una, the fair representative of true religion, who has lost through enchantment her Guardian Knight, and who is wandering disconsolate in the forest : —

> ". . . Her angel's face,
> As the great eye of heaven, shyned bright,
> And made a sunshine in the shady place ;
> Did never mortall eye behold such heavenly grace.

> "It fortuned out of the thickest wood
> A ramping Lyon rushed suddeinly,
> Hunting full greedy after salvage blood.
> Soone as the royall virgin he did spy,
> With gaping mouth at her ran greedily,
> To have att once devoured her tender corse ;
> But to the pray when as he drew more ny,
> His bloody rage aswaged with remorse,
> And with the sight amazd, forgat his furious forse.

> "In stead thereof he kist her wearie feet,
> And lickt her lilly hands with fawning tong,
> As he her wronged innocence did weet.
> O, how can beautie maister the most strong,
> And simple truth subdue avenging wrong !"[1]

The power of beauty has seldom been more vividly described. As we read the succeeding stanzas and see the lion following her, like a faithful dog, to shield her from harm, we feel the power of both beauty and goodness and realize that with Spenser these terms are interchangeable. Each one of the preceding selections shows his preference for the subjective and the ideal to the actual.

A critic rightly says that Spenser repels none but the anti-poetical. His influence upon other poets has been

---

[1] *Faerie Queene*, Book I., Canto 3.

far-reaching. Milton, Dryden, Byron, Wordsworth, Keats, and Shelley show traces of his influence. Spenser has been called the poet's poet, because the more poetical one is, the more one will enjoy him.

Spenser searched for old and obsolete words. He used "eyne" for "eyes," "fone" for "foes," "shend" for "shame." He did not hesitate to coin words when he needed them, like "mercify" and "fortunize." He even wrote "wawes" in place of "waves" because he wished it to rhyme with "jaws." In spite of these peculiarities, Spenser is not hard reading after the first appearance of strangeness has worn away.

III. THE ENGLISH DRAMA

The Rise of the Drama in England. — Like so many things of great moment, our drama took its rise in religion. The rites of the Roman Catholic church have always been marked with much dramatic splendor. Any one may to-day form some idea of the rise of our drama by attending the service of that church on Christmas or Easter Sunday. In many Catholic churches there may still be seen at Christmas time a representation of the manger at Bethlehem. Sometimes the figures of the infant Savior, of Joseph and Mary, of the wise men, of the sheep and cattle, are very lifelike.

The events clustering about the Crucifixion and the Resurrection furnished the most striking material for the early religious drama. Our earliest dramatic writers drew their inspiration from the *New Testament*.

Miracle and Mystery Plays. — A Miracle play is the dramatic representation of the life of a saint and of the miracles connected with him. A Mystery play deals with gospel events which are concerned with any phase of the life of Christ, or with any biblical event that remotely foreshadows Christ or indicates the necessity of a Redeemer. In England there were few, if any, pure Miracle plays, but the term "Miracle" is applied indiscriminately to both Miracles and Mysteries.

The first Miracle play in England was acted probably not far from 1100. In the fourteenth, fifteenth, and sixteenth centuries these plays had become so popular that they were produced in nearly every part of England. Shakespeare felt their influence. He must have had frequent opportunities in his boyhood to witness their production. They were seldom performed in England after 1600, although visitors to Germany have every ten years the opportunity of seeing a modern production of a Mystery in the *Passion Play* at Oberammergau.

The Subjects. — Four great cycles of Miracle plays have been preserved: the York, Chester, and Coventry plays, so called because they were performed in those places, and the Towneley plays. These last take their name from Towneley Hall in Lancashire, where the manuscript was kept for some time. It is probable that almost every town of importance had its own collection of plays.

The York cycle contains forty-eight plays. A cycle or circle of plays means a list forming a complete circle from Creation until Doomsday. The York collection begins with Creation and the fall of Lucifer and the bad angels from Heaven, — a theme which was later to inspire the pen of one of England's greatest poets. The tragedies of Eden and the Flood, scenes from the lives of Abraham, Isaac, and Moses, the manger at Bethlehem, the slaughter of the Innocents, the Temptation, the resurrection of Lazarus, the Last Supper, the Trial, the Crucifixion, and

the Easter triumph, are a few of the Miracle plays that
were acted in the city of York.

The Actors and Manner of Presentation. — At first the
actors were priests who presented the plays either in the
church or in its immediate vicinity on sacred ground.

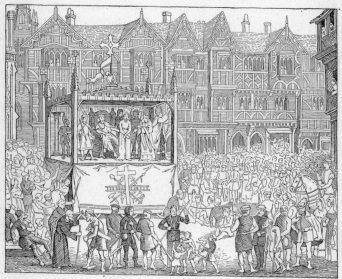

From an old print.

MIRACLE PLAY AT COVENTRY

After a while the plays became so popular that the laity
presented them. When they were at the height of their
popularity, that is, during the fourteenth and fifteenth
centuries, the actors were selected with great care from
the members of the various trades guilds, and each guild
undertook the entire responsibility for the presentation of
some one play, and endeavored to surpass all the other
guilds.

Considerable humor was displayed in the allotment of various plays. The tanners presented the fall of Lucifer and the bad angels into the infernal regions; the ship carpenters, the play of Noah and the building of the ark; the bakers, the Last Supper; the butchers, the Crucifixion.

In their prime, the Miracle plays were acted on wooden platforms mounted on wheels. There were two distinct stories in these movable stages, a lower one in which the actors dressed, and an upper one in which they played. The entrance to the lower story was a terrible pair of dragonlike jaws, painted red. From these issued smoke, flame, and horrible outcries. This entrance was known as Hell Mouth. From it leaped red-coated devils to tempt the Savior, the saints, and men. Into it the devils would disappear with some wicked soul. They would torture it and make it roar with pain, as the smoke poured faster from the red jaws.

In York on Corpus Christi Day, which usually fell in the first week in June, the actors were ordered to be in their places on these movable theaters at half past three in the morning. Certain stations had been selected throughout the city, where each pageant should stop and, in the proper order, present its own play. In this way the enormous crowds that visited York to see these performances were more evenly scattered throughout the city.

The actors did not always remain on the stage. Herod in his magnificent robes used to ride on horseback among the people, boast of his prowess, and overdo everything, so that Shakespeare, who was evidently familiar with the character, speaks of out-Heroding Herod. The Devil also frequently jumped from the stage and availed himself of his license to play pranks among the audience.

Much of the acting was undoubtedly excellent. In 1476

the council at York ordained that four of the best players
in the city should examine with regard to fitness all who
wished to take part in the plays. So many were desirous
of acting, that it was much trouble to get rid of incom-
petents.   The ordinance ran: "All such as they shall
find sufficient in person and cunning, to the honor of the
City and worship of the said Crafts, for to admit and
able; and all other insufficient persons, either in cunning,
voice, or person, to discharge, ammove and avoid."   A
critic says that this ordinance is "one of the steps on
which the greatness of the Elizabethan stage was built,
and through which its actors grew up."[1]

Introduction of the Comic Element in the Miracle Plays. —
While the old drama generally confined itself to religious
subjects, the comic element occasionally crept in, made its
power felt, and disclosed a new path for future playwrights.
In the *Play of Noah's Flood*, when the time for the flood
has come, Noah's wife refuses to enter the ark and a
domestic quarrel ensues.   Finally her children pull and
shove her into the ark.   When she is safe on board, Noah
bids her welcome.   His enraged wife deals him resounding
blows until he calls to her to stop, since his back is nearly
broken.

The *Play of the Shepherds* has a genuine little comedy
inserted, the first comedy worthy of the name to appear in
England.   While watching their flocks on Christmas Eve,
the shepherds are joined by Mak, a neighbor whose reputation for honesty is not good.   Before they go to sleep,
they make him lie down within their circle, but he rises
when he hears them begin to snore, steals a sheep, and
hastens home.   His wife is alarmed, because in that day
the theft of a sheep was punishable by death.   She finally

[1] Smith's *York Plays*.

concludes that the best plan will be to wrap the animal in swaddling clothes and put it in the cradle. If the shepherds come to search the house, she will pretend that she has a child; and, if they approach the cradle, she will caution them against touching it for fear of waking the child and causing him to fill the house with his cries. She speedily hurries Mak away to resume his slumbers among the shepherds. When they wake, they miss the sheep, suspect Mak, and go to search his house. His wife allows them to look around thoroughly, but she keeps them away from the cradle. They leave, rather ashamed of their suspicion. As they are going out of the door, a thought strikes one of them whereby they can make partial amends. He decides to give the child sixpence, and so he returns, lifts up the covering of the cradle, and discovers the sheep. Mak and his wife both declare that an elf has changed their child into a sheep. The shepherds threaten to have the pair hanged. They seize Mak, throw him on a canvas, and toss him into the air until they are exhausted. They then lie down to rest and are roused with the song of an angel from Bethlehem.

To produce this comedy required genuine inventive imagination; for there is nothing faintly resembling this incident in the sacred narrative. These early exercises of the imagination in our drama may resemble the tottering footsteps of a child, but they were necessary antecedents to the strength, beauty, and divinity of movement in Elizabethan times.

The Morality. — The next step in the development of the drama is known as the Morality play. This personified abstractions. Characters like Charity, Hope, Faith, Truth, Covetousness, Falsehood, Abominable Living, the World, the Flesh, and the Devil, — in short, all the Virtues and the

Vices, — came on the stage in the guise of persons, and played the drama of life.

Critics do not agree about the precise way in which the Morality is related to the Miracle play. It is certain that the Miracle play had already introduced some abstractions. In one very important respect, the Morality marks an advance, by giving more scope to the imagination. The Miracle plays had their general treatment absolutely predetermined by the Scriptural version of the action or by the legends of the lives of saints, although diverting incidents could be introduced, as we have seen. In the Morality, the events could take any turn which the author chose to give.

In spite of this advantage, the Morality is in general a synonym for what is uninteresting. The characters born of abstractions are too often bloodless, like their parents. The Morality under a changed name was current a few years ago in the average Sunday-school book. Incompetent writers of fiction to-day often adopt the Morality principle in making their characters unnaturally good or bad, mere puppets who do not develop along the line of their own emotional prompting, but who are moved by machinery in the author's hands.

FOOL'S HEAD [1]

A new character, the Vice, was added as an adjunct to the Devil, to increase the interest of the audience in the Morality play. The Vice represented the leading spirit of evil in any particular play, sometimes Fraud, Covetousness, Pride, Iniquity, or Hypocrisy. It was the business of the Vice to

AIR-BAG FLAPPER [1]

[1] Stage properties of the Vice and Fool.

annoy the Virtues and to be constantly playing pranks. The Vice was the predecessor of the clown and the fool upon the stage. The Vice also amused the audience by tormenting the Devil, belaboring him with a sword of lath, sticking thorns into him, and making him roar with pain. Sometimes the Devil would be kicked down Hell Mouth by the offended Virtues, but he would soon reappear with saucily curled tail, and at the end of the play he would delight the spectators by plunging into Hell Mouth with the Vice on his back.

The Interlude.—Any short dramatic incident, such as the refusal of Noah's wife to enter the ark, or Mak's thievery in the *Play of the Shepherds*, interpolated in Miracle and Mystery plays, to give variety and interest, might be called an Interlude. This type served to bring the drama closer to real life, and became for this reason one of the important foundation stones of the Elizabethan drama. John Heywood, who died about the year 1580, made the Interlude a finished play by itself, and gave it a place of its own in dramatic literature. During the reign of Queen Mary, he supplied the royal court with dramatic amusements, but on account of his religious views he fled to the continent when Elizabeth came to the throne.

The Interlude was short. It was some times given between the courses of a banquet or immediately after it. Such a play could also be acted before guests at the home in connection with other forms of entertainment.

LATH DAGGER [1]

FOOL'S HEAD [1]

[1] Stage properties of the Vice and Fool.

The Interlude shows the modern drama in its chrysalis state. Artistic expansion, complexity, and proportion are yet to come, but the development will now proceed without any great break.

Further Steps toward Shakespeare. — Two early comedies and a tragedy are worthy of note.

Ralph Royster Doyster was written by Nicholas Udall, master of Eton College, and acted in 1551, thirteen years before the birth of Shakespeare. This play, founded on a comedy of Plautus, shows the classical influence which was so powerful in England at this time. Ralph, the hero, is a conceited simpleton. He falls in love with a widow who has already promised her hand to a man infinitely Ralph's superior. Ralph, however, cannot understand why she should not want him, and so persists in his wooing. She makes him the butt of her jokes, and he finds himself in ridiculous positions. The comedy amuses us in this way until her lover returns and marries her. The characters of the play, which is written in rhyme, are of the English middle class.

Gammer Gurton's Needle is probably the work of John Still, Bishop of Bath and Wells. This comedy was acted at Christ's College, Cambridge, in 1566, two years after Shakespeare's birth. This play borrows hardly anything from the classical stage. The most of the characters of *Gammer Gurton's Needle* are from the lowest English working classes, and its language, unlike that of *Ralph Royster Doyster*, which has little to offend, is very coarse.

The tragedy of *Gorboduc*, in part the work of Thomas Sackville, the author of the *Induction*, was acted in 1561, three years before the birth of Shakespeare. This is the first regular English tragedy written in blank verse. *Gor-*

boduc is fashioned after the classical rules of Seneca and the Greeks. There is little action on the stage. There is any amount of bloodshed in the play, but the spectators are informed of the carnage by a messenger, as they are not permitted to witness a bloody contest on the stage.

The Dramatic Unities. — If *Gorboduc* had been taken for a model, the English drama could never have attained Shakespearean greatness. Our drama would then have been crippled by following the classical rules, which prescribed unity of place and time in the plot and the action. The ancients held that the play should not represent actions which would, in actual life, require much more than twenty-four hours for their performance. If one of the characters was a boy, he had to be represented as a boy throughout the entire play. The next act could not introduce him as one who had grown to manhood in the interval. The classical rules further required that the action should be performed in one place, or near it. Anything which happened at a great distance had to be merely related by a messenger, and not acted on the stage.

Had these rules been followed, the English drama could not have painted the growth and development of character, for it is not built or developed in a day. The genius of Marlowe and Shakespeare taught them to disregard these dramatic unities. In *As You Like It*, the action is now at the court, and now in the far-off Forest of Arden. Shakespeare knew that the imagination could traverse the distance. At the beginning of the play Oliver is an unnatural, brutal brother; but events change him, so that in the fourth act, when he is asked if he is the man who tried to kill his brother, Oliver replies : —

"'Twas I ; but 'tis not I."

CHRISTOPHER MARLOWE, 1564-1593

Life. — The year 1564 saw the birth of the two greatest geniuses in the English drama, Marlowe and Shakespeare. There are other great names in the early Elizabethan drama, but we must pass them by for the study of the greatest.

Marlowe, the son of a shoemaker, was born at Canterbury, and educated at Cambridge. When he graduated, the dramatic profession was the only one that gave full scope to genius like his. He became both playwriter and actor. All his extant work was written in about six years. When he was only twenty-nine he was fatally stabbed in a quarrel in a tavern. Shakespeare had at that age not produced his greatest plays. Marlowe unwittingly wrote his own epitaph in that of Dr. Faustus : —

> "Cut is the branch that might have grown full straight,
> And burnéd is Apollo's laurel bough."

Works. — Marlowe's great tragedies are four in number : *Tamburlaine, Dr. Faustus, The Jew of Malta,* and *Edward II.* No careful student of English literature can afford to be unacquainted with any of them. Shakespeare's work appears less miraculous when we know that a predecessor at the age of twenty-four had written plays like *Tamburlaine* and *Dr. Faustus.*

Tamburlaine shows the supreme ambition for conquest, for controlling the world with physical force. It is such a play as might have been suggested to an Elizabethan by watching Napoleon's career. *Dr. Faustus*, on the other hand, shows the desire for knowledge that would give universal power, a desire born of the Renaissance. *The Jew of Malta* is the incarnation of the passion for the world's

wealth, a passion that towers above common greed only by
the magnificence of its immensity. In that play we see
that Marlowe

> "Without control can pick his riches up,
> And in his house heap pearl like pebble stones,
> . . . .
> Infinite riches in a little room."

Edward II. gives a pathetic picture of one of the weakest
of kings. This shows more evenness and regularity of
construction than any of Marlowe's other plays, but it is
the one least characteristic of him. Others manifest more
intensity of imagination, more of the spirit of the age.

Dr. Faustus shows Marlowe's peculiar genius at its best.
The legend on which the play is based came from Germany, but Marlowe breathed his own imaginative spirit
into the tragedy. Faustus is wearied with the barren philosophy of the past. He is impatient to secure at once
the benefits of the New Learning, which seems to him to
have all the powers of magic. If he can immediately
enjoy the fruits of such knowledge, he says : —

> "Had I as many souls as there be stars,
> I'd give them all."

In order to acquire this knowledge and the resulting power
for twenty-four years, he sells his soul to Mephistophilis.
Faustus then proceeds to enjoy all that the new order of
things promised. He commands Homer to come from the
realm of shades to sing his entrancing songs. He summons
Helen to appear before him in the morning of her beauty.
The apostrophe to her shows the vividness and exuberance
of his imagination : —

> "Was this the face that launched a thousand ships
> And burnt the topless towers of Ilium?

> Sweet Helen, make me immortal with a kiss.
> · · · · · · · ·
> Oh! thou art fairer than the evening air
> Clad in the beauty of a thousand stars."

Marlowe left a fragment of a lyrical poem, entitled *Hero and Leander*, which is the finest production of its kind in the language. Shakespeare accorded him the unusual honor of quoting from this poem.

In What Sense is Marlowe a Founder of the English Drama? — His success with blank verse showed Shakespeare that this was the proper versification for the drama. Before Marlowe, rhyme or prose had been chiefly employed in writing plays. Sackville had used blank verse in *Gorboduc*, but his verse and Marlowe's are as unlike as the movements of the ox and the flight of the swallow. The sentences of *Gorboduc* generally end with the line, and the accents usually fall in the same place. Marlowe's blank verse shows great variety. The major pause frequently does not come at the end of the line. The poet can move over the field of dramatic action far more easily than he could if he were tied down to the necessity of making his verses rhyme.

Lines like these from the *Jew of Malta* show the freedom of his verse. The thought is often not allowed to suffer any pause at the end of the line : —

> "Thus, like the sad-presaging raven, that tolls
> The sick man's passport in her hollow beak,
> And in the shadow of the silent night
> Doth shake contagion from her sable wings."

Marlowe cast the dramatic unities to the wind. The action in *Dr. Faustus* occupies twenty-four years, and the scene changes from country to country. He knew that he was speaking to a people whose imaginations could accompany him and interpret what he uttered. The other dramatists followed him in placing imaginative interpretation above measurements by the foot rule of the intellect. Symonds says of him: "It was he who irrevocably decided the destinies of the romantic drama; and the whole subsequent evolution of that species, including Shakespeare's work, can be regarded as the expansion, rectification, and artistic ennoblement of the type fixed by Marlowe's epoch-making tragedies. In very little more than fifty years from the publication of *Tamburlaine*, our drama had run its course of unparalleled energy and splendor."

General Characteristics. — As we sum up Marlowe's general qualities, it is well to note that they exhibit in a striking way the characteristics of the time. In the morning of that youthful age the superlative was possible. *Tamburlaine*, *The Jew of Malta*, and *Dr. Faustus* show in the superlative degree the love of conquest, of wealth, and of knowledge. Everything that Marlowe wrote is stamped with a love of beauty and of the impossible.

Tamburlaine speaks like one of the young Elizabethans

> "That in conceit bear empires on our spears,
> Affecting thoughts co-equal with the clouds."

Marlowe voices the new sense of worth of enfranchised man: —

> "Thinkest thou heaven is such a glorious thing?
> I tell thee, 'tis not half so fair as thou,
> Or any man that breathes upon the earth.
> 'Twas made for man, therefore is man more excellent." [1]

The one who runs may note Marlowe's faults. They are the faults of youth and of the age. There are exaggeration and lack of restraint in almost all his work. In

---

[1] *Dr. Faustus*, Scene 6.

Tamburlaine, written when he was twenty-two, he is often bombastic. He has hardly any sense of humor. He does not draw fine distinctions between his characters.

On the other hand, using the words of Tamburlaine, we may say of other writers : —

> " If all the heavenly quintessence they still
>   From their immortal flowers of poesy,"

were gathered into one vial, it could not surpass the odor from patches of flowers scattered here and there in Marlowe's garden.

WILLIAM SHAKESPEARE, 1564-1616

Parents and Birthplace. — William Shakespeare was the son of John Shakespeare, a merchant, who in 1571 was chosen for the chief office in Stratford-on-Avon, Warwickshire. A few years later he lost the most of his property, and with it his position of commanding influence. The poet's mother was the daughter of Robert Arden, a well-to-do farmer. We are told that she was her father's favorite among seven children.

Stratford, where William Shakespeare was born in 1564, lies in the midst of England's fairest rural scenery. When two Englishmen were asked to name the finest walk in England, one chose the walk from Stratford to Coventry, the other the walk from Coventry to Stratford. A short distance northeast of Stratford are Warwick with its castle, the home of the famous King-Maker, and Kenilworth Castle, whose historic associations were romantic enough to stir the imagination of a boy like Shakespeare.

Home Training. — When we study the greatest writer of all time, it is desirable to learn some of the causes contributing to his greatness. In 1579 the parents of the poet sold a piece of land. The conveyance is thus signed: "The marke + of John Shackspere. The marke + of Marye Shacksper." Some think that such evidence tends to indicate that the poet's parents could neither read nor write. However this may be, it is probable that both of them were better educated than the average well-to-do inhabitants of our best cities at the present day, for his parents learned the world at first hand, through the

SHAKESPEARE'S HOUSE (THE POET'S BIRTHPLACE)

exercise of their own senses and reflective powers, and not at second hand through books. Had the dramatist not been an unusually close observer, he could never have written his plays. Had his parents been in the habit of referring him to books for everything, he could never have become a close observer.

It is probable that his mother was the sympathetic

teacher who trained him to miss nothing that came
within range of his senses. We can fancy her pointing
out to him

> " . . . daffodils,
>> That come before the swallow dares, and take
>> The winds of March with beauty ; violets dim,
>> But sweeter than the lids of Juno's eyes." [1]

We can imagine that from her rude song, as she walked
with him over the Stratford fields, he obtained suggestions which enabled him to hold captive the ear of the
world, when he sang of the pearl in the cowslip's ear, of
the bank where the wild thyme blows, of the greenwood
tree and the merry note of the bird, of the beauty of the
morning, in strains like this :—

> " Hark, hark ! the lark at heaven's gate sings,
>> And Phœbus 'gins arise,
>> His steeds to water at those springs
>> On chaliced flowers that lies ;
>> And winking Mary-buds begin
>> To ope their golden eyes." [2]

What he learned at School. — In all probability Shakespeare entered the Stratford Grammar School at about the
age of seven and continued there until he was nearly
fourteen. The typical course in grammar schools of
that period consisted principally of various Latin authors.
One school in 1583 had twenty-five Latin books on its
list of studies, while the only required works in English
were the *Catechism, Psalter, Book of Common Prayer,*
and *New Testament.* Children were put to studying
Lilly's *Latin Grammar* instead of learning their mother
tongue. Among the works which Shakespeare probably

[1] *The Winter's Tale*, IV., 4.   [2] *Cymbeline*, II., 3.

read in Latin, Æsop's *Fables* and Ovid's *Metamorphoses* may be mentioned.

In the fourth act of *The Merry Wives of Windsor*, Shakespeare ridicules the current study of the schools. Mrs. Page there complains to the parson: "Sir Hugh, my husband says my son profits nothing in the world at his book." In the fifth act of *Love's Labor's*

CLASS ROOM IN STRATFORD GRAMMAR SCHOOL [1]

Lost, we are shown adults making a pedantic display of just such wordy learning as Shakespeare was forced to acquire at school. He has two of his characters thus criticise such "learning":—

"*Moth*. (*Aside to Costard*.) They have been at a great feast of languages, and stolen the scraps.

"*Costard*. O, they have lived long on the alms-basket of words."

Study of Human Nature. — In some way or other Shakespeare managed to learn more about human nature than any other mortal. He learned to watch human beings of every rank with the same sympathetic eyes with which he observed the daffodil and the wild bird. The hopes and fears of others appealed to him almost as strongly as his own. People like to talk with one

[1] Tradition says that Shakespeare occupied the desk in the farthest corner.

who sympathizes with them. No author can become great unless he draws close to the universal heart of humanity, as well without, as within, his own set or coterie. To Shakespeare, the blacksmith was as human as the lord. An eminent critic says: ".He could talk simply and naturally without a touch of patronage or condescension to a hodman on his ladder, a costermonger at his stall, the tailor on his board, the cobbler in his combe, the hen-wife in her poultry-yard, the plowman in his furrow, or the base mechanicals at the wayside country inn." If this had not been the case, the Eliza-bethan drama could not have sounded so many notes of hope, love, fear, ambition, and despair; in other words, the drama could not have been complete. Close observa-tion is the child of sympathy. Lines like these show his power in noting what to most would be trivial: —

> " I saw a smith stand with his hammer, thus,
> The whilst his iron did on the anvil cool,
> With open mouth swallowing a tailor's news ;
> Who, with his shears and measure in his hand,
> Standing in slippers, which his nimble haste
> Had falsely thrust on contrary feet,
> Told of a many thousand warlike French,
> That were embattailed and rank'd in Kent." [1]

Life in London. — In 1582, at the age of eighteen, William Shakespeare married Anne Hathaway, a woman nearly eight years his senior. The next year his first child, Susanna, was born, and two years later Hamnet and Judith, twin children, were added to his family. He and his parents were poor, and he probably real-ized that Stratford was no place for him, if he was

[1] *King John*, IV., 2.

to provide properly for his wife and children, and regain the family estates which his father had lost a few years before. Accordingly, at about the age of twenty-one, he set out for London and attached himself to the theater. A tradition says that he not only shot some of the deer of Sir Thomas Lucy, but also lampooned him in cutting verses when that nobleman prosecuted him, and that, to escape being severely dealt with, Shakespeare fled to London. There is, however, no dispute about the fact that he went to London and that he became both an actor and a writer of plays. He is thought to have acted, for instance, the part of the Ghost in *Hamlet*, of Adam in *As You Like It*, and of Old Knowell in Ben Jonson's *Every Man in His Humor*.

By 1592 Shakespeare had become famous as a dramatist. We know this from the attack of envious contemporaries. He was honored by Queen Elizabeth, and he won the friendship of great men, like the Earl of Southampton, to whom Shakespeare dedicated two of his early poems, *Venus and Adonis* and *Lucrece*.

He became a shareholder in at least two theaters, the Blackfriars and the Globe. He grew wealthy and purchased for his family in Stratford larger estates than had been held before the days of misfortune. In 1597 he bought in Stratford a fine large house, known as New Place. A little later he bought one hundred and seven acres near his birthplace. He occasionally visited Stratford during these years, but the majority of his time was passed in London, where he probably wrote almost all his plays.

Last Days at Stratford. — Not far from 1613 he returned to Stratford, where he seems to have passed the remainder of his days in quiet with his family. We can

infer from his plays that he had for some time looked
forward to such a quiet consummation of his labors.

There was in Shakespeare's time more or less odium
attached to the theatrical profession, to the playwright
as well as to the actor. We cannot wonder that when
he felt assured of his independence, he wished to go
where he could live the life of a country gentleman.

One of his *Sonnets* shows how he smarted under the disgrace attaching to his profession : —

> "O, for my sake do you with Fortune chide,
> The guilty goddess of my harmful deeds,
> That did not better for my life provide
> Than public means, which public manners breeds
> And almost thence my nature is subdued
> To what it works in, like the dyer's hand." [1]

It is probable that he wrote no more for the stage during these years of retirement. In 1616, at the age of fifty-two, this master singer of the world, who, in De Quincey's phrase, was "a little lower than the angels," died and was laid at rest in the parish church at Stratford.

Shakespeare's Non-dramatic Work

Narrative Poems and Sonnets. — Not all of Shakespeare's work is dramatic. He would have stood among the first poets of his age, if he had not written a single drama. The best of his non-dramatic poems are *Venus and Adonis*, *Lucrece*, and one hundred and fifty-four *Sonnets*. In the *Venus and Adonis*, possibly written before he left Stratford, we find frequent allusions to the natural phenomena with which he was familiar in his Warwickshire home : —

> "Once more the ruby-color'd portal open'd,
> Which to his speech did honey passage yield;
> Like a red morn, that ever yet betoken'd
> Wreck to the seaman, tempest to the field,
> Sorrow to shepherds, woe unto the birds,
> Gusts and foul flaws to herdsmen and to herds."

[1] *Sonnet* CXI.

The comparison here indicated between the ruby lips of Adonis and a red morning is more in Lyly's vein and less inevitable than almost any of the similes in Shakespeare's maturer work. In these early non-dramatic poems he shows conscious effort to think of something to write, but before long his verse came to him as easily as song to the skylark.

In his *Sonnets*, which are the productions of a more mature period, many of the references to nature are masterly. The following lines from *Sonnets* XXXIII. and XVIII. are illustrations in point:—

> " Full many a glorious morning have I seen
> Flatter the mountain-tops with sovereign eye,
> Kissing with golden face the meadows green,
> Gilding pale streams with heavenly alchemy."

> " Rough winds do shake the darling buds of May,
> And summer's lease hath all too short a date."

But the chief subject of the *Sonnets* is love, concerning which he speaks in such noble lines as these:—

> " Let me not to the marriage of true minds
> Admit impediments. Love is not love
> Which alters when it alteration finds." [1]

Almost every phase of the emotion of love is expressed in these *Sonnets*. Saintsbury says: " From Sappho and Solomon to Shelley and Mr. Swinburne, many bards have spoken excellently of love: but what they said could be cut out of Shakespeare's *Sonnets* better said than they have said it, and yet enough remain to furnish forth the greatest of poets."

[1] *Sonnet* CXVI.

The Dramas

Classification of the Plays. — Shakespeare's chief work consisted in writing plays, which were acted in the theaters. His dramas may be divided into three classes: comedies, histories, and tragedies. We may indicate the following as some of the best in each class. They will be read by every cultivated person.

Comedies: *A Midsummer Night's Dream, As You Like It, The Merchant of Venice, The Winter's Tale,* and *The Tempest.*
Histories: *Richard III., Henry IV., Henry V., Julius Cæsar.*
Tragedies: *Hamlet, Macbeth, Lear, Othello, Romeo and Juliet.*

Counting plays which have two or more parts as one play, we find that the Globe edition of Shakespeare contains thirty-four different plays.

We may make another classification from a different point of view, according to the time at which the plays were written. In order to trace the growth of Shakespeare's mind, it is necessary to study him chronologically. By such study, says Furnivall, "Shakespeare's mind is shown to have run from the amorousness and fun of youth, through the strong patriotism of early manhood, to the wrestling with the dark problems that beset the man of middle age, to the time of gloom which weighed on Shakespeare, as on so many men, in later life, when, though outwardly successful, the world seemed all against him, and his mind dwelt with sympathy on scenes of faithlessness of friends, treachery of relations and subjects, ingratitude of children, scorn of his kind, till at last in his Stratford home again, peace came to him, Miranda and Perdita, in their lovely freshness and charms, greeted him, and he was laid by his quiet Avon's side."

Four Periods of his Life. — We may mark off four periods in Shakespeare's life, corresponding, in the main, to the
divisions indicated by Furnivall.

(1) There was the sanguine period, showing the exuberance of youthful love and imagination. Among the plays
which are typical of these years are *The Comedy of
Errors*, *A Midsummer Night's Dream*, *Romeo and Juliet*,
Richard II., and *Richard III.* These were probably all
composed before 1595.

(2) The second period, from 1595 to 1601, shows progress in dramatic art. There is less exaggeration, more
real power, and a deeper insight into human nature.
There appears in his philosophy a vein of sadness, such
as we find in the sayings of Jaques in *As You Like It*, and
more appreciation of the growth of character, typified by
his treatment of Orlando and Adam in the same play.
Among the plays of this period are *The Merchant of Venice*, *Henry IV.*, *Henry V.*, and *As You Like It*.

(3) We may characterize the third period, from 1601 to
1608, as one in which he felt that the time was out of
joint, that life was a fitful fever. His father died in
1601, after great disappointments. His best friends suffered what he calls, in *Hamlet*, "the slings and arrows
of outrageous fortune." In 1601 Elizabeth executed the
Earl of Essex for treason and on the same charge threw
the Earl of Southampton into the Tower. Even Shakespeare himself may have been suspected, and he had
probably been deceived by some one whom he had
trusted. The great plays of this period are tragedies,
among which we may instance *Julius Cæsar*, *Hamlet*,
Othello, *Macbeth*, and *King Lear*.

(4) The plays of his fourth period, 1608–1613, are
remarkable for calm strength and sweetness. The fierce-

ness of *Othello* and *Macbeth* is left behind. In 1608 Shakespeare's mother died. Her death and the vivid recollection of her kindness and love may have been strong factors in causing him to look on life with kindlier eyes. The greatest plays of this period are *Cymbeline, The Winter's Tale,* and *The Tempest.*

While the dates of the composition of these plays are not exactly known, the foregoing classification is probably approximately correct, and it should be followed in studying the development and the changing phases of Shakespeare's mind.

Sources of the Plots. — In almost all cases we can find the sources of the plots of Shakespeare's plays in some old chronicle, novel, biography, or older play. We can find in Holinshed's *Chronicles of England, Scotland, and Ireland,* published when Shakespeare was thirteen years old, the stories of Macbeth and Lear. But if Shakespeare's genius had not changed the old tales in vital points, we should not have had at the close of *King Lear* the strongest lines he ever penned. He read Plutarch's *Lives* for aid in writing *Julius Cæsar* and *Antony and Cleopatra,* while an old Italian tale gave him the framework for part of *The Merchant of Venice.*

Even Shakespeare could not make brick without straw. Here we have a fresh application of the psychological truth that the imagination is dependent for its materials on the stores of knowledge gleaned from the world by the exercise of our own senses, by learning from other people, and by thinking over what we have thus learned. When a comparison is made between these dramatic masterpieces and the old chronicles and tales, the student will often find that Shakespeare's plays are as different from their sources as the rose from the soil which nourished it.

General Characteristics of his Dramas

The Comic and the Tragic Spirit. — Shakespeare is equally successful in depicting humor and pathos, comedy and tragedy. The next greatest English writer is lacking in the sense of humor. John Milton could write the tragedies of a *Paradise Lost* and a *Samson Agonistes*, but he could not give us the humor of *A Midsummer Night's Dream*, *The Comedy of Errors*, or *As You Like It*. We have seen that the next greatest dramatic genius, Marlowe, has little sense of humor. Mrs. Browning correctly describes the plays of Shakespeare as filled

"With tears and laughters for all time."[1]

Mastery of his Mother Tongue. — His wealth of expression is another striking characteristic. In a poem on Shakespeare, Ben Jonson wrote: —

"Thou had'st small Latin and less Greek."

Shakespeare is, however, the mightiest master of the English tongue. He uses 15,000 different words, while the second greatest writer in our language employs 7000. A great novelist like Thackeray has a vocabulary of about 5000 words, while many uneducated laborers do not use over 600. The combinations which Shakespeare has made with these 15,000 words are far more striking than their mere number.

Variety of Style. — Shakespeare's style is remarkable. When we speak of the style of Milton, Addison, or Macaulay, we have some definite peculiarities which we can easily classify, but Shakespeare, in holding the mirror

[1] *A Vision of Poets.*

up to nature, has different styles for his sailors, soldiers, courtiers, merchants, kings, shepherds, for the alewife Mistress Quickly, and for Lady Macbeth, for Hamlet the philosopher, and for Bottom the weaver.

To employ so many varied styles requires genius of the highest kind. In the case of the most of us, our style would soon betray our individuality. When Dr. Samuel Johnson tried to write a drama, he made all his little fishes talk like whales, as Goldsmith wittily says.

Breadth of Sympathy. — The most pronounced characteristic in his plays is the extent of his sympathy with human kind. There are few intelligent people who do not build a barrier between the larger part of humanity and themselves. When the glass vessel breaks or the reed fails to sustain the weight, the most feel contempt for the frailty and the weakness. To Shakespeare, frailty and weakness were as absolute facts as strength. The ivy, the myrtle, and the floating water lily met his gaze, as well as the oak. A carpenter might have noticed only the oak, but Shakespeare's sympathy enabled him to see more, to understand more, and to interpret more.

Those err who look for Shakespeare's most striking quality in the myriad directions of his intellectual action. He studied people because he found himself entering into their joy and sorrow, because he sympathized with them. It was his sympathy that gave wings to his intellect and rendered its flight easy. Many Elizabethans thought that Ben Jonson had more cold intellect than Shakespeare, and their judgment in this respect was probably right. Sympathy puts sun and moon and stars in the sky of knowledge. Sympathy may create no new objects, but it throws a matchless light on what was previously dark. By looking at a world thus illumined, Shakespeare was able to read those secrets of the soul which are never revealed to an unsympathetic eye. In one of his great tragedies he wrote : —

> " Thou canst not speak of that thou dost not feel." [1]

The centuries have been strewn with the failures of writers who have not heeded this adage.

In his dramas, Shakespeare enters into the lives of such different characters as Hamlet and Juliet, Lear and Falstaff, Dame Quickly and Perdita, Henry the Fourth and the old servant Adam. Shakespeare identifies himself with the philosophic Hamlet as he voices his dissatisfaction with the world : —

> " O, that this too, too solid flesh would melt,
> Thaw and resolve itself into a dew !
> Or that the Everlasting had not fix'd
> His canon 'gainst self-slaughter !   O God ! O God !
> How weary, stale, flat and unprofitable
> Seem to me all the uses of this world ! "

Shakespeare looks at the world with the hopeful eyes of a lover, as he hears Juliet say : —

> " This bud of love, by summer's ripening breath,
> May prove a beauteous flower when next we meet."

When Lear's daughters have driven him out into the storm, the great dramatist takes us with the helpless old King. We can hear him call to the elements : —

> ". . . here I stand, your slave,
> A poor, infirm, weak, and despised old man :
> But yet I call you servile ministers,
> That have with two pernicious daughters join'd
> Your high engender'd battles 'gainst a head
> So old and white as this."

[1] *Romeo and Juliet*, III., 3.

We descend very far in the social scale when we enter the tavern at Eastcheap and listen to the conversation of the hostess, Dame Quickly, with Falstaff : —

"Thou didst swear to me upon a parcel-gilt goblet, sitting in my Dolphin-chamber, at the round table, by a sea-coal fire, upon Wednesday in Wheeson week, when the prince broke thy head for likening his father to a singing-man of Windsor, thou didst swear to me then as I was washing thy wound, to marry me and make me my lady thy wife. Canst thou deny it? Did not goodwife Keech, the butcher's wife, come in then and call me gossip Quickly? coming in to borrow a mess of vinegar; telling us she had a good dish of prawns; whereby thou didst desire to eat some; whereby I told thee they were ill for a green wound?" [1]

No psychologist has ever given a more lifelike illustration of the working of an uncultivated mind. All things that arrested her attention are dragged into the story, in the order in which they happened, although they have no logical relation to the progress of events. Shakespeare has the same sympathetic insight into her character as into that of Hamlet and of Juliet. From Dame Quickly we may turn to Perdita, the princess of young womanhood. We can almost see Shakespeare's brown eyes glisten as he tells us that

". . . nothing she does or seems
But smacks of something greater than herself." [2]

His portraiture of women of varied types is well-nigh marvelous. Giles says: "The fidelity of Shakespeare to the innermost feelings of woman is one of the wonders of his genius to women themselves. Mrs. Siddons marveled at it. Feminine secrecies, which she thought no masculine imagination could divine, she found that Shakespeare

[1] *King Henry IV., Part I.*, Act. II.   [2] *The Winter's Tale*, IV., 4.

had discovered; and this not alone in the maternal anguish of Constance, or the queenly grief of Katharine, but even in the stony dungeons of Lady Macbeth's bosom."

No class is untouched by the great dramatist's sympathy. The old servant in *As You Like It* is drawn with as kindly a pen as King Henry IV. and Prince Hal.

Shakespeare made this rare discovery: —

> "There is some soul of goodness in things evil,
> Would men observingly distil it out."[1]

When a character like Shylock is presented by a great actor, like Sir Henry Irving, the audience feels flashes of sympathy for the Jew. True disciples of Shakespeare constantly feel those touches of nature which make the whole world seem more closely kin.

Universality. — Other writers may have equaled Shakespeare on some one side, but he has as many sides as life has changes, and he is great in them all. He penetrates almost every sea, harbor, creek, and rivulet of human emotion. He identifies himself with the joys and sorrows of the king and of the shepherd, of youth and of age.

Of him Ben Jonson truly says: —

> "He was not of an age, but for all time."

Shakespeare does not exhibit some popular conceit, folly, or phase of thought which was merely the fashion of the hour and for which succeeding generations would care nothing. He voices those truths which appeal to the universal heart of humanity. The grief of Lear over the

[1] *Henry V.,* IV., I.

dead Cordelia, the ambition of Lady Macbeth, the loves of Rosalind and Juliet, the questionings of Hamlet, interest us as much to-day as they did the people three hundred years ago. Fashions in literature may come and go, but Shakespeare's work remains.

Comparative Rank of his Work. — Shakespeare is the greatest writer of the ages. Goethe says: "I do not remember that any book, or person, or event in my life ever produced so great an effect upon me as Shakespeare's plays. They seem to be the work of some heavenly genius." A cautious critic like Hallam writes: "The name of Shakespeare is the greatest in all literature. No man ever came near to him in the creative powers of the mind; no man ever had such strength at once and such variety of imagination."

True as these criticisms are, we must avoid inferring that Shakespeare has no faults. Some of his earlier work is marred by the shortcomings of the age: exaggeration, lack of pruning, and lack of repression. There are also euphuistic conceits scattered through his work.

His Influence on Thought. — If a person should master Shakespeare and the *Bible*, he would find all that is greatest in human thought. With the exception of the *Scriptures*, Shakespeare's dramas have surpassed all other works in molding modern English thought.

Even when we do not read him, we cannot escape the influence of others who have been swayed by him. For generations, certain modes of thought have crystallized about his phrases. We may instance such expressions as these: "Brevity is the soul of wit." "What's in a name?" "The wish was father to the thought." "The time is out of joint." "There's the rub." "There's a divinity that shapes our ends." "Comparisons are odorous." It would, perhaps, not be too much to say that the play of *Hamlet* has affected the thought of the majority of the English-speaking race.

Shakespeare's influence on the thought of any individual has only two circumscribing factors, the extent of Shakespearean study and the capacity for interpreting the facts of life. No intelligent person can study Shakespeare without becoming a deeper and more varied thinker, without securing a broader comprehension of human existence, its struggles, failures, and successes. If we have before viewed humanity through a glass darkly, he will gradually lead us where we can see face to face the beauty and the grandeur of the mystery of existence. He will also give us an added something difficult of definition; he will alchemize the leaden facts of life. After intimate companionship with him, there will be, in the words of Ariel, hardly any common thing in life

> "But doth suffer a sea-change
> Into something rich and strange."[1]

BEN JONSON, 1573?-1637

Life. — About nine years after the birth of Shakespeare, his greatest successor in the English drama was born in London. Jonson outlived Shakespeare twenty-one years, and helped to usher in the decline of the drama.

The son of a clergyman and the stepson of a master bricklayer, Ben Jonson received a good education at Westminster School, and, unlike Shakespeare, learned much Latin and Greek. In one respect Jonson's training here was unfortunate for a poet. He was taught to write prose

[1] *The Tempest*, I., 2.

Ben: Jonsomus.

exercises first and then to turn them into poetry. In this way he acquired the habit of trying to express unpoetical ideas in verse. Art could change the prose into metrical, rhyming lines, but art could not breathe into them the living soul of poetry. In after times Jonson said that Shakespeare lacked art, but Jonson recognized that the author of *Hamlet* had the magic touch of nature. Jonson's pen rarely felt her all-embracing touch.

If Jonson served an apprenticeship as a bricklayer, as

his enemies afterward said, he did not continue long at such work. He crossed the Channel and enlisted for a brief time as a soldier in the Netherlands. He soon returned to London and became a writer for the theater, and thenceforth lived the life of a writer and a student. He loved to study and translate the classics. In fact, what a novice might think original in Jonson's plays was often borrowed from the classics. Of his relations to the classical writers, Dryden says: "You track him everywhere in their snow." Jonson was known as the most learned poet of the age, because, if his plays demanded any special knowledge, no subject was too hard, dry, or remote from common life for him to attempt to master. He knew the boundaries of Bohemia, and he took pleasure in saying to a friend: "Shakespeare in a play brought in a number of men saying they had suffered shipwreck in Bohemia, where is no sea near, by some hundred miles."

Jonson's personal characteristics partly explain why he placed himself in opposition to the spirit of the age. He was extremely combative. It was almost a necessity for him to quarrel with some person or with some opinion. He killed two men in duels, and he would probably have been hanged, if he had not pleaded benefit of clergy. For the greater part of his life, he was often occupied with pen and ink quarrels.

When James I. ascended the throne in 1603, Jonson soon became a royal favorite, and was often employed to write masques, a peculiar species of drama which called for magnificent scenery and dress, and gave the nobility the opportunity of acting the part of some distinguished or supernatural character. Such work brought Jonson into intimate association with the leading men of the day.

In 1616, the year in which Shakespeare died, Jonson

was made poet laureate. When he died in 1637, he was buried in an upright position in Westminster Abbey. A plain stone with the unique inscription, "O Rare Ben Jonson," marks his grave.

Plays. — Ben Jonson's comedies are his best dramatic work. From all his plays we may select three which will best repay reading: *Volpone*, *The Alchemist*, and *The Silent Woman*. *Volpone* is the story of an old childless Venetian nobleman whose ruling passion is avarice. Everything else in the play is made tributary to this passion. The first three lines in the first act strike the keynote of the entire play. Volpone says: —

> "Good morning to the day; and next, my gold! —
> Open the shrine, that I may see my saint.
> Hail the world's soul and mine!"

The Alchemist makes a strong presentation, not of the "eternal gullible" in human nature, but of certain forms of gullibility and of the special tricks which the alchemists and impostors of that day adopted. One character wants to buy the secret of the helpful influence of the stars; another parts with his wealth to learn the alchemist's secret of turning everything into gold and jewels. The way in which these characters are deceived is very amusing. A study of this play adds to our knowledge of a certain phase of the times. In point of artistic construction of plot, *The Alchemist* is nowhere excelled in the English drama, but the intrusion of Jonson's learning often makes the play tedious reading. He must, for instance, by introducing the technical terms of the so-called science of alchemy, show that he has studied it thoroughly. One character speaks to the alchemist of

> "Your lato, azoch, zernich, chibrit, heautarit,"

and another asks : —

> "Can you sublime and dulcify? calcine?
> Know you the sapor pontic? sapor stiptic,
> Or what is homogene, or heterogene?"

Lines like the following show that Jonson's acute mind had grasped something of the principle of evolution : —

> ". . . 'twere absurd
> To think that nature in the earth bred gold
> Perfect in the instant : something went before.
> There must be remote matter."

The Silent Woman is in lighter vein than either of the plays just mentioned. The leading character is called Morose, and his special whim or "humor" is a horror of noise. His home is on a street "so narrow at both ends that it will receive no coaches nor carts, nor any of these common noises." He has mattresses on the stairs, and he dismisses the footman for wearing squeaking shoes. For a long time Morose does not marry, fearing the noise of a wife's tongue. Finally he commissions his nephew to find him a silent woman for a wife, and the author uses to good advantage the opportunity for comic situations which this turn in the action affords. Dryden preferred *The Silent Woman* to any of the other plays.

Besides the plays mentioned in this section, Jonson wrote during his long life many other comedies and masques, as well as some tragedies.

Marks of Decline. — In Jonson's plays we may study the decline of the drama, and in doing this we shall the better appreciate the genius of Shakespeare. We may change Jonson's line (see p. 164) so that it will state one reason for his not maintaining Shakespearean excellence : —

He was not for all time, but of an age.

His first play, *Every Man in His Humor*, paints, not the universal emotions of men, but some especial humor. He thus defines the sense in which he uses humor : —

> " When some peculiar quality
> Doth so possess a man, that it doth draw
> All his effects, his spirits and his powers,
> In their confluctions, all to run one way,
> This may be truly said to be a Humor."

Unlike Shakespeare, Jonson gives a distorted or incomplete picture of life. In *Volpone* everything is subsidiary to the humor of avarice, which receives unnatural emphasis. In *The Alchemist* there is little to relieve the picture of credibility and hypocrisy, while *The Silent Woman* has for its leading character a man whose principal "humor" or aim in life is to avoid noise.

No drama which fails to paint the nobler side of womanhood can be called complete. In Jonson's plays we do not find a single woman worthy to come near the Shakespearean characters, Cordelia, Imogen, and Desdemona. His limitations are nowhere more marked than in his inability to portray a noble woman.

Another reason why he fails to present life completely is shown in these lines, in which he defines his mission : —

> " My strict hand
> Was made to seize on vice, and with a gripe
> Squeeze out the humor of such spongy souls
> As lick up every idle vanity."

Since the world needs building up rather than tearing down, a remedy for an ailment rather than fault-finding, the greatest of men cannot be mere satirists. Shakespeare displays some fellow feeling for the object of his satire, but Jonson's satire is cold and devoid of sympathy.

Jonson deliberately took his stand in opposition to the romantic spirit of the age. Marlowe and Shakespeare had disregarded the classical unities (see p. 143) and had developed the drama on romantic lines. Jonson resolved to follow classical traditions and to adhere to unity of time and place in the construction of his plots. The action in the play of *The Silent Woman*, for instance, occupies only twelve hours.

Miscellaneous Work. — Jonson also wrote some lyrics, exquisite as well for their delicacy of expression as for the character of the thought. A few lines from one of his songs will show both these qualities : —

> " Drink to me only with thine eyes,
> And I will pledge with mine ;
> Or leave a kiss but in the cup,
> And I'll not look for wine.
> The thirst that from the soul doth rise
> Doth ask a drink divine." [1]

No one should form an estimate of Ben Jonson without reading the pithy prose known as his *Discoveries Made upon Men and Matter*. His critical power, as well as his large, ungainly frame, reminds one of Dr. Samuel Johnson. In the *Discoveries* we meet with thoughts as vigorous and as tersely expressed as we find in the conversations of the Doctor (see pp. 296, 297). The following from the *Discoveries* may be compared with the Doctor's way of stating whatever occurred to him on various subjects, or with the best pedagogic thought of to-day : —

" A youth should not be made to hate study before he know the causes to love it, or taste the bitterness before the sweet ; but called on and allured, entreated and praised."

[1] *To Celia.*

The *Discoveries* contains Jonson's famous criticism on Shakespeare, in which occurs this statement, noteworthy because it shows how a great contemporary regarded him : " I loved the man and do honor his memory on this side idolatry as much as any."

General Characteristics. — Jonson's plays show the touch of a conscientious artist with great intellectual ability. His vast erudition is constantly apparent. He is the satiric historian of his time, and he exhibits the follies and the humors of the age under a powerful lens. He is also the author of dainty lyrics and forcible prose criticism.

Among the shortcomings of his plays, we may specially note lack of feeling and of universality. He fails to comprehend the nature of woman. He is not a sympathetic observer of manifold life, but he presents only what is perceived through the frosted glass of intellect. His art is self-conscious. He defiantly opposed the romantic spirit of the age and he weakened the drama by making it bear the burden of the classical unities.

THE PRESENTATION OF ELIZABETHAN PLAYS

Theaters and Actors. — The first building in England for the public presentation of plays was known as The Theater, and it was built in London in 1576. The Globe Theater, with which Shakespeare's name is so closely identified, was erected across the Thames at Southwark in 1593. The public theaters, with the exception of the stage, were roofless. The pit corresponded to the first floor of our modern theaters, but it had neither chairs nor covering. The great bulk of the audience, all the common people, stood and jostled one another in the pit. There was no floor, and hence the frequenters of the pit were sometimes called the "groundlings." Occasionally an overviolent storm would drive them out of the theater to seek shelter. Around the sides of the theaters were boxes for those who could afford

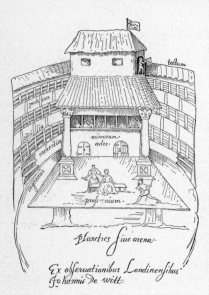

CONTEMPORARY DRAWING OF THE INTERIOR
OF AN ELIZABETHAN THEATER [1]

them. Admission to the pit was often not more than a penny, but the price for the best or the most fashionable seats was sometimes as much as two shillings. The aristocratic young gallants, who went to the theater as much to be seen as to see, paid an extra price for stools on the outer edges of the stage. The play usually began at three o'clock in the afternoon. There was scarcely any scenery. The stage had the same setting for the Forest of

[1] "A rude sketch of the interior of the Swan Theater, London, as it was about the year 1596, was not long since brought to light in the University Library, Utrecht. It is from the hand of a learned Dutchman, Johannes de Witt, who visited England toward the close of the reign of Elizabeth. The stage, strongly supported on timber bulks, is occupied by three actors, and has for all its furniture a bench on which a female figure is seated. Neither curtains nor traverses appear. At the back of the stage, which is open to the weather, is the tiring-room, to which two doors give entrance, and above this rises a covered balcony or row of boxes occupied by spectators, but available at need for the actors. The trumpeter is seen at the door of a covered chamber near the gallery-roof, and from its summit floats a flag, having upon it the figure of a swan. The form of the building is oval. No other drawing of the interior of an Elizabethan theater is known to exist." — EDWARD DOWDEN.

Arden as for the Danish castle of Elsinore.   A board marked "Rome," "Venice," "Athens," or whatever place it might be, announced a change of scene.   Active imagination on the part of the spectator was needed to supply the place of elaborate scenery.

The plays as a rule were probably well acted, and such acting would in a measure make amends for lack of scenery.   The actors also endeavored to produce some scenic effect by elaborate and costly costumes. The occupants of the pit would occasionally throw apples or worse missiles at an unsatisfactory actor. Sometimes the disgusted spectators would rush on the stage to beat all the actors.   If the

THE FOOL OF THE OLD PLAY

fault lay with the playwright, the angry audience might cowhide him or toss him in a blanket.

Excellence in the presentation of plays may seem strange when we know that, prior to the Restoration in 1660, the women's parts were taken by boys.   Ophelia, Lady Macbeth, and Desdemona were acted by boys.   We know that Shakespeare complained of this and other limitations of the stage.   He makes Cleopatra resent the way the stage of future times will deal with her, when she says : —

> "The quick comedians
> Extemporally will stage us, and present
> Our Alexandrian revels, Antony
> Shall be brought drunken forth, and I shall see
> Some squeaking Cleopatra boy my greatness."

These limitations were not without compensation, for they forced the dramatist to do his utmost to produce plays which could hold the attention under the most disadvantageous circumstances. The spectators were also compelled to cultivate their imaginative power by using it. Modern stage settings often leave little for the imagination to supply. No mental power can grow without exercise.

GENERAL SUMMARY

England was vivified by the combined influence of the Renaissance and the Reformation. Knowledge was expanding in every direction and promising to crown human effort with universal mastery. The Reformation removed artificial restraint from the workings of the human mind. To seek for knowledge in every direction was no longer considered impious.

The wonders of the New World, the increase of commerce, the rise of the middle classes, and the spirit of patriotism aroused in England by her enemies and her victories, made the nation feel like a youth capable of all things. The poets caught and reflected the spirit in the air. All forces seemed to work together to inspire the Elizabethans to produce the greatest literature in the world. In reaching this position, they owed much to the literature of Italy, but the English pupils were soon in a position to instruct their Italian teachers.

The prose of the age is far inferior to the poetry. The prose of Lyly is overwrought with conceits, and much of Sidney's is too poetical. Hooker shows advance, but a comparison of his heavy religious prose with the prayer of the King in *Hamlet* or with Portia's words about mercy in *The Merchant of Venice* will show the vast superiority of the poetry in dealing with the same ideas. Bacon's *Essays* are the only prose that has stood the test of time well enough to claim many readers to-day.

Although the poetry covers a wide range, Edmund Spenser is the only great non-dramatic poet. In England the drama underwent a slow growth for centuries, through the Miracle plays, Moralities, and Interludes, to the plays of Shakespeare. Marlowe, Shakespeare, and Ben Jonson are the three greatest Elizabethan dramatists, but they are only the central figures of a group of singers.

The English drama in the hands of Sackville imitated Seneca and followed the rules of the classic stage. Marlowe and Shakespeare threw off the restraints of the classical unities, and the romantic drama, rejoicing in its freedom, speedily told the story of all life. No human being was too high or too low to receive sympathetic attention. This drama was spun out of the very web and woof of life. The master singer of the age set the soul of life to music. Later poetry considers theories and justifications of life. The Shakespearean drama is neither theories nor justifications of life; it is life itself.

The chief excellences of the age consist in the freshness, spontaneity, and universality or sympathetic grasp of all life. An imagination of wonderful activity gave varied concrete interpretation to the manifold facts of life. Such an interpretation was necessary for the drama to gain the ascendency and represent life on an actual stage. Ben Jonson shows a decline in dramatic power because he lacks Shakespeare's universality. The faults of the age sprang naturally from unbridled youthful imagination and the belief that the new forces acting in life would make all things possible. Exaggeration and lack of repression are manifest not only in Marlowe and the minor writers, but

sometimes even in Shakespeare. In the majority of the
minor poets there are exquisite jewels, little known because
of the crude accretions which surround them.

REQUIRED READINGS FOR CHAPTER IV

HISTORICAL

Gardiner,[1] pp. 428–480; Underwood-Guest, pp. 427–441; Green,
Chap. VII.; Guerber, pp. 233–252; Powers's *England and the Reformation*, pp. 88–136; Traill, III., 304–579.

LITERARY

Sackville. — The best parts of Sackville's *Induction* are given in
Ward's *English Poets*, Vol. I., pp. 271–274, and also in Fitzgibbon's
Early English Poetry, pp. 317–326. For Sackville's dramatic work see
p. 180, under *Gorboduc*.

What is there remarkable about Sackville's verse?

Lyly, Sidney, Hooker, and Bacon. — A selection from Lyly's *Euphues*
is given in Craik's *English Prose Selections*, Vol. I., pp. 379–384. A
complete edition is edited by Arber in his *English Reprints*, 478 pp.
Craik also gives in Vol. I. (pp. 409–422) selections from Sidney's
Arcadia and *Apologie for Poetrie*, and (pp. 473–478) from Hooker's
Laws of Ecclesiastical Polity, and in Vol. II., pp. 14–27, from Bacon's
Essays.

Craik's selections from Lyly, Sidney, Hooker, and Bacon will enable
the student to compare the structure of sentence, general style, and
worth of the subject matter of these four authors. Whose prose style
shows most improvement over Mandeville and Malory? In what
respects?

Edmund Spenser. — The *Faerie Queene*, Book I., Canto I., should be
read. Maynard, Merrill, & Co's *English Classic* Series, No. 27 (12
cents), contains this canto. Kitchin's edition of Book I. (Clarendon
Press, 60 cents) is an excellent volume. Ward's *English Poets*, Vol. I.,
pp. 284–340, contains representative selections from all of Spenser's
great poems.

[1] For full titles, see list at end of Chap. I.

The student should select passages that show (*a*) Spenser's melody, (*b*) love of the beautiful, (*c*) nobility of ideals, and (*d*) subjective cast of mind. Instance stanzas that justify calling him the poets' poet. Does he, as the only great non-dramatic poet of the age, show anything of its spirit?

The Drama[1]

Miracle Plays. — Pollard's *English Miracle Plays, Moralities, and Interludes*, 250 pp. (Clarendon Press, $1.90, the best single volume on the subject), gives the two Miracle plays: the Chester *Play of Noah's Flood* (pp. 8–20), and the Towneley *Play of the Shepherds* (pp. 31–43), which best show the germs of English comedy. Manly's *Specimens of the Pre-Shakspearean Drama*, Vol. I., pp. 94–119, also gives this Towneley play. Selections from these two may be found in Morley's *English Writers*, Vol. IV., pp. 71–73 and 95–99. The *Play of the Shepherds* is given almost entire in Morley's *English Plays*, pp. 3–11.

Show how these plays differ from a bald narrative of scriptural facts. Does the *Play of the Shepherds* show constructive plot, apart from mere incident? Give some reasons for calling Miracle plays like these the foundation of our drama. What general purpose did they serve in their time?

Moralities. — The best *Morality* is that known as *Everyman* (Pollard, pp. 77–96). If *Everyman* is not accessible, *Hycke-Scorner* may be substituted (Morley's *English Plays*, pp. 12–18; Manly's *Specimens of the Pre-Shakspearean Drama*, Vol. I., pp. 386–420).

Does the *Morality* show a forward step in the evolution of the drama? What were the favorite characters represented? Is the ethical spirit as prominent in the modern novel as in the early drama?

Interludes. — The best *Interlude* is John Heywood's *The Four P's*. Morley's *English Plays*, pp. 18–20, and Symonds's *Shakspere's Predecessors in the English Drama*, pp. 188–201, give as much of this *Interlude* as is necessary for the student to read.

What were some of the purposes for which *Interludes* were written? How did they aid in the development of the drama?

[1] All the plays mentioned for study in this section, with the exception of those by Shakespeare and Jonson, may be found in Cassell's *Library of English Literature*, Vol. III., *English Plays*, edited by Henry Morley and published by Cassell & Co., London, at eleven and one half shillings.

Ralph Royster Doyster and Gorboduc. — *Ralph Royster Doyster* may be found in Arber's *Reprints* (40 cents), in Morley's *English Plays*, pp. 22–46, and in Manly's *Specimens*, Vol. II., pp. 5–92.

Gorboduc is given in Morley's *English Plays*, pp. 51–64, and, under the title of *Ferrex and Porrex*, in Dodsley's *Old Plays*, Vol. I.

In what different poetic forms are these two plays written? In what does *Gorboduc* resemble classical models? Why would Shakespeare's plays have been impossible if the evolution of the drama had stopped with *Gorboduc*?

Marlowe. — Read *Dr. Faustus*, edited by Gollancz in *The Temple Dramatists*. This play may also be found in Morley's *English Plays*, pp. 116–128, or in Morley's *Universal Library*.

Does this drama observe the classical unities? In what way does it show the spirit of the Elizabethan age? Was the poetic form of the play the regular vehicle of dramatic expression? In what does the greatness of the play consist? What are its defects? Why do young people sometimes think Marlowe the greatest of *all* the Elizabethan dramatists?

Shakespeare. — Students who at this point in their course have sufficient time to read three of Shakespeare's plays should choose one tragedy, either *Hamlet* or *Macbeth*, one historical play, *Julius Cæsar*, and one comedy, *The Merchant of Venice*. These plays, with good explanatory notes, may be found in the *Eclectic English Classics* Series or the Rolfe Series (American Book Co.). Among other good annotated editions of separate plays are those of Clark and Wright, Verity, and Arden. Furness's *Variorum Shakespeare* is the best for exhaustive study.

The student cannot do better than follow the advice of Dr. Johnson: "Let him who is unacquainted with the powers of Shakespeare, and who desires to feel the highest pleasure that the drama can give, read every play, from the first scene to the last, with utter negligence of all his commentators. . . . Let him read on through brightness and obscurity, through integrity and corruption; let him preserve his comprehension of the dialogue and his interest in the fable. And when the pleasures of novelty have ceased, let him attempt exactness and read the commentators."

For effective study, the student must bring to Shakespeare wide sympathy with life, keen observing powers, and the capacity for reflecting on what he sees and reads. To such a student, Shakespeare will speak with myriad tongues. Let the student frequently apply to himself these two lines from Coleridge : —

"O Lady! we receive but what we give,
And in our life does nature live."

What in these plays specially shows Shakespeare's (*a*) variety of style, (*b*) power over laughter and tears, (*c*) strength of imagination, (*d*) breadth of sympathy, (*e*) depth of feeling, and (*f*) universality or myriad-mindedness? Is there anything in Marlowe worthy of Shakespeare? In what special points does Marlowe fail to rank with Shakespeare? Take a certain play and show how Shakespeare treated the classical unities. What did he gain by this treatment?

Ben Jonson. — *The Alchemist* may be found in the *Canterbury Poets* edition of his *Dramatic Works and Lyrics*, edited by Symonds (40 cents) ; also, with *Volpone* and *The Silent Woman*, in Morley's *Universal Library*, No. 20 (40 cents).

Why is the plot of *The Alchemist* called unusually fine? How does Shakespeare's humor differ from Jonson's? Compare Marlowe, Shakespeare, and Jonson in their power of portraying women. How did Jonson regard the classical unities? In what ways does he show a decline in the drama? Why is he called a great dramatist?

Jonson's *Discoveries Made upon Men and Matter* (Cassell's *National Library*, No. 169, 10 cents) contains his striking thoughts on education (pp. 98-101), the oft-quoted criticism of Shakespeare (pp. 47, 48, 169-172), and a number of fine lyrics (pp. 161-192), such as "Drink to me only with thine eyes."

WORKS FOR CONSULTATION AND FURTHER STUDY

(OPTIONAL)

HISTORICAL

Creighton's *The Age of Elizabeth*.
Hall's *Society in the Elizabethan Age*.
Warner's *The People for Whom Shakespeare Wrote*.
Goadby's *The England of Shakespeare*.
Beesley's *Life of Elizabeth*.
Rye's *England as Seen by Foreigners in the Days of Elizabeth and James I*.
Froude's *History of England*.

GENERAL LITERATURE

Saintsbury's *A History of Elizabethan Literature*.
Morley's *English Writers*, Vols. IX., X., XI.
Taine's *English Literature*, Book II., Chaps. II., III., IV.
Whipple's *The Literature of the Age of Elizabeth*.
Minto's *Characteristics of English Poets*, pp. 163–367.
Minto's *English Prose Writers*, pp. 197–251.
Gosse's *A Short History of Modern English Literature*, pp. 73–128.
Phillips's *Popular Manual of English Literature*, Vol. I., pp. 103–284.
Courthope's *History of English Poetry*, Vol. II.
Ward's *English Poets*, Vol. I., pp. 275–566.
Craik's *English Prose Selections*, Vol. I., pp. 267–598.
Schelling's *Elizabethan Lyrics*.

SPECIAL AUTHORS

Lyly, in *Dictionary of National Biography*.
Symonds's *Life of Sidney*.
Sidney's *Apologie for Poetrie* (Arber Reprints).
Walton's *Life of Hooker*.
Hooker, in *Dictionary of National Biography*.
Church's *Life of Bacon*.
Church's *Life of Spenser*.
Dowden's *Transcripts and Studies* (pp. 269–337) contains *Spenser the Poet and Teacher*, and *The Heroines of Spenser*.

THE DRAMA

Pollard's *English Miracle Plays, Moralities, and Interludes* ; *Specimens of the Pre-Elizabethan Drama, with an Introduction, Notes, and Glossary*.
Smith's *York Plays* (Clarendon Press).
Symonds's *Shakspere's Predecessors in the English Drama*.
Bates's *The English Religious Drama*.
Manly's *Specimens of the Pre-Shakspearean Drama*, 3 vols.
Dodsley's *Old Plays*, Vols. I. and II.
Gayley's *Representative English Comedies*.
Collier's *History of English Dramatic Poetry*, 3 vols.

Ward's *A History of English Dramatic Literature*, 3 vols.

Lowell's *The Old English Dramatists*.

Marlowe in *Encyclopædia Britannica* and *Dictionary of National Biography*.

Symonds's *Introduction to Marlowe* in *Mermaid Series of Dramatists*.

Christopher Marlowe in Dowden's *Transcripts and Studies*, pp. 431–453.

Symonds's *Ben Jonson*.

Swinburne's *A Study of Ben Jonson*.

Symonds's *Selections from Ben Jonson* in *Canterbury Poets* Series.

SHAKESPEARE

Sidney Lee's *A Life of William Shakespeare*.

Halliwell-Phillips's *Outlines of the Life of Shakespeare*.

Wilder's *The Life of Shakespeare*.

Fleay's *A Chronicle History of the Life and Work of Shakespeare*.

Williams's *Homes and Haunts of Shakespeare*.

Hudson's *Life, Art, and Characters of Shakespeare*.

Baynes's *Shakespeare Studies and Other Essays*.

How Shakespeare's Senses were Trained, Chap. X., in Halleck's *Education of the Central Nervous System*.

Harting's *The Ornithology of Shakespeare* (excellent for young students).

Rolfe's *Shakespeare the Boy*.

Dowden's *Shakspere Primer*.

Dowden's *Shakspere: A Critical Study of his Mind and Art*.

Coleridge's *Notes and Lectures on the Plays of Shakespeare*.

Brandes's *William Shakespeare: A Critical Study*, 2 vols.

Ten Brink's *Five Lectures on Shakespeare*.

Mrs. Jameson's *Characteristics of Women*.

Weiss's *Wit, Humor, and Shakspeare*.

Gervinus's *Shakespeare Commentaries*.

Dyer's *Folk-Lore of Shakespeare*.

Madden's *The Diary of Master William Silence: A Study of Shakespeare and of Elizabethan Sport*.

Boswell-Stone's *Shakespeare's Holinshed*.

Abbott's *Shakespearian Grammar*.

Bartlett's *Shakespeare Concordance*.

CHAPTER V

THE PURITAN AGE, 1603–1660

Why Termed "Puritan Age." — We call the era following the death of Elizabeth the age of Puritan influence for two reasons: (1) The Puritan standard of morals and of government became triumphant during this period and affected the character of the literature. (2) The greatest writer of the age, the second greatest in English literature, is the Puritan, John Milton.

We must remember that different periods of English literature overlap each other to a considerable extent. To aid the memory, we make classifications which are only roughly true. We have seen that the Elizabethans, Shakespeare, Ben Jonson, and Bacon, lived for a considerable time after the death of Elizabeth. Indeed, some apply the term "Elizabethan" to all the literature written between 1558 and 1660, because some of the influences of the age of Elizabeth are shown in Milton and in the minor poetry of the period here called the Puritan age.

An Age of Controversy. — There are some characteristics which sharply differentiate this age from the preceding one. It was an age of controversy in literature and politics. The pen and the bullet were both used to advance party interests. Milton's *Paradise Lost* is an epic of conflict to the bitter end, an epic which embodies something of the spirit of the times through which he had passed in his manhood.

The Elizabethans did not allow questions of politics and religion to plunge them in civil war. Theirs was a time of intense patriotism, when Englishmen were united to resist the power of Spain. In fifty-four years after the defeat of the Armada, Englishmen were engaged in a war between King and Parliament.

Why the Age was One of Conflict. — Elizabeth with all her faults had the qualities that enabled her to rule well and to keep the affection of her subjects. James I. (1603–1625), the son of Mary Queen of Scots, was the first of the Stuart line to rule in England. He was contemptible and ridiculous in appearance, a coward, and a vain and conceited pedant. He believed that kings governed by divine right, and received from the Deity a title of which no one could lawfully deprive them, no matter how outrageously they ruled.

His son and successor, Charles I. (1625–1649), tenaciously adhered to this view, and tried to govern as he pleased. The resulting struggle between Royalists and Puritans finally led to civil war (1642–1648), in which the Puritans under the leadership of the great Oliver Cromwell were victorious. Charles I. was tried on the charge of being a traitor to the nation, convicted, and beheaded. Oliver Cromwell then ruled as Protector, and the Puritans were in the ascendency until 1660, when the Stuart line of kings was restored in the person of Charles II.

All these events left their mark on our literature, but there was another still more potent factor affecting both the poetry and the prose.

Change of Ideal. — Men took a view of life different from the one held when the New World and the New Learning promised everything that heart could wish. When Raleigh and Drake were sailing on their voyages of discovery, and English vessels were returning with tons of silver from the mines across the sea, almost everything seemed possible. The revival of learning also promised to enable man to unravel the secrets of Nature and command her to serve him as he pleased.

These expectations had not been fulfilled. There were still poverty, disease, and a longing for something that earth had not given. The English, naturally a religious race, reflected much on this. Those who concluded that life could never yield the pleasure which man anticipates, who determined by purity of living to win a perfect land beyond the shores of mortality, who made the New World of earlier dreams a term synonymous with the New Jerusalem, — were called Puritans.

Their guide to this land was the *Bible*. Our *Authorized Version*, the one which is in most common use to-day, was made in the reign of James I. From this time it became much easier to get a copy of the *Scriptures*, and their influence was now more potent than ever to shape the ideals of the Puritans. In fact, it is impossible to estimate the influence which this *Authorized Version* has had on the language and the literature of the English race.

An Imitative Age. — John Milton had the creative capacity of the Elizabethans, but the majority of the literature of this age is imitative. Strange to say, Shakespeare had fewer imitators than John Donne, Ben Jonson, or Edmund Spenser. The foreign models were chiefly Italian, but their influence was not paramount.

John Donne (1573–1631) is of interest to the student of literature chiefly because of the influence which he exerted on the poetry of the age. His verse teems with forced comparisons and analogies between things remarkable for their dissimilarity. An obscure likeness and a worthless conceit were as important to him as was the problem of existence to Hamlet. He acquired the name of "metaphysical" poet because he loved to look at the common things of life through a glass darkened with metaphysical smoke. He wrote some good poetry, but that found fewer imitators.

The lyrics of Ben Jonson were imitated by the minor poets, some of whom claimed the distinction of belonging to the "tribe of Ben." Edmund Spenser exerted an influence for good over the best poetry. Milton called him "our sage and serious Spenser, whom I dare be known to think a better teacher than Scotus or Aquinas."

I. THE PROSE OF THE PURITAN AGE

Variety of Subject. — Prose showed development in several directions during this Puritan age : —

I. The use of prose in argument and controversy was largely extended. Questions of government and of religion were the living issues of the time. Innumerable pamphlets and many larger books were written to present different views. We may instance as types of this class almost all the prose writings of John Milton (1608–1674).

II. English prose dealt with a greater variety of philosophical subjects. Shakespeare had voiced the deepest philosophy in poetry, but up to this time such subjects had found scant expression in prose.

Thomas Hobbes (1588–1679) is the great philosophical writer of the age. In his greatest work, *Leviathan ; or, The Matter, Form, and Power of a Commonwealth*, he considers questions of metaphysical philosophy and of government, in a way that places him on the roll of famous English philosophers.

III. History had an increasing fascination for prose writers. Sir Walter Raleigh's *History of the World* (1614) and Lord Clarendon's *History of the Great Rebellion*, begun in 1646, are specially worthy of mention.

IV. Prose was developing its capacity for expressing delicate shades of humor. In Chaucer and in Shakespeare, poetry had already excelled in this respect. Thomas Fuller (1608–1661), an Episcopal clergyman, displays an almost inexhaustible fund of humor in his *History of the Worthies of England.* We find scattered through his works passages like these: —

THOMAS FULLER

"A father that whipped his son for swearing, and swore at him while he whipped him, did more harm by his example than good by his correction."

Speaking of a pious short person, Fuller says: —

"His soul had but a short diocese to visit, and therefore might the better attend the effectual informing thereof."

Of the lark, he writes: —

"A harmless bird while living, not trespassing on grain, and wholesome when dead, then filling the stomach with meat, as formerly the ear with music."

Before Fuller, humor was rare in English prose writers, and it was not common until the first quarter of the next century.

V. Izaak Walton's *Complete Angler* (1653) is so filled with sweetness and calm delight in nature and life, that one does not wonder that the book has passed through about two hundred editions. It manifests a genuine love of nature, of the brooks, meadows, flowers. In his pages we catch the odor from the hedges gay with wild flowers and hear the rain falling softly on the green leaves:—

"But turn out of the way a little, good scholar, towards yonder high honeysuckle hedge; there we'll sit and sing, whilst this shower falls so gently on the teeming earth, and gives a yet sweeter smell to the lovely flowers that adorn those lovely meadows."

IZAAK WALTON

VI. Of the many authors busily writing on theology, Jeremy Taylor (1613–1667), an Episcopal clergyman, holds the chief place. His imagination was so wide and his pen so facile that he has been called a seventeenth century prose Shakespeare. Taylor's *Holy Living* and *Holy Dying* used to be read in almost every cottage. This passage shows his powers of imagery as well as the Teutonic inclination to consider the final goal of youth and beauty:—

JEREMY TAYLOR

"Reckon but from the sprightfulness of youth, and the fair cheeks and full eyes of childhood, from the vigorousness and strong texture of the joints of five-and-twenty, to the hollowness and dead paleness, to the loathsomeness and horror of a three days' burial, and we shall perceive the distance to be very great and very strange. But so have I seen a rose newly springing from the clefts of its hood, and at first it was fair as morning, and full with the dew of heaven as a lamb's fleece . . . and at night, having lost some of its leaves and all its beauty, it fell into the portion of weeds and outworn faces."

II. The Poetry of the Puritan Age

The Drama. — A number of dramatists who, by some Elizabethan characteristics, partly compensate for much inferior work, wrote plays during the reigns of the first two Stuarts (1603–1649). In so far as strict chronology is concerned, we must remember that Shakespeare produced some of his greatest plays in the reign of James I., and that Ben Jonson did not die until 1637. We shall here consider the most notable of those minor dramatists of the Puritan age, who, showing the decline of the drama, may yet claim some kinship with their greatest predecessors. The one among this group of dramatists who stands nearest to Shakespeare is John Webster. His greatest play, *The Duchess of Malfi*, was acted in 1616. This and *The White Devil*, which ranks second, in their own limited sphere show the working of a master hand. Webster's genius comes to a focus only in depicting the horrible. He found a congenial task in weaving the web of crime and retribution that entangled the Italian Duke Ferdinand, who hired assassins to murder his sister, the Duchess of Malfi, and her children. Just before one of the most terrible scenes in the English drama, a troop of madmen, loosed from the common asylum, bursts in upon the Duchess, and the foremost sings : —

> "O, let me howl some heavy note,
> Some deadly doggéd howl,
> Sounding as from the threatening throat
> Of beast and fatal fowl."

As the assassins tie the cord around her neck, the Duchess says : —

> " Pull, and pull strongly, for your able strength
> Must pull down heaven upon me. —
> Yet stay ; heaven-gates are not so highly arch'd
> As princes' palaces ; they that enter there
> Must go upon their knees [*Kneels*]. — Come, violent death,
> Serve for mandragora to make me sleep ! —
> Go tell my brothers when I am laid out,
> They then may feed in quiet.
>   [*They strangle her*."

When we feel Webster's power in representing the summit of human anguish, we are even then aware of a decline in the drama. We miss Shakespeare's universality, for he has taught us that the world is one of laughter as well as of tears, and that the buds of May are as real as the brown leaves of October.

John Ford (1586?–1639) had Webster's fondness for ghastly subjects. Ford achieved the distinction of writing *Perkin Warbeck*, which is worthy of being placed in a class second only to Shakespeare's historical plays.

Francis Beaumont (1584–1616) and John Fletcher (1579–1625) were collaborators in dramatic work. In their verse we may often find rare flowers of poetry growing out of mire. Lines like these in *Philaster*, one of Beaumont and Fletcher's best plays, might have been uttered by Hamlet : —

> " *Philaster.*   O, but thou dost not know what 'tis to die.
> *Bellario.*   Yes, I do know, my lord.
>   'Tis less than to be born ; a lasting sleep,
>   A quiet resting from all jealousy ;
>   A thing we all pursue ; I know besides
>   It is but giving over of a game
>   That must be lost."

On the whole, the drama during this age steadily pursued a downward course. We miss the earlier creative power and grasp of all life. The plays frequently do not follow the lines of orderly growth in their development. They often seem to be constructed from the outside, and sensational scenes are too frequently introduced abruptly to stimulate temporary interest. The greatest blemish on the drama of the first two Stuarts is the prevailing lack of refinement in thought and language and the frequent neglect of the proper moral sequence to acts, — a sequence which should be as inevitable as any effect, when the efficient cause is operative. Shakespeare shows the moral result indissolubly linked to the deed itself. In *Macbeth*, to name one of many instances, he makes us feel that

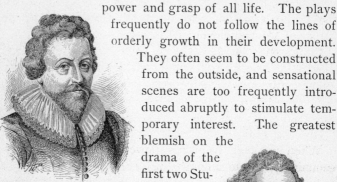

FRANCIS BEAUMONT

JOHN FLETCHER

> "We still have judgment here; that we but teach
> Bloody instructions, which, being taught, return
> To plague the inventor: this even-handed justice
> Commends the ingredients of our poison'd chalice
> To our own lips."

Beaumont and Fletcher, on the other hand, repeatedly neglect the fundamental laws of moral results.

In 1642 the Puritans closed the theaters, and the course of the drama for this age was run. Although the indecent plays of the Restoration flourished for a while, a consideration of the drama hereafter forms but a minor part of the history of the best English literature.

The Caroline Poets. — Carew, Suckling, Lovelace, and Herrick, all adherents of Charles I. (Latin, *Carolus*, hence the adjective *Caroline*), are the best of the Caroline school of poets. They are often called Cavalier poets, because they sympathized with the Cavaliers or Royalists.

The lyric, *Disdain Returned*, of Thomas Carew (1598?– 1639?) shows both the customary type of subject and the serious application sometimes given : —

> " He that loves a rosy cheek,
>   Or a coral lip admires,
>   Or from starlike eyes doth seek
>   Fuel to maintain his fires,
>   As old time makes these decay,
>   So his flames must waste away."

Sir John Suckling (1609?–1642) is a perfect specimen of the Cavalier type. His poem *Constancy* begins : —

> " Out upon it, I have loved
>   Three whole days together;
>   And am like to love three more,
>   If it prove fair weather."

From Richard Lovelace (1618–1658) we have this exquisite stanza, written in prison : —

> " Stone walls do not a prison make,
>   Nor iron bars a cage;
>   Minds innocent and quiet take
>   That for an hermitage;

> If I have freedom in my love,
> And in my soul am free,
> Angels alone, that soar above,
> Enjoy such liberty." [1]

ROBERT HERRICK

By far the greatest of this school is Robert Herrick (1591–1674), a clergyman of the Church of England. He left nearly thirteen hundred poems. He occupies the very front rank of the second class of lyrical poets. The two collections of his poems are entitled *Hesperides* and *Noble Numbers,* the latter a volume of religious poems. His work is uneven, and much of it is unworthy to be read. There is, however, sufficient to merit attention. His *Corinna's Going a-Maying* gives the full freshness of the meadow. His lyric *To the Virgins* is often quoted : —

> "Gather ye rose-buds while ye may :
> Old Time is still a-flying ;
> And this same flower that smiles to-day,
> To-morrow will be dying."

A stanza like this from his religious poem *The Litany* shows his power over melody : —

> "When the passing-bell doth toll
> And the furies in a shoal
> Come to fright a parting soul,
> Sweet Spirit, comfort me."

Characteristics of the School. — The designation " Caroline school " is applied to a group of imitative poets who

[1] *To Althea from Prison.*

flourished chiefly during the reign of Charles I. (1625–1649). The lyrical poems of Ben Jonson and the poetry of John Donne were their chief models. The greatest of the school, Robert Herrick, thus addresses Ben Jonson : —

> "Candles I'll give to thee,
> And a new altar ;
> And thou, Saint Ben, shall be
> Writ in my psalter." [1]

To characterize the Caroline school by one phrase, we might call them lyrical poets in lighter vein. They usually wrote on such subjects as the color in a maiden's cheek and lips, blossoms, meadows, May days, bridal cakes, the paleness of a lover, and

> ". . . wassail bowls to drink,
> Spiced to the brink," [2]

but sometimes religious subjects were chosen, when these lighter things failed to satisfy.

Among the special defects of this school may be mentioned overwrought conceits, strained metaphors and similes, and occasional attempts at obscure philosophical hairsplitting. These conceits and the misuse of figures are seen at their very worst in these two lines from Richard Crashaw (1613?–1649?), in which he calls the weeping eyes of Mary Magdalene

> "Two walking baths, two weeping motions,
> Portable and compendious oceans."

But we find occasional stanzas of such rare sweetness that they are worthy to linger in our memory.

---

[1] *Prayer to Ben Jonson.*
[2] Herrick : *A Thanksgiving to God.*

John Milton

JOHN MILTON, 1608–1674

His Youth. — The second greatest English poet was born in London, eight years before the death of Shakespeare. John Milton's father followed the business of a scrivener and so drew wills and deeds and also invested money for clients. He prospered at this calling, and his family did not suffer for want of money. He was a man of much culture and a musical composer of considerable note.

In 1608 the poet was born and named after his father. The child seems to have given early promise of future greatness. His parents had rare judgment; they believed in the boy, and, seeing that he acted as if guided by a high ideal, they generally allowed him to do whatever he chose. They had the painter to the court execute a portrait of the child at the age of ten. The painting still exists, and shows him to have been "a sweet, serious, round-headed boy." They employed the best of teachers for him at home, and at the age of sixteen he was ready for Cambridge University, where he took both the B.A. and M.A. degrees.

JOHN MILTON, AET. 10

His Early Manhood and Life at Horton. — In 1632 Milton left Cambridge and went to live with his father in a country home at Horton, about twenty miles west of London. Milton had been intended for the church, but he felt that he could not subscribe to its intolerance, and that he had another mission to perform. His father accordingly provided sufficient funds for maintaining him at Horton in a life of studious leisure for over five years. The poet's greatest biographer, David Masson, says: "Until Milton was thirty-two years of age, if even then, he did not earn a penny for himself." Such a course would ruin ninety-nine out of every hundred talented young men, but it was the making of Milton. He spent those years in careful study and in writing his immortal early poems.

In 1638, when he was in his thirtieth year, he determined to broaden his views by travel. He went to Italy, which the Englishman of his day still regarded as the home of art, culture, and song. After about fifteen months abroad, he heard that his countrymen were on the verge of civil war, and he returned home to play his part in the mighty tragedy of the times.

Milton's "Left Hand." — In 1642 the Civil War broke out between the Royalists and the Puritans. He took sides in the struggle for liberty, not with his sword, but with his pen. During this time he wrote little but prose. In doing this, Milton himself says : " I have the use, as I may account it, but of my left hand."

With that " left hand " he wrote much prose. There is one common quality running through all his prose works, although they treat of the most varied subjects. Every one of these works strikes a blow for fuller liberty in some direction ; for more liberty in church, in state, and in home relations, for the freedom of expressing opinions, and for a system of education which should break away from the leading strings of the inferior methods of the past. His greatest prose work is the *Areopagitica: a Speech for the Liberty of Unlicensed Printing.*

Much of his prose is poetic and adorned with grand figures of rhetoric. He frequently follows the Latin order, and inverts his sentences, which are often unreasonably long. Sometimes his "left hand" astonishes us by slinging mud at his opponents, and we eagerly await the loosing of the right hand which was to give us the *Paradise Lost.*

His Blindness. — The English government from 1649 to 1660 is known as the Commonwealth. The two most striking figures of the time were Oliver Cromwell, who in 1653 was styled the Lord Protector, and John Milton, who was the Secretary for Foreign Tongues. All his letters to the various foreign powers were written in Latin. One of the greatest of European scholars, a professor at

Leyden, named Salmasius, had written a book attacking the Commonwealth and upholding the late King. The Council requested Milton to write a fitting answer. His eyes were already failing him, and he had been warned to rest them. He refused to do this, saying that he would willingly sacrifice his eyesight on the altar of liberty. He accordingly wrote in reply his *Pro Populo Anglicano Defensio*, a Latin work, which was published in 1651. This effort cost him his eyesight. In 1652, at the age of forty-three, he was totally blind. In his *Paradise Lost*, he thus alludes to his affliction: —

> " Thus with the year
> Seasons return ; but not to me returns
> Day, or the sweet approach of even or morn,
> Or sight of vernal bloom or summer's rose,
> Or flocks, or herds, or human face divine ;
> But clouds instead and ever-during dark
> Surrounds me, from the cheerful ways of men
> Cut off."

Life after the Restoration. — In 1660, Charles II. was made king. The leaders of the Commonwealth had to flee for their lives. Some went to America for safety and some were caught and executed. The body of Cromwell was taken from its grave in Westminster Abbey, suspended from the gallows, and left to dangle there. Milton was concealed by a friend until the worst of the storm had blown over. Some influential friends interceded for him, and his blindness probably won him sympathy.

During his old age he was largely dependent on the kindness of friends to read to him, and to act as his amanuenses whenever he wished to write anything. Unfortunately he had formed his ideas of woman in the light of the old dispensation. He had not educated his three daughters sufficiently for them to take a sympathetic interest in his work, and they resented his calling on them to help him.

During this period of his life, when he was totally blind, he wrote *Paradise Lost, Paradise Regained*, and *Samson Agonistes*.   He died in 1674, and was buried beside his father in the chancel of St. Giles, Cripplegate, London.

Minor Poems. — In 1629, while Milton was a student at Cambridge, and only twenty-one years old, he wrote a fine lyrical poem, entitled *On the Morning of Christ's Nativity*. These 244 lines of verse show that he did not need to be taught the melody of song any more than a young nightingale.

Four remarkable poems were written during his years of studious leisure at Horton, — *L'Allegro, Il Penseroso, Comus,* and *Lycidas*.   *L'Allegro* describes the charms of a merry social life, and *Il Penseroso* voices the quiet but deep enjoyment of the scholar in retirement.   These two poems have been universal favorites.

Comus is a species of dramatic composition known as a Masque, and it is the greatest of its class.   Some critics, like Taine and Saintsbury, consider this the finest of Milton's productions.   The 1023 lines in *Comus* can soon be read, and there are few poems of equal length that will better repay careful reading.

Comus is an immortal apotheosis of virtue.   While in Geneva in 1639, Milton was asked for his autograph and an expression of sentiment.   He chose the closing lines of *Comus* : —

> " . . . if Virtue feeble were,
> Heaven itself would stoop to her."

Lycidas, one of the world's great elegies, was written on the death of Milton's classmate, Edward King.   Mark

Pattison, one of Milton's biographers, says : " In *Lycidas* we have reached the high-water mark of English poesy and of Milton's own production." The 193 lines in this poem are not to be read lightly, but to be studied. The more one studies them, the more will their greatness become evident. That person is to be pitied who has no sympathetic appreciation for a passage like this : —

> " Ye valleys low, where the mild whispers use
> Of shades, and wanton winds, and gushing brooks,
> On whose fresh lap the swart star sparely looks,
> Throw hither all your quaint enamelled eyes,
> That on the green turf suck the honeyed showers,
> And purple all the ground with vernal flowers.
> Bring the rathe primrose that forsaken dies,
> The tufted crow-toe, and pale jessamine,
> The white pink, and the pansy freaked with jet,
> The glowing violet,
> The musk-rose, and the well-attired woodbine,
> With cowslips wan that hang the pensive head,
> And every flower that sad embroidery wears ;
> Bid amaranthus all his beauty shed,
> And daffadillies fill their cups with tears,
> To strew the laureate hearse where Lycid lies."

Paradise Lost ; Its Inception and Dramatic Plan. — Cambridge University has a list, written by Milton before he was thirty-five, of about one hundred possible subjects for the great poem which he felt it was his life's mission to give to the world. He once thought of selecting Arthur and his Knights of the Round Table, but his final choice was *Paradise Lost*, which stands first on this special list. There are in addition four separate drafts of the way in which he thought this subject should be treated. This proves that the great work of a man like Milton was planned while he was young.

All four drafts show that his early intention was to make the poem a drama, a gigantic Miracle play. The closing of the theaters and the prejudice felt against them during the days of Puritan ascendency may have influenced Milton to forsake the dramatic for the epic form, but he seems never to have shared the common prejudice against the drama and the stage. His sonnet on Shakespeare shows in what estimation he held that dramatist.

Subject Matter and Form. — About 1658, when Milton was a widower, living alone with his three daughters, he began, in total blindness, to dictate his *Paradise Lost*,

Painting by Munkacsy.

MILTON DICTATING PARADISE LOST TO HIS DAUGHTERS

sometimes relying on them but more often on any kind friend who might assist him. The manuscript accordingly shows a variety of handwriting. The work was published in 1667, after some trouble with a narrow-minded censor who had doubts about granting a license.

The subject matter can best be given in Milton's own lines at the beginning of the poem : —

> " Of man's first disobedience, and the fruit
> Of that forbidden tree, whose mortal taste
> Brought death into the World, and all our woe,
> With loss of Eden, till one greater Man
> Restore us, and regain the blissful seat,
> Sing, Heavenly Muse."

The poem treats of Satan's revolt in heaven, of his conflict with the Almighty, and banishment with all the rebellious angels. Their new home in the land of fire and endless pain is described with such a gigantic grasp of the imagination, that the conception has colored all succeeding theology.

The action proceeds with a council of the fallen angels to devise means for alleviating their condition and annoying the Almighty. They decide to strike him through his child, and they plot the fall of man. In short, *Paradise Lost* is an intensely dramatic story of the loss of Eden. The greatest actors that ever sprang from a poet's brain appear before us on the stage, which is at one time the sulphurous pit of hell, at another the bright plains of heaven, and at another the Elysium of our first parents.

In form the poem is an epic in twelve books, containing a total of 10,565 lines. It is written in blank verse of wonderful melody and variety.

Paradise Regained and Samson Agonistes. — After finishing *Paradise Lost*, Milton wrote two more poems, which he published in 1671. *Paradise Regained* is in great part a paraphrase of the first eleven verses of the fourth chapter of *St. Matthew*. The poem is in four books of blank verse and contains 2070 lines. Although it is written with great art and finish, *Paradise Regained* shows a falling off in Milton's genius. There is less ornament and less to arouse human interest.

Samson Agonistes (Samson the Struggler) is a tragedy containing 1758 lines, based on the sixteenth chapter of *Judges*. This poem, modeled after the Greek drama, is hampered by a strict observance of the dramatic unities. It is vastly inferior to the *Paradise Lost*. *Samson Agonistes* contains scarcely any of the glorious imagery of Milton's earlier poems. It has been called "the most unadorned poem that can be found."

Characteristics of Milton's Poetry

Variety in his Early Work. — A line in *Lycidas* says : —

"He touched the tender stops of various quills,"

and this may be said of Milton. His early poems show great variety. We have not only the soul-stirring dirge notes in *Lycidas*, but we also find the lines of the most of his minor poems fresh with the sights, sounds, and odors of the country. We have our own perception of the beauties of nature quickened, as we catch sight in *L'Allegro* of

". . . beds of violets blue
And fresh-blown roses washed in dew,"

as we inhale the matchless odors from

"The frolic wind that breathes the spring,"

and as we find ourselves listening

"While the plowman near at hand
Whistles o'er the furrow'd land,
And the milkmaid singeth blithe,
And the mower whets his scythe."

Although Milton is noted for his seriousness and sublimity, we must not be blind to the fact that his minor poems show great delicacy of touch. The epilogue of the Spirit at the end of *Comus* is an instance of exquisite airy fancy passing into noble imagination at the close. In 1638 Sir Henry Wotton wrote this intelligent criticism of *Comus* to its author: "I should much commend the tragical part, if the lyrical did not ravish me with a certain Doric delicacy in your Songs and Odes, whereunto I must plainly confess to have seen yet nothing parallel in our language: *Ipsa mollities*."

Limitations. — In giving attention to Milton's variety, we should not forget that his limitations are apparent when we judge him by Elizabethan standards. As varied as his excellences are, his range is far narrower than Shakespeare's. Milton has little sense of humor. All sorts and conditions of men, with the ruddy glow of life, do not throng his pages. We feel that he is farther from human life than either Shakespeare or Burns. We find that Milton, unlike those poets, became acquainted with flowers through the medium of a book before he noticed them in the fields. In speaking of flowers and birds, he sometimes makes those mistakes to which the bookish man is more prone than the child who first hears the story of Nature from her own lips. Unlike Shakespeare and Burns, Milton had the misfortune to spend his childhood in a large city. Again, while increasing age seemed to impose no limitations on Shakespeare's genius, since his touch is as delicate in *The Tempest* as in his first plays, Milton's style, on the other hand, grew frigid and devoid of imagery toward the end of his life.

Sublimity. — The most striking characteristic of Milton's poetry is sublimity, and this consists, first, in the subject

matter.   In the opening lines of *Paradise Lost* he speaks
of his "adventrous song"

> "That with no middle flight intends to soar
> Above the Aonian mount, while it pursues
> Things unattempted yet in prose or rhyme."

Milton succeeded in his intention.   The English language
has not another epic poem, or a poem of any other kind,
which approaches *Paradise Lost* in sustained sublimity.

In the second place, we must note the sublimity of treatment.   Milton's own mind was cast in a sublime mold.
His very figures of rhetoric frequently throb with sublimity.   Thus, the Milky Way is spoken of as the royal
highway to heaven : —

> "A broad and ample road, whose dust is gold,
> And pavement stars."

When Death and Satan meet, Milton wishes the horror
of the scene to manifest something of the sublime.
What other poet could, in fewer words, have conveyed
a stronger impression of the effect of the frown of those
terrible powers?

> "So frowned the mighty combatants, that Hell
> Grew darker at their frown."

The pictures painted by Milton show strength and magnificence of touch, as well when the canvas discloses a lurid
sea of flame that gives

> "No light; but rather darkness visible,"

as when Eden with its atmosphere of a spring dawn presents her

> "Flowers of all hue, and without thorn the rose."

In the first part of *Paradise Lost*, Satan is not the crawling fiend that he becomes later: —

> " His form had yet not lost
> All her original brightness, nor appeared
> Less than Archangel ruined."

Harmony. — A pronounced characteristic of Milton's verse is harmony. Any one can detect the exquisite harmony of such lines as these by reading them aloud: —

> " It was the winter wild,
> While the heaven-born child
> All meanly wrapt in the rude manger lies.

> " The winds, with wonder whist,
> Smoothly the waters kissed,

> " The oracles are dumb ;
> No voice or hideous hum
> Runs through the archéd roof in words deceiving." [1]

His blank verse has never been surpassed in harmonious rhythm. Lines like these show the melody of which this verse is capable : —

> " Heaven opened wide
> Her ever-during gates, harmonious sound
> On golden hinges moving." [2]

How the Paradise Lost has affected Thought. — Few persons realize how profoundly this poem has influenced men's ideas of the hereafter. The conception of hell for a long time current was influenced by those pictures which Milton painted with darkness for his canvas and the lightning for his brush. Our pictures of Eden and of heaven have also felt his touch. Theology has often looked through Milton's imagination at the fall of the rebel angels and of

---

[1] *Hymn on the Nativity.*   [2] *Paradise Lost*, Book VII., lines 207–9.

man. Huxley says that the cosmogony which stubbornly resists the conclusions of science, is due rather to the account in *Paradise Lost* than to *Genesis*.

Many of Milton's expressions have become crystallized in modern thought. Among such we may mention : —

> " The mind is its own place, and in itself
> Can make a Heaven of Hell, a Hell of Heaven,
> What matter where, if I be still the same?" [1]

> " To reign is worth ambition, though in Hell :
> Better to reign in Hell, than serve in Heaven." [2]

> " . . . Who overcomes
> By force hath overcome but half his foe." [3]

> " . . . Abashed the Devil stood
> And felt how awful goodness is, and saw
> Virtue in her shape how lovely." [4]

The Embodiment of High Ideals. — No other poet has embodied in his verse higher ideals than Milton. He thought that he owed the world something which he was determined to repay. When twenty-three, he wrote that he intended to use his talents

> " As ever in my great Taskmaster's eye." [5]

Milton's poetry is not universally popular. He deliberately selected his audience. These lines from *Comus* show to whom he would speak : —

> " Yet some there be that by due steps aspire
> To lay their just hands on that golden key
> That opes the palace of eternity.
> To such my errand is."

[1] *Paradise Lost*, Book I., line 254.
[2] *Ibid.*, l. 262.
[3] *Ibid.*, l. 649.
[4] *Ibid.*, Book IV., l. 846.
[5] Sonnet: *On His Having Arrived at the Age of Twenty-three.*

He kept his promise of writing something which the world would not willingly let die. That something still speaks for liberty and for nobility of soul. No man with his thoughts on the ground can appreciate Milton. His ideals react on us and raise us higher than we were. To him we may say with Wordsworth : —

> " Thy soul was like a star and dwelt apart ;
> Thou hadst a voice whose sound was like the sea,
> Pure as the naked heavens, majestic, free." [1]

SUMMARY

The Puritan age was one of conflict in religious and political ideals. The color of the Elizabethan dawn had faded into leaden skies. Men realized that neither lands beyond the sea nor the New Learning could fill the aspirations of the soul. The Puritans turned their attention to the life beyond. They felt that their ideals of this life should be such as their great Taskmaster would approve. Life became a ceaseless battle of the right against the wrong. Hence much of the literature in both poetry and prose is polemical. Milton's *Paradise Lost* is an epic of war between good and evil.

The prose deals with a variety of subjects. There are argumentative, philosophical, historical, biographical, and theological prose works, but only the fine presentation of nature and life in *The Complete Angler* interests the general reader of to-day, although the grandeur of Milton's *Areopagitica*, the humor of Thomas Fuller, and the imagery and variety of Jeremy Taylor deserve more readers.

The drama shows a steady decline from the summit of Elizabethan greatness. Webster and Ford manifest great

[1] *Milton : A Sonnet.*

power in dealing with horrible subjects, and the plays of Beaumont and Fletcher are sprinkled with beautiful passages, but the dramatists of this age lack universality. Their plays are often coarse, and fail to show orderly development and the natural unfolding of moral law.

John Milton is the only great poet of this period. In sublimity of subject matter and cast of mind, in nobility of ideals, in expressing the conflict between good and evil, he is the fittest representative of the Puritan spirit in literature. Even in his minor poems, we see the young Puritan pointing to

> " . . . the crown that Virtue gives
> After this mortal change, to her true servants." [1]

In order to appreciate the difference in ideals between this and the preceding age, it is instructive to compare the aim of the heroes of Marlowe's *Faustus* and *Tamburlaine* with that which animates Milton's *Comus*. While Milton manifests much of the greatness of the Elizabethan age, he lacks its universality and close association with life.

With the exception of Milton, the poets display little creative originality. They are mainly imitators of John Donne, Ben Jonson, and Edmund Spenser. The minor poets of this period exhibit few traces of Shakespearean influence.

REQUIRED READINGS FOR CHAPTER V

HISTORICAL

Gardiner,[2] pp. 481-577; Green, Chap. VIII.; Underwood-Guest, pp. 442-476; Guerber, pp. 252-275; Wakeling's *King and Parliament* (*Oxford Manuals*), pp. 1-68; Frederic Harrison's *Oliver Cromwell* (228 pp., 50 cents); Traill, IV., 1-345.

[1] *Comus*, l. 9.   [2] For full titles, see list at end of Chap. I.

LITERARY

Prose. — The student will obtain a fair idea of the prose of this age by reading Milton's *Areopagitica* (Morley's *National Library*, No. 123, 10 cents ; Craik's *English Prose Selections*, Vol. II., pp. 471–475) ; the selections from Thomas Hobbes, in Craik, II., 214–221 ; from Thomas Fuller, in Craik, II., 377–387 ; from Jeremy Taylor, in Craik, II., 529–542 ; and from Izaak Walton, in Craik, II., 343–349. The student who has the time will wish to read *The Complete Angler* entire (Cassell's *National Library*, No. 4, 10 cents).

Compare (*a*) the sentences, (*b*) general style, and (*c*) worth of the subject matter of these authors ; then, to note the development of English prose, in treatment of subject as well as in form, compare these works with those of (1) Wycliffe and Mandeville in the fourteenth century, (2) of Malory in the fifteenth, and (3) of Tyndale, Lyly, Sidney, Hooker, and Bacon (*e.g.* essay *Of Study*, 1597), in the sixteenth.

The Caroline Poets. — Specimens of the best work of Carew, Suckling, Lovelace, and Herrick may be found in Ward's *English Poets*, Vol. II., pp. 115–187, also in *Cavalier Poets* (Maynard, Merrill, & Co.'s *English Classics*, 12 cents). The influence of John Donne, Ward, I., 558–566, and of Ben Jonson, Ward, II., 8–23, should be noted.

John Milton. — *L'Allegro, Il Penseroso, Comus, Lycidas* (American Book Co.'s *Eclectic English Classics*, 20 cents), and *Paradise Lost*, Books I. and II. (same series) should be read.

Which is the greatest of his minor poems? Why? Is the keynote of *Comus* in accord with Puritan ideals? Are there qualities in *Lycidas* which justify calling it "the high-water mark" of English lyrical poetry? Which poem has most powerfully affected theological thought? Which do you think is oftenest read to-day? Why? What is the most striking characteristic of his poetry? Contrast Milton's greatness, limitations, and ideals of life, with Shakespeare's.

WORKS FOR CONSULTATION AND FURTHER STUDY

(OPTIONAL)

Gardiner's *The First Two Stuarts and the Puritan Revolution.*
Masson's *The Life of John Milton, Narrated in Connection with the Political, Ecclesiastical, and Literary History of his Time* (6 vols.).

Chapter VI. of Vol. I. gives a valuable survey of British literature when Milton was a young man.

Masterman's *The Age of Milton* gives in 254 pages a survey of all the literature of the age.

General works on literature by Taine, Gosse, Saintsbury, and Phillips. Saintsbury's *A History of Elizabethan Literature* comes down to 1660.

Ward's *English Poets*, Vol. II., pp. 24-379.

Craik's *English Prose Selections*, Vol. II.

Minto's *Manual of English Prose Literature*, pp. 261-295.

Pattison's *Life of Milton*.

Garnett's *Life of Milton*.

Stopford Brooke's *Milton*.

Masson's *Poetical Works of John Milton*, 3 vols., contains excellent introductions and notes, and is the standard edition.

Addison's criticisms on Milton, beginning in number 267 of *The Spectator*, are suggestive.

Macaulay's *Essay on Milton*.

The Idealism of Milton, pp. 454-473, in Dowden's *Transcripts and Studies*.

Scherer's *Milton and Paradise Lost*, in *Essays on English Literature*.

Arnold's *Essays in Criticism*, Second Series.

For accounts of life and works of minor authors, consult *Dictionary of National Biography*.

CHAPTER VI

THE AGE OF THE RESTORATION, 1660-1700

Change in Morals. —With the Restoration, a tremendous reaction against the Puritanic view of life set in. Reaction always results when excessive restraint in any direction is removed. The court of Charles II. was the vilest ever known in England. Any one who insisted on purity of life was mocked and called a hypocrite. The Puritan virtues were laughed to scorn by the ribald courtiers who attended Charles II. In 1663 Samuel Butler published a famous satire, entitled *Hudibras*. Its object was to ridicule everything that savored of Puritanism. This satire became extremely popular in court circles, and it was the favorite reading of Charles II.

SAMUEL BUTLER

The change in morals is reflected in no branch of literature more than in the drama of this age. The popular plays show almost no respect for the great ethical laws of life. The dramatists seemed unable to grasp the truth presented with such emphasis in Shakespeare's plays, that human society rests on moral foundations, on the virtues of the home, on fidelity, kindness, sympathy. The indecent drama of the Restoration, in endeavoring to paint life out of harmony with these conditions, has fortunately paid the penalty by remaining for the most part unread to-day.

Change in the Subject Matter of Literature. — The Elizabethan age impartially held the mirror up to every type of human emotion. The writers of the Restoration, as a class, avoided any subject which demanded a portrayal of deep and noble feeling. In this age, we catch no glimpse of a Lear bending over a dead Cordelia, or of the heroic characters of a *Paradise Lost*.

The popular subjects were those which appealed to cold intellect, and these were, for the most part, satirical, didactic, and argumentative. John Dryden, the ruling poet of the Restoration, affords a typical instance of one who usually chose such subjects. John Locke (1632–1704), a great prose writer of this age, shows in the very title of his most famous work, *The Conduct of the Understanding*, what he preferred to discuss. That book opens with the statement: "The last resort a man has recourse to in the conduct of himself is his understanding." This declaration embodies a pronounced tendency of the age. It could not realize that the world of feeling is no less real than that of the understanding.

Neglect of Nature. — A striking way in which the change of subject matter manifested itself was in the neglect of references to nature. Shakespeare says: —

> "I know a bank where the wild thyme blows,
> Where oxlips and the nodding violet grows." [1]

In his pages we catch the gleam of the glowworm's eyes, we see the summer's velvet buds, we inhale the odor of the musk rose and the eglantine. "Everything that pretty is" in the world of nature greets our senses

[1] *A Midsummer Night's Dream*, II., I.

in his plays.   With all his bookishness, Milton takes us out
of doors

> ". . . early, ere the odorous breath of morn
> Awakes the slumbering leaves," [1]

to visit inspiring scenery.

The poets of the Restoration, on the other hand,
pay but little attention to the charms of nature.   Wordsworth says of Dryden : " There is not a single image from
nature in the whole of his works."   Poetry which affects
a contempt for nature is lacking in an important element
of greatness.

The Study of Science. — One of the best characteristics
of the period was its love of scientific investigation.   An
age devoted to intellectual activity must seek various out-
lets.   Some of the most important of these were found in
scientific fields.   The Royal Society was founded in 1662
to investigate natural phenomena and to penetrate into the
hidden mysteries of philosophy and life.

When we remember that Locke was paid for his essay,
The Conduct of the Understanding, a volume of only
about a hundred pages, three times as much as Milton
received for the *Paradise Lost*, we may realize that the
taste of the age preferred the productions of cold intellect
to the noble creations of thought and imagination, in conjunction with feeling.

Change in Foreign Influence. — Of all foreign influences
from the beginning of the Renaissance to the Restoration, the literature of Italy had been the most important.
French influence now gained the ascendency.

There were several reasons for this change.   (1) France
under the great Louis XIV. was increasing her political importance.   (2) She now had among her writers

---

[1] *Arcades.*

men who were by force of genius fitted to exert wide influence. Among such, we may instance Molière (1622–1673), who stands next to Shakespeare in dramatic power. (3) Charles II. and many Cavaliers had passed the time of their exile in France. They became familiar with French literature, and when they returned to England in 1660, their taste had been influenced by French models.

More Attention paid to Form of Expression. — A great genius like Shakespeare, by the worth of what he says, more than atones for any deficiencies of form. In the Puritan age the metaphysical poets had nothing original to utter, but even what they copied often lacks correctness of form. Their shallow thoughts are frequently stated obscurely; their figurative language is often extravagant or absurd. The readers of the Restoration demanded that if a writer had nothing original to offer, his second-hand thoughts should at least be presented in artistic form, and that obscurity should no longer be employed as a cloak to cover shallowness.

It is well for the student to be reminded frequently that influences are often operative for a long while before their results are widely felt. In the early part of the century, Edmund Waller (1606–1687), a poet very popular after the Restoration, but little read to-day, had put in practice the French idea that too much attention cannot be paid to the formal excellence of poetry. Before 1630 he had used the same French rhyming couplets which Dryden, and especially Pope (see p. 234), brought to a high degree of formal perfection in English verse. The following couplet, the best that Waller ever wrote, will show its form: —

> " The soul's dark cottage, battered and decayed,
>   Lets in new light through chinks that time hath made." [1]

[1] *Old Age and Death*, from *Divine Poems*.

Waller, however, found few pupils until the Restoration opened wide the door to French influence, which in this age and the next was potent in causing writers to pay more attention to polished forms of expression. French critics did not object to a commonplace thought, if the style was clear, incisive, and attractive.

JOHN DRYDEN, 1631-1700

Life. — John Dryden was born in 1631 in the small village of Aldwinkle, in the northern part of Northamptonshire. Few interesting facts concerning his life have come down to us. His father was a baronet; his mother, the daughter of a rector. Young Dryden graduated from Cambridge in 1654.

From a print.

BIRTHPLACE OF DRYDEN

During his entire life, Dryden was a professional literary man, and with his pen he made the principal part of his living. This necessity often forced him against his own better judgment to cater to the perverted taste of the Restoration. The theaters were opened soon after the return of Charles II., and Dryden found that plays had more market value than any other kind of literature. He agreed to furnish three plays a year for the King's actors, but was unable to produce that number. For fifteen years in the prime of his life, Dryden did little but write plays, the majority of which are seldom read to-day.

At the age of fifty, he showed the world where his genius lay, by writing the greatest political satire in the language. During the last twenty years of his life, he produced but few plays. His greatest satires, didactic poems, and lyrics belong to this period. In his last years he wrote a spirited translation of Virgil, and retold in his own inimitable way various stories from Chaucer and Boccaccio. Dryden died in 1700 and was buried in Westminster Abbey beside Chaucer.

It is difficult to speak positively of Dryden's character. He wrote a poem in honor of the memory of Cromwell, and a little later another welcoming Charles II. He argued in stirring verse in favor of the Episcopal religion, when that was the faith of the court. James II. was a Roman Catholic, and, after his accession, Dryden wrote another poem to prove the Catholic Church the only true one. He had been appointed poet laureate in 1670, but the Revolution of 1688, which drove James from the throne, caused Dryden to lose the laureateship. He would neither take the oath of fealty to the new government nor change his religion. In spite of adversity and the loss of an income almost sufficient to support him, he remained a Catholic for the rest of his life and reared his sons in that faith.

He seems to have been of a forgiving disposition, and ready to acknowledge his own faults. He admitted that

Jon: Dryden.

his plays were disfigured with coarseness.   He was very kind to young writers and willing to help them with their work.   In his chair at Will's Coffee House, discoursing to the wits of the Restoration about matters of literary art, he was one of the most prominent figures of the age.

His Prose. — Although to the majority of people Dryden is known only as a poet, his influence on prose has been so far-reaching as to entitle him to be called one of the founders of modern prose style.

The shortening of sentences has been a striking feature in the development of modern English prose.   Edmund

Spenser averages about fifty words to each of his prose sentences; Richard Hooker, about forty-one. One of the most striking sentences in Milton's *Areopagitica* contains ninety-five words, although he crowds over three hundred words into some of his long sentences. The sentences in some of Dryden's pages average only twenty-five words in length. We turn to Macaulay, one of the most finished masters of modern prose, and find that his sentences average twenty-two words. Dryden also helped to free English prose from the inversions, involutions, and parenthetical intricacies of earlier times.

Dryden's prose deals chiefly with literary criticism. The most of his prose is to be found in the prefaces to his plays and poems. His most important separate prose composition is his *Essay of Dramatic Poesy*, a work which should be read by all who wish to know some of the foundation principles of criticism.

Satiric Poetry. — No English writer has surpassed Dryden in satiric verse. His greatest satire is *Absalom and Achitophel*, in which, under the guise of Old Testament characters, he satirizes the leading spirits of the Protestant opposition to the succession of James, the brother of Charles II., to the English throne. Dryden thus satirizes Achitophel, the Earl of Shaftesbury : —

> " Great wits are sure to madness near allied,
>   And thin partitions do their bounds divide,
>   Else, why should he, with wealth and honor blest,
> ' Refuse his age the needful hours of rest?
>   Punish a body which he could not please,
>   Bankrupt of life, yet prodigal of ease?
>   And all to leave what with his toil he won
>   To that unfeathered two-legged thing, a son.
>   . . . .
>   In friendship false, implacable in hate,
>   Resolved to ruin or to rule the state."

Zimri, the Duke of Buckingham, is immortalized thus : —

> "Stiff in opinions, always in the wrong,
> Was everything by starts, and nothing long."

Mac Flecknoe is another satire of almost as great merit, directed against a certain Whig poet by the name of Shadwell. He would have been seldom mentioned in later times, had it not been for two of Dryden's lines : —

> "The rest to some faint meaning make pretence,
> But Shadwell never deviates into sense."

All for Love, one of Dryden's greatest plays, shows the delicate keenness of his satire in characterizing the cold-blooded Augustus Cæsar, or Octavius, as he is there called. Antony has sent a challenge to Octavius, who replies that he has more ways than one to die. Antony rejoins : —

> "He has more ways than one ;
> But he would choose them all before that one.
> *Ventidius.* He first would choose an ague or a fever.
> *Antony.* No ; it must be an ague, not a fever ;
> He has not warmth enough to die by that."

Dryden could make his satire as direct and blasting as a thunderbolt. He thus describes his publisher : —

> "With leering looks, bull-faced, and freckled fair,
> With two left legs, and Judas-colored hair,
> And frowsy pores that taint the ambient air."

Argumentative or Didactic Verse. — Dryden is a master in arguing in poetry. He was not a whit hampered by the restrictions of verse. They were rather an advantage to him, for in poetry he could make more telling arguments in briefer compass than in prose. The best two examples of his power of arguing in verse are *Religio Laici*, written in 1682, to uphold the Episcopal religion, and *The Hind and the Panther*, composed in 1687, to vindicate the Catholic Church. Verse of this order is called didactic, because it endeavors to teach or to explain something. The age of the Restoration delighted in such exercises of the intellect vastly more than in flights of fancy or imagination.

Lyrical Verse. — While the most of Dryden's best poetry is either satiric or didactic, he wrote three fine lyrical poems: *Alexander's Feast, A Song for St. Cecilia's Day*, and *An Ode to Mrs. Anne Killigrew.* All are distinguished by remarkable beauty and energy of expression. *Alexander's Feast* is the most widely read of Dryden's poems. The opening lines of the *Ode to Mrs. Killigrew* seem almost Miltonic in their conception, and they show his power in the field of lyrical poetry. Mistress Killigrew was a young lady of rare accomplishments in both poetry and painting. She died at the age of twenty-five, and Dryden thus begins her memorial ode: —

> "Thou youngest virgin daughter of the skies,
> Made in the last promotion of the blest;
> Whose palms, new plucked from Paradise,
> In spreading branches more sublimely rise,
> Rich with immortal green above the rest:
> .   .   .   .
> Thou wilt have time enough for hymns divine,
> Since Heaven's eternal year is thine."

Some of his plays have songs and speeches instinct with lyrical force. The following famous lines on the worth of existence are taken from his tragedy of *Aurengzebe:* —

> "When I consider'd life, 'tis all a cheat,
> Yet, fool'd with hope, men favor the deceit,
> Trust on, and think to-morrow will repay:
> To-morrow's falser than the former day,

Lies worse ; and while it says, we shall be blest,
With some new joys, cuts off what we possest.
Strange cozenage! none would live past years again ;
Yet all hope pleasure in what remain.
And, from the dregs of life, think to receive
What the first sprightly running could not give.
I'm tir'd with waiting for this chemic gold,
Which fools us young and beggars us when old."

General Characteristics. — In point of time, Dryden is the first great poet of the school of literary artists. His verse does not tolerate the unpruned irregularities and exaggerations of many former English poets. His command over language is remarkable. He uses words almost as he chooses, but he does not invest them with the warm glow of feeling. He is, however, something more than a great word artist. Many of his ideas bear the stamp of marked originality.

In the field of satiric and didactic poetry, he is a master. The intellectual, not the emotional, side of man's nature appeals strongly to him. He heeds not the song of the bird, the color of the rose, or the clouds of evening.

Although more celebrated for his poetry than for his prose, he is the earliest of the great modern prose stylists and he displays high critical ability.

JOHN BUNYAN, 1628-1688

Life. — The Bedfordshire village of Elstow saw in 1628 the birth of one who in his own peculiar field of literature was to lead the world. The father, Thomas Bunyan, was a brazier, a mender of pots and pans, and he reared his son John to the same trade. In his autobiography, John Bunyan says that his father's house was of "that rank that is meanest and most despised of all the families in the land."

John Bunyan

The boy went to school for only a short time and soon forgot what little he had learned. The father, by marrying a second time within a year after his wife's death, wounded the feelings of his sixteen year old son sufficiently to cause him to enlist as a soldier in the civil war. At about the age of twenty, he married, when neither he nor his wife had so much as a dish or a spoon.

Bunyan tells us that in his youth he was very wicked, and he would probably have been so regarded from the point of view of a strict Puritan. His worst offenses seem to have been dancing on the village green, playing hockey on Sundays, ringing bells to rouse the neighborhood, and swearing. When he repented, his vivid imagination made him think that he had committed the unpardonable sin. In the terror which he felt at the prospect of the loss of his soul, he passed through much of the experience which enabled him to write the *Pilgrim's Progress*.

Bunyan became a preacher of God's word. Under trees, in barns, on the village green, wherever people resorted, he told them the story of salvation. Within six months after the Restoration, he was arrested for preaching without Episcopal sanction. The officers took him away from his little blind daughter. The roisterers of the Restoration thought a brazier was too coarse to have feelings, but he dropped tears on the paper when he wrote of "the many hardships, miseries, and wants that my poor family were like to meet with, should I be taken from them, especially my poor blind child, who lay nearer to my heart than all besides. Oh, the thoughts of the hardship my poor blind one might undergo, would break my heart to pieces." In spite of his dependent family and the natural right of the freedom of speech, Bunyan was thrust into Bedford jail and kept a prisoner for nearly twelve years. Had it not been for his imprisonment in this "squalid den," of which he speaks in the *Pilgrim's*

BEDFORD BRIDGE, SHOWING GATES AND JAIL

From an old print.

Progress, we should probably be without that famous work. Part of it, at least, was written in the jail.

In 1672, as a step toward restoring the Catholic religion, Charles II. suspended all penal statutes against the dissenting clergy, and Bunyan was released from jail.

After his release, he settled down to his life's work of spreading the Gospel by both pen and tongue. He sometimes visited London to preach, and it was not uncommon for twelve hundred persons to come to hear him at seven o'clock in the morning of a week day in winter.

The immediate cause of his death was a cold caught by riding in the rain, on his way to try to reconcile a father and son. In 1688 Bunyan died as he uttered these words: "Take me, for I come to Thee."

His life and works are a necessary supplement to an account of the Restoration period, for they show how one-sided an opinion of English life and literature might be formed from a study of the dissolute court alone. All the moral greatness of the Commonwealth period was not obliterated in a day. Men like John Bunyan still lived to exert a powerful influence over English life and thought.

His Work. — Bunyan achieved the distinction of writing the greatest of all allegories, the *Pilgrim's Progress*. This is the story of Christian's journey through this life, the story of meeting Mr. Worldly Wiseman, of the straight gate and the narrow path, of the Delectable Mountains of Youth, of the valley of Humiliation, of the encounter with Apollyon, of the wares of Vanity Fair, "kept all the year long," of my lord Time-server, of Mr. Anything, of imprisonment in Doubting Castle by Giant Despair, of the flowery land of Beulah, lying beyond the valley of the Shadow of Death, through which a deep, cold river runs, and of the city of All Delight on the other side. This story still has absorbing interest for human beings, for the child and the old man, the learned and the ignorant.

Bunyan wrote many other works, but none of them equals the *Pilgrim's Progress*. His *Holy War* is a powerful allegory, and it has been called a prose *Paradise Lost*. Bunyan produced a strong piece of realistic fiction, the *Life and Death of Mr. Badman*. This shows the descent of a soul along the broad road. The story is the counterpart of his great masterpiece, and ranks second to it in point of merit.

From an old print.   BUNYAN'S BIRTHPLACE

General Characteristics. — Since the *Pilgrim's Progress* has been more widely read in England than any other book except the *Bible*, it is well to investigate the secret of Bunyan's power.

In the first place, his style is simple. Secondly, rare earnestness is coupled with this simplicity. He had something to say, and in his inmost soul he felt that this something was of supreme importance for all time. Only a great man can tell such truths without a flourish of language, or without straining after effect. At the most critical part of the journey of the Pilgrims, when they approach the river of death, note that Bunyan avoids the tendency to indulge in fine writing, that he is content to rely on the power of the subject matter, simply presented, to make us feel the terrible ordeal : —

"Now I further saw that between them and the gate was a river; but there was no bridge to go over, and the river was very deep. . . . The pilgrims then, especially Christian, began to despond in their mind, and looked this way and that, but no way could be found by them by which they might escape the river. . . . They then addressed themselves to the water, and entering, Christian began to sink. . . . And with that, a great darkness and horror fell upon Christian, so that he could not see before him. . . .

"Now, upon the bank of the river, on the other side, they saw the two shining men again, who there waited for them. . . . Now you must note, that the city stood upon a mighty hill; but the pilgrims went up that hill with ease, because they had these two men to lead them up by the arms; they had likewise left their mortal garments behind them in the river; for though they went in with them, they came out without them."

Of all the words in the above selection, eighty per cent. are monosyllables. Few authors could have resisted the tendency to try to be impressive at such a climax. One has more respect for this world, on learning that it has set the seal of its approval on such earnest simplicity and neglected works that strive with every art to attract attention.

Thirdly, Bunyan has a rare combination of imagination and dramatic power. His abstractions become living persons. They have warmer blood coursing in their veins than many of the men and women in modern fiction. Giant Despair is a living giant. We can hear the clanking of the chains and the groans of the captives in his dungeon. We are not surprised to learn that Bunyan imagined that he saw and conversed with these characters. The *Pilgrim's Progress* is a prose drama. Note the vivid dramatic presentation of the tendency to evil, which we all have at some time felt threatening to wreck our nobler selves: —

"Then Apollyon straddled quite over the whole breadth of the way, and said, 'I am void of fear in this matter; prepare thyself to die; for I swear by my infernal den that thou shalt go no further; here will I spill thy soul.'"

It would be difficult to find English prose more simple, earnest, strong, imaginative, and dramatic than this. Bunyan's style felt the shaping influence of the *Bible* more than of all other works combined. He knew the *Scriptures* almost by heart.

SUMMARY

The Restoration introduced a change in both the subject matter and the form of literature. With the Elizabethans and their successors, intellectual action was but the prelude to a richness of emotional life. They regarded man as a being who could love and feel joy and grief. The Restoration, on the other hand, looked at man chiefly from the coldly intellectual side. The masterpieces are for the most part couched in a satiric and a didactic vein. The finest work of Dryden, the great representative of the age, is his satiric and didactic verse. To the voice of nature speaking through the buds of spring, the russet leaves of autumn, or the song of bird, the poetry of the Restoration turns a deaf ear.

France exerted the predominating foreign literary influence. Increasing attention was paid to the manner of expressing thought. Literature began its long period of worship at the shrine of formal excellence.

In prose there was a decided advance. Dryden's prose might have been written by a modern hand. Few modern writers have surpassed Bunyan in simplicity, energy, and imaginative power.

REQUIRED READINGS FOR CHAPTER VI

HISTORICAL

Gardiner,[1] pp. 578–671 ; Green, pp. 616–700 ; Underwood-Guest, pp. 477–507 ; Guerber, pp. 275–290 ; Wakeling's *King and Parliament*, pp. 69–115 ; Traill, IV., 346–511.

LITERARY

Prose. — An idea of the best prose of the age may be gained from the following works : —

Bunyan's *Pilgrim's Progress* (Craik's *English Prose Selections*, Vol. III., pp. 84–96), Dryden's critical *Essays* (Craik, III., 148–166, or No. 161 in Cassell's *National Library*, 10 cents), Locke's *Conduct of the Understanding* (Craik, III., 180–183).

In what does the secret of Bunyan's popularity consist — in his style, or in his subject matter, or in both? What is specially noteworthy about his style? In what respect was his style appreciably affected by his familiarity with any other work? Select and comment on some of Dryden's best critical dicta. Why is Locke's work considered a classic? How does it indicate the spirit of the age? In what respects does the prose of this age show advance?

Poetry. — Read the selections from Butler's *Hudibras*, in Ward's *English Poets*, Vol. II., pp. 400–408 ; from Dryden's *Alexander's Feast* (Ward, II., 478) ; from *Absalom and Achitophel* (Ward, II., 454). As a specimen of Dryden's argumentative or didactic verse, read the opening lines of *Religio Laici* (Cassell's *National Library*, No. 98), or the selections in Ward, II., 463–468.

---

[1] For full titles, see list at end of Chap. I.

What characteristic of the age is reflected in *Hudibras?* What are the qualities of this new school of poetry, of which Dryden is the most famous exponent? What are his special excellences and defects? Compare him with Shakespeare and Milton.

WORKS FOR CONSULTATION AND FURTHER STUDY

(OPTIONAL)

Sydney's *Social Life in England from the Restoration to the Revolution*.

Macaulay's *History of England*.

Taine's *History of English Literature*, Book III., Chaps. I., II., III.

Gosse's *History of Eighteenth Century Literature* begins with 1660.

Garnett's *The Age of Dryden*.

Phillips's *Popular Manual of English Literature*, Vol. I., pp. 375–434.

Minto's *Manual of English Prose Literature*, pp. 312–341.

Saintsbury's *Life of Dryden*.

Macaulay's *Essay on Dryden*.

Lowell's *Essay on Dryden*, in *Among My Books*.

Dryden's *Essays on the Drama*, edited by Strunk.

Fowler's *Life of Locke*.

Ward's *English Poets*, Vol. II., pp. 396–496.

Craik's *English Prose Selections*, Vol. III., pp. 1–229.

Froude's *Life of Bunyan*.

Venable's *Life of Bunyan*.

Macaulay's *Essay on Southey's Edition of the Pilgrim's Progress*.

CHAPTER VII

THE FIRST FORTY YEARS OF THE EIGHTEENTH CENTURY, 1700–1740

Ideals of the Age. — The greater part of the eighteenth century in England was marked by the existence of a low moral standard. It was an age of double dealing and corruption. The political situation was partly responsible for this. In 1688 James II. was driven from England because of his tyrannical and lawless methods. His son-in-law and daughter, William and Mary, succeeded him. For more than fifty years after James had been dethroned, he, and after him his son and grandson, made repeated efforts to return. Many of the leading men of the nation tried to keep the favor of the exiled princes as well as of the actual rulers. It was at times impossible to tell in which direction the balance would turn, hence double dealing was resorted to by many whose example had wide influence because of their prominent position.

The age was dull, unimaginative, and brutal. Drunkenness was extremely common. Not only the lower classes, but also ministers of state and women of fashion drank to excess. Bribery was the rule. The greatest prime minister of the age had for a motto : " Every man has his price."

Although hanging was the penalty for stealing a few shillings and for numerous other offenses, this punishment

seemed to have little restraining power.   Men and women
of fashion would go out in parties to see droves of poor
wretches hanged.   For minor offenses, the culprits were
tied fast in the pillory and often maimed for life with
stones, bricks, and other missiles.   All ranks of society
felt the degrading influence of such brutality.   In this
soil nobility of soul and sympathy with one's kind did not
thrive.   The eighteenth century furnished Swift sufficient
suggestions for his pictures of the Yahoos.   Those who
object to such pictures are merely resenting the fact that
the ideals of the age left their mark on the literature.
There was not a single writer with Bunyan's moral power,
no Milton calling through a silver trumpet : —

> "Mortals, that would follow me,
> Love Virtue; she alone is free."[1]

Literary Form preferred to Matter. — The desire for
polish and veneer, which had become marked during the
age of the Restoration, now attained the greatest intensity.
There was no poetic masterpiece of true creative imagination.   The age was in one sense a critical one; that is,
it was very particular about the way in which a thing was
said.   The matter was considered of far less importance.

The age lacked enthusiasm and moral earnestness; it
lacked imaginative comprehension of higher realities.   In
poetry there was nothing to correspond to the Shakespearean conception as embodied in the following lines : —

> "The poet's eye, in a fine frenzy rolling,
> Doth glance from heaven to earth, from earth to heaven;
> And as imagination bodies forth
> The forms of things unknown, the poet's pen
> Turns them to shapes, and gives to airy nothing
> A local habitation and a name."[2]

[1] *Comus*, line 1018.   [2] *A Midsummer Night's Dream*, V., 1.

Pope struck the keynote of the age when he said : —

> "True Wit is Nature to advantage dress'd,
>   What oft was thought, but ne'er so well express'd." [1]

A new thought was not so much desired as an excellent dress for an old one.

The Rhyming Couplet. — Almost all of the best poetry of the age was written in lines of five iambic feet. The two adjacent lines rhyme, and they are called a couplet. There is generally a pause at the end of each line, and each couplet, when detached from the context, will usually make complete sense. Such lines catch the ear and they are easily retained in the memory. The following couplet from Pope is an example : —

> " A *little learning* is a dang'rous thing;
>   Drink deep, or taste not the Pierian spring." [2]

A strict adherence to the rules of the couplet cramps both the reason and the imagination. Such leading strings narrow freedom of movement. The greatest passages in Shakespeare and Milton do not rhyme, and there is frequently no pause in the sense at the end of a line. These lines from *Macbeth* show how the ending of a line is not allowed to interfere with the sense : —

> ". . . Besides, this Duncan
>   Hath borne his faculties so meek, hath been
>   So clear in his great office, that his virtues
>   Will plead like angels, trumpet-tongued against
>   The deep damnation of his taking-off."

It is, however, easier for a small mind to catch the running sense in Pope than in Shakespeare.

[1] *Essay on Criticism*, line 297.   [2] *Ibid*, line 215.

The influence of French writers was still in the ascendency. Boileau (1636–1711), a French critic and poet, whom Voltaire called the Legislator of Parnassus, advised poets to compose the second line of the couplet first. No better rule could have been given for dwarfing poetic power and for making poetry artificial.

The Classic School. — The literary lawgivers of the first part of the eighteenth century held that a rigid adherence to certain narrow rules was the prime condition of producing a masterpiece. Indeed, the belief was common that a knowledge of rules was more important than genius.

The men of this school are called *classicists* because they held that a study of the best works of the ancients would disclose the necessary guiding rules. No style which did not closely follow these rules was considered good. Horace was the one classical author most copied by this school. His *Epistles* and *Satires* were considered models. The writers of this age were not the first classicists. In the days of Elizabeth, a determined effort was made to have the English drama develop on classic lines (p. 143). The classicists then tried to laugh down any play that did not observe the rules of Seneca and regard the classical unities of time and place. The Elizabethans turned away from the laughers to listen to Shakespeare. The first part of the eighteenth century had no such genius, and all writers in order to be popular followed the classical rules.

The motto of this school, of which Pope was the chief, was polished regularity. The classicists cared little for the fields, the flowers, and the birds. The writers closed their ears to the great symphony of nature. They despised enthusiasm and the fire of passion. They disliked anything that was romantic, irregular, or improbable. We find them condemning the *Arabian Nights* on the score of improbability. Voltaire, a French classicist, says: " I do not like the monstrous irregularities of Shakespeare." An eighteenth century classicist endeavored to improve Hamlet's soliloquy by putting it in rhyming couplets. These lines show his attempt at improvement: —

> " My anxious soul is tore with doubtful strife,
> And hangs suspended betwixt death and life;
> Life! death! dread objects of mankind's debate!
> Whether superior to the shocks of fate,
> To bear its fiercest ills with steadfast mind,
> To Nature's order piously resigned," etc.[1]

Pope was appealed to by an Episcopal bishop to polish some of Milton's poetry.

Such views could not remain in the ascendency very long, if imagination and fancy were to make their existence felt. In 1730 James Thomson (1700–1748) published a romantic poem entitled *The Seasons*. This deals with the fields, flowers, woods, and streams. It takes us where

> " The hawthorn whitens; and the juicy groves
> Put forth their buds." [2]

This poem shows the revolt against the narrowness of the classical school. In the next chapter we can trace the progress of the revolt.

The Prevalence of Satire. — The satirist is a critic who searches for defects in order to ridicule them. Criticism that concerns itself exclusively with faults is a mark of deterioration in an age or in an individual. The highest criticism is constructive, not destructive; that is, it shows the way to better achievements, instead of contenting itself with merely holding existing things up to scorn.

[1] William Hamilton of Bangour: *Poems and Songs*, p. 65.
[2] *Spring*, from *The Seasons*.

The greatest writers of this age, in both poetry and prose, were satirists. Dean Swift, Joseph Addison, and Alexander Pope excelled in satirizing the existing order of things. Much of their work is of the very highest order of excellence as satire, but the point to be remembered is that satire can never be the highest type of literature.

The intense party strife between Whigs and Tories increased the tendency toward satire, for the leaders of each party were eager to get the services of the greatest writers to satirize the opposition. Men of the rank of Swift and Defoe employed their pens in political satire.

An Age of Prose. — In each preceding age, if we except the work of Bunyan, the masterpieces were poetry, but the prose of the first half of the eighteenth century far surpasses the poetry. Daniel Defoe (pp. 277–279), the author of *Robinson Crusoe*, Dean Swift, the author of *Gulliver's Travels*, Richard Steele and Joseph Addison, the great essayists, are the principal prose writers of the period. The question has been often discussed whether Alexander Pope, the greatest writer in verse, is a true poet.

Matthew Arnold says : " The glory of English literature is in poetry, and in poetry the strength of the eighteenth century does not lie. Nevertheless the eighteenth century accomplished for us an immense literary progress, and its very shortcomings in poetry were an instrument to that progress, and served it. The example of Germany may show us what a nation loses from having no prose style. . . . French prose is marked in the highest degree by the qualities of regularity, uniformity, precision, balance. . . . The French made their poetry also conform to the law which was molding their prose. . . . This may have been bad for French poetry, but it was good for French prose." It is unquestionably true that French writers exerted a powerful influence in changing the cumbersome style of Milton's prose to the polished, neatly turned sentences of Addison. The same influence which gave vigor, point, and definiteness to the prose, necessary for the business of the world, helped to dwarf the poetry. If both could not advance together, we may be thankful that the eighteenth century gave us a varied prose of such high excellence.

JONATHAN SWIFT, 1667-1745

Life. — Swift, one of the greatest prose writers of the eighteenth century, was born of English parents in Dublin in 1667. It is absolutely necessary to know something of his life in order to pass proper judgment on his writings. A cursory examination of his life will show that heredity and environment were responsible for many of his peculiarities. Swift's father died a few months before the birth of his son, and the boy saw but little of his mother.

Swift's school and college life were passed at Kilkenny School and Trinity College, Dublin. For his education he seems to have been dependent on the charity of an uncle, who made the boy feel the bitterness of receiving something at another's hand. In after times he said that his uncle treated him like a dog. Swift's early experience seems to have made him misanthropic and hardened to consequences, for he neglected certain studies and came near failing to take his A. B. degree.

After his graduation in 1688, he spent almost ten years as the private secretary of Sir William Temple, at Moor Park in Surrey, about forty miles southwest of London. Temple had been asked to furnish some

employment for the young graduate because Lady
Temple was related to Swift's mother. Here, Swift was
probably treated as a dependent, and he had to eat
at the second table. Finally, this life became so intoler-
able that he took holy orders and went to a little parish
in Ireland, a country that he hated. After a stay of
eighteen months there, he returned to Moor Park, where
he remained until Temple's death in 1699.
Swift then went to another little country
parish in Ireland. From

From a print.

MOOR PARK

there he went to
London on a mission
in behalf of the Episcopal church in Ireland. He quarreled with the Whigs, became a Tory, and assisted that
party by writing many political pamphlets. The Tory
ministry soon felt that it could scarcely do without him.
He dined with ministers of state, and was one of the most
important men in London. He advanced the interests of
his friends much better than his own, for he got little from
the government except the hope of becoming a bishop.
In 1713 he was made dean of St. Patrick's Cathedral,

Dublin. In 1714 Queen Anne died, the Tories went out of power, and Swift returned to Ireland a disappointed man. He passed the rest of his life there, with the exception of a few visits to England.

Swift championed the Irish cause when English politicians endeavored to oppress Ireland with unjust laws. A man who knew him well, says: "I never saw the poor so carefully and conscientiously attended to as those of his cathedral." He gave up a large part of his income every year for the poor. In Dublin he was looked upon as a hero. When a certain person tried to be revenged on Swift for a satire, a deputation of Swift's neighbors proposed to thrash the man. Swift sent them home, but they boycotted the man and lowered his income £1200 a year.

During the last years of his life, Swift was hopelessly insane. He died in 1745, leaving his property for an asylum for lunatics and incurables.

There are unsolved mysteries in Swift's life. He suffered from an unknown brain disease for the principal part of his existence. This affection, the galling treatment received in his early years, and the disappointments of his prime, largely account for his misanthropy, for his coldness, and for the almost 'brutal treatment of the women who loved him — treatment against which Thackeray inveighs powerfully.

Swift's attachment to the beautiful Hester Johnson, known in literature as Stella, led him to write to her that famous series of letters known as the *Journal to Stella*, in which he gives much of his personal history during the three sunniest years of his life, from 1710 to 1713, when he was a lion in London. Thackeray says: "I know of nothing more manly, more tender, more exquisitely touch-

ing, than some of these brief notes, written in what Swift calls his 'little language' in his *Journal to Stella*."

A Tale of a Tub. — Swift's greatest satiric allegory is known as *A Tale of a Tub*. The purpose of the work is to satirize Romanists and Calvinists, and to uphold the Episcopalians. For those not interested in theological arguments, there is much entertaining philosophy, as the following quotation will show : —

"If we take an examination of what is generally understood by happiness, as it has respect either to the understanding or the senses, we shall find all its properties and adjuncts will herd under this short definition, that it is a perpetual possession of being well deceived. And first, with relation to the mind or understanding, it is manifest what mighty advantages fiction has over truth; and the reason is just at our elbow, because imagination can build nobler scenes and produce more wonderful revolutions than fortune or nature will be at expense to furnish."

Swift's satiric definition of happiness as the art "of being well deceived" is a characteristic instance of a combination of his humor and pessimistic philosophy.

Gulliver's Travels. — The world is always ready to listen to any one who has a good story to tell. Neither children nor philosophers have yet wearied of reading the adventures of Captain Lemuel Gulliver in Lilliput and Brobdingnag. *Gulliver's Travels* is Swift's most famous work.

In Lilliput we are introduced to a race of men about six inches high. Everything is on a corresponding scale. Gulliver eats a whole herd of cattle for breakfast and drinks several hogsheads of liquor. He captures an entire fleet of war ships. A rival race of pygmies endeavors to secure his services so as to obtain the balance of power. The quarrels between those little people seem ridiculous, and so petty as to be almost beneath contempt.

The voyage to Brobdingnag shows all this to be changed. Men are there sixty feet tall, and the affairs of an ordinary human being appear petty and insignificant. The cats are as large as three oxen, and the dogs attain the size of four elephants. Gulliver eats on a table thirty feet high, and he trembles lest he may fall and break his neck. The baby seizes Gulliver and tries to swallow his head. Afterward the hero fights a desperate battle with two rats. A monkey catches him and carries him to the almost infinite height of the house top. Cer-

tainly the voyages to Lilliput and Brobdingnag merit
Leslie Stephen's criticism of being "almost the most delightful children's book ever written."

The voyage to Laputa satirizes the philosophers. We
are taken through the academy at Lagado and are shown
a typical philosopher : —

"He had been eight years upon a project for extracting sunbeams
out of cucumbers, which were to be put in vials, hermetically sealed,
and let out to warm the air in raw, inclement summers. He told me
he did not doubt that in eight years more he should be able to supply
the governor's gardens with sunshine at a reasonable rate."

In this voyage the Struldbrugs are described. They
are a race of men who, after the loss of every faculty and
of every tie that binds them to earth, are doomed to continue living. Dante never painted a stronger or a ghastlier
picture. The voyage to the country of the Houyhnhnms
describes the Yahoos, who are the embodiment of all the
detestable qualities of human beings. The last two voyages are not pleasant reading, and one might wish that
the author of two such inimitable tales as the adventures
in Lilliput and Brobdingnag had stopped with these.

Children read *Gulliver's Travels* for the story, but
there is more than a story in the work. In its pages
the historian finds allusions and side lights that reveal
the age more distinctly. Among the Lilliputians, there is
one party, known as the Bigendians, which insists that all
eggs shall be broken open at the big end, while another
party, called the Littleendians, contends that eggs shall be
opened only at the little end. These differences typify the
quarrels of the age concerning religion and politics. The
Travels also contains much human philosophy. The lover
of satire is constantly delighted with the keenness of the
thrusts.

General Characteristics. — Swift is one of the greatest of English prose humorists. He is also noted for wit of that satiric kind which enjoys the discomfiture of the victim. A typical instance is shown in the way in which he, under the assumed name of Isaac Bickerstaff, dealt with an astrologer and maker of prophetic almanacs, whose name was Partridge. Bickerstaff claimed to be an infallible astrologer, and he predicted that Partridge would die March 29, 1708, at 11 P.M. When that day had passed, Bickerstaff issued a pamphlet giving a circumstantial account of Partridge's death. Partridge, finding that his customers began to decrease, protested that he was alive. Bickerstaff promptly replied that Partridge was dead by his own infallible rules of astrology, and that the man now claiming to be Partridge was a vile impostor.

Swift's wit frequently left its imprint on the thought of the time. The results of this special prank with the astrologer were: first, to cause the wits of the town to join in the hue and cry that Partridge was dead; second, to increase the contempt for astrologers; and, third, in the words of Scott: "The most remarkable consequence of Swift's frolic was the establishment of the *Tatler*." Richard Steele, its founder, adopted the popular name of Isaac Bickerstaff (p. 248).

Taine says of Swift: "He is the inventor of irony, as Shakespeare of poetry." The most powerful instance of Swift's irony is shown in his attempt to make the Irish understand the brutality of rearing large families in ignorance, rags, hunger, and crime. His *Modest Proposal* for relieving such distress is to have the children at the age of one year served as a new dish on the tables of the great. So apt is irony to be misunderstood and to fail of its mark, that the Irish thought that Swift was brutal, instead of themselves. His ironical remarks on *The Abolishing of Christianity* were also misunderstood.

We shall search Swift's work in vain for examples of pathos or sublimity. We shall find his pages caustic with wit, satire, and irony, and often disfigured with coarseness. One of the great pessimists of all time, he is yet tremendously in earnest in whatever he says, from his *Drapier's Letters*, written to protect Ireland from the schemes of English politicians, to his *Gulliver's Travels*, where he describes the court of Lilliput. This earnestness and circumstantial minuteness throw an air of reality around his most grotesque creations.

Although sublimity and pathos are outside of his range, his style is remarkably well adapted to the special subject matter that he chose. While reading his works, one scarcely ever thinks of his style, unless the attention is specially directed to it. Only a great artist can thus conceal his art. A style so natural as this has especial merits which will repay study. Three of its chief characteristics are simplicity, flexibility, and energetic directness.

JOSEPH ADDISON, 1672-1719

Life. — Joseph Addison was born in the paternal rectory at Milston, a small village in the eastern part of Wiltshire. He was educated at Oxford, and he intended to become a clergyman, but he had attracted attention

From an old print.

ADDISON'S BIRTHPLACE

J. Addison.

by his graceful Latin poetry, and he was dissuaded by influential court friends from entering the service of the church. They persuaded him to fit himself for the diplomatic service, and they secured for him a yearly pension of £300. He then went to France, studied the language of that country, and traveled extensively, so as to gain a knowledge of foreign courts. The death of King William in 1702 stopped the pension, and Addison was forced to return to England and seek employment as a tutor.

The great battle of Blenheim was won by Marlborough in 1704. As Macaulay says, the ministry was mortified to see such a victory celebrated by so much bad poetry, and he instances these lines from one of the poems : —

> " Think of two thousand gentlemen at least,
>   And each man mounted on his capering beast ;
>   Into the Danube they were pushed by shoals."

The Chancellor of the Exchequer went to Addison's humble lodgings and asked him to write a poem in honor of the battle.   Addison took the town by storm with a simile in which the great general was likened to the calm angel of the whirlwind.   When people reflected how calmly Marlborough had directed the whirlwind of war, they thought that no comparison could be more felicitous.   From that time Addison's fortunes rose.   Since his day no other man relying on literary talents alone has risen so high in state affairs.   He was made assistant Secretary of State, Secretary for Ireland, and finally chief Secretary of State.

Though Addison was a prominent figure in the political world, his literary life most concerns us.   In his prime he wrote for *The Tatler* and *The Spectator*, famous newspapers of Queen Anne's day, many inimitable essays on contemporary life and manners.   Most newspaper work is forgotten with the setting sun, but these essays are eagerly read by the most cultivated people of to-day. His own age thought his tragedy of *Cato*, a drama observing the classical unities, his most famous production.   This fact shows how unreliable contemporary opinion may be concerning the merit of an author's works, for *Cato* is now little read.   Some of his *Hymns* are much finer.   Lines like these, written of the stars, linger in our memories : —

> "Forever singing as they shine,
>   The hand that made us is divine."

Addison had a singularly pleasing personality. Though he was a Whig, the Tories admired and applauded him. He was a good illustration of the truth that if one smiles in the mirror of the world, it will answer him with a smile. Swift said he believed the English would have made Addison king, if they had been requested to place him on the throne. Pope's jealous nature

From an old print.

ADDISON'S HOME AT BILTON, WARWICKSHIRE

strove to quarrel with Addison, but the quarrel was chiefly on one side. Men like Macaulay and Thackeray have exerted their powers to do justice to the kindliness and integrity of Addison.

Addison died at the age of forty-seven, and was buried in Westminster Abbey.

Collaborates with Steele. — Under the pen name of Isaac Bickerstaff, Richard Steele (1672–1729), a former schoolmate and friend of Addison, started in 1709 *The Tatler*, a periodical published three times a week. This discussed matters of interest in society and politics, and occasionally published an essay on morals and manners. Steele was a good-natured, careless individual, who had had experience as a soldier, playwright, moralist, keeper of the official gazette, and pensioner. He says that he always "preferred the state of his mind to that of his fortune," but his mental state was often fickle, and too much dependent on bodily luxuries, though he was patriotic enough to sacrifice his personal fortune for what he considered his country's interest.

RICHARD STEELE

We find Addison a frequent contributor to *The Tatler* after its seventeenth number. Steele says: "I fared like a distressed prince who calls in a powerful neighbor to his aid; I was undone by my auxiliary; when I had once called him in, I could not subsist without dependence on him."

The Tatler was discontinued in 1711, and the more famous *Spectator* was begun two months later. Addison wrote the first number, but the second issue, which came from Steele's pen, contains sketches of those characters which have become famous in the *Sir Roger de Coverley Papers*. While Steele should have full credit for the first bold sketches, the finished portraits in the de Coverley gallery are due to Addison. In many respects, each seemed to be the complement of the other. Steele's writings have not the polish or delicate humor of Addison's, but they have more strength and pathos. From the neglect of Steele and the enduring interest in Addison, the student should learn the valuable lesson that artistic finish, as well as excellence of subject matter, has become almost a necessity for a prose writer who would not be soon neglected.

Addison, however, needed as a starting point the suggestive originality of Steele. Of Addison, Steele says: "I claim to myself the merit of having extorted excellent productions from a person of the greatest abilities, who would not have let them appear by any other means." If it is true that the majority of readers to-day neglect Steele's work, it is also true that but for him they would not have Addison's best essays with which to charm many an idle hour.

Addison's Essays. — The greatest of Addison's *Essays* appeared in *The Spectator*, which was published every week day for 555 issues. The subject matter of these *Essays* is extremely varied. On one day there is a pleasant paper on witches; on another, a chat about the new woman; on another, a discourse on clubs. Addison is properly a moral satirist, and his pen did much more than the pulpit to civilize the age and make virtue the fashion. In *The Spectator*, he says: "If I meet with anything in city, court, or country, that shocks modesty or good manners, I shall use my utmost endeavors to make an example of it." He accomplished his purpose, not by heated denunciations of vice, but by holding it up to kindly ridicule. He remembered the fable of the different methods employed by the north wind and the sun to make a man lay aside an ugly cloak.

Addison also stated that one of his objects was to bring "philosophy out of closets and libraries, schools and colleges, to dwell in clubs and assemblies, at tea tables and coffeehouses." His papers on Milton did much to diminish that great poet's unpopularity in an age that loved form rather than matter, art rather than natural strength.

The Sir Roger de Coverley Papers. — The most famous of Addison's productions are his papers which appeared in *The Spectator*, describing a typical country gentleman, Sir Roger de Coverley, and his friends and servants. Taine **says** that Addison here invented the novel without suspecting it. This is an overstatement, but these papers certainly have the interest of a novel from the moment Sir Roger appears until his death, and the delineation of character is far in advance of what the majority of modern novels can show. We find ourselves rereading the *de Coverley* papers more than once, a statement that can be made of but few novels.

General Characteristics. — Before we have read many of Addison's essays, we shall discover that he is a humorist of high rank. His humor is of the kind that makes one smile, rather than laugh aloud. We are amused, for instance, by this sentence from *Spectator* No. 112 : —

" As Sir Roger is landlord to the whole congregation, he keeps them in very good order, and will suffer nobody to sleep in it besides himself ; for, if by chance he has been surprised into a short nap at sermon, upon recovering out of it, he stands up and looks about him, and, if he sees anybody else nodding, either wakes them up himself, or sends his servants to them."

The paper, *Of Clubs in General*, is highly entertaining because of its humor : —

" When a set of men find themselves agree in any particular, though never so trivial, they establish themselves into a kind of fraternity, and meet once or twice a week upon the account of such a fantastic resemblance. I know a considerable market town, in which there was a club of fat men. . . . The room where the club met was something of the largest, and had two entrances, — the one by a door of a moderate size, and the other by a pair of folding doors. If a candidate for this corpulent club could make his entrance through the first, he was looked upon as unqualified ; but if he stuck in the passage, and could not force his way through it, the folding doors were immediately thrown open for his reception, and he was saluted as a brother. . . .

" In opposition to this society, there sprang up another, composed of scarecrows and skeletons, who, being very meager and envious, did all they could to thwart the designs of their bulky brethren." [1]

[1] *The Spectator*, No. 9.

Some of the *Rules for the Twopenny Club* show Addison's humor at its best : —

"If any member absents himself, he shall forfeit a penny for the use of the club, unless in case of sickness or imprisonment.

"If any member brings his wife into the club, he shall pay for whatever she drinks or smokes.

"If any member's wife comes to fetch him home from the club, she shall speak to him without the door.

"None shall be admitted into the club that is of the same trade with any member of it."

It is well to notice in the preceding quotations the peculiarity of Addison's humor, for to this quality chiefly he owes his legions of readers. His wit is never used against morality. He is a satirist, but his satire is not personal, like Pope's, or misanthropical, like Swift's.

Of his style, Dr. Samuel Johnson says : "Whosoever wishes to attain an English style, familiar but not coarse, and elegant but not ostentatious, must give his days and nights to the study of Addison." This is stronger praise than the present century would accord. His sentences are smooth and elegant, but they need the additional qualities of variety, incisiveness, energy, and, occasionally, of precision, to perfect them.

ALEXANDER POPE, 1688-1744

Life. — Alexander Pope was born in London in 1688. His father was a merchant and a devout believer in the Roman Catholic religion. The future poet was not allowed to go either to a public school or to a university. He picked up almost all of his education in a haphazard way, reading those authors that pleased his fancy.

A. Pope

In his childhood, his parents removed from London to Binfield, a village in Berkshire, nine miles from Windsor. When nearly thirty, he went to Twickenham, a rural place on the Thames, near London. Here he indulged his fancy for landscape gardening and lived in quiet for the chief part of the rest of his life.

He was a very precocious child. At the age of twelve he was writing an *Ode on Solitude*. He chose his vocation early, for writing poetry was the business of his life.

On the basis of what he wrote, we may divide his life into three periods. During his first thirty years, he produced various kinds of verse, like the *Essay on Criticism* and *The Rape of the Lock*. The middle period of his life was marked by his translation of Homer's *Iliad* and *Odyssey*. In his third period, he wrote moral and didactic poems, like the *Essay on Man*, and satires, like the *Dunciad*.

By nature he was secretive and given to double dealing. It was said that he could hardly drink tea without stratagem. His vanity prompted him to take steps to have published a volume of his letters to various friends. Fearing that he would be criticised if he gave these letters to the public himself, he arranged to have them stolen and published apparently against his will. While accomplishing this, he became involved in a network of falsehoods. Leslie Stephen says of him: "He would instinctively snatch at a lie even when a moment's reflection would have shown that the plain truth would be more convenient, and therefore he had to accumulate lie upon lie, each intended to patch up the other."

In spite of such failings, Pope had some admirable traits. By his indomitable will he showed the world what careful workmanship could accomplish, and his devotion to his aged mother was remarkable.

Some Poems of the First Period : Essay on Criticism and The Rape of the Lock. — In 1711 Pope gave to the world a poem entitled *Essay on Criticism*. This is merely an exquisite setting of a number of gems of criticism which had for a long time been current. Pope's intention in writing this poem may be seen from what he himself says : "It seems not so much the perfection of sense to say things that have never been said before, as to express those best that have been said oftenest."

From this point of view, the poem is a remarkable one. No other writer, save Shakespeare, has in an equal num-

From an old print.

POPE'S HOME AT BINFIELD

ber of lines said so many things which have passed into current quotation. Rare perfection in the form of state-ment accounts for this. The poem abounds in such lines as these : —

"For fools rush in where angels fear to tread."

"To err is human, to forgive divine."

"All seems infected that th' infected spy,
As all looks yellow to the jaundiced eye."

"In words, as fashions, the same rule will hold,
Alike fantastic, if too new, or old :
Be not the first by whom the new are tried,
Nor yet the last to lay the old aside."

The Rape of the Lock is Pope's masterpiece. It was a favorite with Oliver Goldsmith, and Lowell rightly says : "The whole poem more truly deserves the name of a creation than anything Pope ever wrote." The poem is a mock epic, and it has the supernatural machinery which was supposed to be absolutely necessary for an epic. In place of the gods and goddesses of the great epics, the fairylike sylphs help to guide the action of this mock epic.

The poem describes a young lord's theft of a lock of hair from the head of a court beauty. Such an incident actually happened, and Pope composed *The Rape of the Lock* to soothe her indignation and to effect a reconciliation. This poem, which should now be read entire by the student, is a vivid satiric picture of fashionable life in Queen Anne's reign.

Translation of Homer. — Pope's chief work during the middle period of his life was his translation of the *Iliad* and the *Odyssey* of Homer. From a financial point of view, these were the most successful of his labors. They brought him in nearly £9000, and made him independent of bookseller or of nobleman.

The remarkable success of these translations is strange when we remember that Pope's knowledge of Greek was very imperfect, and that he was obliged to consult translations before attempting any passage. The Greek scholar Bentley, a contemporary of Pope, delivered a just verdict on the translation : " A pretty poem, Mr. Pope, but you must not call it Homer." The historian Gibbon said that the poem had every merit except faithfulness to the original.

Homer is simple and direct. He abounds in concrete terms. Pope dislikes a simple term and loves a circumlocution and an abstraction. We have the concrete " herd of swine " translated into "a bristly care," " skins," into "furry spoils." The concrete was considered common and undignified. Homer says in simple language : " His father wept with him," but Pope translates this: "The father poured a social flood."

Pope used to translate thirty or forty verses of the *Iliad* before rising, and then to spend a considerable time in polishing them. But half of the translation of the *Odyssey* is his own work. He employed assistants to finish the other half. It is by no means easy to distinguish his work from theirs. To imitate the work of a genius is not so easy.

Some Poems of his Third Period: Essay on Man, and Satires. — The *Essay on Man* is a philosophical poem with the avowed object of vindicating the ways of God to man. The entire poem is an amplification of the idea contained in these lines: —

> " All nature is but art unknown to thee ;
> All chance, direction which thou canst not see ;
> All discord, harmony not understood ;
> All partial evil, universal good.
> And spite of pride, in erring reason's spite,
> One truth is clear, Whatever is, is right."

The chief merit of the poem consists in throwing into polished form many of the views current at the time, so that they may be easily understood. Before we read very far we come across such old acquaintances as

> " The proper study of mankind is man."

> " An honest man's the noblest work of God."

> " Vice is a monster of so frightful mien
> As, to be hated, needs but to be seen ;
> Yet, seen too oft, familiar with her face,
> We first endure, then pity, then embrace."

The *Epistle to Dr. Arbuthnot* and the *Dunciad* are Pope's greatest satires. In the *Dunciad*, an epic of the dunces, he holds up to ridicule every person and writer who had offended him. These were in many cases scribblers who had no business with a pen. In a few instances they were the best scholars of that day. A great deal of the poem is now very tiresome reading. Much of it is brutal. Pope was a powerful agent, as Thackeray says, in rousing much of that obloquy which has ever since pursued a struggling author.

General Characteristics. — For a long time there was considerable dispute in regard to whether Pope's verse is genuine poetry. He has not strong imagination, a keen feeling for nature, or wide sympathy with man. Leslie Stephen correctly says : " Pope never crosses the undefinable, but yet ineffaceable line, which separates true poetry from rhetoric." No student can ever be a good critic of poetry until he can both understand and feel the force of this remark. Many readers are to-day more pleased with rhetoric than with true poetry.

He is the poet who best expresses the classical spirit of the eighteenth century. His works show the preference of his age for subjects and form of treatment. He excels in satiric and didactic verse, expresses in as perfect a form as possible his ideas, which are frequently not original, and embodies them in classical couplets, sometimes styled "rocking-horse meter," but he shows no power of fathoming the emotional depths of the soul.

In the history of literature, he holds an important place because, more than any other writer, he calls attention to the importance of correctness of form, and of avoiding slovenliness of expression. He is the prince of artificial poets. Though he erred in exalting form above matter, the lesson of careful workmanship which he taught his age, was a needed one.

SUMMARY

The first part of the eighteenth century was marked by a low moral standard in both church and state. This standard had its effect on literature. We find no such sublime outbursts of song as characterize the Elizabethan and Puritan ages. The writers chose satiric or didactic subjects, and avoided pathos, deep feeling, and sublimity.

The age was molded by classical influence. Horace in his *Epistles* and *Satires* was the patron saint of criticism. The classical school loved polished regularity. An old idea, dressed in exquisite form, was as welcome as a new one. Anything strange, irregular, romantic, full of feeling, highly imaginative, or improbable to the intellect, was unpopular. Even in *Gulliver's Travels*, Swift endeavored to be as realistic as if he were demonstrating a geometrical proposition. Pope is the great poetic exponent of this school.

The age is far more remarkable for its prose than for its poetry. French influence helped to develop a concise, flexible, energetic prose style. The deterioration in poetry was partly compensated for by the rapid advances in prose, which needed the influences working toward artistic finish. Of all the prose writers since Swift's time, few have equaled him and still fewer surpassed him in simplicity, flexibility, directness, and lack of affectation. In grace of style, delicate humor, and the power of awakening and retaining interest, Addison's *Essays* have no superiors.

The influence of this age was sufficient to raise permanently the standard level of artistic literary expression. The unpruned, shapeless, and extravagant forms of earlier times will no longer be tolerated.

REQUIRED READINGS FOR CHAPTER VII

HISTORICAL

Gardiner,[1] pp. 671–729; Green, pp. 701–734; Underwood-Guest, pp. 508–523; Guerber, pp. 291–303; Wakeling's *King and Parliament*, pp. 115–128; and Hassall's *Making of the British Empire*, pp. 7–30 (*Oxford Manuals*); Traill, IV., 511–622, V, 1–171; John Morley's *Walpole* (251 pp., 50 cents).

LITERARY

Swift. — Craik's *English Prose Selections*, Vol. III., pp. 391–424, contains representative selections from Swift's prose. The best of these are *The Philosophy of Clothes*, from *A Tale of a Tub* (Craik, III., 398); *A Digression concerning Critics*, from the same (Craik, III., 400); *The Emperor of Lilliput* (Craik, III., 417), and *The King of Brobdingnag* (Craik, III., 419), from *Gulliver's Travels*.

Is Swift's a good prose style? Does he use ornament? Can you find a passage where he strives after effect? In what respects do the subjects which he chooses and his manner of treating them show the spirit of the age? Why is *Gulliver's Travels* so popular? What are the most important lessons which a young writer may learn from Swift? In what is he specially lacking?

Addison. — From the *Sir Roger de Coverley Papers* the student should not fail to read *Spectator* No. 112, *A Country Sunday*. He may then read *Spectator* No. 2, by Steele, which sketches the de Coverley characters, and compare the style and characteristics of the two authors. The student who has the time at this point should read all the *de Coverley Papers* (*Eclectic English Classics*, American Book Co.).

What are the excellences and defects of Addison's style? Why may his *Essays* be called a prelude to the novel of life and manners? What qualities draw so many readers to the *de Coverley Papers?* Select passages which will serve to bring into sharp contrast the style and humor of Swift and of Addison.

Pope. — Read *The Rape of the Lock* (printed with the *Essay on Man* in *Eclectic English Classics*, American Book Co., 20 cents). Selections from this are given in Ward's *English Poets*, Vol. III., pp. 73–82.

---

[1] For full titles, see list at end of Chap. I.

The *Essay on Man*, Book I. (Ward, III., 85–91) will serve as a specimen of his didactic verse. The *Epistle to Dr. Arbuthnot* (Ward, III., 103–105) will illustrate his satire, and the lines from the *Iliad* in Ward, III., 82, will show the characteristics of his translation.

How does Pope show the spirit of the classical school? What are his special merits and defects? Does an examination of his poetry convince you that Leslie Stephen's criticism (p. 258) is right? Select specimens of true poetry from as many of Pope's predecessors as possible. Place beside these selections some of Pope's best lines, and see if you have a clearer idea of the difference between rhetoric and true poetry.

WORKS FOR CONSULTATION AND FURTHER STUDY

(Optional)

Ashton's *Social Life in the Reign of Queen Anne*.
Sydney's *England and the English in the Eighteenth Century*.
Lecky's *History of England in the Eighteenth Century*.
Stephen's *History of Thought in the Eighteenth Century*.
Thackeray's *Henry Esmond*.
Taine's *History of English Literature*, Book III., Chaps. IV. and V.
Gosse's *History of English Literature in the Eighteenth Century*.
Perry's *English Literature in the Eighteenth Century*.
Minto's *Manual of English Prose Literature*, pp. 342–408.
Clarke's *Study of English Prose Writers*, pp. 82–198.
Dennis's *The Age of Pope*.
Phillips's *Popular Manual of English Literature*, Vol. I., pp. 437–564.
Ward's *English Poets*, Vol. III., pp. 1–182.
Craik's *English Prose Selections*, Vol. III., pp. 355–595.
Thackeray's *English Humorists*.
Stephen's *Life of Swift*.
Craik's *Life of Swift*.
Courthope's *Life of Addison*.
Macaulay's *Essay on Addison*.
Stephen's *Life of Pope*.
De Quincey's *Essay on Pope*, and *On the Poetry of Pope*.
Johnson's *Lives of the Poets*.
Gosse's *From Shakespeare to Pope*.

CHAPTER VIII

THE SECOND FORTY YEARS OF THE EIGHTEENTH CENTURY, 1740–1780

An Age of Changing Standards. — The second forty years of the eighteenth century are more remarkable for the foundations which they laid for future changes than for original literary productions. Moral, religious, political, and literary standards began to change. There was more diversity of opinion in regard to all these subjects. These years were a flight of stairs leading up to the romantic age, and to the entire nineteenth century.

In 1742 Robert Walpole's long term as prime minister came to a close. His political code contained two rules of action: (1) to secure by bribery, whenever necessary, the adoption of his measures, and (2) never to attempt to remedy abuses or to change any existing state of affairs, unless the demand for such change was too strong to be resisted. In 1757 William Pitt became, in effect, prime minister (though not so in name). Walpole had tried to bribe him in various ways and had utterly failed. In politics, Pitt was in a certain sense the counterpart of Wesley in religious life. Pitt appealed to the patriotism and to the sense of honor of his countrymen, and many heard his appeal. Under Walpole, Great Britain was a third-rate insular power; under Pitt, she became one of the foremost powers of the world. Between 1750 and 1760, Clive was making Great Britain mistress of the vast empire of India, and in 1759 Wolfe shattered the power of France in Canada. England was expanding to the eastward and the westward and taking her literature with her. As Wolfe advanced on Quebec, he was reading Gray's *Elegy*.

Change in Religious Influence. — The church had become too lukewarm and respectable to endeavor to bring in the masses, and they saw nothing in the church to attract them to it. When religious influence was at the lowest ebb, two eloquent preachers, John Wesley and George Whitefield, started a movement which is still gathering force. Although anything like enthusiasm or appeal to the emotions from the pulpit had for some time been considered in bad taste, Wesley did not ask his audience to listen to a sermon on the favorite bloodless abstractions of the eighteenth century pulpit, such as Charity, Faith, Duty, Holiness, abstractions which never moved a human being an inch heavenward. His sermons were emotional. They dealt largely with the emotion of love, God's love for man. He did not ask his listeners to engage in intellectual disquisitions about the aspects of infinity. He did not talk free-will metaphysics or trouble his hearers with a satisfactory philosophical account of the origin of evil. He spoke about things which reached not only the understanding but also the feelings of plain men.

About the same time, Whitefield was preaching to the miners near Bristol. Tears streamed down the cheeks of these rude men as he eloquently told them the story of salvation, and made many resolve to lead better lives.

This religious awakening may have been accompanied with too much appeal to the feelings and some unhealthy emotional excitement, but some vigorous movement was absolutely necessary to quicken the spiritual life of such an age.

Change in Literary Standards: Romanticism

What is Romanticism?— It is important to understand the meaning of the romantic movement in order to comprehend the dominating spirit of the next age. The years from 1740 to 1780 nowhere show romantic literature at the height of its excellence, but they indicate how the foundations of the movement were laid.

The best short definition of romanticism is that of Victor Hugo, who called it "liberalism in literature." Although this definition is incomplete, it has the merit of covering all kinds of romantic movements. In this period and the far more glorious one that followed, romanticism made its influence felt for the better in four different ways. An understanding of each of these will make us more intelligent critics.

In the first place, the romantic spirit is opposed to the prosaic. The romantic yearns for the light that never was on sea or land and longs to attain the unfulfilled ambitions of the soul, even when these in full measure are not possible. Sometimes these ambitions are so unrelated to the possible that the romantic has in certain usage become synonymous with the impractical or the absurd, but this is not its meaning in literature. The romantic may not always be "of imagination all compact," but it has a tendency in that direction. A reality of the imagination is as satisfying to romanticists as a reality of the prosaic reason, hence they, unlike the classicists, can enjoy *The Tempest* and *A Midsummer Night's Dream*. The events in these plays could not have been objective realities in an actual world, but they have the necessary element of subjective truth. The imagination is the only power that can grasp the unseen. Any movements which stimulate imaginative activity must give the individual more points of contact with that part of the world that does not obtrude itself on the physical senses, and especially with many facts of existence which cold intellectual activity can never comprehend. Hence, romanticism leads to greater breadth of view.

In the second place, the romantic is the opposite of the hackneyed. Hence, too much repetition may take a necessary quality away from what was once considered romantic. The epithets "ivory" and "raven," when applied to "brow" and to "tresses," respectively, were at first romantic, but much repetition has deprived them of this quality. If an age is to be considered romantic, it must look at things from a point of view somewhat different from that of the age immediately preceding. This change may be either in the character of the thought or in the manner of its presentation, or in both. An example of the formal element of change which appeared, consists in the substitution of blank verse and the Spenserian stanza for the classical couplets of the French school. In the next age, we shall find that the subject matter is no longer chiefly of the satiric or the didactic type.

In the third place, the highest type of romanticism must contain something of the subjective element (see p. 130) peculiar to the individual. This often appears in the ideals that we fashion and in our characteristic conceptions of the spiritual significance of the world and its deepest realities. Two writers of this period by investing nature with a spirit of melancholy (see p. 270) illustrate one of the many phases which this subjective element can assume.

In the fourth place, we shall see that the romantic movement tended toward deeper feeling. Sometimes the movement was injured and subjected to caricature by

exhibitions of unbridled and ridiculous passion. Of
course, the best romantic works are not mere seas of
rippling sensibility or stormy passion, but the great
romanticists never avoid expressions of profound feeling,
like the love of Juliet or the jealousy of Othello. The
classic school shunned as vulgar all exhibitions of enthusiasm and strong emotion.

The Influence of Spenser, Shakespeare, and Milton. — The
classicists had turned away from the great English authors
and had gone to French models for instruction in polish
and form. Spenser exerted a powerful influence on the
romanticists, for he is to the core a romantic poet. His
far-off forest world with its enchantment of bowers,
streams, glorious maidens, and heroic knights, is the
very fairyland of romance. Before 1750 there was only
one eighteenth century edition of Spenser's work published in England. In 1758, three editions of the *Faerie
Queene* appeared. Spenser's readers and imitators were
becoming very numerous.

Much of the mid-eighteenth century influence of
Shakespeare came from the masterly performance of
his plays on the stage. In 1741 the great actor David
Garrick captivated London audiences by his presentation
of Shakespeare's dramas. Before Garrick retired in 1776,
he had produced twenty-four of these plays, and so he
brought some of the influences of the romantic Elizabethan age to bear on the taste of eighteenth century
England. The presentation of Shakespeare by a master
like Garrick affected the imaginations of the people far
more vividly than a mere reading of the plays. We have
seen that the classicists did not like the "monstrous
irregularities of Shakespeare," but, later in the century,
he found a larger and more delighted audience. No age

with its eye on Shakespeare can tolerate a literature without romance and spirituality.

Milton's influence for romanticism was also strong. At first thought, it may seem strange that a poet saturated as he was with the study of Greek and Latin literature, should have such influence, but his *Paradise Lost* is a work of the creative imagination, and the subject matter satisfies the romantic requirement in being strange and instinct with strong feeling. His minor poetry, especially his *Il Penseroso*, was most important in the new movement, although the blank verse of *Paradise Lost* was often adopted as a welcome relief from "the rocking-horse" verse of the rhyming couplet.

Ossian. — Between 1760 and 1764 James Macpherson, a Highland schoolmaster, published a series of poems, which he claimed to have translated from an old manuscript, the work of Ossian, a Gaelic poet of the third century. These may have been forged in whole or in part, but the question of their genuineness does not alter the fact that they powerfully affected the romantic movement. The so-called translation of the poems is in prose, and it won for Macpherson a grave in the Poets' Corner of Westminster Abbey.

The qualities in *Ossian* which appealed to the age were its wildness, its vague suggestions to the imagination, its disregard of conventional forms, the profusion of its rhetorical figures, and the deep feeling of melancholy. Gray was profoundly impressed with the strange work. He praised highly the following quotation from it : —

> "Ghosts ride on the tempest to-night ;
>   Sweet is their voice between the gusts of wind ;
>   Their songs are of other worlds."

Ossian also influenced Byron. Professor W. L. Phelps found Byron's copy of *Ossian* with notes and comments in Byron's own handwriting. In some respects Byron considered *Ossian* equal to Homer. But the Ossianic poems have not stood the test of time. They are mentioned here only because they were so pronounced a factor in ushering in the romantic movement.

Horace Walpole and The Castle of Otranto. — "The great resources of fancy have been dammed up, by a strict adherence to common life," said Horace

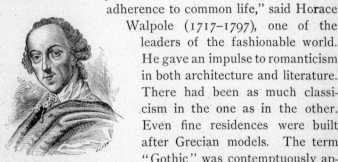

HORACE WALPOLE

Walpole (1717–1797), one of the leaders of the fashionable world. He gave an impulse to romanticism in both architecture and literature. There had been as much classicism in the one as in the other. Even fine residences were built after Grecian models. The term "Gothic" was contemptuously applied to whatever was mediæval or out of date, whether in art, philosophy, or general literature. About 1750 he erected a Gothic residence, which became the talk of fashionable England and soon found many imitators. People began to study mediæval architecture and to turn their attention to other things that were old as well as good.

In 1764 a book was published, entitled *The Castle of Otranto: A Gothic Romance*. This professed to be a translation from an old black-letter volume. The scene of the story is laid in a Gothic castle, in whose mysterious labyrinths and trap doors the strangest adventures occur. The weirdness and improbabilities of the romance were welcomed by readers weary of the prosaic works that had been so unsparingly produced. No name was placed on the title page of the first edition. Walpole was afraid of being sneered at for breaking the classical rules prescribing conventional regularity and probability. The pronounced success of the story soon led him to acknowledge the authorship, not, however, before some had ascribed it to Thomas Gray, the poet. This work gave a pronounced impetus to ultra-romantic tales. Its influence was felt across the Atlantic, by an early American novelist, Charles Brockden Brown (1771–1810).

Percy's Reliques and Translation of Mallet's Northern Antiquities. — In 1765 Thomas Percy (1729–1811) published *The Reliques of Ancient English Poetry*, an epoch-making work in the history of the romantic movement. The *Reliques* is a collection of old English ballads and songs, many of which have a story to tell, and a very romantic one, too. Scott drew inspiration from them, and Wordsworth acknowledged his indebtedness to their influence. So important was this collection that it has been called "the Bible of the Romantic Reformation."

In 1770 Percy's translation of Mallet's *Northern Antiquities* appeared. For the first time the English world was given an easily accessible volume which disclosed the Norse mythology in all its strength and weirdness. Classical mythology had become hackneyed, and poets like Gray rejoiced that there was a new fountain to which they could turn. Thor and his invincible hammer, the Frost Giants, Bifrost or the Rainbow Bridge, Odin, the Valkyries, Valhal, the sad story of Baldur, and the Twilight of the Gods, have appealed strongly to a race which takes pride in its own mythology, to a race which to-day loves to hear Wagner's translation of these myths into the music of *Die Walküre*, *Siegfried*, and *Götterdämmerung*.

The Literature of Melancholy. — The choice of subjects in which the emotion of melancholy was given full sway shows one direction taken by the romantic movement. Here, the influence of Milton's *Il Penseroso* can often be traced. The exquisite *Ode to Evening*, by William Collins (1721–1759) shows the love for nature's solitudes where this emotion may be nursed. Lines like these: —

> "... be mine the hut,
> That, from the mountain's side,
> Views wilds and swelling floods,
> And hamlets brown, and dim-discovered spires;
> And hears their simple bell; and marks o'er all
> Thy dewy fingers draw
> The gradual dusky veil,"

caused Swinburne to say: "Corot on canvas might have signed his *Ode to Evening*."

THOMAS GRAY

The high-water mark of the poetry of melancholy of this period was reached in Thomas Gray's (1716–1771) *Elegy written in a Country Churchyard* (1751). The poet with great art selected those natural phenomena which cast additional gloom upon the scene. We may notice in the very first stanza that the images were chosen with this end in view: —

> "The curfew tolls the knell of parting day,
> The lowing herd winds slowly o'er the lea,
> The plowman homeward plods his weary way,
> And leaves the world to darkness and to me."

Then we listen to the droning flight of the beetle, to the drowsy tinklings from a distant fold, to the moping owl in an ivy-mantled tower. Each natural object, either directly or by contrast, reflects the mood of man. Nature is a background for the display of emotion. Later poets cultivated her for her own beauties, but that time had not yet arrived.

STOKE POGES CHURCHYARD (GRAY'S BURIAL PLACE AND SCENE OF HIS ELEGY)

Gosse says in his *Life of Gray:* "The *Elegy* has exercised an influence on all the poetry of Europe, from Denmark to Italy, from France to Russia. With the exception of certain works of Byron and Shakespeare, no English poem has been so widely admired and imitated abroad."

The Conflict between Romanticism and Classicism. — The influences of this period were not entirely in the direction of romanticism. Samuel Johnson, the literary dictator of the age, was unsparing in his condemnation of the movement. The weight of his opinion kept many romantic

tendencies in check. Even authors like Gray were afraid
to adopt the new creed in its entirety. In one stanza of
his *Hymn to Adversity* we find four capitalized abstractions, after the manner of the classical school: Folly,
Noise, Laughter, Prosperity; and the following two lay
figures, little better than abstractions:—

> "The summer Friend, the flattering Foe."

These abstractions have little warmth or human interest.
After Gray had studied the Norse mythology, we find him
using such strong expressions as "Iron-sleet of arrowy
shower." Collins's ode on *The Passions* contains seventeen personified abstractions, from "pale Melancholy" to
"brown Exercise."

In Oliver Goldsmith (1728–1774) the conflict between
romanticism and classicism is marked. Goldsmith's natural taste in many directions preferred the romantic, but
the influence of the age in general, and of Dr. Johnson in
particular, modified this preference and made his work a
mixture of both the romantic and the classic. Goldsmith
wrote his two great poems, *The Traveller* and *The Deserted
Village*, in the classical couplet. To show how he could
combine words with art, Matthew Arnold quotes from *The
Traveller* the line:—

> "No cheerful murmurs fluctuate in the gale,"

and says: "There is exactly the poetic diction of our
prose century: rhetorical, ornate, and, poetically, quite
false. Place beside it a line of genuine poetry, such as
the
> 'In cradle of the rude imperious surge'

of Shakespeare; and all its falseness instantly becomes
apparent."

Oliver Goldsmith

On the other hand, one could not ask for pictures lighted up with finer romantic touches than those of the village preacher and the village master in *The Deserted Village*. Every cultivated person ought to experience the luxury of knowing those by heart. Swinburne happily says: "In Goldsmith's verse there is a priceless and adorable power of sweet human emotion." This is warm enough to be felt in spite of the chilling effects of classical influence. The hearty humor of his great comedy, *She Stoops to Conquer*, would satisfy Victor Hugo's ideal of "liberalism in literature" (p. 264).

The conflict between these two schools still continues. Indeed, there are many people who still think that any poetry which shows polished regularity must be excellent. To prove this statement, we have only to turn to the magazines and glance at the current poetry, which often consists of words rather artificially strung together without the soul of feeling or of thought.

THE DEVELOPMENT OF THE MODERN NOVEL

Story-telling an Old Art. — It is true that the modern novel was not developed until the middle of the eighteenth century, but the modern novel is the flower of a plant which had been growing for a long time. Authentic history does not take us back to the time when human beings were not solaced by stories. We are to-day interested in tales from the old Aryan, Grecian, and Norse mythologies. As we read the adventures of Ulysses with the Cyclops and with Circe, we are charmed with the tales which Homer tells. The *Bible* contains stories of marked interest. The church often put the lives of saints in the form of a story. It is primarily the business of the novelist to tell a story, but a history of fiction shows that there are different ways in which to tell stories, just as a study of art from early times discloses differences in the ways of drawing and painting human figures.

Mediæval Romances. — The original meaning of romance was a story in verse in some one of the Romance languages. The majority of the early romances read in England were of French origin. There were four cycles of French romance especially popular in England before Chaucer's time. These were tales of the remarkable adventures of King Arthur and his Knights, Charlemagne and his

Peers, Alexander the Great, and the heroes at the siege of Troy.

An account of the adventures of a knight, as he rode about in his armor, often made interesting reading. Writers soon began to imagine adventures for him, and the literature of fiction received vast additions in this way. Chaucer's *Knightes Tale* holds the place of honor in his magnificent collection of stories.

We have an inventory of the library of a gentleman in the reign of Edward IV. (1461–1483). About one half of this library consisted of story-telling literature. Prominent in this class were two of Chaucer's poetic tales, the celebrated romance, *Guy, Earl of Warwick*, *Sir Gawayne and the Green Knight*, *The Death of King Arthur*, a collection of extravagant adventures attributed to Richard the Lion-hearted, and a religious allegory. The point to be noticed is that for several hundred years the favorite type of romance consisted of tales crowded with marvelous incidents, in which giants, fairies, enchanters, and all-powerful knights figure. The adventures in *Sir Gawayne and the Green Knight* may serve to illustrate the characteristics of some of these stories. At the court of King Arthur, Gawayne cuts off the Green Knight's head. The decapitated giant picks up his head and rides away, challenging his foe to meet him a year hence at a certain Green Chapel. Gawayne presents himself at the appointed time and barely resists many fatal enchantments. Relying on the protection of a magic belt, he fights the Green Knight. It is well to notice that the wound which Gawayne receives is the result of deception which he practices. The moral element thus introduced gives dignity to the story.

The knight who meets with all kinds of adventures and

rescues everybody, is admirably burlesqued in the *Don
Quixote* of the Spanish author Cervantes, which appeared
at the beginning of the seventeenth century. This world-
famous romance shows by its ridicule that the taste for
the impossible adventures of chivalry was beginning to
pall. The following title to one of the chapters of *Don
Quixote* is sufficiently suggestive: " Chapter LVIII. —
Which tells how Adventures came crowding on Don
Quixote in Such Numbers that they gave him No Breath-
ing Time."

The Romances of the Sixteenth Century. — The Elizabethan age shows an advance in the development of prose
fiction. Mention has already been made of Lyly's *Euphues*,
in which he strings his philosophy and curious knowledge
on a slight thread of romance, and of Sidney's *Arcadia*,
which furnished a model for pastoral romances.

Two of the novelists of the sixteenth century, Robert
Greene (1560?–1592) and Thomas Lodge (1558?–1625),
helped to give to Shakespeare the plots of two of his
plays. Greene's novel *Pandosto* suggested the plot of
The Winter's Tale, and Lodge's *Rosalind* was the immediate source of the plot of *As You Like It*.

Although Greene died in want at the age of thirty-two,
he was the most prolific of the Elizabethan novelists. His
most popular stories deal with the passion of love as well
as with adventure. He was also the pioneer of those
realistic novelists who go among the slums to study life at
first hand. Greene made a careful study of the sharpers
and rascals of London and published his observations in
a series of realistic pamphlets.

Thomas Nash (1567–1601) was the one who introduced
into England the picaresque novel in *The Unfortunate
Traveller, or the Life of Jacke Wilton* (1594). The

picaresque novel (Spanish, *pícaro*, a rogue) is a story of adventure in which rascally tricks play a prominent part. This type of fiction came from Spain and attained great popularity in England. Jacke Wilton is page to a noble house. Many of his sharp tricks were doubtless drawn from real life. Nash is a worthy predecessor of Defoe in narrating adventures which seem to be founded on actual life.

Fiction in the First Part of the Eighteenth Century. — Although there were in the seventeenth century the powerful religious allegories of Bunyan and the romances of Mrs. Behn, yet this century does not show much progress in the development of the novel. But the essay of life and manners at the beginning of the eighteenth century presents us at once with various pigments necessary for the palette of the novelist. Students on turning to the second number of *The Spectator* will find sketches of six different types of character which are worthy to be framed and hung in a permanent gallery of English fiction. The portrait of Sir Roger de Coverley may even claim one of the places of honor on the walls.

In 1719 Daniel Defoe (1661?–1731) gave to the world *Robinson Crusoe*, one of the most remarkable tales of adventure ever written. There has never appeared another work which has been so great a favorite with as large a number of boys.

In treatment of character and in style, Defoe takes a forward step in the development of fiction. *Robinson Crusoe* shows the way in which circumstance and environment react on character. We note with admiration the logical way in which Crusoe sets to work to solve the problems of his environment and the patience which he displays in overcoming difficulties. No magic belt is introduced to

aid him. Obstacles merely develop additional will power to surmount them. We do not, however, find in this story the development and progress of the passion of love, which is the chief element in modern novels.

In the second place, Defoe does not show a trace of the grandiloquence of chivalry. The overwrought poetic fancies of the *Arcadia* never appear in his writings. He has no superior in telling a plain unvarnished tale about a shipwrecked mariner, or about sharpers and cheats, such as figure in his picaresque stories entitled *Moll Flanders* and *Colonel Jack*, or in describing with minute circumstantial detail the events chronicled in his fanciful *Journal of the Plague Year*.

He is a great realist. He never shunned any labor in mastering every detail necessary to make his narratives appear absolutely true. Leslie Stephen rightly calls his stories " simple history minus the facts." Swift also has something of this quality, as we may note in his *Gulliver's Travels* (1726).

Distinction between the Romance and the Modern Novel. — The romances and tales of adventure which had been so long in vogue differ widely from the modern novel. Many of them pay but little attention to probability, but those which do not offend in this respect generally rely on a succession of stirring incidents to secure attention. Novels showing the analytic skill of Thackeray's *Vanity Fair*, or the development of character in George Eliot's *Silas Marner*, would have been little read in competition with the stirring tale of adventure, if they had appeared before a taste for them had been developed by habits of trained observation and thought.

We may broadly differentiate the romance from the modern novel by saying that the romance primarily deals with incident and adventure for their own sake, while the novel concerns itself with these only in so far as they are necessary for a faithful picture of life or for showing the development of character. Again, as a general rule, the leading characters of the romances which we have been considering are kings, princesses, knights, or members of the nobility. The ordinary type of human being, the type that does the most of the world's work, usually either occupies an insignificant position or is held up to scorn in the romance.

For the first time the eighteenth century novel undertook to do for humanity what the Elizabethan drama had already accomplished, to paint all human life, to neglect neither the lord nor the servant. Pamela, a waiting maid, is the heroine of the first eighteenth century novel, while the aristocratic Sir Charles Grandison is the hero of another tale. The romance, the ballad, and the drama had all taught the novelist. In his endeavor to draw as near to human life as the great dramatists of the sixteenth century, the novelist has in a great measure supplanted the dramatist, because a good novel can entertain one at home, without the necessity for living actors and elaborate scenery.

From an old print.

RICHARDSON'S HOME AT NORTH END, HAMMERSMITH

The First Great English Novelist. — Samuel Richardson (1689–1761) was born in Derbyshire. When he was only thirteen years old some of the young women of the neighborhood unconsciously began to train him for a novelist. They employed him to conduct their love correspondence, and they were well satisfied with his success. This early training partly accounts for the fact that every one of

S. Richardson

his novels is merely a collection of letters written by the chief characters to each other and to their friends to narrate the progress of events.

At the age of fifteen he went to London and learned the printer's trade, which he followed for the rest of his life. When he was about fifty years old, some publishers asked him to prepare a letter writer which would be useful to country people and others who could not think how to express themselves with a pen. The idea of making these letters tell a connected story occurred to him. The result was the first modern novel, *Pamela*, published in four volumes in 1740.   This was followed by *Clarissa Harlowe*, in seven volumes, in 1748, and this by *Sir Charles Grandison*, in seven volumes, in 1753.

The affairs in the lives of the leading characters are so minutely dissected, the plot is evolved so slowly and in a way so unlike the astonishing bounds of the old romance, that one is tempted to say, before starting the seventh volume of *Clarissa Harlowe*, that Richardson's novels progress more slowly than events in life.   One secret of his success depends on the fact that we feel that he is deeply interested in all his characters.   He is as much interested in the heroine of his masterpiece, *Clarissa Harlowe*, as if she were his own daughter.   He has the remarkable power of so thoroughly identifying himself with his various characters that, after we are thoroughly introduced to them, we can name them when we hear selections read from their letters.

The length and slow development of his novels repel modern readers, but there was so little genuinely interesting matter in the middle of the eighteenth century that many were sorry his novels were no longer.   The novelty of productions of this type also added to their interest.   His many faults are largely those of his age.   He wearies his readers with his didactic aims.   He is narrow and prosy. He poses as a great moralist, but he teaches the morality of direct utility.

Richardson may be called the inventor of the modern novel in the same way that a man is said to be the inventor of a new machine.   The inventor does not discover the principles of leverage.   He is not the original finder of the metals necessary for construction.   He merely takes, combines, and applies in a new way certain things which others have discovered.   Such a man is rightly called an inventor.

He introduces the world to something new. Some one
else may immediately improve his invention. This was
the case with the novel, but this improvement could not
have been made unless some one had taken the first step,
and furnished something for improvement.

Henry Fielding, 1707–1754. — The greatest novelist
of the eighteenth century, and one of the greatest that
England ever produced, was born in Sharpham Park, Som-

ersetshire.   After graduating at the University of Leyden,
he became a playwriter, a lawyer, a judge of a police court,
and, most important of all, a novelist, or an historian of
society, as he preferred to style himself.

When Richardson's *Pamela* appeared, Fielding determined to write a story caricaturing its morality and sentiment, which seemed hypocritical to him.   Before he had
gone very far he discovered where his abilities lay, and,
abandoning his narrow, satiric aims, he wrote *Joseph
Andrews* (1742), a novel far more interesting than *Pamela*.
In 1749 he published his masterpiece, *Tom Jones*, and in
1751 his third and last novel, *Amelia*.

Fielding's novels show several points of improvement
over Richardson's.   In the first place, every one of Fielding's novels displays a remarkable sense of humor.
Richardson has no humor, and no man can enter the very
first rank of novelists without this quality.

In the second place, Fielding is a master of plot.   From
all literature Coleridge selected for perfection of plot,
The Alchemist, *Œdipus Tyrannus*, and *Tom Jones*.

In the third place, Fielding writes with his eye sharply
fixed on the world.   The most of his characters seem alive
and vigorous.   Richardson's Sir Charles Grandison is an
impossible conglomeration of abstract virtues.   Richardson
is more subjective and his own personality is much in
evidence in most of his characters.   Except in the cases
of Tom Jones and Captain Booth, who are Fielding himself, Fielding appears to be listening with considerable
curiosity to the conversations of his characters, and wondering what they will do next.

Fielding shows the eighteenth century love of satire.   He
hates that hypocrisy which tries to conceal itself under a
mask of morality.   In the evolution of the plots of his

novels, he invariably puts such characters in positions which
tear away their mask.   He displays almost savage pleasure
in making them ridiculous.   Perhaps the lack of spirituality of the age finds the most ample expression in his pages,
but the finest creations of both Chaucer and Fielding, the
Parish Priest of the *Prologue* (p. 79) and Parson Adams of
Joseph Andrews, are typical of those persisting moral forces
which have bequeathed a heritage of power to England.

Sterne and Smollett. — With Richard and Fielding
it is customary to associate two other mid-eighteenth century novelists, Laurence Sterne (1713–
1768) and Tobias Smollett (1721–
1771).   Between 1759 and 1767
Sterne wrote his first novel, *The
Life and Opinions of Tristram
Shandy, Gentleman*, which presents the delightfully comic and
eccentric members of the Shandy
family, among whom Uncle
Toby is the masterpiece.   In
1768 Sterne gave to the world
that compound of fiction, essays,

LAURENCE STERNE

and sketches of travel known as *A Sentimental Journey
through France and Italy*.   The adjective "sentimental"
in the title should be specially noted, for it defines Sterne's
attitude toward everything in life.   He is habitually sentimental in treating not only those things fitted to awaken
deep emotion, but also those trivial incidents which
ordinarily cause scarcely a ripple of feeling.   Although
he is sometimes a master of pathos, he frequently gives
an exhibition of weak and forced sentimentalism.   He
more uniformly excels in subtle humor, which is his next
most conspicuous characteristic.

Roderick Random (1748), *Peregrine Pickle* (1751), and *The Expedition of Humphrey Clinker* (1771) are Smollett's  best novels. They are composed mainly of a succession of stirring or humorous incidents. In relying for interest more on adventure than on the drawing of character, he reverts to the picaresque (see p. 277) type of story.

The Relation of Richardson, Fielding, Sterne, and Smollett to Subsequent Fiction. — Although the modern reader frequently complains that these older novelists

TOBIAS SMOLLETT

often seem heavy, slow in movement, unrefined, and too ready to draw a moral or preach a sermon, yet these four men hold an important place in the history of fiction. With varying degrees of excellence, Richardson, Fielding, and Sterne all have the rare power of portraying character from within, of interpreting real life. Some novelists resort to the far easier task of painting merely external characteristics and mannerisms. Smollett belongs to the latter class. He is so effective at focusing external peculiarities and caricaturing exceptional individuals, that his influence has been far-reaching. It may be traced in the work of so great a novelist as Charles Dickens. On the other hand, Thackeray learned much from Fielding, and this great Victorian novelist has recorded in *The English Humorists* his admiration for his earlier fellow-craftsman.

Although subsequent English fiction has invaded many new fields, although it has entered the domain of history and of sociology, it is not too much to say that later novelists have advanced on the general lines marked out by these four mid-eighteenth century pioneers. We may even affirm with Gosse that "the type of novel invented in England about 1740-50 continued for sixty or seventy years to be the only model for Continental fiction; and criticism has traced on every French novelist, in particular, the stamp of Richardson, if not of Sterne and Fielding."

The Vicar of Wakefield. — In 1766, there was published a delightful romantic novel, of which Oliver Goldsmith, its author, said: "There are an hundred faults in this thing, and an hundred things might be said to prove them beauties. But it is needless. A book may be amusing with numerous errors, or it may be very dull without a single absurdity." This is sound criticism. *The Vicar of Wakefield* has faults, but it is amusing enough to be immortal in spite of them. The plot shows that Goldsmith did not have Fielding's constructive genius. In fact, the plot is so poorly constructed that the novel would have been almost a failure, had other qualities not insured success. But the story is such a compound of sweet human emotion and rare humor that we overlook some defects in the framework.

The Vicar, who is the hero of the story, is a country clergyman. We have delightfully entertaining pictures of his virtues and failings. We are interested in his domestic life, in his wife, his credulous son Moses, his good but somewhat aspiring daughters, and his happy little ones. It would be difficult to enumerate all the reasons which have made the tale such a favorite, but the chief are its inimitable humor, the grace and ease of the style, the excellent way in which some of the characters draw their own portraits, and the air of naturalness and good nature diffused throughout the work.

Philosophical, Historical, and Political Prose

Philosophy. — Although the majority of eighteenth century writers disliked speculative thought and resolutely
turned away from it, yet the age produced some remarkable philosophical works, which are still discussed, and
which have powerfully affected nineteenth century thought.
David Hume (1711–1776) is the greatest metaphysician
of the century. He took for his starting point the conclusions of a contemporary philosopher, George Berkeley
(1685–1753).

Berkeley had said that ideas are the only real existing
entities, that matter is merely another term for the ideas
in the Mind of the Infinite, and that matter has no existence outside of mind. He maintained that if every quality
should be taken away from matter, no matter would remain;
e.g., if color, sweetness, sourness, form, and all other qualities, should be taken away from an apple, there would be
no apple. Now, a quality is a mental representation based
on a sensation, and this quality varies as the sensation
varies; in other words, the object is not a stable immutable
something. It is only a something as I perceive it.
Berkeley's idealistic position was taken to crush atheistic
materialism.

Hume took Berkeley's position and attempted to rear
on it an impregnable citadel of skepticism. He accepted
Berkeley's conclusion that we know nothing of matter,
and then attempted to show that inferences based on ideas
might be equally illusory. Hume attacked the validity
of the reasoning process itself. He endeavored to show
that there is no such thing as cause and effect in either
the mental or the material world.

Hume's *Treatise of Human Nature* (1739–1740), in which

these views are stated, is one of the world's epoch-making works in philosophy. Its conclusion startled the great German metaphysician Kant and roused him to action. The questions thus raised by Hume have never been answered to the satisfaction of all philosophers.

Hume's skepticism is the most thoroughgoing that the world has ever seen, for he attacks the certainty of our knowledge of both mind and matter. But he dryly remarks that his own doubts disappear when he leaves his study. He avoids a runaway horse and inquires of a friend the way to a certain house in Edinburgh, relying as much on the evidence of his eyes and on the directions of his friend, as if these philosophic doubts had never been raised.

Historical Prose. — In carefully elaborated and highly finished works of history, the eighteenth century surpasses its predecessors. *The History of England* by David Hume, the philosopher, is the first work of the kind to add to the history of politics and the affairs of state an account of the people and their manners. His *History* is distinguished for its polished ease and clearness. Unfortunately, his work is written from a partisan point of view. Hume was a Tory, and took the side of the Stuarts against the Puritans. He sometimes misrepresents facts if they do not uphold his views. His *History* is consequently read more to-day as a literary classic than as an authority.

Edward Gibbon (1737–1794) is the greatest historian of the century. His monumental work, *The History of the Decline and Fall of the Roman Empire*, in six volumes, begins with the reign of Trajan, A.D. 98, and closes with the fall of the Eastern Roman Empire at Constantinople in 1453. Gibbon constructed a "Roman road" through nearly fourteen centuries of history, and he built it so well that another on the same plan has not yet been found

E Gibbon.

necessary.   E. A. Freeman says: "He remains the one historian of the eighteenth century whom modern research
has neither set aside nor threatened to set aside."   In preparing his *History*, Gibbon spent fifteen years.   Every
chapter was the subject of long-continued study and careful original research.   From the chaotic materials which
he found, he constructed a history remarkable as well for
scholarly precision as for the vastness of the field covered.

His sentences follow one another in magnificent procession. One feels that they are the work of an artist. They are thickly sprinkled with fine-sounding words derived from the Latin. The 1611 version of the first four chapters of the *Gospel* of John averages 96 per cent of Anglo-Saxon words, and Shakespeare 89 per cent, while Gibbon's average of 70 per cent is the lowest of any great writer. He has all the coldness of the classical school, and he shows but little sympathy with the great human struggles described in his pages. He has been well styled "a skillful anatomical demonstrator of the dead framework of society." With all its excellences, his work has, therefore, those faults which are typical of the eighteenth century.

Political Prose. — Edmund Burke (1729–1797) was a distinguished statesman and member of the House of Commons in an important era of English history — a time when the question of the independence of the American colonies was paramount, and when the spirit of revolt against established forms was in the air. He is the greatest political writer of the eighteenth century.

Burke's best productions are *Speech on American Taxation* (1774) and *Speech on Conciliation with America* (1775). His *Reflections on the Revolution in France* is also noteworthy. His prose marks a great advance in the following directions : (1) He is one of the greatest masters of metaphor and imagery in English prose. Only Carlyle (p. 415) surpasses him in the use of metaphorical language. (2) Burke's breadth of thought and wealth of expression enable him to present an idea from many different points of view, so that if his readers do not comprehend his exposition from one side, they may from another. He endeavors to attach what he says to something in the experience of his hearers or readers and he remembers that the experience of all is not the same. (3) As a corollary of

the preceding, it follows that his imagery and figures lay
all kinds of knowledge under contribution. At one time
he draws an illustration from manufacturing; at another,
from history; at another, from the butcher shop. (4) His
work displays intense earnestness, love of truth, strength
of logical reasoning, vividness of imagination, and breadth
of view, all of which are necessary qualities in prose which
is to mold the opinions of men.

It is well to note that Burke's careful study of English
literature contributed largely to his success as a writer.

His use of Bible phraseology and his familiarity with poetry led a critic to say that any one "neglects the most valuable repository of rhetoric in the English language, who has not well studied the English Bible. . . . The cadence of Burke's sentences always reminds us that prose writing is only to be perfected by a thorough study of the poetry of the language."

SAMUEL JOHNSON, 1709-1784

Early Struggles. — Michael Johnson, an intelligent book-seller in Lichfield, Staffordshire, was in 1709 blessed with a son who was to occupy a unique position in literature, a position gained not so much by his written as by his spoken words and great personality.

Samuel was prepared for Oxford at various schools and in the paternal bookstore, where he read widely and voraciously, but without much system. He said that at the age of eighteen, the year before he entered Oxford, he knew almost as much as at fifty-three. Poverty kept him from remaining at Oxford long enough to take a degree. He left the university, and, for more than a quarter of a century, he struggled doggedly against poverty. When he was twenty-five, he married a widow of forty-eight. With the money which she brought him, he opened a private school, but failed. He never had more than eight pupils, one of whom was David Garrick (p. 266).

In 1737 Johnson went to London and sought employment as a hack writer. Sometimes he had no money with which to hire a lodging, and was compelled to walk the streets all night to keep warm. Johnson reached London in the very darkest days for struggling authors. They often slept on ash heaps, and begged something for a

Sam. Johnson.

meal. They were the objects of a general contempt,
to which Pope's *Dunciad* had largely contributed.

During this period Johnson did much hack work for
the *Gentleman's Magazine*. He was also the author of
two satirical poems, *London* (1738) and *The Vanity of
Human Wishes* (1749), which won much praise.

Later Years. — By the time he had been for ten years
in London, his abilities were sufficiently well known to
the leading booksellers for them to hire him to compile
a *Dictionary of the English Language* for £1575. He
was seven years at this work, finishing it in 1755.

Between 1750 and 1760 he wrote the matter for two periodicals, *The Rambler* (1750–1752) and *The Idler* (1758–1760), which contain papers on manners and morals. He intended to model these papers on the lines of *The Tatler* and *The Spectator*, but his essays are for the most part ponderously dull and uninteresting.

In 1762, for the first time, he was really an independent man, for then George III. gave him a life pension of £300 a year. Even as late as 1759, in order to pay his mother's funeral expenses, Johnson had been obliged to dash off the romance of *Rasselas* in a week, but from the time he received his pension, he had leisure "to cross his legs and have his talk out" in some of the most distinguished gatherings of the eighteenth century. During the rest of his life he produced little besides *The Lives of the Poets*, which is his most important contribution to literature. In 1784 he died, and was buried in Westminster Abbey, among the poets whose lives he had written.

A Man of Character. — Any one who will read Macaulay's *Life of Johnson*[1] may become acquainted with some of Johnson's most striking peculiarities, but these do not constitute his claims to greatness. He had qualities that made him great in spite of his peculiarities. He knocked down a publisher who insulted him, and he would never take insolence from a superior, but there is no case on record of his ever having been unkind to an inferior. Goldsmith said : "Johnson has nothing of a bear but the skin." When some one manifested surprise that Johnson should have assisted a worthless character, Goldsmith promptly replied : "He has now become miserable, and that insures the protection of Johnson."

[1] To be found in *Encyclopædia Britannica*, Vol. XIII., or in Macaulay's collected *Essays*.

When Johnson came home late at night, he would sometimes see homeless street Arabs asleep on a doorstep.
In order that they might
find something for
breakfast when
they awoke, he
would frequent-
ly slip a coin
into their hands.
He spent the
greater part of
his pension on
the helpless, sev-
eral of whom he
received into his
own house.

From an old print.

SAMUEL JOHNSON'S BIRTHPLACE

There have
been many
broader and
more scholarly
Englishmen,
but there never
walked the streets of London a man who battled more
courageously for what he thought was right. The more
we know of him, the more certain are we to agree with
this closing sentence from Macaulay's *Life of Johnson:*
"And it is but just to say that our intimate acquaintance
with what he would himself have called the anfractuosities
of his intellect and of his temper serves only to strengthen
our conviction that he was both a great and a good man."

A Great Converser and Literary Lawgiver. — By nature
Johnson was fitted to be a talker. He was happiest when
he had intelligent listeners. Accordingly, he and Sir

Joshua Reynolds, the artist, founded the famous Literary Club in 1764. During Johnson's lifetime this had for members such men as Edmund Burke, Oliver Goldsmith, Charles James Fox, James Boswell, Edward Gibbon, and David Garrick. Macaulay says: "The verdicts pronounced by this conclave on new books were speedily known all over London, and were sufficient to sell off a whole edition in a day, or to condemn the sheets to the service of the trunk maker and the pastry cook. . . . To predominate over such a society was not easy; yet even over such a society Johnson predominated."

He was consulted as an oracle on all kinds of subjects, and his replies were generally the pith of common sense. So famous had Johnson become for his conversations, that George III. met him on purpose to hear him talk. A committee from forty of the leading London booksellers waited on Johnson to ask him to write the *Lives of the Poets*. There was then in England no other man with so much influence in the world of literature.

JAMES BOSWELL

Boswell's Life of Johnson. — In 1763 James Boswell (1740– 1795), a Scotchman, met Johnson and devoted much time to copying the words that fell from the great Doctor's lips and to noting his individual traits. We must go to Boswell's *Life of Johnson*, the greatest of all biographies, to read of Johnson as he lived and talked; in short, to learn those facts which render him far more famous than his written works.

Leslie Stephen says: " I would still hope that to many readers Boswell has been what he has certainly been to some, the first writer who gave them a love of English literature, and the most charming of all companions long after the bloom of novelty has departed. I subscribe most cheerfully to Mr. Lewes's statement that he estimates his acquaintances according to their estimate of Boswell."

A Champion of the Classical School. — Johnson was a powerful adherent of classicism, and he did much to defer the coming of romanticism. His poetry is formal, and it shows the classical fondness for satire and aversion to sentiment. The first two lines of his greatest poem, *The Vanity of Human Wishes*, —

> " Let observation with extensive view
>   Survey mankind from China to Peru,"

show the classical couplet, which he employs, and they afford an example of poetry produced by a sonorous combination of words. " Observation," " view," and " survey " are nearly synonymous terms. Such conscious effort centered on word building subtracts something from poetic feeling.

His critical opinions of literature manifest his preference for classical themes and formal modes of treatment. He says of Shakespeare : " It is incident to him to be now and then entangled with an unwieldy sentiment, which he cannot well express . . . the equality of words to things is very often neglected."

In *The Lives of the Poets*, Johnson writes thus of Milton's great elegy : " One of the poems on which much praise has been bestowed is *Lycidas ;* of which the diction is harsh, the rhymes uncertain, and numbers unpleasing. . . . Its form is that of a pastoral, easy, vulgar, and there-

fore disgusting." Johnson felt positive repugnance to
Milton's flocks and shepherds going forth

"Under the opening eyelids of the Morn,"

amid the cowslips wan, the primroses dying forsaken, and
the daffodils with tear-filled cups. Johnson preferred the
streets of London to the finest spring landscape.

General Characteristics. — While he is best known in
literary history as the great converser whose full-length
portrait is drawn by Boswell, Johnson left the marks
of his influence on much of the prose written within nearly
a hundred years after his death. On the whole, this influence has, for the following reasons, been bad.

First, he loved a ponderous style in which there was
an excess of the Latin element. He liked to have his
statements sound well. He once said in forcible Saxon :
" *The Rehearsal* has not wit enough to keep it sweet,"
but a moment later he translated this into : " It has not
sufficient vitality to preserve it from putrefaction." In
his *Dictionary* he defined " network " as " anything re-
ticulated or decussated at equal distances with interstices
between the intersections." Some wits of the day said
that he used long words to make his *Dictionary* a necessity. If we read much of Johnson, we are in danger of
imitating him unconsciously. A critic in the latter part
of the nineteenth century, describing Johnson's style,
says : " He delivers himself with severe majestical dignity
and vigorous authoritative brevity." This critic was unconsciously writing Johnsonese.

In the second place, Johnson loved formal balance so
much that he used too many antitheses. Many of his
balancing clauses are out of place or add nothing to the
sense. The following shows excess of antithesis : —

"If the flights of Dryden, therefore, are higher, Pope continues longer on the wing. If of Dryden's fire the blaze is brighter, of Pope's the heat is more regular and constant. Dryden often surpasses expectation, and Pope never falls below it. Dryden is read with frequent astonishment, and Pope with perpetual delight." [1]

As a rule, Johnson's prose is too abstract and general, and it awakens too few images. This is a characteristic failing of his essays in *The Rambler* and *The Idler*. Even in *Rasselas*, his great work of fiction, he speaks of passing through the fields and seeing the animals around him, but he does not mention definite trees, flowers, or animals. Shakespeare's wounded stag or "winking Mary-buds" would have given a touch of life to the whole scene.

Johnson's latest and greatest work, *The Lives of the Poets*, is comparatively free from most of these faults. The sentences are energetic and full of meaning. Although we may not agree with much of the criticism, we shall find it stimulating and suggestive. Before he gave these critical essays to the world, he had been doing little for years except talking in a straightforward manner. His constant practice in speaking English reacted on his later written work. Unfortunately this work has been the least imitated.

SUMMARY

The second part of the eighteenth century was a time of changing standards in church, state, and literature. The downfall of Walpole, the religious revivals of Wesley, the victories of Clive in India and of Wolfe in Canada, show the progress that England was making at home and abroad.

[1] *Lives of the Poets.*

There began to be a revolt against the narrow classical standards in literature. A longing gradually manifested itself for more freedom of imagination, such as we find in *Ossian*, *The Castle of Otranto*, Percy's *Reliques*, and translations of the Norse mythology. There was a departure from the hackneyed forms and subjects of the preceding age and an introduction of more of the subjective and ideal element, such as can be found in Gray's *Elegy* and Collins's *Ode to Evening*. The progress toward romanticism was neither uniform nor constant. Dr. Johnson threw his powerful influence against the movement, and curbed somewhat the romantic tendencies in Goldsmith, who, nevertheless, gave fine romantic touches to *The Deserted Village* and to much of his other work. This period was one of preparation for the glorious romantic outburst at the end of the century.

In prose, the most important achievement of the age was the creation of the modern novel. In addition to Richardson's *Pamela* and *Clarissa Harlowe*, Fielding's *Tom Jones*, Sterne's *Tristram Shandy*, Smollett's *Humphrey Clinker*, and Goldsmith's *Vicar of Wakefield*, there were noted prose works in philosophy and history by Hume and Gibbon, in politics by Burke, and in criticism by Johnson.

REQUIRED READINGS FOR CHAPTER VIII

HISTORICAL

Gardiner,[1] pp. 730–792; Green, pp. 735–786; Underwood-Guest, pp. 523–535; Guerber, pp. 303–308; Hassall's *Making of the British Empire*, pp. 30–82; Traill, V., 172–365.

[1] For full titles, see list at end of Chap. I.

LITERARY

The Romantic Movement. — In order to note the difference in feeling, imagery, and ideals, between the romantic and the classic schools, it will be advisable for the student to make a special comparison of Dryden's and Pope's satiric and didactic verse with Spenser's *Faerie Queene* and Milton's *Il Penseroso*. What is the difference in the general atmosphere of these poems? See if the influence of *Il Penseroso* is noticeable in Collins's *Ode to Evening* (Ward's *English Poets*, Vol. III., p. 287), and in Gray's *Elegy* (Ward, III., 331).

What element foreign to Dryden and Pope appears in Thomson's *Seasons* (Ward, III., 173)?

What signs of a struggle between the romantic and the classic are noticeable in Goldsmith's *Deserted Village* (Ward, III., 373-379)? Pick out the three finest passages in the poem, and give the reasons for the choice.

Read pp. 173-176 of *Ossian* (*Canterbury Poets* series, 40 cents), and show why it appealed to the spirit of romanticism.

Read the opening of Walpole's *Castle of Otranto* (Cassell's *National Library*, No. 9, 10 cents), and explain why the time welcomed a romance of that order.

In Percy's *Reliques*, read the first ballad, that of *Chevy Chase*, and explain how the age could turn from Pope to read such rude verse.

The Novel. — *Guy, Earl of Warwick* is given in Morley's *Early Prose Romances* (pp. 331-408). An easily accessible Elizabethan novel is Greene's *Pandosto*, which may be found at the end of the Cassell *National Library* edition of Shakespeare's *Winter's Tale* (No. 101, 10 cents). Selections from Lodge's *Rosalind* are given in Craik's *English Prose Selections*, Vol. I., pp. 544-549. These should be compared with the parallel parts of *As You Like It*. (*Rosalind* may be found complete in No. 62 of Cassell's *National Library*.) Selections from Nash's *The Unfortunate Traveller* are given in Craik, I., 573-576, and selections from Sidney's *Arcadia* in the same volume, pp. 409-419.

For the preliminary sketching of characters that might serve as types in fiction, read *The Spectator's Club* by Steele (Cassell's *National Library*, No. 28, pp. 21-29, 10 cents). Defoe's *Robinson Crusoe* will be read entire by almost every one.

In Craik, IV., read the following selections from these four great novelists of the middle of the eighteenth century: from Richardson, pp. 59–66; from Fielding, pp. 118–125; from Sterne, pp. 213–219; and from Smollett, pp. 261–264 and 269–272.

Goldsmith's *Vicar of Wakefield* should be read entire by the student (*Eclectic English Classics*, American Book Co.). Selections may be found in Craik, IV., 365–370.

Sketch the general lines of development in fiction, from the early romance to Fielding. What type of fiction did *Don Quixote* ridicule? Compare Greene's *Pandosto* with Shakespeare's *Winter's Tale*, and Lodge's *Rosalind* with *As You Like It*. In what relation do Steele and Addison stand to the novel? Why is the modern novel said to begin with Richardson? Why is the novel a dangerous rival of the drama?

Philosophy. — Two selections from Berkeley in Craik, IV., 34–39, give some of that philosopher's subtle metaphysics. The same volume, pp. 189–195, gives a selection from Hume's *Treatise of Human Nature*. Can the subject matter in these be readily comprehended, or is the style involved and metaphysical?

Gibbon. — Read Aurelian's campaign against Zenobia, which constitutes the last third of Chap. XI. of the first volume of *The Decline and Fall of the Roman Empire*. Other selections may be found in Craik, IV., 460–472.

What is the special merit of Gibbon's work? Compare his style, either in description or in narration, with Bunyan's.

Burke. — Let the student who has not the time to read all the speech on *Conciliation with America* (*Eclectic English Classics*, 20 cents) read the selection in Craik, IV., 379–385, and also the selection referring to the decline of chivalry, from *Reflections on the Revolution in France* (Craik, IV., 402).

Point out in Burke's writings the four characteristics mentioned on pp. 291, 292. Compare his style with Bacon's, Swift's, Addison's, and Gibbon's.

Johnson. — Representative selections are given in Craik, IV., 141–185. Those from *The Lives of the Poets* (Craik, IV., 175–182) will best repay study. Let the student who has the time read Dryden's Life entire (Cassell's *National Library*, No. 36, 10 cents). As much as possible of Boswell's *Life of Johnson* should be read (Craik, IV., 482–495).

Compare the style of Johnson with that of Gibbon and Burke. For what reasons does Johnson hold a high position in literature?

WORKS FOR CONSULTATION AND FURTHER STUDY
(Optional)

Lecky's *History of England in the Eighteenth Century*.
Thackeray's *The Four Georges*.
Taine's *History of English Literature*, Book III., Chap. VI.
Phillips's *Popular Manual of English Literature*, Vol. II., pp. 3–84.
Minto's *Manual of English Prose Literature*, pp. 409–486.
Baldwin's *Introduction to the Study of English Literature*, Vol. II., pp. 134–258.
Clark's *Study of English Prose Writers*, pp. 199–322.
Gosse's *History of English Literature in the Eighteenth Century*.
Perry's *English Literature in the Eighteenth Century*, pp. 282–419.
Saintsbury's *A Short History of English Literature*, pp. 567–636.
Stephen's *History of Thought in the Eighteenth Century*.
Jusserand's *The English Novel in the Time of Shakespeare*.
Cross's *The Development of the English Novel*.
Raleigh's *The English Novel*; Lanier's *The English Novel*.
Dunlop's *History of Fiction*.
Beers's *English Romanticism, XVIII. Century*.
Phelps's *Beginnings of the English Romantic Movement*.
Ward's *English Poets*, Vol. III., pp. 245–381.
Craik's *English Prose Selections*, Vol. IV., pp. 25–421.
Stephen's *Hours in a Library*.   Vol. I. contains an excellent essay on Samuel Richardson, and Vol. II. one on Henry Fielding.
Traill's *The New Fiction and Other Essays* contains *Samuel Richardson* (pp. 104–136), and *The Novel of Manners* (pp. 137–169).
Dobson's *Life of Fielding*.
Thackeray's *English Humorists*.
Huxley's *Life of Hume*.
Morison's *Life of Gibbon*.
Forster's, Dobson's, or Black's *Life of Goldsmith*.
Stephen's *Life of Johnson*; Grant's *Life of Johnson*.
Dr. Johnson's Writings in Vol. II. of Stephen's *Hours in a Library*.
Boswell's *Life of Johnson*.
Macaulay's *Essay on Croker's Edition of Boswell's Life of Johnson*.
Fitzgerald's *Life of Boswell*.
Gosse's *Life of Gray*.
Morley's *Life of Edmund Burke.*

CHAPTER IX

The Victory of Romanticism. — We have traced in the preceding age the beginnings of the romantic movement. Its ascendency over classical rules was complete in the period between 1780 and the Victorian age. The romantic victory brought to literature more individuality, deeper feeling, a less artificial form of expression, and an added sense for the appreciation of the beauties of nature and their spiritual significance.

Swinburne says that the new poetic school, "usually registered as Wordsworthian," was "actually founded at midnight by William Blake [1757–1827] and fortified at sunrise by William Wordsworth." These lines from Blake's *To the Evening Star* (1783) may be given to support this statement : —

> " Thou fair-haired Angel of the Evening,
> Smile on our loves ; and while thou drawest the
> Blue curtains of the sky, scatter thy silver dew
> On every flower that shuts its sweet eyes
> In timely sleep.   Let thy West Wind sleep on
> The lake."

If any one wishes to become a critic sufficiently intelligent to appreciate the differences in the work of English poets, it will be an excellent step for him to compare the poetry of this romantic school — beginning with the above lines, for instance — with the verse of Pope.

If we except the verse of Milton, we may say that the poetry of this age is more genuine and unaffected than any other produced in England since the time of Elizabeth. The eyes of honest Cowper looked face to face on nature and on rural life. To express strong feeling was unfashionable in the time of Pope, but in the romantic age there was no more hesitancy than in Elizabethan days in voicing the deepest and most varied emotions of the soul. Wordsworth, the greatest representative of the romantic age, boldly said: "All good poetry is the spontaneous overflow of powerful feelings." We hear from the lips of Burns immortal songs of intense love, which make all seasons seem like spring.

Increased Range of Literary Activity. — Because of its lack of polish and of conventionality, the classicists had looked upon England's past as a rude age, worthy of contempt. Writers now began to regard that past as the parent of the present and to enrich literature with pictures of bygone times. At his magic bidding, Scott made the knightly past don the garb of life for the entertainment of the world. Charles Lamb (p. 312) increased the influence of the Elizabethan age by an excellent volume of selections from the half-forgotten dramatists of that time.

CHARLES LAMB

The union of strong imagination with intellect gave more variety to literature than resulted in the first part of the eighteenth century from the union of intellect with weak or repressed imagination. We consequently find a greater variety in the song notes of the poets, from George Crabbe (1754–1832), who sings of the miseries of the poor, to Shelley and Byron, who at one moment voice intense desire for individual liberty and at another paint the delicate traceries of cloud or the ocean mirror

> ". . . where the Almighty's form
> Glasses itself in tempests." [1]

Such was the power of imagination that a new world then burst from the chrysalis of the old. Wordsworth heard from the common flowers, the pansy at his feet, the primrose by a river's brim, truths newer and more weighty than fell from the lips of any lord or lady mentioned in Pope's verses. Keats could utter with new meaning : —

> " The poetry of earth is never dead." [2]

We may say of the poetry of this age what Coleridge's Ancient Mariner said of the music that filled the sea and air around him : —

> " And now 'twas like all instruments,
> Now like a lonely flute ;
> And now it is an angel's song,
> That makes the heavens be mute."

After a thorough study of the romantic age, each one may truthfully apply to himself this line from Keats : —

> "Much have I travel'd in the realms of gold." [3]

As varied as was the imaginative activity of the poets, it was for the most part confined to regarding Nature and Man from a new point of view. Let us next try to note more specifically in what this change consists.

---

[1] Byron : *Childe Harold*, Canto IV.   [2] *To a Grasshopper*.
[3] *On First Looking into Chapman's Homer*.

Growth of Appreciation of Nature. — In the appreciation of Nature and in sympathetic interpretation of her various moods, every preceding age, even the Elizabethan, is surpassed. For more than a century after Milton, the majority of references to nature were made in general terms and were borrowed from the stock illustrations of older poets, like Virgil. We find the conventional lark, nightingale, and turtledove. Nothing new or definite is said of them. In many cases the poets had probably neither heard nor seen them. Increasing comforts and safety in travel now took more people where they could see for themselves the beauties of nature. Gradually, observation became more exact, after the most obvious aspects of natural objects had been commonly noted. In the new poetry of nature we find more definiteness. We can hear the whir of the partridge, the chatter of magpies, the caw of the rook, the whistling of the quail. Poets speak not only in general terms of a tree, but they also note the differences in the shade of the green of the leaves and the peculiarities of the bark. Previous to this time, poets borrowed from Theocritus and Virgil piping shepherds reclining in the shade, whom no Englishman had ever seen. Wordsworth pictures a genuine English shepherd in *Michael*.

The love for mountains and wild nature is of recent growth. One writer in the seventeenth century considered the Alps as so much rubbish swept together by the broom of nature to clear the plains of Italy. A seventeenth century traveler thought the Welsh mountains better than the Alps because the former would pasture goats. Dr. Johnson asked: "Who can like the Highlands?" The influence of the romantic movement developed the love for wild scenery, which is so conspicuous in Wordsworth and Byron. The poetry of wonder and mystery naturally followed this sympathetic feeling for wild and solitary nature. Coleridge's *Ancient Mariner* is a romantic masterpiece, filled with the mystery of the lonely sea.

The eighteenth century classicists loved the town and despised the country, but the spread of romanticism changed this feeling. Burns could say:—

> "The Muse, na Poet ever fand her
> Till by himsel he learn'd to wander
> Adown some trottin burn's [1] meander." [2]

As the eighteenth century closed, we may notice that Nature was loved more and more for herself, and not merely because she was useful to man or appeared to flatter him by reflecting his emotions. To William Wordsworth, the greatest romantic poet, nature seemed to possess a conscious soul, which expressed itself in the primrose, the rippling lake, or the cuckoo's song, with as much intelligence as human lips ever displayed in whispering a secret to the ear of love.

Influence of the Democratic Spirit on the Poetry of Man. — In the age of Pope, the only type of man considered worthy of a place in literature was the aristocratic, cultured class. The ordinary laborer was an object too contemptible even for satire. The democratic movement had for some time been gathering force. In 1789 this movement culminated in the French Revolution against the tyranny of the nobility. The youth of all Europe responded to the cry of the French people for Liberty, Fraternity, Equality, and looked forward rapturously to the time when mankind should be united under the universal democracy of Man, without regard to nationality, birth, or religion.

[1] stream.   [2] *To William Simpson.*

Such feelings completely changed the way of looking at the begrimed, hard-handed laborer. He was no longer simply a burden bearer or a machine, but a friend and a brother. In 1795 Burns could proclaim thoughts which would have been laughed to scorn early in the century : —

> "Is there, for honest poverty,
>   That hangs his head and a' that?
>   The coward slave, we pass him by,
>   We dare be poor for a' that !
> .   .   .   .
>   The rank is but the guinea's stamp;
>   The man's the gowd[1] for a' that." [2]

To the ardent young spirits of the time, this French Revolution meant the downfall of the old dynasty of tyranny, and the birth of a new dynasty of world-wide liberty. The English poets struck on their lyres notes of hope, of promise, of boundless possibilities, not heard since the days of the Elizabethans. Like the Elizabethans, the poets of the Revolution saw the rising of a new sun and dreamed of what would be when it reached its glorious meridian, and liberty was at every hearth. The very buoyancy of youth was in the earth, and her poets caught the new spirit.

> "Bliss was it in that dawn to be alive,
>   But to be young was very Heaven!"[3]

cried the usually sober-minded Wordsworth. Shelley's poetry is colored with rosy dreams of an enfranchised humanity.

All the influences exerted by statesmen, poets, and philanthropists gradually brought fuller freedom to Great Britain. Before Victoria ascended the throne, the House

---

[1] gold.   [2] *For a' That and a' That.*   [3] *The Prelude*, Book XI.

of Lords had been forced to withdraw its opposition to the passage of the Reform Bill, which gave to the middle classes more voice in the government; negro slavery had been abolished; and even the unfortunate and the criminal classes had found their champions.

Philosophical Thought. — While the French revolutionists were proclaiming the equal rights of all men, and the British Parliament was gradually realizing the force of this view, the philosophers were not confining their attention entirely to metaphysics, as had been the custom too often in the past, but they were laying the foundations for the new science of political economy and endeavoring to ascertain how the condition of the masses could be improved. While investigating this subject, Malthus (1766–1834) announced his famous proposition, since known as the Malthusian theorem, that population tends to increase faster than the means of subsistence.

In moral philosophy, Jeremy Bentham (1748–1832) laid down the principle that happiness is the prime object of existence. He shocked the upper classes of society generally by announcing the revolutionary principle that the happiness of any one person, whether lord or bishop, is no more important than the happiness of any other individual, although he may be a factory hand. Bentham insisted that the basis of legislation should be the greatest happiness to the greatest number, instead of to the privileged few. He measured the morality of actions by their efficiency in securing this happiness, and he said that pushpins are as good as poetry, if they give as much pleasure. Such novel statements set men to thinking. He was followed by James Mill (1773–1836), who maintained that the morality of actions is measured by their utility.

Coleridge abhorred the destructive doctrine of Hume and the utilitarian dogmas of Bentham and Mill. To Coleridge, only the modern teachings of German philosophers, like Kant and Schelling, were congenial, and he propounded an idealistic philosophy and urged upon his common-sense generation that mind alone is the force in the world and that God reveals himself to every mind directly. To Coleridge is largely due the introduction of German influence on English philosophic thought.

We find in Shelley striking poetic expression of the belief in the immanence of the Divine Spirit in everything, from the flower to the storm. Such lines as these on the death of Keats express a philosophy almost pantheistic : —

> " He is made one with Nature : there is heard
> His voice in all her music, from the moan
> Of thunder to the song of night's sweet bird.
> . . . .
> Dust to the dust ! but the pure spirit shall flow
> Back to the burning fountain whence it came,
> A portion of the Eternal." [1]

The Position of Prose. — The eighteenth century until near its close was, broadly speaking, an age of prose. In excellence and variety, the prose surpassed the poetry, but in this age (1780–1837) their position was reversed, and poetry regained almost an Elizabethan ascendency. Toward the close of this era, the Victorian giants of prose, Carlyle and Macaulay, began their work, but the chief prose writers belonging to this age are Scott, Lamb, Southey, Coleridge, De Quincey, and Landor.

The works of Scott alone, among this group, are widely read to-day, although the delicate humor and unique literary flavor of Charles Lamb's (1775–1834) *Essays of Elia*

[1] *Adonais.*

still charm many devotees. Coleridge has, perhaps, a thousand readers for his *Ancient Mariner* to one for his prose. Southey (1774–1843), usually classed with Wordsworth and Coleridge as one of the three so-called Lake Poets, wrote much better prose than poetry. His *Life of Nelson* ranks better as prose than his *Curse of Kehama* as poetry. It is probable that, had he lived in an age of prose ascendency, he would have written little poetry, for he distinctly says that the desire of making money "has already led me to write sometimes in poetry what would perhaps otherwise have been better written in prose." This statement shows

· ROBERT SOUTHEY

in a striking way the spirit of those times. To-day one who wishes to make money avoids writing poetry.

The prose of the age is often the vehicle of romantic adventure, as in Scott, and of romantic humor, as in Lamb's *Dissertation on Roast Pig* and De Quincey's *Murder considered as one of the Fine Arts*. The prose of one writer, Walter Savage Landor, is the embodiment of conscious style and classical polish. These qualities are conspicuous in his *Imaginary Conversations*. Some of the critical prose is well worth study, especially Wordsworth's *Prefaces* and parts of Coleridge's *Biographia Literaria*, which expound the literary philosophy of the new school of poetry.

WILLIAM COWPER, 1731–1800

Life. — It is usual to associate the idea of overpowering enthusiasm or of intrepid fearlessness with the leaders of all new movements. But with the name of Cowper, one

of the earliest among the romantic poets, neither characteristic can be coupled.   He was one of the shyest and
most shrinking of men.   He had none of the aggressive
traits that make a reformer, and the thought of inaugura-
ting a revolt from the standard subjects of verse would
have frightened him into silence.   He was merely a child
of nature who passed his life among rural scenes and
wrote of what he knew best.

His life is a tale of almost continual sadness, caused by
his morbid timidity.   He was born at Great Berkhamp-

stead, Hertfordshire, in 1731. At the age of six, he lost his mother and was placed in a boarding school. Here his sufferings began. The child was so especially terrified by one rough boy that he could never raise his eyes to the bully's face, but knew him unmistakably by his shoe buckles.

There was some happiness for Cowper at his next school, the Westminster School, and also during the twelve succeeding years, when he studied law; but the short respite was followed by the gloom of madness. Owing to his ungovernable fear of a public examination, which was necessary to secure the position offered by an uncle, Cowper underwent days and nights of agony, when he tried in many ways to end his miserable life. The frightful ordeal unsettled his reason, and he spent eighteen months in an insane asylum.

Upon his recovery, he was taken into the house of a Rev. Mr. Unwin, whose wife tended Cowper as an own son during the rest of her life. He was never supremely happy, and he was sometimes again thrown into madness by the terrible thought of God's wrath, but his life was passed in a quiet manner in the villages of Weston and Olney, where he was loved by every one. The simple pursuits of gardening, carpentering, visiting the sick, caring for his numerous pets, rambling through the lanes, and studying nature, occupied his sane moments when he was not at prayer.

Works. — Cowper's first works were the *Olney Hymns*. His religious nature is manifest again in the volume which consists of didactic poems upon such subjects as *The Progress of Error*, *Truth*, *Charity*, *Table Talk*, and *Conversation*. These are in the spirit of the formal classical poets, and contain sententious couplets such as,

> "An idler is a watch that wants both hands,
>   As useless when it goes as when it stands."[1]

> "Vociferated logic kills me quite;
>   A noisy man is always in the right."[2]

The bare didacticism of these poems is softened and sweetened by the gentle, devout nature of the poet, and is enlivened by a vein of pure humor.

He is one of England's most delightful letter writers because of his humor, which ripples occasionally over the stream of his constitutional melancholy. *The Diverting History of John Gilpin* is extremely humorous. The poet seems to have forgotten himself in this ballad and to have given full expression to his sense of the ludicrous.

The work which has made his name famous is *The Task*. He gave it this title half humorously because his friend, Lady Austen, had bidden him write a poem in blank verse upon some subject or other, the sofa, for instance; and he called the first book of the poem *The Sofa*. *The Task* is chiefly remarkable because it turns from the artificial and conventional subjects which had been popular, and describes simple beauties of nature and the joys of country life. Cowper says:—

> "God made the country, and man made the town."

To a public acquainted with the nature poetry of Burns, Wordsworth, and Tennyson, Cowper's poem does not seem a wonderful production. Appearing as it did, however, during the ascendency of Pope's influence, when aristocratic city life was the only theme for verse, *The Task* is a strikingly original work. It marks a change from the artificial style of eighteenth century poetry and

[1] *Retirement.*   [2] *Conversation.*

proclaims the dawn of the natural style of the new school.
He who could write of

> " . . . rills that slip
> Through the cleft rock, and chiming as they fall
> Upon loose pebbles, lose themselves at length
> In matted grass, that with a livelier green
> Betrays the secret of their silent course,"

was a worthy forerunner of Shelley and Keats.

General Characteristics. — Cowper's religious fervor was
the strongest element in both his life and his writings.
Perhaps that which next appealed to his nature was
the pathetic. He had considerable mastery of pathos, as
may be seen in the drawing of "crazed Kate" in *The
Task*, in the lines *To Mary*, and in the touchingly beautiful
poem *On the Receipt of My Mother's Picture out of Nor-
folk*, beginning with that well-known line : —

> "Oh that those lips had language ! "

The two most attractive characteristics of his works are
refined, gentle humor and a simple and true manner of
picturing rural scenes and incidents. He says that he
described no spot which he had not seen, and expressed
no emotion which he had not felt. In this way, he re-
stricted the range of his subjects and displayed a somewhat literal mind, but, what he had seen and felt, he
touched with a light fancy and with considerable imaginative power.

ROBERT BURNS, 1759-1796

Life. — The greatest of Scottish poets was born in a
peasant's clay-built cottage, a mile and a half south of
Ayr. His father was a man whose morality, industry, and
zeal for education made him an admirable parent. For

a picture of the father and the home influences under which the boy was reared, *The Cotter's Saturday Night* should be read. The poet had little formal schooling, but under paternal influence he learned how to teach himself.

Until his twenty-eighth year, Robert Burns was an ordinary laborer on one or another of the Ayrshire tenant farms which his father or brothers leased. At the age of

BIRTHPLACE OF ROBERT BURNS

fifteen, the future poet was worked beyond his strength in doing a man's full labor. He called his life on the Ayrshire farms "the unceasing toil of a galley slave." All his life he fought a hand-to-hand fight with poverty.

In 1786, when he was twenty-seven years old, he resolved to abandon the struggle and seek a position in the far-off island of Jamaica.   In order to secure money for his passage, he published some poems which he had thought out while following the plow or resting after the day's toil. Six hundred copies were printed at three shillings each. All were sold in a little over a month. At the end of the nineteenth century a copy of this edition was sold in Edinburgh for £572. His fame from that little volume has grown as much as its monetary value.

Some Edinburgh critics praised the poems very highly and suggested a second edition. He abandoned the idea of going to Jamaica and went to Edinburgh to arrange for a new edition. Here he was entertained by the foremost men of the town, some of whom wished to see how a plowman would behave in polite society, while others desired to gaze on what they regarded as a freak of nature. The new volume appeared in 1787, and contained but few poems which had not been published the previous year. The following winter he again went to Edinburgh, but he was almost totally neglected by the leaders in literature and society.

In 1788 Burns married Jean Armour and took her to a farm which he leased in Dumfriesshire. The first part of this new period was the happiest in his life. She has been immortalized in his songs : —

> "I see her in the dewy flowers,
> I see her sweet and fair :
> I hear her in the tunefu' birds,
> I hear her charm the air :
> There's not a bonie flower that springs
> By fountain, shaw, or green ;
> There's not a bonie bird that sings,
> But minds me o' my Jean." [1]

This farm proved unprofitable. He appealed to influential persons for some position that would enable him to

[1] *I Love My Jean.*

Robert Burns

support his family and write poetry. This was an age of
pensions, but not a farthing of pension did he ever get.
He was made an exciseman or gauger, at a salary of £50
a year, and he followed that occupation for the few remaining years of his life.

Robert Burns wrote much and did much unworthy of
a great poet; but when Scotland thinks of him, she quotes
the lines which he wrote for *Tam Samson's Elegy:* —

· "Heav'n rest his saul, whare'er he be!
Is th' wish o' mony mae than me:

> He had twa faults, or maybe three,
> Yet what remead ?[1]
> Ae social, honest man want we."

Burns's Poetic Creed. — We can understand and enjoy Burns much better if we know his object in writing poetry and the point of view from which he regarded life. It would be hard to fancy the intensity of the shock which the school of Pope would have felt on reading this statement of the poor plowman's poetic creed : —

> "Give me ae spark o' Nature's fire,
> That's a' the learning I desire ;
> Then tho' I drudge thro' dub an' mire
> At pleugh or cart,
> My Muse, though hamely in attire,
> May touch the heart."[2]

Burns's heart had been touched with the loves and sorrows of life, and it was his ambition to sing so naturally of these as to touch the hearts of others.

With such an object in view, he did not disdain to use in his best productions much of the Scottish dialect, the vernacular of the plowman and the shepherd. The literary men of Edinburgh, who would rather have been convicted of a breach of etiquette than of a Scotticism, tried to induce him to write pure English, but the Scotch words which he first heard from his mother's lips seemed to possess more "o' Nature's fire." He ended by touching the heart of Scotland and making her feel more proud of this dialect, of him, and of herself.

Union of the Elizabethan with the Revolutionary Spirit. — In no respect does the poetry of Burns more completely part company with the productions of the classical school

----

[1] remedy.   [2] *Epistle to John Lapraik.*

than in the expression of feeling. The emotional fire of Elizabethan times was restored to literature. No other poet except Shakespeare has ever written more nobly impassioned love songs. Burns's song beginning : —

"Ae fond kiss and then we sever"

seemed to both Byron and Scott to contain the essence of a thousand love tales. This unaffected, passionate treatment of love had long been absent from our literature, but intensity of genuine feeling reappeared in Burns's *Highland Mary*, *I Love My Jean*, *Farewell to Nancy*, *To Mary in Heaven*, and *O Wert Thou in the Cauld Blast*, which last Mendelssohn thought exquisite enough to set to music. The poetry of Burns throbs with varying emotions. It has been well said that the essence of the lyric is to describe the passion of the moment. Burns is a master in this field.

The spirit of revolution against the bondage and cold formalism of the past made the poor man feel that his place in the world was as dignified, his happiness as important, as that of the rich. A feeling of sympathy for the oppressed and the helpless also reached beyond man to animals. Burns wrote touching lines about a mouse whose nest was, one cold November day, destroyed by his plow. When the wild eddying swirl of the snow beat around his cot, his heart went out to the poor sheep, cattle, and birds.

Burns can, therefore, claim kinship with the Elizabethans because of his love songs, which in depth of feeling and beauty of natural utterance show something of Shakespeare's magic. In addition to this, the poetry of Burns voices the democratic spirit of the Revolution.

Treatment of Nature. — In his verses, the autumn winds

blow over yellow corn; the fogs melt in limpid air; the birches extend their fragrant arms dressed in woodbine; the lovers are coming through the rye; the daisy spreads her snowy bosom to the sun; the "westlin" winds blow fragrant with dewy flowers and musical with the melody of birds; the brook flows past the lovers' Eden, where summer first unfolds her robes and tarries longest, because of the rarest bewitching enchantment of the poet's tale told there.

In his poetry those conventional birds, the lark and the nightingale, do not hold the chief place. His verses show that the source of his knowledge of birds is not to be sought in books. We catch glimpses of grouse cropping heather buds, of whirring flocks of partridges, of the sooty coot and the speckled teal, of the fisher herons, of the green-crested lapwing, of clamoring craiks among fields of flowering clover, of robins cheering the pensive autumn, of lintwhites chanting among the buds, of the mavis singing drowsy day to rest.

It is true that on the poetic stage of Burns, man always stands in the foreground. Nature is employed in order to give human emotion a proper background. He chose those aspects of nature which harmonized with his present mood, but the natural objects in his pages are none the less enjoyable for that reason. Sometimes his songs complain if nature seems gay when he is sad, but this contrast is employed to throw a stronger light on his woes.

General Characteristics. — It is said that the birthplace of Burns is visited each year by more people than go to see Shakespeare's House. What qualities has Burns sufficient to account for this?

The fact that the Scotch are an unusually patriotic people and make many pilgrimages to the land of Burns is only a partial answer to this question. The complete answer is to be found in a study of his characteristics. In the first place, with his "spark o' Nature's fire," he has touched the hearts of more of the rank and file of humanity than even Shakespeare himself. The songs of Burns minister in the simplest and most direct way to every one of the common feelings of the human heart. Shakespeare surpasses all others in painting universal human nature, but he is not always simple. Sometimes his audience consists of only the cultured few.

Especially enjoyable is the humor of Burns, which usually displays a kindly and intuitive sympathy with human weaknesses. *Tam o' Shanter*, his greatest poem, keeps the reader smiling or laughing from beginning to end. When the Scottish Muse proudly placed on his brow the holly wreath, she happily emphasized two of his conspicuous qualities, his love and mirth, when she said : —

> "I saw thee eye the gen'ral mirth
> With boundless love."[1]

Burns is one of the great masters of lyrical verse. He preferred that form. He wrote neither epic nor dramatic poetry. He excels in "short swallow flights of song."

There are not many ways in which a poet can keep larger audiences or come nearer to them than by writing verses which naturally lend themselves to daily song. There are few persons, from the peasant to the lord, who have not sung some of Burns's songs, such as *Auld Lang Syne*, *Coming through the Rye*, *John Anderson my Jo*, or *Scots Wha hae wi' Wallace Bled*. Since the day of his death, the audiences of Robert Burns have for these reasons continually grown larger.

---

[1] *The Vision.*

Walter Scott

SIR WALTER SCOTT, 1771-1832

Life. — Walter Scott, the son of a solicitor, was born in Edinburgh in 1771. He was such an invalid in childhood that he was allowed to follow his own bent without much attempt at formal education. He was taken to the country, where he acquired a lasting fondness for animals and wild scenery. With his first few shillings he bought the collection of early ballads and songs known as Percy's *Reliques of Ancient English Poetry*. Of this he says: "I do not believe I ever read a book half so frequently, or with half the enthusiasm." His grandmother used to delight him with tales of adventure on the Scottish border.

Later, Scott went to the Edinburgh High School and to the University. At the High School he showed wonderful genius for telling stories to the boys. "I made a brighter figure in the *yards* than in the *class*," he says of himself at this time. This early practice in relating tales and noting what held the attention of his classmates was excellent training for the future Wizard of the North.

After an apprenticeship to his father, the son was called to the bar and began the practice of law. He often left his office to travel over the Scottish counties in search of legendary ballads, songs, and traditions, a collection of which he published under the title of *Minstrelsy of the Scottish Border*. In 1799 he married a Miss Charlotte Carpenter, who had an income of £500 a year. He was shortly after appointed sheriff of Selkirkshire at an annual salary of £300, and he found himself able to neglect the law for literature. His early freedom from poverty is in striking contrast to the condition of his fellow-Scotsman, Robert Burns.

During the period between thirty and forty, he wrote his best poems. Not until he was nearly forty-three did he discover where his greatest powers lay. He then published *Waverley*, the first of a series of novels known by that general name. During the remaining eighteen years of his life, he wrote twenty-nine novels, besides many other works, such as the *Life of Napoleon*, in nine volumes, and an entertaining work on Scottish history, under the title of *Tales of a Grandfather*.

The crisis which showed Scott's sterling character came in the winter of 1825–1826, when an Edinburgh publishing firm in which he was interested failed and

left on his shoulders a debt of £117,000. Had he been
a man of less honor, he might have taken advantage of
the bankrupt law, and then his future earnings would
have been free from past claims. He refused to take any
step which would remove his obligation to pay the debt.
At the age of fifty-four, he abandoned his happy dream
of founding the house of Scott of Abbotsford and sat

ABBOTSFORD, HOME OF SIR WALTER SCOTT

down to pay off the debt with his pen. The example of
such a life is better than the finest sermon on honor.
He wrote with almost inconceivable rapidity. His novel
Woodstock, the product of three months' work, brought
£8228. In four years he paid £70,000 to his creditors.
One day the tears rolled down his cheeks because he
could no longer force his fingers to grasp the pen. The
King offered him a man of war in which to make a voyage

to the Mediterranean. Hoping to regain his health, Scott made the trip, but the rest came too late. He returned to Abbotsford in a sinking condition, and died in 1832, at the age of sixty-one.

Poetry. — Scott's three greatest poems are *The Lay of the Last Minstrel* (1805), *Marmion* (1808), and *The Lady of the Lake* (1810). They belong to the distinct class of story-telling poetry. Like many of the ballads in Percy's collection, these poems are stories of old feuds between the Highlander and the Lowlander, and between the border lords of England and Scotland. These romantic tales of heroic battles, thrilling incidents sometimes supernatural, and love adventures, are told in fresh, vigorous verse, which breathes the free air of wild nature and moves with the prance of a war horse. Outside of Homer, we can nowhere find a better description of a battle than in the sixth canto of *Marmion: A Tale of Flodden Field :* —

> "They close, in clouds of smoke and dust,
>   With sword sway and with lance's thrust ;
>   And such a yell was there,
>   Of sudden and portentous birth,
>   As if men fought upon the earth,
>   And fiends in upper air,
>   . . . .
>   And in the smoke the pennons flew,
>   As in the storm the white sea mew."

The Lady of the Lake, an extremely interesting story of romantic love and adventure, has been the most popular of Scott's poems. Loch Katrine and the Trossachs, where the scene of the opening cantos is laid, have since his day been thronged with tourists.

The most prominent characteristic of Scott's poetry is its energetic movement. Many schoolboys know by heart those dramatic lines which express Marmion's defiance of Douglas, and the ballad of *Lochinvar*, which is alive with the movements of tireless youth. These poems have an interesting story to tell, not of the thoughts, but of the deeds, of the characters. Scott is strangely free from nineteenth century introspection.

He delights in wild outdoor life and in observing nature. In his verses we find that his eye has rested lovingly on the gray birch, the mountain ash with its narrow leaves and red berries, the dew on the heath flower, and the speckled thrush singing a good morning to the water lily and to the green leaves just stirring from their breezeless sleep in the gray mist. He does not implant his emotions in nature, like Burns, or put there a nature spirit, like Wordsworth.

We feel that Scott lacks the penetration and the spirituality of Wordsworth. We can hardly imagine Scott saying with Wordsworth : —

> " To me the meanest flower that blows can give
> Thoughts that do often lie too deep for tears." [1]

Like Burns, Scott appeals to the simpler feelings, but Burns's plummet fathoms far deeper recesses of the human heart. Nevertheless, Scott's poems are specially well adapted to develop an appreciation for poetry that probes deeper into life. He holds the attention of the young at a time when a study of more philosophical poetry might awaken a lasting distaste for all verse.

Historical Fiction. — Scott began in verse his story telling, which he continued more effectively in prose. He stopped writing poetry not only because he saw that Byron was surpassing him in this field. Scott had also discov-

---

[1] *Ode on Intimations of Immortality.*

ered that his own great power lay in writing prose tales which no living competitor could equal. In 1814 he published *Waverley*, a story of the attempt of the Jacobite Pretender to recover the English throne in 1745. Seventeen of Scott's works of fiction are historical.

When the young wish a vivid picture of the time of Richard Cœur de Lion, of the knight and the castle, of the Saxon swineherd Gurth and of the Norman master who ate the pork, they may read *Ivanhoe*. If one desires some reading which will make the Crusaders live again, one finds it in the pages of *The Talisman*. When we wish an entertaining story of the brilliant days of Elizabeth, we turn to *Kenilworth*. If we are moved by admiration for the Scotch Convenanters to seek a story of their times, we have Scott's finest historical tale, *Old Mortality*. Shortly after this story appeared, Lord Holland was asked his opinion of it. "Opinion!" he exclaimed; "we did not one of us go to bed last night — nothing slept but my gout." The man who could thus charm his readers was called the Wizard of the North.

Scott is the creator of the historical novel, which has advanced on the general lines marked out by him. Carlyle tersely says: "These historical novels have taught all men this truth, which looks like a truism, and yet was as good as unknown to writers of history and others till so taught : that the by-gone ages of the world were actually filled by living men, not by protocols, state papers, controversies, and abstractions of men."

The history in Scott's novels is not always absolutely accurate. To meet the exigencies of his plot, he sometimes takes liberties with the events of history, and there are occasional anachronisms in his work. Readers may rest assured, however, that the most prominent strokes of his brush will convey a sufficiently accurate idea of certain phases of history. Although the hair lines in his pictures may be neglected, most persons can learn more truth from studying his gallery of historic scenes than from poring over volumes of documents and state papers. Scott does not look at life from every point of view. The reader of *Ivanhoe*, for instance, should be cautioned against thinking that Scott presents a complete picture of the Middle Ages. He shows the bright, the noble side of chivalry, but not all the brutality, ignorance, and misery of the times.

Novels which are not Historical.—Twelve of Scott's novels contain but few attempts to represent historic events. The greatest of these novels are *Guy Mannering*, *The Heart of Midlothian*, *The Antiquary*, and *The Bride of Lammermoor*.

Scott said that his most rapid work was his best. The finest product of his pen, *Guy Mannering*, was written in six weeks. It is an admirable picture of Scottish life and manners. Many of its characters, like Dominie Sampson, the pedagogue, Meg Merrilies, the gypsy, and Dick Hatteraick, the smuggler, have more life than half the people we meet.

A century before, Pope said that most women had no characters at all. His writings tend to show that this was his real conviction, as it was that of many others during the time when Shakespeare was little read. *The Heart of Midlothian* presents in Jeanie Deans a woman whose character and feminine qualities have won the admiration of the world. Scott could not paint women in the higher walks of life. He was so chivalrous that he was prone to make such women too perfect, but his humble Scotch lass Jeanie Deans is one of his greatest creations.

When we note the vast number of characters drawn by his pen, we are astonished to find that he repeats so little.

Many novelists write only one original novel.   Their succeeding works are merely repetitions of the first.   The
hero may have put on a new suit of clothes and the
heroine may wear a new style of bonnet, or each may be
given a new mannerism, or a peculiar form of expression,
but there is nothing really new in character or in incident.
For year after year, Scott wrote with wonderful rapidity,
without repeating his characters or his plots.

General Characteristics. — All critics are impressed with
the healthiness of Scott's work, with its freedom from what
is morbid or debasing.   His stories display marked energy
and movement.   There is little subtle analysis of feelings
and motives.   He aimed at broad and striking effects.
We do not find much development of character in his
pages.   "His characters have the brilliance and the fixity
of portraits."

Scott does not particularly care to delineate the intense
passion of love.   Only one of his novels, *The Bride of
Lammermoor*, is aflame with this overmastering emotion.
He delights in adventure.   He places his characters in
unusual and dangerous situations, and he has succeeded in
making us feel his own interest in the outcome.   He has
on a larger scale many of the qualities which we may note
in the American novelist Cooper, whose best stories are
tales of adventure in the forest or on the sea.   Like him,
Scott shows lack of care in the construction of sentences.
Few of the most cultured people of to-day could, however,
write at Scott's breakneck speed and make as few slips.
Scott has far more humor and variety than Cooper.

Scott's romanticism is seen in his love for supernatural
agencies, which figure in many of his stories.   His fondness for adventure, for mystery, for the rush of battle, for
color and sharp contrast, and his love for the past are also

romantic traits. He, however, sometimes falls into the classical fault of over-description and of leaving too little to the imagination.

In the variety of his creations, he is surpassed by no other novelist. He did more than any other pioneer to aid fiction in dethroning the drama. His influence can be seen in the historical novels of almost every nation.

JANE AUSTEN, 1775-1817

Life and Works. — While Sir Walter Scott was laying the foundations of his large family estates and recounting the story of battles, chivalry, royalty, and brigandage, a quiet, sunny little woman, almost unmindful of the great world, was enlivening her father's parsonage and writing about the clergy, the old maids, the short-sighted mothers, the marriageable daughters, and other people that figure in village life. This cheery, sprightly young woman, whom her acquaintances never once suspected of the guilt of authorship, was Jane Austen, a daughter of the rector of Steventon, Hampshire.

The life of Jane Austen was simple, wholesome, unpretending, and happy. She possessed both wit and beauty, and was ready to enjoy any festivities which her small world afforded. She was clever in turning out tales for her nephews and nieces and quick to seize upon the leading points in character. She studied carefully the folk about her, and she was one of the first of novelists to chronicle the lives of homely, commonplace people.

Pride and Prejudice is generally considered her best novel, though *Sense and Sensibility*, *Emma*, and *Mansfield Park* all have their ardent admirers. The scenes of these stories are laid in small English towns, with which

J. Austen

the author was thoroughly familiar, and the characters are taken from the middle class and the gentry.

There are no startling discoveries and mysterious secrets in her works. Simple domestic episodes and ordinary people, living somewhat monotonous and narrow lives, satisfy her, and she exhibits wonderful skill in fashioning these into slight but entertaining narratives. In *Pride and Prejudice*, for example, she creates some refreshing situations by opposing Philip Darcy's pride to Elizabeth Bennet's prejudice, and manages the long-delayed reconciliation between these two lovers with a tact which shows true genius and a knowledge of the human heart.

A strong feature of Jane Austen's novels is her subtle, careful manner of drawing character. She perceives with an intuitive refinement the delicate shadings of emotion, and describes them with the utmost care and detail. Her heroines are especially fine, each one having an interesting individuality, thoroughly natural and womanly. The minor characters in Miss Austen's works are usually quaint and original. She sees the oddities and foibles of people with the insight of the true humorist, and paints them with most dexterous cunning.

Walter Scott sums up Jane Austen's chief characteristics when he says in his big-hearted way: "That young lady has a talent for describing the involvements of feelings and characters of ordinary life, which is to me the most wonderful I ever met with. The big bow-wow strain I can do myself, like any one going; but the exquisite touch which renders ordinary commonplace things and characters interesting from the truth of the description and the sentiment is denied to me. What a pity such a gifted creature died so early!"

WILLIAM WORDSWORTH, 1770-1850

Early Education. — William Wordsworth was born in Cockermouth, Cumberland, in 1770. He came from a North of England family, sound and healthy in its moral tone, and vigorous physically. Losing his parents early in life, he was left to the care of uncles who discharged their trust in a praiseworthy manner.

He went to school in his ninth year at Hawkshead, a village on the banks of Esthwaite Water. These school

Wm Wordsworth

days were happy ones.   He boarded in the village with a
kindly old dame, whom he has fondly described in his
Prelude, and, out of school hours, he was free from the
supervision of tutors.   He writes: "I was left at liberty
then, and in the vacation, to read whatever books I liked."
He was free also to go about as he pleased, and he
roamed early and late over the mountains.

The healthy out of door life hardened the fibers of his
sturdy frame and kept him vigorous, and the constant
sight of nature in the wondrous beauty of the Lake
District awoke love and reverence in him.   He enjoyed

the sports of hunting, skating, and rowing, but he says, in the *Prelude:* —

> "Not seldom from the uproar I retired
> Into a silent bay, or sportively
> Glanced sideway, leaving the tumultuous throng,
> To cut across the reflex of a star
> That fled, and, flying still before me, gleamed
> Upon the glassy plain."

At such a moment, almost as a revelation to his throbbing heart, the

> ". . . common face of nature spake to him
> Rememberable things."

He says that in one of these moments of solitude

> ". . . the calm
> And dead still water lay upon my mind
> Even with a weight of pleasure, and the sky,
> Never before so beautiful, sank down
> Into my heart, and held me like a dream."

Little by little, the glories of Nature grew upon him, until his soul seemed flooded with unutterable delight when in her presence. This profound passion was fostered by his life in these early years, and grew steadily with his youth. At seventeen, he went to Cambridge and, for a time, was dazzled by the intercourse with town-bred men, but the infatuation was of short duration, and his four years at college were the least congenial of his life.

Influence of the French Revolution. — His travels on the continent in his last vacation and after his graduation brought him in contact with the French Revolution, and he came under its spell, as did most of the young, enthusiastic men of the time. His hopes were stirred and his imagination fired with dreams of an ideal republic, which he fancied would arise from the Revolution. He says: —

> " I gradually withdrew
> Into a noisier world, and thus ere long
> Became a patriot ; and my heart was all
> Given to the people, and my love was theirs." [1]

He was prepared to throw himself personally into the struggle, when his relatives recalled him to England to face the ugly specter of poverty. The rude shock came too suddenly upon his ardent aspirations, and, following closely upon it, came the failure of the revolutionists, the period of anarchy and imperialism in France. He sank into a dejection as deep as his hopes had been high, and, as he slowly recovered from his disappointment, he became more and more conservative in his politics, and less in sympathy with any violent reactions. For this he was censured by Byron, Shelley, and other strong adherents of liberty, but such moderation was more natural to Wordsworth than the excitement of his early years. To the end of his days, he never failed to utter for genuine liberty a hopeful, though calm and tempered note.

Maturity and Declining Years. — He returned from France in 1792. In 1795 a bequest of £900 relieved the financial strain which had caused him anxiety, and secured for him and his sister Dorothy a modest maintenance. They went back to the Lake District, in which, save for an occasional tour, they passed the rest of their lives. The two places most associated with the poet are Grasmere, where he wrote the best of his poetry between the years 1798 and 1808, and Rydal Mount, where he lived in his later years. Dorothy was his lifelong companion. She won him back from his hopelessness over the Revolution and urged upon him the duty of devoting himself to poetry. Their favorite pastime was walking.

---

[1] *The Prelude*, Book IX.

De Quincey estimates that Wordsworth, during the course of his life, must have walked as many as 175,000 miles.

WORDSWORTH'S HOME AT GRASMERE — DOVE COTTAGE

In 1802 Wordsworth married Mary Hutchinson. With her income, the payment of a debt with its long accruing interest, and the salary from the office of Distributor of Stamps for the counties of Cumberland and Westmoreland, Wordsworth was insured against annoyance from debt, and given the leisure to devote his whole time to the production of poetry.

This peaceful, retired life, away from the passionate contests of men in crowded towns, prevented Wordsworth from gaining an accurate knowledge of his fellowmen. His absorbing concentration of mind upon poetry made him self-centered, and caused him to disparage all views and ideals of life which differed from his own. His temper remained "stiff," but his earnestness and purity of life made him, as his mother had prophesied, "remarkable for good."

His poetry was too far removed from the formal classical style to be at once popular with the public. The critics ridiculed him harshly. He lived, however, to see his work appreciated and to be rewarded with the laureateship by the nation. He died six years later, in 1850, and was buried in the Grasmere churchyard.

A Poet of Nature. — Wordsworth is one of the world's most loving, penetrative, and thoughtful poets of Nature. He found much of his greatest joy in the presence of her calm, her beauty, her external revelations of a divine hand. For him, Nature possessed a soul, a conscious existence, an ability to feel joy and love. In these *Lines Written in Early Spring*, he expresses his faith in her power to be happy : —

> " And 'tis my faith that every flower
> Enjoys the air it breathes."

Again, he says in *The Leech-Gatherer* : —

> " All things that love the sun are out of doors ;
> The sky rejoices in the morning's birth."

The *Intimations of Immortality* also incorporates this belief in the conscious soul of nature : —

> " The moon doth with delight
> Look round her when the heavens are bare."

This manner of investing nature with sentiency is peculiarly characteristic of Wordsworth. He was not content to experience only that childlike joy which satisfied Cowper and Burns, or, like Keats and Tennyson, to

paint only the external features of nature. With rare
skill Wordsworth looked beyond the color of the flower,
the outline of the hills, the beauty of the clouds, to the
spirit which breathed through them, and he communed
with "Nature's self which is the breath of God." Nature,
therefore, did more than please his senses; she appealed
to his heart; she aroused his noblest feelings and filled
him with a worship that was a part of his religion.

In his close study of her secrets, he learned her outward
appearances, and he wrote some beautiful descriptions,
such as the following upon a dandelion seed : —

> "Suddenly halting now, a lifeless stand!
> And starting off again with freak as sudden;
> In all its sportive wanderings, all the while
> Making report of an invisible breeze,
> That was its wings, its chariot, and its horse,
> Its very playmate and its moving soul."

But Wordsworth is not preëminently the purely descriptive poet, as Tennyson is. Wordsworth was too much
engrossed with the feeling inspired by the scene, and
with its imaginative interpretation, to attend strictly to
sketching the outlines. Note these lines from one of his
sonnets : —

> "The gentleness of Heaven is on the sea:
> Listen! the mighty Being is awake
> And doth with his eternal motion make
> A sound like thunder — everlastingly." [1]

There is not here a vivid picture of the sea, such as
Tennyson would have given, but there is the impression,
the feeling, the thought inspired in an imaginative mind
by the sea. Wordsworth is unrivaled in his capacity to

[1] *Sonnet :* "It is a beauteous evening, calm and free."

present the inherent atmosphere and spirit of a scene. In the lines

> "With heart as calm as lakes that sleep,
>   In frosty moonlight glistening;
>   Or mountain rivers, where they creep
>   Along a channel smooth and deep,
>   To their own far-off murmurs listening," [1]

he suggests the very soul of solitude. Nothing else could have done this so ideally as the streams that hear no sound but the echo of their own lonely murmurings. It is in this contemplative and imaginative interpretation of nature that Wordsworth is a master poet.

Narrative Poems: Poetry of Man. — Wordsworth is a poet of man as well as of nature. The love for nature came to him first, but out of it grew his regard for the people who lived near to nature.

He traces the growth of these feelings in *The Prelude* (1850), an autobiographical poem, unrivaled in its class. Wordsworth also tells in this poem how the French Revolution roused him to the worth of each individual soul and to a sense of the equality of all humanity at the bar of character and conscience. As his lyrics show the sympathy which he had for the outside world, so his narrative poems illustrate the second dominant characteristic of the age, the strong sense of the brotherhood of man.

Michael, one of the very greatest of his productions, displays a tender and living sympathy with the humble shepherd. The simple dignity of Michael's character, his frugal and honorable life, his affection for his son, for his sheep, and for his forefathers' old home, appealed to the heart of the poet. He loved his subject and wrote the poem with that indescribable simplicity which makes

---

[1] *Memory.*

the tale, the verse, and the tone of thought and feeling form together one perfect and indissoluble whole. *The Leech-Gatherer* and the story of "Margaret" in the *Excursion* also deal with lowly characters and exhibit Wordsworth's power of pathos and simple earnestness. He could not present complex personalities, but these characters, which belonged to the landscapes of the Lake District and partook of its calm and its simplicity, he drew with a sure hand.

His longest narrative poem is the *Excursion* (1814), which is in nine books. It contains fine passages of verse and some of his sanest and maturest philosophy, but the work is not the masterpiece which he hoped to make. It is tedious, prosy, and without action of any kind. The style is heavy, for the most part, and becomes pure and easy only in some description of a mountain peak or in the recital of a tale, like that of "Margaret."

General Characteristics. — "Meditation and sympathy, not action and passion, were the two main strings of his serene and stormless lyre. On these no hand ever held more gentle yet sovereign rule than Wordsworth's," says Swinburne. Wordsworth possessed no dramatic power, no ability to enter into another's personality. His genius was introspective. Moreover, he seemed a stranger to tempestuous passions and fierce burning love. His nature was strong, restrained, and calm. The joys of nature, the elemental emotions of humanity, and the necessity of obeying the moral law, are his subjects. This last subject is treated with wonderful elevation of language in his *Ode to Duty* and *Character of the Happy Warrior*.

Wordsworth's compass is limited, but within that compass he is surpassed by no poet since Milton. On the other hand, no great poet ever wrote more that is worthless.   Matthew Arnold did much for Wordsworth's renown by collecting his priceless poems and publishing them apart from the mediocre work.   Among the fine productions, his sonnets occupy a high place.   Only Shakespeare and Milton in our language excel him in this form of verse.

The most pronounced characteristic of Wordsworth's style is its austere simplicity.   When he was most truly great, he seemed to write as he breathed, not only naturally but involuntarily.   He was unconscious of the power which he wielded.   When he attempted to command it at will, he failed, as in the dull, lifeless lines of the *Excursion*.   On the contrary, of such a work as *Michael*, *The Solitary Reaper*, or *The Fountain*, we may say with Matthew Arnold: "It might seem that Nature not only gave him the matter for his poem, but wrote his poem for him."

We may take this line from Wordsworth : —

"This Sea that bares her bosom to the moon,"[1]

and compare it with Tennyson's line in *The Princess :* —

"A full sea glazed with muffled moonlight."

Tennyson's is harmonious and the imagery is exceptionally true and beautiful, but the line seems to have been elaborated and polished in the study, while Wordsworth's artless figure has the breath of inspiration about it.   An excellent craftsman might have produced Tennyson's line, but only a genius could have displayed Wordsworth's frequent natural directness and ease.   He ranks among the greatest poets of English literature ; only the very mightiest tower above him.   If Shakespeare occupies the first place, Milton the next, and Chaucer the third, Wordsworth is entitled to follow closely after them.

[1] *Sonnet:* "The World is too much with us."

S. T. Coleridge

SAMUEL TAYLOR COLERIDGE, 1772–1834

Life. — The troubled career of Coleridge is in striking contrast to the peaceful life of Wordsworth. Coleridge, the thirteenth child of a clergyman, was born in the year 1772, in Ottery St. Mary, Devonshire. Early in his life, the future poet became a dreamer. Before he was five years old, he had read the *Arabian Nights*. A few years later, the boy's appetite for books was so voracious that he is said to have devoured an average of two volumes a day. So omnivorous was his reading and so broad the fields which his studies finally covered, that a recent biographer is led to say that Coleridge's education "outstrides the intellectual equipment of every Englishman since Bacon." In this opinion contemporaries concurred.

Coleridge went to Cambridge, but he did not remain to graduate. From this time he seldom completed anything that he undertook. It was characteristic of him, stimulated by the spirit of the French Revolution, to dream of founding with Southey a Pantisocracy on the banks of the Susquehanna. In this ideal village across the sea, the dreamers were to work only two hours a day and to have all goods in common. The demand for poetry was at this time sufficiently great for a bookseller to offer Coleridge, although he was as yet comparatively unknown, thirty guineas for a volume of poems and a guinea and a half for each hundred lines after finishing that volume. With such wealth in view, Coleridge married a Miss Fricker of Bristol, because no single people could join the new ideal commonwealth. Southey married her sister, but the young enthusiasts were forced to abandon the project because they did not have sufficient money to procure passage across the ocean.

But the tendency to dream never forsook Coleridge. One of his favorite poems begins with this line : —

"My eyes make pictures when they are shut." [1]

He recognized his disinclination to remain long at work on prearranged lines, when he said : "I think that my soul must have preëxisted in the body of a chamois chaser."

In 1797–1798 Coleridge lived with his young wife at Nether-Stowey in Somerset. Wordsworth and his sister Dorothy moved to a house in the neighborhood in order to

[1] *A Day-Dream.*

be near Coleridge. The two young men and Dorothy Wordsworth seemed to be exactly fitted to stimulate one another. Together they roamed over the Quantock Hills, gazed upon the sea, and planned *The Rime of the Ancient Mariner,* which is one of the few things that Coleridge ever finished. In not much more than a year he wrote nearly all the poetry which has made him famous. Had he died when he was twenty-five, like Keats, the world would probably be won-

COLERIDGE'S COTTAGE AT NETHER-STOWEY

dering what heights of poetic fame Coleridge might have reached. He became addicted to the use of opium and passed a wretched existence of thirty-six years longer, partly in the Lake District, but chiefly in London, without adding to his poetic fame. During his later years in London, he did hack work for papers, gave occasional lectures, wrote critical and philosophical prose, and became a talker almost as noted as Dr. Johnson.

Poetry. — *The Ancient Mariner* (1798) is Coleridge's poetical masterpiece. It is also one of the world's master-pieces. The supernatural sphere into which it introduces the reader is a remarkable creation, with its curse, its polar spirit, the phantom ship, the seraph band, and the magic breeze. The mechanism of the poem is almost flawless. The meter, the rhythm, and the music are superb. Almost every stanza shows not only exquisite harmony, but also the easy mastery of genius in dealing with those weird scenes which romanticists love. This poem should by all means be read entire by the student.

His next greatest poem is the unfinished *Christabel*, which in parts surpasses *The Ancient Mariner*. The lovely maiden Christabel falls under the enchantments of a mysterious Lady Geraldine : —

> " And Geraldine in maiden wise,
>   Casting down her large bright eyes,
>   With blushing cheek and courtesy fine
>   She turn'd her from Sir Leoline ;
>   . . . .
>   And looked askance at Christabel —
>   Jesu, Maria, shield her well !
>   A snake's small eye blinks dull and shy,
>   And the lady's eyes they shrunk in her head,
>   Each shrunk up to a serpent's eye."

too little

Even so did Coleridge's poetical powers shrink up in what should have been his prime.

The fragment ends with Christabel under the spell of Geraldine's enchantments. We miss the interest of a finished story, which draws so many readers to *The Ancient Mariner*, but *Christabel* is thickly sown with gems. Lines like these are filled with the airiness of nature : —

> " There is not wind enough to twirl
>   The one red leaf, the last of its clan,
>   That dances as often as dance it can,
>   Hanging so light, and hanging so high,
>   On the topmost twig that looks up at the sky."

In all literature there has been no finer passage written on the wounds caused by broken friendship than the lines in *Christabel* relating to the estrangement of Roland and Sir

Leoline. After reading this poem and *Kubla Khan*, an unfinished dream fragment of fifty-four lines, we feel that the closing lines of *Kubla Khan* are peculiarly applicable to Coleridge : —

> " For he on honey dew hath fed
> And drunk the milk of Paradise."

Swinburne says of *Christabel* and *Kubla Khan :* " When it has been said that such melodies were never heard, such dreams never dreamed, such speech never spoken, the chief things remain unsaid, unspeakable. There is a charm upon these poems which can only be felt in silent submission and wonder."

General Characteristics of his Poetry. — Unlike Wordsworth, Coleridge is not the poet of the earth and the common things of life. He is the poet of air, of the regions beyond the earth, and of dreams. The supernatural has never been invested with more charm.

He has rare feeling for the beautiful, whether in the world of morals, or of nature, or of the harmonies of sound. The motherless Christabel in her time of danger dreams a beautiful truth of this divinely governed world : —

> " But this she knows, in joys and woes,
> That saints will aid if men will call :
> For the blue sky bends over all."

Coleridge throws his whole soul into the beautiful picture of friendship, painted on the living canvas of *Christabel*.

His nature poetry is less remarkable for photographic details than for its suggestiveness. Note this picture of a dell : —

> "A green and silent spot, amid the hills,
> A small and silent dell ! O'er stiller place,
> No singing skylark ever poised himself." [1]

[1] *Fears in Solitude.*

The details of this picture must be filled in by imagination.
He invests natural objects with bewitching color, and, in
the lines following this quotation, he proceeds to clothe the
dell in a soft green light like that from the setting sun
shining through vernal cornfields.   He revels in the grace
and beauty of coloring of even the water snakes : —

> " Blue, glossy green, and velvet black,
>   They coiled and swam ; and every track
>   Was a flash of golden fire." [1]

His melody is best described in his lines from *The Eolian
Harp :* —

> " Such a soft floating witchery of sound,
>   As twilight Elfins make, when they at eve
>   Voyage on gentle gales from Fairy Land."

Prose. — Coleridge's prose, which is almost all of the
philosophic type, left its influence on the work of the
younger generation.   He was an idealist and a student of
the German metaphysicians, whose idealistic teachings he
introduced to combat the utilitarian and sense-bound philosophy of Bentham, Malthus, and Mill.   We pass by
Coleridge's *Aids to Reflection* (1825), the weightiest of his
metaphysical works, to consider those works which possess
a more vital interest for the student of literature.

Coleridge's great work on criticism is entitled *Biographia
Literaria* (2 vols., 1817).   J. C. Shairp, late Professor of
Poetry at Oxford, used to say to his students : " There is
more to be learned about poetry from a few pages of that
dissertation, confined though it is to a specific kind of poetry, than from all the reviews that have been written in
English on poets and their works from Addison to the
present hour. . . .   These principles, few or none at that

[1] *The Ancient Mariner.*

time acknowledged, but they have since won the assent of all competent judges." Coleridge's general point of view is that of the romantic Wordsworthian school, but he does not hold Wordsworth's belief that the language of poetry and of common speech should be identical, and he protests against not a little of Wordsworth's poetical practice. The work abounds in statements as suggestive and as stimulating as these : —

"Not the poem which we have read, but that to which we return with the greatest pleasure, possesses the genuine power and claims the name of essential poetry. . . . Our genuine admiration of a great poet is a continuous undercurrent of feeling; it is everywhere present, but seldom anywhere as a separate excitement. . . . For poetry is the blossom and the fragrancy of all human knowledge, human thoughts, human passions, emotions, language."

His *Lectures and Notes on Shakespeare* was an epoch-making work in the criticism of that dramatist. Professor Shairp says: "Coleridge was the first who clearly saw through and boldly denounced the nonsense that had been talked about Shakespeare's irregularity and extravagance. . . . Any one who shall master these notes on Shakespeare, taken as a whole, will find in them more fine analysis of the hidden things of the heart, more truthful insight into the workings of passion, than are to be found in whole treatises of psychology."

One of Coleridge's finest prose sentences, filled with the romantic appreciation of the living forms of nature, may be found in the marginal notes to *The Ancient Mariner* : —

"In his loneliness and fixedness he yearneth towards the journeying Moon, and the stars that still sojourn, yet still move onward; and everywhere the blue sky belongs to them, and is their appointed rest, and their native country, and their own natural homes, which they enter unannounced, as lords that are certainly expected, and yet there is a silent joy at their arrival."

GEORGE NOEL GORDON, LORD BYRON, 1788-1824

Life. — Byron was born in London in 1788. His father
was a reckless, dissipated spendthrift, who deserted his
wife and child.   Mrs. Byron convulsively clasped her son
to her one moment and threw the scissors and tongs at
him the next, calling him "the lame brat," in reference to
his club foot.   Such treatment drew neither respect nor
obedience from Byron, who inherited the proud, defiant
spirit of his race.   His accession to the peerage in 1798

did not tend to tame his haughty nature, and he grew up passionately imperious and combative.

He was ambitious, and he made excellent progress in his studies at Harrow, but when he entered Cambridge he devoted much of his time to shooting, swimming, and other sports, for which he was always famous. In 1809 he started on a two years' trip through Spain, Greece, and the far East. Upon his return, he published two cantos of *Childe Harold's Pilgrimage*, which describe his journey.

This poem made him immediately popular. London society neglected its old favorite, Scott, and eagerly sought out the beautiful young peer who had burst suddenly upon it. Poem after poem was produced by this lion of society, and each one was received with enthusiasm and delight. Probably no other English poet knew such instant widespread fame as Byron.

Suddenly and unexpectedly this adulation turned to hatred. In 1815 Byron married Miss Milbanke, an heiress, and she left him a year later. No reason for the separation was given, but the public fastened all the blame upon Byron. The feeling against him grew so strong that he was warned by his friends to prepare for open violence, and finally, in 1816, he left England forever.

His remaining eight years were spent mostly in Italy. Here, his great beauty, his exile, his poetry, and his passionate love of liberty made him a prominent figure throughout Europe. Notwithstanding this fame, life was a disappointment to Byron. Baffled but defiant, he threw himself for a time into a vortex of dissolute, licentious living, and enjoyed the shock it gave to his countrymen.

The closing year of his life shone the brightest of all. His main activities had hitherto been directed to the selfish pursuit of his own pleasure, and he had failed to obtain

happiness.   The Greeks were battling with Turkey for
their independence, and in 1823 Byron went to Greece to
aid them.   He poured his whole energies into this struggle
for freedom, and he displayed "a wonderful aptitude for
managing the complicated intrigues and plans and selfish-

NEWSTEAD ABBEY, BYRON'S HOME

nesses which lay in the way."   His efforts cost him his
life.   He contracted fever, and, after restlessly battling
with the disease, he said quietly, one April morning in
1824: "Now I shall go to sleep."   The proud, imperious
spirit awoke no more to dash itself against the cage of life.
He was buried in the family vault at Hucknall, Notting-
hamshire, not far from Newstead Abbey.

Early Works. — The poems which Byron wrote during his brilliant sojourn in London, amid the whirl of social gayeties, are *The Giaour, The Bride of Abydos, The Corsair, Parisina, Lara*, and *The Siege of Corinth*. These narrative poems are romantic tales of oriental passion and coloring which show the influence of Scott. They are told with a dash and a fine-sounding rhetoric well fitted to attract immediate attention; but they lack the qualities of sincere feeling, lofty thought, and subtle beauty, which give lasting fame.

His next publication, *The Prisoner of Chillon* (1816), is a much worthier poem. The pathetic story is feelingly told in language which often displays remarkable energy and mastery of expression and versification. His picture of the oppressive vacancy which the Prisoner felt is a well-executed piece of very difficult word painting : —

> "There were no stars — no earth — no time —
> No check — no change — no good — no crime —
> But silence, and a stirless breath
> Which neither was of life or death ;
> A sea of stagnant idleness,
> Blind, boundless, mute, and motionless!"

Dramas. — Byron wrote a number of dramas, the best of which are *Manfred* (1817) and *Cain* (1821). His spirit of defiance and his insatiable thirst for power are the subjects of these dramas. Manfred is a man of guilt who is at war with humanity, and who seeks refuge on the mountain tops and by the wild cataract. He is fearless and untamed in all his misery, and even in the hour of death does not quail before the spirits of darkness, but defies them with the cry : —

> "Back to thy hell!
> Thou hast no power upon me, *that* I feel!
> Thou never shalt possess me, *that* I know :

> What I have done is done; I bear within
> A torture which could nothing gain from thine:
> .   .   .   .
>   Back, ye baffled fiends !
> The hand of death is on me — but not yours ! "

Cain, while suffering remorse for the slaying of Abel, is borne by Lucifer through the boundless fields of the universe. Cain yet dares to question the wisdom of the Almighty in bringing evil, sin, and remorse into the world. A critic has remarked that " Milton wrote his great poem to justify the ways of God to man ; Byron's object seems to be to justify the ways of man to God."

The very soul of stormy revolt breathes through both *Manfred* and *Cain*, but *Cain* has more interest as a pure drama. It contains some sweet passages and presents one lovely woman, — Adah. But Byron could not interpret a character wholly at variance with his own. He possessed but little constructive skill, and he never overcame the difficulties of blank verse. A drama that does not show wide sympathy with varied types of humanity, and the constructive capacity to present the complexities of life, is lacking in essential elements of greatness.

Childe Harold, The Vision of Judgment, and Don Juan. — His best works are the later poems which require only a slight framework or plot, such as *Childe Harold's Pilgrimage*, *The Vision of Judgment*, and *Don Juan*.

The third and fourth cantos of *Childe Harold*, published in 1816 and 1818, respectively, are far superior to the first two. These later cantos continue the travels of Harold, and contain some of Byron's most splendid descriptions of nature, cities, and works of art. Rome, Venice, the Rhine, the Alps, and the sea inspired the finest lines. He wrote of Venice as she

" .   sate in state, throned on her hundred isles!
She looks a sea Cybele, fresh from ocean,
Rising with her tiara of proud towers
At airy distance."

He calls Rome

" The Niobe of nations! there she stands,
Childless and crownless, in her voiceless woe;
An empty urn within her wither'd hands,
Whose holy dust was scattered long ago."

The following description of a wild stormy night in the
mountains is very characteristic of his nature poetry and
of his own individuality : —

" And this is in the night : — Most glorious night!
Thou wert not sent for slumber! let me be
A sharer in thy fierce and far delight —
A portion of the tempest and of thee!
How the lit lake shines, a phosphoric sea,
And the big rain comes dancing to the earth!
And now again 'tis black, — and now, the glee
Of the loud hills shakes with its mountain-mirth
As if they did rejoice o'er a young earthquake's birth."

When George III. died, Southey wrote a poem filled
with absurd flattery of that monarch. Byron had such
intense hatred for the hypocrisy of society that he wrote
his *Vision of Judgment* (1822), to parody Southey's poem
and to make the author the object of satire. Pungent wit,
vituperation, and irony were here handled by Byron in a
brilliant manner, which had not been equaled since the
days of Dryden and Pope. The parodies of most poems
are quickly forgotten, but we have here the strange case
of Byron's parody keeping alive Southey's original.

Don Juan (1819–1824), a long poem in sixteen cantos, is
Byron's greatest work. It is partly autobiographic. The

sinister, gloomy Don Juan is an ideal picture of the author, who was sore and bitter over his thwarted hopes of liberty and happiness. Therefore, instead of strengthening humanity with hope for the future, this poem tears hope from the horizon, and suggests the possible anarchy and destruction toward which the world's hypocrisy, cant, tyranny, and universal stupidity are tending.

The poem is unfinished. Byron followed Don Juan through all the phases of life known to himself. The hero has exciting adventures and passionate loves, he is favored at courts, he is driven to the lowest depths of society, he experiences a godlike happiness and demoniacal despair.

Don Juan is a scathing satire upon society. All its fondest idols, love, faith, and hope, are dragged in the mire. There is something almost grand in the way that this titanic scoffer draws pictures of love only to mock at them, sings patriotic songs only to add : —

> " Thus sung, or would, or could, or should have sung
> The modern Greek in tolerable verse,"

and mentions Homer, Milton, and Shakespeare only to show how accidental and worthless fame is.

Amid the splendid confusion of pathos, irony, passion, mockery, keen wit, and brilliant epigram, which display Byron's versatile and spontaneous genius at its height, there are some beautiful and powerful passages. There is an ideal picture of the love of Don Juan and Haidee : —

> " Each was the other's mirror, and but read
> Joy sparkling in their dark eyes like a gem."

> " . . . they could not be
> Meant to grow old, but die in happy spring,
> Before one charm or hope had taken wing."

As she lightly slept, —

> " . . . her face so fair
> Stirr'd with her dream, as rose-leaves with the air ;
> Or as the stirring of a deep clear stream
> Within an Alpine hollow, when the wind
> Walks o'er it."

General Characteristics. — The poetry of Wordsworth and Coleridge shows the revolutionary reaction against classicism in literature and tyranny in government, but their verse raises no cry of revolt against the proprieties and moral restrictions of the time. Byron was so saturated with the revolutionary spirit that he rebelled against these also, and for this reason England would not allow him to be buried in Westminster Abbey.

Byron frequently wrote in the white heat of passionate revolt, and his verse shows the effects of lack of restraint. Unfortunately he did not afterwards take the trouble to improve his subject matter, or the mold in which it was cast. Swinburne says : " His verse stumbles and jingles, stammers and halts, where is most need for a swift and even pace of musical sound."

The great power of Byron's poetry consists in its wealth of expression, its vigor, its rush and volume of sound, its variety, and its passion. Lines like the following show the vigorous flow of the verse, the love for lonely scenery, and a wealth of figurative expression : —

> "Mont Blanc is the monarch of mountains,
> They crowned him long ago
> On a throne of rocks, in a robe of clouds,
> With a diadem of snow."[1]

Scattered through his works we find rare gems such as the following : —

[1] *Manfred*, Act I.

> "... when
> Music arose with its voluptuous swell,
> Soft eyes looked love to eyes which spake again,
> And all went merry as a marriage bell."[1]

We may also frequently note the working of an acute intellect, as, for instance, in the lines in which he calls his own gloomy type of mind

> "... the telescope of truth,
> Which strips the distance of its phantasies,
> And brings life near in utter nakedness,
> Making the cold reality too real!"[2]

The answers to two questions which are frequently asked, will throw more light on Byron's characteristics : —

I. Why has his poetic fame decreased so much in England? In the eyes of his contemporaries he seemed worthy of a place beside Goethe. The reason for such an estimate is to be sought in the fact that Byron reflected so powerfully the mood of that special time. That reactionary period in history has passed and with it much of Byron's influence and fame. He was, unlike Shakespeare, specially fitted to minister to a certain age. Again, much of Byron's verse is rhetorical, and that kind of poetry does not wear well. On the other hand, we might reread *Hamlet*, *Lycidas*, and the *Intimations of Immortality* every month for a lifetime, and discover some hidden beauty and deep truth at every reading.

II. Why does the continent of Europe still class Byron among the very greatest English poets, next even to Shakespeare ? There is more liberty in England than on the continent. To the Europeans, Byron's poetry still voices the desire for freedom from tyranny and conven-

---

[1] *Childe Harold*, Canto III.   [2] *The Dream.*

tionality.   Swinburne gives as another reason the fact that
Byron actually gains by translation into a foreign tongue.
His faulty meters and careless expressions are improved,
and his vigorous way of stating things and his rolling
rhetoric are easily comprehended.   On the other hand, the
delicate shades of thought in *Hamlet* cannot be translated
into French without a distinct loss.

PERCY BYSSHE SHELLEY, 1792-1822

Life. — Another fiery spirit of the Revolution was
Shelley, born in 1792, of rich parentage, at Field Place,
near Horsham, Sussex.   He was one of the most ardent,
independent, and reckless English poets inspired by the
French Revolution.   He was a man who could face
infamy and defy the conventionalities of the world, and,
at the same moment, extend a helpful hand of sympathy
to a friend or sit for sixty hours beside the sick bed of
his dying child.   Tender, pitying, fearless, full of a desire
to reform the world, and of hatred for any form of tyranny,
Shelley failed to adjust himself to the customs and laws
of his actual surroundings.   He was calumniated and despised by the public at large, and almost idolized by his
intimate friends.

At Eton he denounced the tyranny of the larger boys.
At Oxford he decried the tyranny of the church over freedom of thought, and he was promptly expelled for his
article on *The Necessity of Atheism*.   Immediately after
this, he married a schoolgirl of inferior birth, to relieve
her from parental tyranny.   These acts alienated his family and forced him to forfeit his right to Field Place.

His repeatedly avowed ideas upon religion, government,
and marriage brought him into conflict with his country's

Percy B. Shelley

laws. When he finally left England in 1818, never to return, he was, like Byron, practically an exile.

The remaining four years of Shelley's life were passed in Italy, and they were comparatively peaceful. With length of days, he might have learned moderation and have gained the ear of the English people, but he died in his thirtieth year, when he was still in the fervor of youthful extravagance. He was drowned in the Bay of

Spezia in 1822 and was buried in Rome, near the spot where Keats lay (p. 369).

Works. — *Alastor, or the Spirit of Solitude* (1816), is a magnificent expression of Shelley's own restless, tameless spirit, wandering among the grand solitudes of nature in search of the ineffably lovely dream maiden, who was his ideal of beauty. He travels through primeval forests, stands upon dizzy abysses, plies through roaring whirlpools, all of which are symbolic of the soul's wayfaring, until at last, —

"When on the threshold of a green recess,"

his dying glance rests upon the setting moon and the sufferer finds eternal peace. The general tone of this poem is painfully despairing, but this is relieved by the grandeur of the natural scenes and by many imaginative flights.

The year 1819 saw the publication of a work unique among Shelley's productions, *The Cenci*. This is a drama based upon the baleful story of Beatrice Cenci. The poem deals with human beings, human passions, real acts, and the natural world, whereas Shelley usually preferred to treat of metaphysical theories, personified abstractions, and worlds of fancy. This strong drama was the most popular of his works during his lifetime.

He returned to the ideal sphere again in his greatest poem, the lyrical drama *Prometheus Unbound* (1820). This poem is the apotheosis of the Revolution. Prometheus, the friend of mankind, lies tortured and chained to the mountain side. As the hour of redemption approaches, his beloved Asia, the symbol of nature, arouses the soul of Revolution, represented by Demogorgon. He rises, hurls down the enemies of progress and freedom, releases Prometheus, and spreads liberty and happiness through all the world. Then the Moon, the Earth, and the Voices of the Air break forth into a magnificent chant of praise. The most delicate fancies, the most gorgeous imagery, and the most fiery, exultant emotions are combined in this poem with something of the stateliness of its Greek prototype. The swelling cadences of the blank verse and the tripping rhythm of the lyrics are the product of a nature rich in rare and wonderful melodies.

The Witch of Atlas (1820), *Epipsychidion* (1821), *Adonais* (1821), and the exquisite lyrics, *The Cloud, To a Skylark*, and *Ode to the West Wind* are the most beautiful of the remaining works. The first two mentioned are the most elusive of Shelley's poems. With scarcely an echo in his soul of the shadows and discords of earth, the poet paints, in these works, lands

> " . . . 'twixt Heaven, Air, Earth, and Sea,
>   Cradled, and hung in clear tranquillity;"

where all is

> "Beautiful as a wreck of Paradise."[1]

Adonais is a lament for the early death of Keats, and it stands second in the language among elegiac poems, *Lycidas*, of course, coming first. Shelley makes all nature mourn for the poet who had written of her with such adoration: —

> "Morning sought
> Her eastern watch tower, and her hair unbound,
> Wet with the tears which should adorn the ground,
> Dimmed the aerial eyes that kindle day;
> Afar the melancholy thunder moaned,
> Pale Ocean in unquiet slumber lay,
> And the wild winds flew round, sobbing in their dismay."

[1] *Epipsychidion.*

There is an intensely thrilling beauty about the poem. It is a sad, impassioned, spontaneous burst of song in which one poet crowns another with unfading laurel. Nothing that Shelley ever wrote surpasses this poem in roundness, completeness, and perfection of artistic finish.

A Great Lyric Poet. — Shelley is one of the supreme lyrical geniuses in the language. In his lyrics he sings with airy ease in strains of overflowing ecstasy. They seem to float and soar as naturally as the Æolian harp gives forth sound. They have an entrancing lightness and grace, and their melody is glorious. This stanza from the poem *To Night* shows Shelley's fine lyrical qualities : —

> " Swiftly walk over the western wave,
> Spirit of Night!
> Out of the misty eastern cave,
> Where, all the long and lone daylight,
> Thou wovest dreams of joy and fear,
> Which make thee terrible and dear, —
> Swift be thy flight! "

This same fragile, spiritlike beauty is shown again in *Prometheus Unbound.* One of the most exquisite, impassioned passages is the following, where Asia approaches her lover in

> " An ivory shell, inlaid with crimson fire,
> Which comes and goes within its sculptured rim
> Of delicate strange tracery,"

and where Asia's wondrous beauty dazzles the eye of her sister : —

> " Child of Light! thy limbs are burning
> Through the vest that seems to hide them,
> As the radiant lines of morning
> Through the clouds, ere they divide them ;
> And this atmosphere divinest
> Shrouds thee wheresoe'er thou shinest."

The Cloud, To a Skylark, and the *Ode to the West Wind* are lyrics which partake of this same charming witchery. The first stanza of *The Cloud* is a fine example : —

> " I bring fresh showers for the thirsting flowers,
>   From the seas and streams ;
> I bear light shade for the leaves when laid
>   In their noonday dreams.
> From my wings are shaken the dews that waken
>   The sweet buds every one,
> When rocked to rest on their mother's breast,
>   As she dances about the sun.
> I wield the flail of the lashing hail,
>   And whiten the green plains under ;
> And then again I dissolve it in rain,
>   And laugh as I pass in thunder."

The reader feels like saying of Shelley what he says of the skylark : —

> " Higher still and higher
>   From the earth thou springest,
> Like a cloud of fire ;
>   The blue deep thou wingest,
> And singing still dost soar, and soaring ever singest."

Treatment of Nature. — In many of his lyrics Shelley seems to have forgotten humanity and to have entered with wonderful intuition into the heart of nature. He makes the cloud, the bird, and the wind sing, not as the ordinary man would, simply as a reflection of his own mood, but as these embodiments of nature might themselves be supposed to sing. In the *Ode to the West Wind*, one of the most exquisite things Shelley wrote, he cries out : —

> " Make me thy lyre, even as the forest is :
>   What if my leaves are falling like its own ?
> The tumult of thy mighty harmonies
>   Will take from both a deep autumnal tone
> Sweet though in sadness."

We can fancy that the spirit forms of nature which appear in cloud and night, in mist and western wind, are content to have found in Shelley a lyre that responded in such entrancing notes to their touch.

General Characteristics. — Shelley is the purest, the most hopeful, and the noblest voice of the Revolution. Wordsworth and Coleridge lost their faith and became Tories, and Byron was a selfish, lawless creature, but Shelley had the martyr spirit of sacrifice, and he trusted to the end in the wild hopes of the revolutionary enthusiasts. His *Queen Mab*, *Revolt of Islam*, *Ode to Liberty*, *Ode to Naples*, and, above all, his *Prometheus Unbound*, are some of the works inspired by a trust in the ideal Democracy which was to be based on universal love and the brotherhood of man. This faith gives a bounding elasticity and buoyancy to Shelley's thought, but also tinges it with that disgust for the old, that defiance of restraint, and that boyish disregard for experience which mark a time of revolt.

The other subject which Shelley treats most frequently in his verse is ideal beauty. He yearned all his life for some form beautiful enough to satisfy the aspirations of his soul. *Alastor*, *Epipsychidion*, *The Witch of Atlas*, and *Prometheus Unbound*, all breathe this insatiate craving for that "Spirit of Beauty," that "awful Loveliness."

Some of his efforts to describe in verse this democracy and this ideal beauty are impalpable, obscure, and difficult to follow. Symonds says that Shelley "flew at the grand, the spacious, the sublime ; and did not always succeed in realizing for his readers what he had imagined." It is difficult to clothe such shadowy abstractions in clear, simple form. Sometimes his thoughts seem to have emerged but partly from the cloud lands which gave them birth.

Like Byron, Shelley is sometimes careless, and his poetry often shows the "negligence of nature." Neither poet was in the habit of subjecting his work to that careful revision which leaves every word in its exact place.

We shall, however, search in vain for these faults in some of Shelley's lyrics. His greatest title to fame rests on his rare lyric gift. Of all the lyric poets of England, he is the greatest master of an ethereal, evanescent, and phantomlike beauty. Many of his lyrics are wonderfully successful in portraying the elusive spirit of nature, whether in the changing lights of the dawn, the transient glory of the rainbow, or the breath of autumn, which turns the leaves

> "Yellow, and black, and pale, and hectic red,
> Pestilence-stricken multitudes."[1]

JOHN KEATS, 1795–1821

Life. — John Keats was born at Moorfields, London, in 1795. He attended school at Enfield, and was apprenticed at fifteen to a surgeon. One day, when Keats should have been listening to a surgical lecture, "there came," he says, "a sunbeam into the room and with it a whole troop of creatures floating in the ray; and I was off with them to Oberon and fairy land."

While he made a moderately good surgeon, he found that his heart was constantly with "Oberon and the fairy land" of poesy, so at nineteen he gave up his profession and began to study hard, preparatory to a literary career. Greek mythology and art were his favorite studies, and the ones from which his poetry drew most freely. His first volume was published in 1817, and his last in 1820. He

---

[1] *Ode to the West Wind.*

John Keats

died of consumption in 1821, when he was twenty-five years old. He breathed his last in Rome, whither he had gone to recuperate, and he lies buried in the Protestant cemetery there.

Works. — Keats's third volume of poetry, entitled *Lamia, Isabella, The Eve of St. Agnes, Hyperion, and Other Poems* (1820), is the one upon which his fame rests. In his earlier works, notably in *Endymion* (1817), the immaturity of his mind and art is shown by a boyish sentimentality, a confusion of details, and an overabundance of ornament.

These blemishes are not present in his third volume, which reveals a mastery of poetic form, and establishes his right to stand in the front rank of British poets.

Lamia is one of the most faultless of these poems. Keats's nature was in sympathy with this beautiful enchantress, Lamia, who, upon turning from a serpent into a radiant woman, filled every sense with joy and rapture; and he condemned the philosopher Apollonius for discovering her sorceries and causing her to vanish from sight. Keats says : —

> " . . . Do not all charms fly
> At the mere touch of cold philosophy?
> There was an awful rainbow once in heaven :
> We know her woof, her texture ; she is given
> In the dull catalogue of common things.
> Philosophy will clip an Angel's wings,
> Conquer all mysteries by rule and line,
> Empty the haunted air, and gnomed mine —
> Unweave a rainbow, as it erewhile made
> The tender-person'd Lamia melt into a shade."

Keats revels in the intoxicating and bewildering charms which he gives to his enchantress and to her magic palace. His language describing them is full of seductive beauty.

Isabella, or the Pot of Basil, is a romantic tale of love, taken from a story in Boccaccio. The narration of this tale is not well handled, but it contains incidents which are beautifully told. The young, impulsive love of Isabella and Lorenzo makes a sweet idyl, and the pitiful grief of Isabella, when she learns, through a vision, that her lover has been murdered, is painted with a tender pathos nowhere else surpassed in Keats.

The Eve of St. Agnes is an exquisite and brilliant gem, fashioned out of the slightest of themes. The subject is merely the visions of love which St. Agnes gives to one of her votaries, and the manner in which those visions are realized. It can hardly be said that this poem tells a tale; it rather paints a picture, vivid and highly colored. It should be read entire.

The beautiful fragment of *Hyperion* differs widely from *The Eve of St. Agnes*. *Hyperion* is an epic, planned on lines of severity and simplicity.

> "Deep in the shady sadness of a vale
> Far sunken from the healthy breath of morn,
> Far from the fiery noon, and eve's one star,
> Sat gray-hair'd Saturn, quiet as a stone,
> Still as the silence round about his lair."

These opening lines of *Hyperion* show with what a stately march the verse is to bear along this story of Gods and Titans. There are repose, dignity, and majesty in the poem. The characters tower above human proportions, as though cut from the polished marble by Michael Angelo. Byron says of Keats: "His fragment of *Hyperion* seems actually inspired by the Titans, and is as sublime as Æschylus."

In addition to these works, there are many shorter poems which exhibit the powers of Keats at their height. Among these poems are the ballad *La Belle Dame sans Merci* and those glorious odes, *On a Grecian Urn*, *To Autumn*, and *To a Nightingale*.

General Characteristics. — In the judgment of Keats, philosophy, politics, and ethics were not suitable subjects for verse. While, therefore, Wordsworth and Coleridge were reflecting upon the moral law of the universe, while Byron was voicing the political ideals of Europe in his poetry of revolt, and Shelley was writing of an enfranchised humanity, the muse of Keats was luxuriating in classic myths and mediæval legends, and was inspired by an insatiable love of beauty.

> "A thing of beauty is a joy forever,"

he says in *Endymion*. In the *Ode on a Grecian Urn*, he
writes : —

> "' Beauty is truth, truth beauty,' — that is all
> Ye know on earth, and all ye need to know."

His poetry has rarely been equaled in descriptions of the
beauties perceptible to the senses, such as form, color,
perfume, or music. It was his mission to interpret, not
the highest spiritual life, but the highest type of sensuous
beauty. Such beauty has its moral side, and its power to
elevate and purify. Since all the higher operations of the
intellect rest upon sensory foundations, it is well that the
latter should be built of the most beautiful masonry that
nature can offer.

The sensitiveness of Keats to all sense impressions
made him an ardent admirer of nature. In his verse, the
color, the form, and the sounds of nature possess Circean
charms. He delights to paint the "self-folding" flower, —

> "The coming musk-rose full of dewy wine,
> The murmurous haunt of flies on summer eves,"[1]

and —

> "Sweet birds antheming the morn."[2]

Because most of the poetry of Keats is full of a youthful
beauty, it is a mistake to suppose that he has no deep and
serious vein. The following lines have the old Saxon
seriousness, although it is softened into gentler strains
than we have before heard : —

> "Darkling I listen ; and, for many a time
> I have been half in love with easeful Death,
> Call'd him soft names in many a muséd rime,
> To take into the air my quiet breath."[3]

[1] *Ode to a Nightingale.*   [2] *Fancy.*   [3] *Ode to a Nightingale.*

These lines have appealed to many a tired soul and made it "half in love with easeful Death."

Keats is akin to the Elizabethans in his fondness for imagery. His poetry abounds in figurative language. He is also a master of melody. His verse is full of deep, rich harmonies. It has, in places, more of the epic quality than any contemporary work possesses.

THOMAS DE QUINCEY, 1785-1859

Life. — Thomas De Quincey was born in Manchester in 1785. He was a precocious child, and he became quite a student at the age of eight. When he was only eleven, his Latin verses were the envy of the older boys at the Bath school, which he was then attending. At the age of fifteen, he was so thoroughly versed in Greek that his professor said of him to a friend: "That boy could harangue an Athenian mob better than you or I could address an English one." De Quincey was sent in this year to the Manchester grammar school, but his mind was in advance of the instruction given there, and he unceremoniously left the school on his seventeenth birthday.

For a time he tramped through Wales, living on an allowance of a guinea a week. Hungering for books, he suddenly posted to London. He feared that his family would force him to return to school, so he did not let them know his whereabouts. He therefore received no money from them, and was forced to wander hungry, sick, and destitute, through the streets of the metropolis, with its outcasts and waifs. He describes this part of his life in a very entertaining manner in his *Confessions of an English Opium-Eater*.

Thomas de Quincey.

When his family found him, a year later, they prevailed on him to go to Oxford; and, for the next four years, he lived the life of a recluse at college, scarcely raising his head from his books to talk to any one.

In 1808 he took the cottage at Grasmere which Wordsworth had quitted, and enjoyed the society of the three Lake poets (p. 313). Here De Quincey married and lived his happiest years.

The latter part of his life was clouded by his indulgence in opium, which he had first taken while at college to relieve acute neuralgia. At one time he took 8000 drops of laudanum a day. Owing to a business failure, his money was lost, and it became necessary for him to throw off the influence of the narcotic sufficiently to earn a livelihood. In 1821 he began to write. From that time until his death, in 1859, his life was devoted mainly to literature.

Works. — Nearly all of De Quincey's writings were contributed to magazines. His first and greatest contribution was *The Confessions of an English Opium-Eater*, published in the *London Magazine*. These *Confessions* are most remarkable for the brilliant and elaborate style in which the author's early life and his opium dreams are related. His splendid, yet melancholy, dreams are the most famous in the language.

De Quincey's wide reading, especially of history, supplied the material for many of them. In these dreams he saw the court ladies of "the unhappy times of Charles I.," witnessed Marius pass by with his Roman legions, "ran into pagodas" in China, where he "was fixed, for centuries, at the summit, or in secret rooms," and "was buried for a thousand years, in stone coffins, in narrow chambers at the heart of eternal pyramids" in Egypt.

His dreams were affected also by the throngs of people whom he had watched in London. He was haunted by "the tyranny of the human face." He says: —

"Faces imploring, wrathful, despairing, surged upwards by thousands, by myriads, by generations, by centuries: my agitation was infinite, my mind tossed, and surged with the ocean."

Sound also played a large part in the dreams. Music, heart-breaking lamentations, and pitiful echoes recurred frequently in the most magnificent of these nightly pageants. One of the most distressing features of the dreams was their vastness. The dreamer lived for centuries in one night, and space " swelled, and was amplified to an extent of unutterable infinity."

To present with such force and reality these grotesque and weird fancies, these vague horrors, and these deep oppressions required a powerful imaginative grasp of the intangible, and a masterly command of language.

In no other work does De Quincey reach the eminence attained in the *Confessions*, although his scholarly acquirements enabled him to treat philosophical, critical, and historical subjects with wonderful grace and ease.   His biographer, Masson, says : " De Quincey's sixteen volumes of magazine articles are full of brain from beginning to end."   The wide range of his erudition is shown by the fact that he could write such fine literary criticisms as *On Wordsworth's Poetry* and *On the Knocking at the Gate in Macbeth*, such clear, strong, and vivid descriptions of historical events and characters as *The Cæsars*, *Joan of Arc*, and *The Revolt of the Tartars*, and such acute essays on unfamiliar topics as *The Toilette of a Hebrew Lady*, *The Casuistry of Roman Meals*, and *The Spanish Military Nun*.

He had a contemplative, analytic mind which enjoyed knotty metaphysical problems and questions far removed from daily life, such as the first principles of political economy, and of German philosophy.   While he was a clear thinker in such fields, he added little that was new to English thought.

The works which rank next to *The Confessions of an English Opium-Eater* are all largely autobiographical, and reveal charming glimpses of this dreamy, learned sage. These works are *Suspiria de Profundis* (Sighs from the Depths), *The English Mail Coach*, and *Autobiographic Sketches*.   None of them contains any striking or unusual experience of the author. Their power rests upon their marvelous style. *Levana and Our Ladies of Sorrow* in *Suspiria de Profundis* and the *Dream Fugue* in the *Mail Coach* are among the most musical, the most poetic, and the most imaginative of the author's productions.

General Characteristics. — One of the most prominent characteristics of De Quincey's style is precision. There are but few English essayists who can compare with him in scrupulous precision of expression. He qualifies and elaborates a simple statement until its exact meaning becomes plainly manifest. His vocabulary is extraordinary. In any of the multifarious subjects treated by him, the right word seems always at hand. The extreme care which he takes to get the best word may be seen in the following passage from *Levana and Our Ladies of Sorrow* : —

"These Sisters — by what name shall we call them? If I say simply 'The Sorrows,' there will be a chance of mistaking the term; it might be understood of individual sorrow, — separate cases of sorrow, whereas I want a term expressing the mighty abstractions that incarnate themselves in all individual sufferings of man's heart, and I wish to have these abstractions presented as impersonations, — that is, as clothed with human attributes of life, and with functions pointing to flesh. Let us call them, therefore, *Our Ladies of Sorrow*."

Such elaborate explanation of expressions is met with frequently in De Quincey.

Another characteristic, which is very striking in all his works, is stateliness. His long, periodic sentences move with a quiet dignity, adapted to the treatment of lofty themes. In contrasting the simplicity of Swift with the elegance of De Quincey, Leslie Stephen humorously remarks that if Swift's plain, direct subjects had been attempted by De Quincey, " he would have resembled a king in his coronation robes, compelled to lead a forlorn hope up the scaling ladders." When, however, De Quincey describes a magnificent dream, a fine landscape, or an incident in his own experience, the floating "coronation robes" of his style have the proper regal sweep.

A further striking quality of De Quincey's style is harmony. His language is so full of rich harmonies that it challenges comparison with poetry. He shared the enjoyment of Keats in the rhythm and sound of a sentence, apart from its meaning. He sometimes gains his effects by the repetition of words. He says : —

"The sound was reverberated — everlasting farewells ! and again and yet again reverberated — everlasting farewells ! "[1]

De Quincey's work possesses also a light, ironic humor, which is happiest in parody. The essay upon *Murder Considered as One of the Fine Arts* is the best example of his humor. This selection is one of the most whimsical : —

"For, if once a man indulges himself in murder, very soon he comes to think little of robbing ; and from robbing he comes next to drinking and Sabbath breaking, and from that to incivility and procrastination. Once begin upon this downward path, you never know where you are to stop."

De Quincey's gravest fault is digression. He frequently leaves his main theme and follows some line of thought that has been suggested to his well-stored mind. These digressions are often quite lengthy, and sometimes one digression leads to another, until several subjects receive treatment in one paper. He, however, always returns to the subject in hand, and he always defines very sharply the point of digression and of return. Another of his faults is an indulgence in involved sentences, which weaken the vigor and simplicity of the style.

[1] *Confessions of an English Opium-Eater.*

Despite these faults, De Quincey is a great master of language. He deserves study for the three most striking characteristics of his style, — precision, stateliness, and harmony.

SUMMARY

The tide of reaction, which had for some time been gathering force, swept triumphantly over England in this age of Romanticism.

Men rebelled against the aristocracy, the narrow conventions of society, the authority of the church and of the government, against the supremacy of cold classicism in literature, against confining intellectual activity to tangible commonplace things, and against the repression of imagination and of the soul's aspirations. The two principal forces behind these changes were the Romantic Movement, which culminated in changed literary ideals, and the spirit of the French Revolution, which emphasized the close kinship of all ranks of humanity.

The age was preëminently poetic. The Elizabethan period alone excels it in the glory of its poetry. The subjects of verse in the age of Romanticism were external nature and an ideal humanity. Cowper, Burns, Scott, Wordsworth, Coleridge, Byron, Shelley, and Keats constitute a group of nature poets that cannot be paralleled in English literature. The democratic spirit of the age is shown in the poetry of man. Burns sings of the Scotch peasant, Wordsworth pictures the life of shepherds and dalesmen, Byron's lines ring with a cry of liberty for all, and Shelley immortalizes the dreams of a universal brotherhood of man.

While the prose does not take such high rank as the poetry, there are some writers who will not soon be forgotten. Scott will be remembered as the great master of

the historical novel, Jane Austen as the skillful interpreter
of commonplace character, De Quincey for the brilliancy
of his style and the vigor of his imagination in presenting
his opium dreams, and Lamb for his exquisite humor.   In
philosophical prose, Mill, Bentham, and Malthus made important contributions to moral, social, and political philosophy, while Coleridge opposed their utilitarian and
materialistic tendencies, and codified the principles of
criticism from a romantic point of view.

REQUIRED READINGS FOR CHAPTER IX

HISTORICAL

Gardiner,[1] pp. 792–914; Green, pp. 786–836; Underwood-Guest,
pp. 536-556; Guerber, pp. 309–320; Hassall's *Making of the British
Empire*, pp. 82–142; Traill, V., 366–627, VI., 1-110.

LITERARY

Cowper. — Read the opening stanzas of Cowper's *Conversation* and
note the strong influence of Pope in the cleverly turned but artificial
couplets.   Compare this poem with the one *On the Receipt of my
Mother's Picture* or with *The Task*, Book IV., lines 1–41 and 267–332,
and point out the marked differences in subject matter and style.   Is
there a forward movement in literature indicated by the change in
Cowper's manner? *John Gilpin* should be read for its fresh, beguiling
humor.

Burns. — Read *The Cotter's Saturday Night, For a' That and a'
That, To a Mouse, Highland Mary, To Mary in Heaven, Farewell to
Nancy, I Love My Jean, A Red, Red Rose.*   The teacher should read
to the class parts of *Tam o' Shanter*.

In what ways do the first three poems mentioned above show Burns's
sympathy with democracy? Quote some of Burns's fine descriptions
of nature and describe the manner in which he treats nature.   How
does he rank as a writer of love songs?   What qualities in his poems

---

[1] For full titles, see list at end of Chap. I.

have touched so many hearts? Compare his poetry with that of Dryden, Pope, and Shakespeare.

Scott. — Read *The Lady of the Lake*, Canto III., stanzas iii.–xxv., or *Marmion*, Canto VI., stanzas xiii.–xxvii., (American Book Co.'s *Eclectic English Classics*, or Cassell's *National Library*, Nos. 14 and 136). Read in Craik's *English Prose Selections*, Vol. V., "The Gypsy's Curse," pp. 14–17, "The Death of Madge Wildfire," pp. 30–35, and "The Grand Master of the Templars," pp. 37–42. The student should put on his list for reading at his leisure : *Guy Mannering, Old Mortality, Ivanhoe, Kenilworth,* and *The Talisman.*

In what kind of poetry does Scott excel? Quote some of his spirited lines, and point out their chief excellences. How does his poetry differ from that of Burns? In the history of fiction does Scott rank as an imitator or a creator? As a writer of fiction in what do his strength and his weakness consist? Has he those qualities that will cause him to be popular a century hence? What can be said of his style?

Jane Austen. — In Craik's *English Prose Selections*, Vol. V., read the two selections from *Pride and Prejudice*, pp. 59–66.

In delineation of character, how does Jane Austen differ from Scott?

Wordsworth. — From the uneven work of Wordsworth such poems as the following may be selected : *Michael*, from the narrative poems ; *The Solitary Reaper, Glen Almain, To a Highland Girl, Lines Composed a Few Miles above Tintern Abbey,* and *Daffodils*, from the lyrics ; " It is a beauteous evening, calm and free," " Milton! thou should'st be living at this hour," and " The world is too much with us, late and soon," from the sonnets ; and the *Ode on Intimations of Immortality,* from the odes.

In which of these poems does Wordsworth show his belief in the consciousness of nature? Are these poems of nature more remarkable for their power of description or for their spiritual, imaginative beauty? Are the characters in *Michael* as clearly marked as those in *The Cotter's Saturday Night* ? Was Matthew Arnold justified in saying of Wordsworth : " It might seem that nature not only gave him the matter for his poem, but wrote his poem for him "? Indicate some passages where Wordsworth's reflective genius is best displayed.

Coleridge. — Read *The Ancient Mariner* and *Christabel* (Ward, IV., 128–154 ; *The Ancient Mariner* may also be had in the *Eclectic English Classics* Series).

In what way do these poems display the influence of romanticism? Is Wordsworth's influence noticeable in any of Coleridge's poetry of nature? What feeling, almost unknown in early poetry, is common in Coleridge's *The Ancient Mariner*, Wordsworth's *Hart-Leap Well*, Burns's *To a Mouse, On Seeing a Wounded Hare Limp by Me, A Winter Night*, and Cowper's *On a Goldfinch Starved to Death in his Cage*?

Coleridge's prose criticisms upon Wordsworth in *Biographia Literaria* and on Shakespeare in the first and second volumes of *Literary Remains* should be read by the student. The cream of these works will be found in Henry A. Beers's carefully edited *Selections from the Prose Writings of Samuel Taylor Coleridge*, 146 pp., 50 cents.

Note how fully Coleridge unfolds the principles of romantic criticism in these essays.

Byron. — Read *The Prisoner of Chillon* (*Selections from Byron, Eclectic English Classics*), *Childe Harold*, Canto III., stanzas xxi.–xxv. and cxiii., Canto IV., stanzas lxxviii. and lxxix., "Oh, Snatch'd away in Beauty's Bloom," "There's not a joy the world can give like that it takes away," and from *Don Juan*, Canto III., the song inserted between stanzas lxxxvi. and lxxxvii. All these poems will be found in the two volumes of Byron's works in the *Canterbury Poets'* series.

From these stanzas of *Childe Harold* select, first, the passages which best illustrate the spirit of revolt, and, second, the passages marked by most poetic beauty. Is Byron a poet of despair? What natural phenomena appeal most to Byron?

Shelley. — Read *Adonais, The Cloud, To a Skylark, Ode to the West Wind, The Sensitive Plant*.

Does either the *Adonais* of Shelley or the *Lycidas* of Milton express a deep, personal sorrow? Under what different aspects do these two elegiac poems view the life after death? Did Shelley see the spiritual side of nature like Wordsworth? What is the most striking quality of Shelley's poetic gift?

Keats. — Read *The Eve of St. Agnes, La Belle Dame sans Merci, Ode on a Grecian Urn, To a Nightingale*.

In what respects is Keats a great poet of nature? Does he teach any ethical lesson? How is he more nearly akin to the Elizabethans than any of his contemporaries?

De Quincey. — Read *Levana and Our Ladies of Sorrow*, which will be found in Craik's *English Prose Selections*, Vol. V., pp. 264–270. The first few chapters of *The Confessions of an English Opium-Eater* (Morley's *Universal Library*, No. 35, 40 cents) are so entertaining that they will well repay reading, if the student has the time.

Do his writings show the influence of a romantic and poetic age?

Compare his style with that of Addison, Gibbon, and Burke. In what respects does De Quincey succeed, and in what does he fail, as a model for a young writer?

Lamb. — From the *Essays of Elia*, read the *Dissertation on Roast Pig.* Selections from the *Essays* may be found in Craik, V., pp. 116-126.

In what does Lamb's chief charm consist? Point out resemblances and differences between his *Essays* and Addison's.

WORKS FOR CONSULTATION AND FURTHER STUDY

(OPTIONAL)

Herford's *The Age of Wordsworth*, 315 pp. (the best short work).

Oliphant's *Literary History of England in the End of the Eighteenth and Beginning of the Nineteenth Century.*

Saintsbury's *History of Nineteenth Century Literature*, pp. 1–137.

Shairp's *Poetic Interpretation of Nature* and *Aspects of Poetry.*

Brooke's *Theology in the English Poets.*

Hancock's *French Revolution and the English Poets.*

The French Revolution and Literature and *The Transcendental Movement and Literature*, in Dowden's *Studies in Literature.*

Scudder's *Life of the Spirit in the Modern English Poets.*

Arnold's *Essays in Criticism.*

Noel's *Essays on Poetry and Poets.*

Swinburne's *Essays and Studies* and *Miscellanies.*

Masson's *Wordsworth, Shelley, and Keats.*

Bagehot's *Literary Studies.*

Lowell's *Among My Books.*

Phillips's *Popular Manual of English Literature*, Vol. II., pp. 87–402.

Ward's *English Poets*, Vol. III., pp. 422-608; Vol. IV., pp. 1–488.

Craik's *English Prose Selections*, Vol. V., pp. 1–273.

Clark's *Study of English Prose Writers*, pp. 323–419.

Wright's *Life of Cowper.*

Goldwin Smith's *Life of Cowper.*

Cowper and Rousseau, in Stephen's *Hours in a Library*, Vol. II.

Shairp's *Life of Burns.*

Blackie's *Life of Burns.*

Carlyle's *Essay on Burns.*

Lockhart's *Life of Scott.*

Hutton's *Life of Scott.*

Yonge's *Life of Scott*.

Sir Walter Scott, in Stephen's *Hours in a Library*, Vol. I.

Jack's *Essays on the Novel as Illustrated by Scott and Miss Austen*.

Goldwin Smith's *Life of Jane Austen*.

Knight's *Life of William Wordsworth*, 3 vols.

Myers's *Life of Wordsworth*.

Wordsworth: the Man and the Poet, in Shairp's *Studies in Poetry and Philosophy*.

Wordsworth's Ethics, in Stephen's *Hours in a Library*, Vol. II.

Knight's *Through the Wordsworth Country*, illustrated.

Reynold's *The Treatment of Nature in English Poetry between Pope and Wordsworth*.

George's *Preface* to *The Prelude* and *Preface* to *Selections from Wordsworth*.

Pater's *Appreciations* (Wordsworth and Coleridge).

Traill's *Life of Coleridge*.

Caine's *Life of Coleridge*.

Samuel Taylor Coleridge in Shairp's *Studies in Poetry and Philosophy*.

Brandl's *Samuel Taylor Coleridge and the English Romantic Movement*.

Coleridge: Prose Extracts, edited by H. A. Beers.

Nichol's *Life of Byron*.

Noel's *Life of Byron*.

Macaulay's *Essay on Byron*.

Mathilde Blind's *Introduction to the Poetical Works of Lord Byron* in *Canterbury Poets*.

Dowden's *Life of Shelley*.

Symonds's *Life of Shelley*.

Shairp's *Life of Shelley*.

Shelley's Philosophical Views of Reform and *Last Words on Shelley*, in Dowden's *Transcripts and Studies*.

Brooke's *Preface* to *Poems of Shelley*.

Godwin and Shelley, in Stephen's *Hours in a Library*, Vol. III.

Colvin's *Life of Keats*.

Rossetti's *Life of Keats*.

Masson's *Life of De Quincey*.

Page's *Life and Writings of De Quincey*.

Study of *Thomas De Quincey*, in Minto's *Manual of English Prose Literature*, pp. 31–75.

De Quincey, in Stephen's *Hours in a Library*, Vol. I.

CHAPTER X

A Literature of Variety. — Before Queen Victoria ascended the throne in 1837, Coleridge, Scott, Shelley, Byron, and Keats had passed away. The old order had given place to a new one. At the end of the eighteenth century, the spirit of revolt against classical literary forms and tyrannical methods of government was animating the poets. The Victorian age has been inspired by no overmastering impulse, without which no age can reach the greatest heights, although it may do much excellent and necessary work in the evolution of literature.

While no one type of literature has received its consummate expression in this period, a greater variety of efforts has attained eminence than in any previous time. In poetry, prose fiction, essays, history, philosophy, and scientific treatises, the Victorian age has done good work. The most eminent writers of the period are Browning and Tennyson in poetry; Thackeray, Dickens, and George Eliot, in prose fiction; Carlyle, Macaulay, Ruskin, and Matthew Arnold, in essay writing; Herbert Spencer, Cardinal Newman, and Sir William Hamilton in various types of philosophy; and Darwin, Tyndall, and Huxley in science. This many-sided, restless modern life has found literary expression as varied as its aims and moods.

Prose takes higher comparative rank in the Victorian than in the preceding age. In special fields, the prose of Bunyan, Swift, and Burke has not been surpassed, but the Victorian age stands first in the extent, variety, and finished style of its prose. The novel is the most widely popular, the most prolific, and the most characteristic type of nineteenth century prose. The changed character of the reading public furnishes one reason for the unprecedented growth of fiction. The spread of education among all classes of society, through public schools, newspapers, and cheap magazines, gradually enabled the masses to become the readers of books not too abstruse or philosophical. The lives of the majority of people are spent in hard toil and their culture is limited. If such are to find much amusement, it must come from reading matter within their comprehension. The novel has also the advantage of being able to present life in all its variety.

If those epochs represented by only one great poet, like Chaucer or Milton, are not considered, it is probable that posterity will assign third place to the Victorian age for its poetry and rank it below the poetry of the age of Elizabeth and of Romanticism. The Victorian poets, unlike the Elizabethan, could not sit at the feet of all human life, listen to its wonderful tale, and repeat it unmarred by special theories and philosophies, nor could the later poets "recapture the first fine careless rapture" of the earlier singers. In some respects the Victorian poets surpass their more gifted brothers. The exaggeration and lack of self-control in the Elizabethan age have been largely avoided. Unlike the poets of the first part of the eighteenth century, Tennyson combines rare artistic power with feeling and close observation of life. The Victorian poets are less buoyant and imaginative than the Romantic school which immediately preceded them, but in regard to government, social reformation, and human capability, they display the characteristics of a saner, wiser, and more moderate age.

The Victorian period may also be differentiated from others by the extent of the influence of science on literature. This influence has been so powerful that it demands special consideration.

A Scientific Age. — The growth of science has been one of the foremost influences to shape the thought of the age. Steam has been put to a thousand uses. Wonderful machines have been invented to do what was impossible for human hands. The year of Victoria's accession to the throne saw the operation of the first telegraph line in England. Electricity made a reality of Puck's boast to girdle the earth in forty minutes. Friend conversed with friend across a thousand miles of space. Things which the Elizabethans would have called the wildest dreams became prosaic realities.

Some of the most acute thinkers of the century devoted their lives to scientific investigation. Men like Charles Darwin (1809–1882), Thomas Huxley (1825–1895), John Tyndall (1820–1893), and Herbert Spencer (1820– ——) endeavored to build the stray bricks of scientific knowledge into a philosophical structure.

CHARLES DARWIN

The Victorian age was the first to set forth clearly the evolution hypothesis, which teaches the orderly development of life from simple to complex forms. While the idea of evolution had suggested itself to many naturalists, Darwin was the first to gain a wide hearing for the theory. His *Origin of Species by Natural Selection* (1859) was an epoch-making book. Spencer carried the doctrine of evolution into broader fields. In his *Synthetic Philosophy* he applied it to the structure, not only of plants and animals, but also of society, morality, and religion. Of all the scientific thought of the age, the doctrine of evolution has had the most influence on both prose and poetry. A great scientist like Tyndall becomes almost poetic in presenting his conception of evolution. He says: —

" Not alone the more ignoble forms of animalcular or animal life, not alone the nobler forms of the horse and lion, not alone the exquisite and wonderful mechanism of the human body, but the human mind itself — emotion, intellect, will, and all their phenomena — were once latent in a fiery cloud. . . . All our philosophy, all our poetry, all our science, and all our art — Plato, Shakespeare, Newton, and Raphael — are potential in the fires of the sun." [1]

With this we may contrast Tennyson's poetic exposition of the nebular hypothesis : —

" This world was once a fluid haze of light
Till toward the center set the starry tides,
And eddied into suns, that wheeling cast
The planets ; then the monster, then the man." [2]

" Out of the deep, my child, out of the deep,
Where all that was to be in all that was,
Whirl'd for a million æons thro' the vast
Waste dawn of multitudinous-eddying light." [3]

We shall now proceed to note more specifically some of the ways in which science has affected literature. We shall find that science has influenced the idea of growth, the search for truth, the way of regarding the problems of existence, religious faith, ethical and social aims, and the tendency toward analytical modes of thought.

[1] *The Imagination in Science.*   [2] *The Princess*, Canto II.   [3] *De Profundis.*

The Idea of Growth. — Evolution has impressed on literature and on social philosophy what might be termed the "growth idea." In these two lines Browning thus expresses this new idea of the working of the Divine Power : —

> "He fixed thee 'mid this dance
> Of plastic circumstance."[1]

Evolution teaches the slow development of the lower into the higher. Preceding literature, with the conspicuous exception of Shakespeare's work, had, for the most part, presented individuals whose character was already fixed. We are introduced to them as monsters of wickedness, or as embodiments of strong will and fine character, but we are not shown the various steps which complete the moral perversion or develop the strength of character. George Eliot, Thackeray, and Robert Browning, instead of taking us into a gallery of completed statues, show us the sculptors at work upon the newly quarried marble. These sculptors, whose names are Heredity, Environment, Will Power, Moral Feeling, and Trial, in both failure and success, are chiseling out their statues in the world studio. We can see the figures in process of development, and note the stage at which the flaw in the marble appears and mars the work.

The idea of growth explains why this age has taken a different view of social problems. Science has caused the abandonment of the idea that men can be permanently uplifted as the result of a sudden revolution, like the one in France. Enlightened men no longer think that such measures as the killing of a Catiline, a Cæsar, or the French nobles, or the imprisonment of some members of a corrupt city government, can cure the evils in a state. There has been a wider realization of the fact that there

[1] *Rabbi Ben Ezra.*

must be, under the proper stimulating influences, an orderly growth from the former condition into a new one. Vast progress is shown by the nineteenth century in its realization of the fact that changes in the character of an individual or in the reformation of a government are not the result of a few minutes' exposure to some strain or of a sudden upheaval. Science has shown the necessity of time in the development of all things. Tennyson voices this new belief : —

> "Man as yet is being made, and ere the crowning Age of ages,
> Shall not æon after æon pass and touch him into shape?"[1]

Browning also emphasizes it : —

> ". . . progress is
> The law of life, man is not Man as yet.
> Nor shall I deem his object served, his end
> Attained, his genuine strength put fairly forth,
> While only here and there a star dispels
> The darkness, here and there a towering mind
> O'erlooks its prostrate fellows."[2]

The Search for Truth. — Man increased his dominion over nature in proportion as he learned scientific truth. The beneficent results of understanding natural laws and of acting in harmony with them have impelled many to join in the search for truth in this direction. Some few have caught fresh glimpses of the fact that the laws of the spiritual world, as well as of the natural world, must be understood, if man would not introduce discordant notes into the larger harmony of both worlds. The age is distinguished by a groping after truth in every direction. Physics, geology, biology, psychology, religion, sociology, ethics, government, and every other subject that seemed

[1] *Making of Man.*   [2] *Paracelsus*, Act V.

to point toward truth, — all have had patient investigators.

We see everywhere a determination to learn the truth, irrespective of where it may lead. There has been the firm consciousness that even the heavens rest on pillars of truth, that the truth can harm no righteous cause. Geologists investigated the records of creation as carefully as historians searched the state papers of a bygone reign. Philosophers sought the origin of conscience, the foundation of belief, the underlying truths of every science. Men believed that all these truths, when woven together, would give new unity, dignity, and fullness to life.

Science and Imagination. — Some have insisted with Keats that science would clip the wings of imagination. Since a great imaginative poet does not make his appearance on an average of once in a century, it is too early yet to tell what the final outcome will be. In the first flush of scientific discoveries, it was thought that all the mystery would soon be eliminated from existence, and that the sphere of imaginative activity would necessarily be lessened. This view is less common to-day, for it is now generally recognized that evolution has merely substituted a greater mystery in place of a lesser one.

Has any preceding age offered to the imagination wider views with more unfathomed mystery than astronomy and the æons of geology present? In Shakespeare's theater, we see the seven ages of man passing across the stage; in the theater of the universe, we behold all the offspring of creation playing their parts. It seems safe to predict that lack of genius will remain the only factor capable of limiting the workings of imagination.

It is well to note that as philosophical a nineteenth century scientist as John Tyndall wrote one of his greatest essays, *The Imagination in Science,* to show that even science could not dispense with imagination. He says:—

"Philosophers may be right in affirming that we cannot transcend experience; but we can at all events carry it a long way from its origin. We can also magnify, diminish, qualify, and combine experiences, so as to render them fit for purposes entirely new. We are gifted with the power of imagination, and by this power we can lighten the darkness which surrounds the world of the senses. . . . Bounded and conditioned by coöperant reason, imagination becomes the mightiest instrument of the physical discoverer. Newton's passage from a falling apple to a falling moon was, at the outset, a leap of the imagination."

Problems of Existence. — The hypothesis of evolutionary development has caused men to regard from a new point of view the origin of life, its worth here, and its destiny hereafter. On one side, evolution means continuous progress from a lower to a higher and a nobler form of life, and the entire world thus seems to be on the royal highway to Eden. Tennyson proclaims that the human beings of the future shall be

> "No longer half akin to brute,
>   For all we thought and loved and did,
>   And hoped, and suffer'd, is but seed
> Of what in them is flower and fruit." [1]

But the message of evolution is not entirely optimistic. When men pondered over Darwin's famous demonstration of the survival of the fittest, they saw that there were two sides to the evolutionary shield, that for every fit one who survived to reach the heights, perhaps a thousand perished, and that success might be as dear to each of the prostrate thousand as to the fortunate one. Tennyson perceived the ruthless destructiveness of the natural world. Of "Nature, red in tooth and claw with ravine," he says:—

[1] *In Memoriam,* CXXXI.

"So careful of the type she seems,
So careless of the single life.
. . . . . .
"'So careful of the type?' but no.
   From scarpéd cliff and quarried stone
   She cries, 'A thousand types are gone:
I care for nothing, all shall go.'"[1]

One school of evolutionists denied any freedom to will power. They taught that everything is potential in the nebular mist (see p. 388), and that its development is under the control of a law as inexorable as that which determines the path of a rifle ball. Since Shakespeare and Benedict Arnold were both potential in the nebula, it had to evolve them exactly as they were evolved. They were, under this view, as powerless to change themselves, as undeserving of either praise or blame, as a bullet which cannot determine whether it shall strike a target or kill a child. This school taught that man, like every other product which the nebula was under the necessity of evolving, is merely a bubble floating on the stream of an eternal Energy, a powerless spectator of a current which bears him helplessly onward toward a great sea, in which the bubble will change its form and lose its individual existence. Such theories have led toward materialism, and the thought of the age has been profoundly impressed by them. Some writers, like Matthew Arnold, never escaped from the doubts thus raised.

ALGERNON C. SWINBURNE

Lines like these from Swinburne present a gloomy picture of "the sleep eternal," with which materialism endeavors to solace the weary: —

[1] *In Memoriam*, LV., LVI.

> " We thank with brief thanksgiving
>   Whatever gods may be
>   That no life lives forever ;
>   That dead men rise up never ;
>   That even the weariest river
>   Winds somewhere safe to sea.
>
> " Then star nor sun shall waken,
>   Nor any change of light ;
>   Nor sound of waters shaken,
>   Nor any sound or sight :
>   Nor wintry leaves nor vernal,
>   Nor days nor things diurnal ;
>   Only the sleep eternal
>   In an eternal night." [1]

Materialistic fatalism leads naturally to pessimistic theories of life.   The question, " Is life worth living ? " has been asked on all sides.   On the supposition that this life ends all, the verdict of Tennyson, who perhaps more than any other poet reflects the moods of the age, is that

> " . . . earth is darkness at the core,
>   And dust and ashes all that is." [2]

Outcome in Religious Thought. — Science has certainly tended to inspire the belief that the world's development is the result of a growth more orderly than former ages had imagined.   On examining the works of many of the greatest writers of the period, we shall, however, find that they do not accept the hypothesis of a blind Energy that cares nothing for a sparrow's fall, an Energy that says : " Thy brother shall not rise again, but like a raindrop he shall forever lose his identity in the great Ocean of Eternity."

The vastness of scientific discovery merely stunned certain minds, while it served to stimulate others to reach

---

[1] *The Garden of Proserpine.*   [2] *In Memoriam*, XXXIV.

greater heights of spiritual truth.   While some writers never emerged from the shadow of doubt, we can still say that the greatest literature of the age is resonant with the voices of faith and hope.   Carlyle and Ruskin are powerful religious teachers.   Carlyle says : —

"The man who cannot wonder (and worship), were he President of innumerable Royal Societies, and carried the whole *Mécanique Céleste* and Hegel's *Philosophy*, and the epitome of all laboratories and observatories with their results in his single head, is but a pair of spectacles behind which there is no eye.   Let those who have eyes look through him, then he may be useful." [1]

The greatest poets of this age used the vast stores of fact which the scientist had gathered, as lenses for deciphering more clearly the message from a divine hand. Sometimes this message proved too complex for complete human grasp, and Tennyson exclaims : —

> "I falter where I firmly trod,
>   And falling with my weight of cares
>   Upon the great world's altar-stairs
> That slope thro' darkness up to God." [2]

However dark these stairs may be, his creed is

> "That nothing walks with aimless feet ;
>   That not one life shall be destroyed,
>   Or cast as rubbish to the void,
> When God hath made the pile complete." [3]

And Browning, combining most splendidly his scientific knowledge with his emotional intensity, exclaims with joyous hopefulness : —

> ". . . all's love, yet all's law.
>
> I but open my eyes, — and perfection, no more and no less,
> In the kind I imagined, full-fronts me, and God is seen God
> In the star, in the stone, in the flesh, in the soul and the clod.

[1] *Sartor Resartus.*   [2] *In Memoriam*, LV.   [3] *Ibid.*, LIV.

> And thus looking within and around me, I ever renew
> (With that stoop of the soul which in bending upraises it too)
> The submission of man's nothing perfect to God's all complete,
> As by each new obeisance in spirit I climb to his feet." [1]

Evolution impressed on both Browning and Tennyson the necessity of a hand that never wearies or guides wrong in the labyrinthine mazes of eternity. Tennyson, who had wrestled with all the doubts of the century concerning the hereafter, wrote just before his final voyage across the Unknown Sea: —

> "I hope to see my Pilot face to face
> When I have crost the bar." [2]

The Ethical and Social Spirit. — A striving for better government, for higher moral ideals, and for the general uplifting of the masses is a marked feature of the age. The spirit of individualism reached its culmination at the time of the French Revolution. That spirit exalted individual effort and looked on the individual as unrelated to the mass or to the movements of the age. In the latter part of the nineteenth century, we may note more organized ethical effort in the direction of an altruism that concerns itself more with upward social movements and less with stray individuals. Men have realized more than ever before that they are their brothers' keepers. The wrongs in industrialism, the inequalities in birth and opportunity, have received increased attention. In no preceding age was the philanthropic spirit so eager to cure social evils.

Nearly all the great works of the Victorian age are imbued with an ethical purpose. The novels of Dickens paint the horrors of poverty-stricken neighborhoods and champion the cause of helpless school children under

[1] *Saul*, XVII.   [2] *Crossing the Bar*.

brutal masters. George Eliot shows the influences of heredity and environment, and teaches a needed moral lesson based on those scientific truths. The novel has proved the most effective ethical text-book of the century.

The poetry does something more than paint beautiful pictures. It is mindful of our duty to the unfortunate. Tennyson asks: —

> "Is it well that while we range with Science, glorying in the time,
> City children soak and blacken soul and sense in city slime?"[1]

Browning shows how character is tested and developed. Both he and Tennyson have strengthened the moral courage of many who were wavering. There is high ethical aim in such lines as these: —

> "Follow Light, and do the Right — for man can half control his doom —
> Till you find the deathless Angel seated in the vacant tomb."[2]

If, perchance, an author turned aside from the serious questions of existence to the enjoyment of mere beauty, he seemed to feel that he was a truant from one of life's lessons and shirking a responsibility. The seriousness and significance of existence were felt with an oppressive weight by some writers, notably by George Eliot; and all the strongest spirits uttered earnest ringing words upon conduct, ideals of living, and the duty of man to man. The age is remarkable for ethical teachers. Carlyle, Ruskin, Browning, and George Eliot stand among the greatest of those who have been inspired with a desire to uplift and beautify life.

An Analytical Age.— Science turned the spectroscope on the stars and determined their constituent elements. The chemist analyzed the bubbling fountain and resolved it into

---

[1] *Locksley Hall Sixty Years After.*   [2] *Ibid.*

hydrogen and oxygen. The botanist dissected the rose, the daffodil, and the violet. Science has infused into Victorian literature the analytical spirit, the desire to dissect life in order to discover the underlying springs of action.

The Elizabethans had preferred to watch throbbing life in its wonderful variety rather than to subject it to minute dissection. In this characteristic, the two ages differ widely. Dowden says: "Shakespeare had cared to see what things are, all of pity and terror, all of beauty and mirth, that human life contains,— Lear in the storm, and Falstaff in the tavern, and Perdita among her flowers. He had said: 'These things are,' and had refused to put the question: 'How can these things be?'" The Victorian age, on the other hand, has demanded theories of life, an analysis of all the reasons why Hamlet did not kill the King, or why Romeo loved Juliet.

The Elizabethans had loved to present strong lights and gloomy shadows, the fury of a Tamburlaine and the jealousy of an Othello, Macbeth as subject, murderer, and king. The uneventful lives of the rank and file of humanity had few charms for the Elizabethans. The nineteenth century alone has more adequately described the multitudinous host of the commonplace, which includes the vast majority of people. The common types of life acquire new interest for us as we analyze them. A scientist who can present an intelligent analysis of a grasshopper may be as interesting as a novelist. The keen, searching, analytical genius of a modern artist is required to point out interesting features in ordinary people and to present them with the necessary subtlety, such as George Eliot displays in her *Scenes from Clerical Life*. Thackeray shows a special gift in analyzing the motives of those whom he met in everyday life. Dickens lacks this analytical faculty, but it is possessed by far the greater number of modern novelists. So pronounced has been the tendency to dissect character, that the psychological novel is as typical of the Victorian age as the drama of the Elizabethan.

Victorian poetry is largely introspective and it presents a record of thoughts rather than of actions. It is full of complexities, analyses, and critical judgments. Browning is the prince of analytical poets. Tennyson and Arnold are at their best when meditating upon nature or reflecting upon life. The poetry in general is marked not by a comprehensive grasp of life as a whole, but by a power of analyzing certain problems, feelings, motives, and types of character to serve as stepping stones toward the temple of truth and as a foundation for theories of existence.

THOMAS BABINGTON MACAULAY, 1800-1859

Life. — A prominent figure in the social and political life of England during the first part of the century was Thomas Babington Macaulay, a man of brilliant intellectual powers, strict integrity of character, and enormous capacity for work. He loved England and gloried in her liberties and her commercial prosperity. He served her for many years in the House of Commons, and he bent his whole energy and splendid forensic talent in favor of the Reform Bill of 1832, which secured greater political liberty for England.

He was not a theorizer, but a practical man of affairs. Notwithstanding the fact that his political opinions were ready made for him by the Whig party, his career in the House was never "inconsistent with rectitude of intention and independence of spirit." He voted conscientiously

for measures, although he personally sacrificed hundreds
of pounds by so doing.

He was a remarkable talker. A single speech of his has
been known to change an entire vote in Parliament. Unlike Coleridge, he did not indulge in monologue, but
showed to finest advantage in debate. His power of
memory was wonderful. He often startled an opponent
by quoting from a given chapter and page of a book. He
repeated long passages from *Paradise Lost ;* and it is said
he could have restored it complete, had it all been lost.

His disposition was sweet and his life altogether fortunate. His biographer says of him: " Descended from Scotch Presbyterians — ministers many of them — on his father's side, and from a Quaker family on his mother's, he probably united as many guarantees of 'good birth,' in the moral sense of the word, as could be found in these islands at the beginning of the century."

He was born at Rothley Temple, Leicestershire, in 1800. He was prepared for college at good private schools, and sent to Cambridge when he was eighteen. He studied law and was admitted to the bar in 1825, but, in the following year, he determined to adopt literature as a profession, owing to the welcome given to his *Essay on Milton*. He had written epics, histories, and metrical romances prior to the age of ten, so that his choice of a profession was neither hasty nor unexpected.

He continued from this time to write for the *Edinburgh Review*, but literature was not the only field of his activity. He had a seat in Parliament, and he held several positions under the Government. He was never unemployed. Many of his *Essays* were written before breakfast, while the other members of the household were asleep.

He was a voracious reader. If he walked in the country or in London, he always carried a book to read. He spent some years in the Government's service in India. On the long voyage over, he read incessantly, and on the return trip he studied the German language.

He was beyond the age of forty when he found the leisure to begin his *History of England*. He worked uninterruptedly and broke down early. He was but fifty-nine years old at the time of his death in 1859.

With his large, fine physique, his sturdy common sense, his interest in practical matters, and his satisfaction in the physical improvements of the people, Macaulay was a fine specimen of the English gentleman.

Essays and Poetry. — Like De Quincey, Macaulay was a frequent contributor to periodicals. He wrote graphic essays on men of action and historical periods. The essays most worthy of mention in this class are *Sir William Temple*, *Lord Clive*, *Warren Hastings*, and *William Pitt, Earl of Chatham*. Some of his essays on English writers and literary subjects are still classic. Among these are *Milton*, *Dryden*, *Addison*, *Southey's Edition of Pilgrim's Progress*, *Croker's Edition of Boswell's Life of Johnson*, and the biographical essays on *Bunyan*, *Goldsmith*, and *Johnson*, contributed to the *Encyclopædia Britannica*. Although they may lack deep spiritual insight into the fundamental principles of life and literary criticism, these essays are still deservedly read by most students of English history and literature.

Gosse says: "The most restive of juvenile minds, if induced to enter one of Macaulay's essays, is almost certain to reappear at the other end of it gratified, and, to an appreciable extent, cultivated." These *Essays* have developed a taste for general reading in numbers who could not have been induced to begin with anything dry or hard. Many who have read Boswell's *Life of Johnson* during the past fifty years say that Macaulay first turned their attention to that fascinating work. In the following quotation from an essay on that great biography, we may note his love for interesting concrete statements, presented in a vigorous and clear style : —

"Johnson grown old, Johnson in the fullness of his fame and in the enjoyment of a competent fortune, is better known to us than any other man in history. Everything about him, his coat, his wig, his figure, his face, his scrofula, his St. Vitus's dance, his rolling walk, his blinking eye, the outward signs which too clearly marked his approbation of his dinner, his insatiable appetite for fish sauce and veal pie with plums, his inextinguishable thirst for tea, his trick of touching the posts as he walked . . . all are as familiar to us as the objects by which we have been surrounded from childhood."

Macaulay wrote some stirring ballad poetry, known as *Lays of Ancient Rome*, which gives a good picture of the proud Roman Republic in its valorous days. These ballads have something of Scott's healthy, manly ring. They contain rhetorical and martial stanzas which boys love, but Macaulay lacked that spirituality and passion for beauty which are necessary in a great poet.

History of England. — Macaulay had for some time wondered why some one should not do for real history what Scott had done for imaginary history. Macaulay accordingly proposed to himself the task of writing a history which should be more accurate than Hume's and possess something of the interest of Scott's historical romances. In 1848 appeared the first two volumes of *The History of England from the Accession of James II.* Macaulay had the satisfaction of seeing his work, in sales and popular appreciation, surpass the novels. He intended to trace the development of English liberty from James II. to the death of George III., but his minute method of treatment allowed him to unfold only sixteen years of that important period, from 1685 to 1701.

Macaulay's pages are not a graveyard for the dry bones of history. The human beings that figure in his chapters have been restored to life by his touch. We see Charles II. "before the dew was off in St. James's Park striding among the trees, playing with his spaniels, and flinging corn to his ducks." We gaze for a moment with the English courtiers at William III. : —

" They observed that the King spoke in a somewhat imperious tone, even to the wife to whom he owed so much, and whom he sincerely loved and esteemed. They were amused and shocked to see him, when the Princess Anne dined with him, and when the first green peas of the year were put on the table, devour the whole dish without offering a spoonful to her Royal Highness, and they pronounced that this great soldier and politician was no better than a low Dutch bear." [1]

Parts of the *History* are masterpieces of the narrator's art. A trained novelist, unhampered by historical facts, could scarcely have surpassed the last part of Macaulay's eighth chapter in relating the trial of the seven Bishops. Our blood tingles to the tips of our fingers as we read in the fifth chapter the story of Monmouth's rebellion and the Bloody Assizes of Judge Jeffreys.

Macaulay shirked no labor in preparing himself to write the *History*. He read thousands of pages of authorities and he personally visited the great battlefields in order to give accurate descriptions. Notwithstanding such preparation, the value of his *History* is impaired, not only because he sometimes displays partisanship, but also because he fails to appreciate the significance of underlying social movements. He does not adopt the modern idea that history is a record of social growth, moral as well as physical. While a graphic picture of the exterior aspects of society is presented, we are given no profound insight into the interior movements of a great constitutional epoch. We may say of both Gibbon and Macaulay that they are too often mere surveyors, rather than geologists, of the historic field.[2] The popularity of the *History* is not injured by this method.

Macaulay's grasp of fact never weakens, his love of

[1] *History of England*, Vol. III., Chap. XI.
[2] Morison's *Life of Macaulay*, p. 139.

manly courage never relaxes, his joy in bygone time never fails, his zeal for the free institutions of England never falters, and his style is never dull. While scholars may study other works, the generality of mankind will prefer to read Macaulay.

General Characteristics. — The chief quality of Macaulay's style is its clearness. Contemporaries said that the printers' readers never had to read his sentences a second time to understand them. This clearness is attained, first, by the structure of his sentences. He avoids entangling clauses, obscure references in his pronouns, and long sentences whenever they are in danger of becoming involved and causing the reader to lose his way. In the second place, if the idea is a difficult one or not likely to be apprehended at its full worth, Macaulay repeats his meaning from a different point of view and throws additional light on the subject by varied illustrations. In the third place, his works abound in concrete ideas, which are more readily grasped than abstract ones. He is not content to write: "The smallest actual good is better than the most magnificent promise of impossibilities," but he gives the concrete equivalent: "An acre in Middlesex is worth a principality in Utopia."

It is possible for style to be both clear and lifeless, but his style is as energetic as it is clear. In narration he takes high rank. His erudition, displayed in the vast stores of fact which his memory retained for effective service in every direction, is worthy of special mention.

While his excellences may serve as a model, he has faults which admirers would do well to avoid. His fondness for contrast often leads him to make one picture too bright and the other too dark. His love of antithesis has the merit of arousing attention in his readers and of crystallizing some thoughts into enduring epigrammatic form, but he is often led to sacrifice exact truth in order to obtain fine contrasts, as in the following : —

"The Puritan hated bear-baiting, not because it gave pain to the bear, but because it gave pleasure to the spectators."

Macaulay lacked sympathy with theories and aspirations which could not accomplish immediate practical results. His works are confined to the treatment of the material world. They are not illumined with the spiritual glow that sheds luster on the pages of Coleridge, Carlyle, and Ruskin.

CARLYLE'S BIRTHPLACE

THOMAS CARLYLE, 1795-1881

Life. — In striking contrast to the placid temperament and realistic common sense of Macaulay, are the passionate eagerness and idealism of Carlyle. This son of Scotch peasants was bred upon the stern doctrines of the Kirk of Scotland; he was surrounded by "an inflexible element of authority" in his cheerless home; he was acquainted with the stings of poverty; he endured the sufferings of acute dyspepsia; and he knew the bitterness of a doubting soul.

He was born at Ecclefechan, Dumfriesshire, in 1795. His parents destined him for the church, so they sent him to the University of Edinburgh. He soon discovered that his views were not in accord with the church's teachings, and, with much sadness, he assured his parents that he could not realize their ambitions. His somber, passionate nature suffered intensely during the following years of religious doubt. He lost faith both in himself and in a God, and shrank from the pains of life. Carlyle's long and troubled vigils were finally crowned with joy. He seemed suddenly to pierce the gloom and to find his God. This inner conflict left its traces upon Carlyle's entire life. A powerful record of his experience is found in *Sartor Resartus*.

During this dark period, Carlyle was writing for magazines and striving to succeed in the uncongenial drudgery of teaching. In 1819 he began the study of German. He translated Goethe's novel, *Wilhelm Meister*, and wrote a *Life of Schiller*. Together with Coleridge and De Quincey, Carlyle was instrumental in acquainting the English public with German philosophy and literature.

He married in 1826. His wife, Jane Welsh, was a woman of brilliant intellectual attainments. She recognized her husband's genius, and by her timely words of praise strengthened him against the ridicule of the critics. Despite her quick temper, which took fire at Carlyle's

Thomas Carlyle

querulousness, she was the ideal wife for him. They
loved each other passionately. In 1828 they went to
her lonely farm at Craigenputtock, where, for six years,
Carlyle was immersed in study. They moved to London
in 1834, and lived very quietly at Chelsea, where Carlyle
continued his literary labors.

Carlyle did not attain Macaulay's sudden and widespread popularity. Carlyle had to wait years for a public,
but he finally won it. In 1865 he was highly honored
by the Edinburgh University, which elected him Lord
Rector. He was inaugurated in 1866. His gruff but

kindly heart was deeply touched, and his speech of acceptance was full of emotion.

A few weeks later, his happiness was blighted by the announcement of his wife's death during his stay in Scotland. He lived fifteen lonely years after this loss. His sad life ended in 1881, and on a bleak February day he was laid beside his father in Ecclefechan.

Sartor Resartus. — Carlyle's most daring and original work is *Sartor Resartus* (1833–1834), which means "the tailor patched." It pretends, half humorously, to be a confused assortment of some German philosopher's manuscripts; but it is, in reality, Carlyle's own mystical interpretation of life. He calls the work a Philosophy of Clothes, using the word "clothes" symbolically to signify the outward expression of the spiritual. For example, since man's spirit expresses itself in thoughts and deeds, these are the clothes of the human spirit; and since God reveals himself in the physical universe, therefore it is the clothing of the divine spirit. Carlyle says:—

"It is written, the Heavens and the Earth shall fade away like a Vesture; which indeed they are: the Time-vesture of the Eternal. Whatsoever sensibly exists, whatsoever represents Spirit to Spirit, is properly a Clothing, a suit of Raiment, put on for a season, and to be laid off. Thus in this one pregnant subject of CLOTHES, rightly understood, is included all that men have thought, dreamed, done, and been: the whole External Universe and what it holds is but Clothing; and the essence of all Science lies in the PHILOSOPHY OF CLOTHES."

The message that Carlyle delivers to his generation in *Sartor Resartus* is that man must tear away these vestments, which are but semblances, and pierce to the inner spirit, which is the reality. The century's material progress, which was such cause of pride to Macaulay, afforded

Carlyle no sense of gratification. He emphasizes the need of a quickening spirit for his time. He denounces the money-making basis of modern life, the selfishness of industrialism, the material explanations which science finds for the sacred emotions of duty, sacrifice, and worship. He holds up to scorn the philosophy which takes pleasure in a nation's commercial welfare, when her people's heart is still hard and unloving. He says of the utilitarian philosophy, which he hated intensely:—

"It spreads like a sort of Dog-madness; till the whole World-kennel will be rabid."

He uses all the power of his grotesque and caustic humor to satirize the lack of spirituality in the age, and he does not shrink from mere ugliness of expression when he is aroused. He writes:—

"But what, in these dull unimaginative days, are the terrors of Conscience to the diseases of the Liver! Not on Morality, but on Cookery, let us build our stronghold: there brandishing our frying pan as censer, let us offer sweet incense to the Devil, and live on the fat things *he* has provided for his Elect!"

The gospel of Carlyle's teaching is work. He teaches that all men are ennobled by work, honestly performed, no matter how humble it is. In his peculiarly emphatic way, he says:—

"Be no longer a Chaos, but a World, or even Worldkin. Produce! Produce! Were it but the pitifullest infinitesimal fraction of a Product, produce it, in God's name! 'Tis the utmost thou hast in thee: out with it, then."

This production of Carlyle, which hurls satiric denunciations at the shams and trivialities of the world, and calls men to earnest activity, proved a powerful stimulant to the younger generation of Englishmen. Many were thus roused from their lethargy and complacency to action, to reforms, and to a trust in eternal spiritual truth.

The French Revolution. — Carlyle's manner of handling incidents and characters is so extremely dramatic that his histories have been said to resemble more closely the historical plays of Shakespeare than the works of ordinary historians. *The French Revolution* (1837) is perhaps the most dramatic of all Carlyle's works. It is not a flowing, connected narrative like Macaulay's *History of England*, but a succession of striking pageants that are alive with action and lifelike characters. Carlyle used the romancer's privilege of selection ; and, from out a mass of material which would have bewildered men of less ability, he chose for powerful presentation a limited number of significant and picturesque incidents.

The death of Louis XV., the storming of the Bastille, the insurrection of the women, the march of the mob to Versailles in search of royalty, the horrors of the Reign of Terror, and other equally ghastly scenes, are presented with distinctness and dramatic force. The individuals who were the life of the Revolution are all strongly drawn. Lafayette, Mirabeau, Danton, Robespierre, and many another stand forth like the flesh and blood realities which they once were.

Carlyle seems to get into the very midst of a mob and catch its feelings, and to reach the hearts of his characters and know their springs of action. He neither describes men, assemblages, and crowds from the outside, like Macaulay, nor submits them to careful dissection, like De Quincey. Carlyle describes everything as though he had been a participator, so that there is a warm personal element in all his men and scenes. In the following passage, he bears the reader with the mob as it breaks into Versailles : —

"The terrorstruck Bodyguards fly, bolting and Barricading; it follows. Whitherward? Through hall on hall: wo, now! toward the Queen's Suite of Rooms, in the furthest room of which the Queen is now asleep. Five sentinels rush through that long Suite; they are in the Anteroom knocking loud: 'Save the Queen!' Trembling women fall at their feet with tears; are answered: 'Yes, we will die; save ye the Queen!'

"Tremble not, women, but haste: for, lo, another voice shouts far through the outermost door, 'Save the Queen!' and the door is shut. It is brave Miomandre's voice that shouts this second warning. He has stormed across imminent death to do it; fronts imminent death, having done it. . . . She [the Queen] flies for her life, across the Œil-de-Bœuf; against the main door of which, too, Insurrection batters. She is in the King's Apartment, in the King's arms, she clasps her children amid a faithful few."

The dramatic excitement, the vividness, and the vigor of treatment which this selection shows, combine to make *The French Revolution* a stirring recital.

Carlyle's power of making some great personality the center of every movement adds much to the interest of his work. Mirabeau is one of the most imposing figures. He is made known by a few bold, graphic touches. He is described as a man

"Through whose shaggy beetle-brows, and rough-hewn, seamed, carbuncled face, there look natural ugliness, smallpox, incontinence, bankruptcy, — and burning fire of genius.

"But now if Mirabeau is the greatest, who of these Six Hundred may be the meanest? Shall we say, that anxious, slight, ineffectual-looking man, under thirty, in spectacles; his eyes (were the glasses off) troubled, careful?"

This is the "greenish coloured" Robespierre. Carlyle delights in bringing out such contrasts in character as these men afford.

Whatever found lodgment in Carlyle's brain seems to have taken some definite form and to have become a picture. It is his manner of painting distinct pictures that constitutes his chief power in historical writing. It is by means of his pictorial vividness that the reader gains such an intense realization of the wild chaos, the frenzy, and the blood-curdling madness of the French Revolutionists.

Carlyle's "Real Kings." — Carlyle believed that "universal history, the history of what man has accomplished in this world, is at bottom the history of the great men who have worked here." In accordance with this belief, he studied, not the slow growth of the people, but the lives of the world's great geniuses.

In his course of lectures entitled *Heroes and Hero Worship* (1841), he considers *The Hero as Prophet*, *The Hero as Poet*, *The Hero as Priest*, and *The Hero as King*, and shows how history has been molded by men like Mohammed, Shakespeare, Luther, and Napoleon. It is such men as these whom Carlyle calls "kings," beside whom "emperors," "popes," and "potentates" are as nothing. He believed that there was always living some man worthy to be the "real king" over men, and such a kingship was Carlyle's ideal of government. The difficulty lay only in the discovery of the rightful king.

Oliver Cromwell was one of Carlyle's great heroes. The edition of *Cromwell's Letters and Speeches* (1845) is Carlyle's most valuable book from a scholar's point of view, because this work was the first to present the character of the Protector in its full strength and greatness. In opposition to the rankest prejudices of the public, Carlyle proved once for all that Cromwell was a "real king" whose memory all Englishmen should honor.

The Life of John Sterling (1851) is a fair, true, and

touching biography. Carlyle knew Sterling well and described his faults and virtues, alike, with tender sympathy. After reading the book, George Eliot said she wished that more men of genius would write biographies.

Carlyle's next attempt at biography grew into the massive *History of Friedrich II.* (1858–1865), which includes a survey of European history in that dreary century which preceded the French Revolution. " Friedrich is by no means one of the perfect demigods." He is "to the last a questionable hero." However, "in his way he is a Reality," one feels "that he always means what he speaks; grounds his actions, too, on what he recognizes for the truth; and, in short, has nothing of the Hypocrite or Phantasm." Despite his tyranny and his bloody career, he, therefore, is another of Carlyle's "real kings." While this work is a history of modern Europe, Friedrich is always the central figure. He gives to these six volumes a human note, a glowing interest of personal adventure, and a oneness that are remarkable in so vast a work.

General Characteristics. — Carlyle has been called the " Censor of the age." With biting satire and contemptuous scorn, he lashes this "swine's trough" of a world, with its " Pig science, Pig enthusiasm and Devotion." He is the champion of spiritual truth in opposition to the material tendencies which gave Macaulay so much satisfaction. Carlyle urges men to cease yearning for "pig's wash," by which he means material comfort, and to seek after the everlasting light of truth and duty. " Do thy Duty, the Duty that lies nearest thee," he says again and again.

A subject had to possess strong human interest in order to appeal to Carlyle. Metaphysics, technical literary criticisms, and economic histories had no attraction for him. *Sartor Resartus* is not a bare philosophical treatise. The fears, doubts, beliefs, and ideals of Carlyle's own palpitating heart are the subject of the work. His literary criticisms of Burns, Voltaire, Johnson, and Goethe judge the men by their characters and purposes and not by their purely literary skill. His histories are not made up of abstract movements and scientific economic causes, but of living, suffering men and women, whose passions, characters, and sacrifices have led to the movements which constitute history. Carlyle is not a cool, logical reasoner, but a seer and a revealer who quickens history and philosophy with the breath of imagination, and who speaks with the authority of a prophet and a priest.

He has wonderful richness of figurative language. It seems more natural for him to use metaphors than simple terms. In describing Daniel Webster, Carlyle speaks of "the tanned complexion, that amorphous crag-like face; the dull black eyes under their precipice of brows, like dull anthracite furnaces needing only to be blown, the mastiff-mouth, accurately closed." His vocabulary abounds in unusual metaphorical epithets, rare or new compounds, and words which he coined himself and engrafted upon the language.

In style, as in philosophy, he presents a striking contrast to Macaulay. Carlyle's sentences are loose, disjointed, and broken by frequent interjections. He is declamatory and rugged and seldom attains smoothness or harmony. His style, on the whole, is like the man, original, earnest, fiery, and forceful. It has the directness of a personal spoken appeal. While this style is frequently discordant, and sometimes theatrical, it can become, in his intensest moments, poetic, full of deepest invective or noble figure, and ablaze with words that come "flamingly from the heart of a living man."

JOHN RUSKIN, 1819-1900

Life. — The great disciple of Thomas Carlyle was John Ruskin, also a man of earnest and dogmatic nature, and of lofty and inspiring ideals. Like his master, Ruskin regretted the mechanical humdrum and the spiritual dullness of society, and he labored to construct a social system founded upon nobler objects than those of trade.

Ruskin was born in London in 1819. Both of his parents were Scotch, and both possessed the honesty, piety, and unbending will characteristic of the best element of that race. John Ruskin was their only child and their one idol. He had the best tutors, the choicest books and paintings, and the most costly education which Oxford could afford. He gratefully returned this care with unfailing attention to his parents throughout their lives.

Ruskin's home training was rigidly Puritanical. He says: "Nothing was ever promised me that was not given; nothing ever threatened me that was not inflicted; and nothing ever told me that was not true." Another molding power in his early education was his daily lesson in the *Bible*. The *Scriptures* became so familiar to him that quotations from them slipped unconsciously into his speech, and his early writings are strongly tinged with the eloquence of the Hebrew Prophets.

While still a small child, Ruskin traveled with his parents through England, Scotland, Italy, and Switzerland. His passion for nature was thus early fostered. He became a close student of the sky, the mountains, the rivers, and the fields. These trips mark an important epoch in his career, for they led him to keep a diary in which we find him dwelling fondly on the description of landscapes and the criticism of art. He thus acquired practice in the special field of literature in which he afterwards became so famous. His first great volume of art criticism was published when he was twenty-four. This was followed by repeated successes in the same field, until he became one of the most noted of art critics.

After 1860 Ruskin eschewed art studies in order to better the conditions of humanity. This decision was perhaps the only one which he ever made in open defiance of his parents. They could not sympathize with his founding of libraries, museums, art schools, his building of sanitary tenement houses, and his manual labor. It is said that his fortune of £180,000 amounted to only £18,000 after his expenditures for the poor had been deducted. He taught art at the Workingmen's College. With his own hands he wielded a pick, and he influenced some other Oxford enthusiasts to aid in building for farmers a road leading into London. His greatest undertaking was the founding of an ideal village. The project was known as St. George's Guild. All competition was discarded, and a healthy, unselfish, out-of-door life was encouraged. Some men and women appreciated the benefits of this community, but, on the whole, the experiment proved little more than an expensive luxury.

Ruskin's noble endeavors were so misunderstood by his neighbors that he was thought to be insane. He says in *Fors Clavigera:* " Because I have passed my life in almsgiving, not in fortune hunting; because I have labored always for the honor of others, not of my own, and have chosen rather to make men look at Turner and Luini, than to form or exhibit the skill of my own hand; because I have lowered my rents, and assured the comfortable lives of my poor tenants, instead of taking from them all I could force for the roofs they needed; because I love a wood walk better than a London street; and would rather watch a sea gull fly than shoot it, and rather hear a thrush sing than eat it; finally, because I never disobeyed my mother, because I have honored all women with solemn worship, and have been kind even to the unthankful and evil; therefore, the hacks of English art and literature wag their heads at me." Ruskin did not permit the criticism of the "hacks" to interfere with his reforms. The relieving of the poor remained his chief work, until broken health and shattered nerves drove him into retirement at his beautiful home of Brantwood on Coniston Water, in the Lake District. He died in 1900.

RUSKIN'S HOME ON CONISTON WATER

Art Criticism. — Ruskin is noted as a critic of art. His *Modern Painters* (1843–1860) and his two works on architecture, *The Seven Lamps of Architecture* (1849), and *The Stones of Venice* (1851–1853), are his chief productions in the criticism of art. The greatest of these is *Modern Painters*, which deals primarily with landscape painting. In a masterly survey of ancient and modern artists, he shows the great superiority of the landscapes of the modern school over those of the old masters. He compares the landscapes of different artists with real mountains, clouds, water, and vegetation, and shows how inaccurate and stereotyped are most of the supposed copies of nature. The only painter who filled all of Ruskin's requirements in reproducing nature was J. M. W. Turner. In a lecture on painting Ruskin says : —

"By Shakespeare humanity was unsealed to you; by Verulam, the *principles* of nature; and by Turner, her *aspect*. All these were sent to unlock one of the gates of light, and to unlock it for the first time. . . . none before Turner had lifted the veil from the face of nature; the majesty of the hills and forests had received no interpretation, and the clouds passed unrecorded from the fall of the heaven which they adorned, and of the earth to which they ministered."

Before the revolution in landscape painting was complete, a noted critic, on looking at a canvas where the trees were green, asked in surprise: "But where is your brown tree?" Leafy trees appeared green to Ruskin and he insisted that they should be painted green, no matter what color the conventional school declared was the proper one.

In *Modern Painters*, Ruskin enters into a careful study of the phenomena of nature. He describes, for example, the form and arrangement of clouds at certain elevations. He explains the structure, angles, and surfaces of various kinds of rocks. He sets forth in a minutely scientific manner the manifold aspects of water. He also describes the arrangement of boughs, the laws of foliage, the effects of distance, and the wonders of color.

In ridiculing those who do not found on exact observation their criticism of art, he shows the influence of the scientific spirit of the age. In the first part of *Modern Painters*, he says:—

"Ask the connoisseur, who has scampered all over Europe, the shape of the leaf of an elm, and the chances are ninety to one that he cannot tell you; and yet he will be voluble of criticism on every painted landscape from Dresden to Madrid, and pretend to tell you whether they are like nature or not. Ask an enthusiastic chatterer in the Sistine Chapel how many ribs he has, and you get no answer; but it is odds that you do not get out of the door without his informing you that he considers such and such a figure badly drawn!"

But *Modern Painters* is something more than a criticism of art. The work is a gospel of the beautiful in nature as the expression of the Divine Mind. Later in life Ruskin himself said : "*Modern Painters* taught the claim of all lower nature on the hearts of men ; of the rock, and wave, and herb, as a part of their necessary spirit life." In *Modern Painters* he also expounds the object of his sermons on art, when he says of this dull world : "I do verily believe it will come, finally, to understand that God paints the clouds and shapes the moss fibers, that men may be happy in seeing Him at His work." Ruskin's works on architecture are also less valuable for technical criticism than for magnificent descriptions of beautiful objects, and for an exposition of the intellectual and moral significance of the beautiful in architecture.

Social Questions. — By turning from the criticism of art to consider the cause of humanity, Ruskin shows the influence of the ethical and social forces of the age. In middle life he was overwhelmed with the amount of human misery and he determined to do his best to relieve it. He wrote : —

"I simply cannot paint, nor read, nor look at minerals, nor do anything else that I like, and the very light of the morning sky, when there is any, — which is seldom, nowadays, near London, — has become hateful to me, because of the misery that I know of, and see signs of, where I know it not, which no imagination can interpret too bitterly." [1]

After 1860 his main efforts with both pen and purse were devoted to improving the condition of his fellow-men. His books written with this end in view bear strangely fanciful titles, such as *Unto this Last* and *Munera Pulveris*, which explain political economy, *Crown of Wild Olive*,

[1] *Fors Clavigera*, Letter I.

which treats of "Work, Traffic, and War," and *Fors Clavigera*, a series of letters to workingmen. Some of his economical theories and plans for bettering the world are as fanciful and as unrelated to what is possible as the titles of these works are to their contents.

These works deserve attention, not because of the excellence of their working theories of social regeneration, but because Ruskin here voices grand ethical truths of sufficient power to play a part in placing humanity on a higher spiritual plane.

General Characteristics. — As the high priest of beauty, Ruskin occupies a secure place in prose literature. Many have testified that their power to perceive new beauties in cloud and mist, meadow and stream, waterfall and mountain, tree and flower, has been tripled through the influence of his teaching. The spirit of the age is shown in the fact that Ruskin achieves this result less by a direct appeal to feeling, after the manner of the poets, than by teaching us to observe more closely and to discover the beautiful for ourselves through the exercise of our perceptive and reasoning powers on the world around us. He once said : " All my work is to help those who *have* eyes and see not." The æsthetic movement of the last part of the nineteenth century owes more to Ruskin than to any other single man.

In the second place, Ruskin is a great ethical teacher, in his works on art as well as in those on social amelioration. He is not the apostle of merely sensuous beauty, but rather of that beauty which ennobles the spiritual life and ministers to the highest needs of the soul. His very conception of beauty is founded on a high ethical standard. Like Carlyle he opposed sordid materialism. Unlike Carlyle, Ruskin's social philosophy led to his following the example of the Good Samaritan in the actual walks of life. His utterances may sometimes be dogmatic and self-contradictory, and his economic theories, absurd; but his noble ethical teachings overarch all, like a rainbow promising a new covenant of good will to earth.

Ruskin's best prose is written in a descriptive, ornate, almost poetic style. He is remarkable for his power of word painting. The following description of the Rhone deserves to be ranked with a fine oil painting: —

"There were pieces of wave that danced all day as if Perdita were looking on to learn; there were little streams that skipped like lambs and leaped like chamois; there were pools that shook the sunshine all through them, and were rippled in layers of overlaid ripples, like crystal sand; there were currents that twisted the light into golden braids, and inlaid the threads with turquoise enamel; there were strips of stream that had certainly above the lake been mill streams, and were busily looking for mills to turn again."[1]

Word painting naturally lends itself to a descriptive style, for the writer desires to aid the reader in the realization of what is described. By employing language as varied as a painter's pigments, Ruskin enables us to realize the color of the Rhone with its

". . . ever-answering glow of unearthly aquamarine, ultra-marine, violet blue, gentian blue, peacock blue, river-of-paradise blue, glow of a painted window melted in the sun, and the witch of the Alps flinging the spun tresses of it forever from her snow."[2]

In breadth of sympathetic observation, joined to rare ability for describing the beauties of nature, of painting, and of architecture with something of the power usually possessed by poets alone, Ruskin is surpassed by no other English prose writer.

[1] *Præterita*, Vol. II., Chap. V. [2] *Ibid*.

MATTHEW ARNOLD, 1822-1888

Life. — Matthew Arnold was born in 1822, at Laleham, Middlesex. His father, Dr. Thomas Arnold, was the eminent head master of Rugby School, and the author of *History of Rome*, *Lectures on Modern History*, and *Sermons*. Under the guidance of such a father, Matthew Arnold enjoyed unusual educational advantages. In 1837 he entered Rugby, and from there he went to Baliol College, Oxford. He was so ambitious and studious that he won two prizes at Oxford, graduated with honors, and, a year later, was elected fellow of Oriel College. Arnold's name, like Thomas Gray's, is associated with university life.

From 1847 to 1851, Arnold was private secretary to Lord Lansdowne. In 1851 he married the daughter of Justice Wightman. After relinquishing his secretaryship, Arnold accepted a position which took him again into educational fields. He was made lay inspector of schools, a position which he held to within two years of his death. This office called for much study in methods of education, and he visited the continent three times to investigate the systems in use there. In addition, he held the chair of poetry at Oxford for ten years, between 1857 and 1867. One of the most scholarly courses of lectures that he delivered there was *On Translating Homer*. From this time until his death, in 1888, he was a distinguished figure in English educational and literary circles.

MATTHEW ARNOLD'S GRAVE IN LALEHAM CHURCHYARD

Poetical Works. — Matthew Arnold's poetry belongs to the middle of the century, that season of doubt, perplexity, and unrest, when the strife between the church and science was bitterest and each threatened to overthrow the other. In his home, Arnold was taught a devout faith in revealed religion, and at college he was thrown upon a world of inquiring doubt. Both influences were strong. His feelings yearned after the early faith, and his intellect sternly demanded scientific proof and explanation. He was, therefore, torn by a conflict between his emotions and reason, and he was thus eminently fitted to be the poetic exponent of what he calls

> " . . . this strange disease of modern life,
> With its sick hurry, its divided aims,
> Its heads o'ertaxed, its palsied hearts." [1]

Arnold felt that there were too much hurry and excitement in the age. In the midst of opposing factions, theories, and beliefs, he cries out for rest and peace. We rush from shadow to shadow, —

> "And never once possess our soul
> Before we die." [2]

Again, in the *Stanzas in Memory of the Author of "Obermann,"* he voices the unrest of the age : —

> "What shelter to grow ripe is ours?
> What leisure to grow wise?
> Like children bathing on the shore,
> Buried a wave beneath,
> The second wave succeeds, before
> We have had time to breathe."

But Arnold is not the seer to tell us how to enter the vale of rest, how to answer the voice of doubt. He passes through life a lonely figure, —

> "Wandering between two worlds, one dead,
> The other powerless to be born." [3]

The only creed that he offers humanity is one born of the scientific temper, a creed of stoical endurance and un-

---

[1] *The Scholar-Gypsy.*　　　　[2] *A Southern Night.*
[3] *The Grande Chartreuse.*

swerving allegiance to the voice of duty. While these might support his own lofty spirit, they are little better than stones to a people crying for the bread of life. Arnold himself was far from satisfied, but his cool reason refused him the solace of an unquestioning faith.

Arnold has been called "the poet of the Universities," because of the reflective, scholarly thought in his verse. It breathes the atmosphere of books and the study. Such poetry cannot appeal to the masses. It is for the thinker.

The style of verse which lends itself best to Arnold's genius is the elegiac lyric. *The Scholar-Gypsy* and its companion piece *Thyrsis, Memorial Verses, Stanzas from the Grande Chartreuse,* and *Stanzas in Memory of the Author of "Obermann,"* are some of his best elegies.

Sohrab and Rustum and *Balder Dead* are Arnold's finest narrative poems. They are stately, dignified recitals of the deeds of heroes and gods. The series of poems entitled *Switzerland* and *Dover Beach* are among Arnold's most beautiful lyrics. A fine description of the surf is contained in the last-named poem : —

> "Listen ! you hear the grating roar
> Of pebbles which the waves draw back, and fling,
> At their return, up the high strand,
> Begin, and cease, and then again begin,
> With tremulous cadence slow, and bring
> The eternal note of sadness in."

Neither the movement of the narrative nor the lightness of the lyric is wholly congenial to Arnold's introspective melancholy muse.

Prose Works. — Although Arnold's first works were in poetry, he won recognition as a prose writer before he was widely known as a poet. His works in prose comprise such subjects as literary criticism, education, theology, and social ethics. As a critic of literature, he surpasses all his great contemporaries. Neither Macaulay nor Carlyle possessed the critical acumen, the taste, and the cultivated judgment of literary works, in such fullness as Matthew Arnold.

His greatest contributions to critical literature are the various magazine articles which were collected in the two volumes entitled *Essays in Criticism* (1865–1888). Arnold displays great breadth of culture and fairness of mind in these essays. He rises superior to the narrow provincialism and racial prejudices which he deprecates in other criticisms of literature, and gives the same sympathetic consideration to the German Heine and the Frenchman Joubert as to Wordsworth. Arnold further insists that Frenchmen should study English literature for its serious ethical spirit, and that Englishmen would be benefited by a study of the lightness, precision, and polished form of French literature.

Arnold's object in all his criticisms is to discover the best in both prose and poetry, and his method of attaining this object is another illustration of his scholarship and mental reach. He says in his *Introduction* to Ward's *English Poets:* —

"Indeed, there can be no more useful help for discovering what poetry belongs to the class of the truly excellent, and can therefore do us most good, than to have always in one's mind lines and expressions of the great masters, and to apply them as a touchstone to other poetry."

When Arnold seeks to determine an author's true place in literature, his keen critical eye seems to see at a glance all the world's great writers, and to compare them with the man under discussion. In order to ascertain Wordsworth's literary stature, for example, his height is measured by that of Homer, of Dante, of Shakespeare, and of Milton.

Another essential quality of the critical mind which Arnold possessed, is "sweet reasonableness." His judgments of men are marked by a moderation of tone. His strong predilections are sometimes shown, but they are more often restrained by a clear, honest intellect. Arnold's calm, measured criticisms are not marred by such stout partisanship as Macaulay shows for the Whigs, by the hero worship which Carlyle expresses, or by the exaggerated praise and blame which Ruskin sometimes bestows. On the other hand, Arnold loses what these men gain, for while his intellect is less biased than theirs, it is also less colored and warmed by the glow of feeling.

The analytical quality of Arnold's mind shows the spirit of the age. His subjects are minutely classified and defined. Facts seem to divide naturally into brigades, regiments, and battalions of marching order. His literary criticisms note subtleties of style, delicate shadings in expression, and many technical excellences and errors that Carlyle would have passed over unheeded. In addition to the *Essays in Criticism*, the other works of Arnold which possess his fine critical qualities in highest degree are *On Translating Homer* (1861) and *The Study of Celtic Literature* (1867).

General Characteristics. — The impression which Arnold has left upon literature is mainly that of a keen, brilliant intellect. In his poetry there is more emotion than in his prose, but even in his poetry there is no passion or fire. The sadness, the loneliness, the unrest of life, and the irreconcilable conflict between faith and doubt are most often the subjects of his verse. His range is narrow, but within it he attains a pure, noble beauty. His introspective, analytical poetry is distinguished by a "majesty of grief," depth of thought, calm, classic repose, and a dignified simplicity.

In prose, Arnold attains highest rank as a critic of literature. His culture, the breadth of his literary sympathies, his scientific analyses, and his lucid literary style, place his critical works second to none in the language. He has a light, rather fanciful, humor, which gives snap and spice to his style. He is also a master of irony, which is galling to an opponent. He himself never loses his suavity or good breeding. Arnold's prose style is as far removed from Carlyle's as the calm simplicity of the Greeks is from the powerful passion of the Viking. The ornament and poetic richness of Ruskin's style are also missing in Arnold's. His style has a classic purity and refinement. He has a terseness, a crystalline clearness, and a precision which have been excelled in the works of few even of the greatest masters of English prose.

CHARLES DICKENS, 1812-1870.

Life. — Out of the vast host of Victorian novelists, the three greatest, Dickens, Thackeray, and George Eliot, will be selected for special study. The first of these to achieve fame was Charles Dickens. This man, who was to become a great portrayer of child life, had a sad, painful childhood. He was born in 1812 at Landport, a district of the city of Portsmouth, Hampshire, where his father was a clerk in the Navy Pay Office. John Dickens, the prototype of Mr. Micawber, was a kind, well-intentioned man, who knew far better how to harangue his large household of children than to supply it with the necessities of life. He moved from place to place,

sinking deeper into poverty and landing finally in a debtors' prison.

The dreams of a fine education and a brilliant career which the future novelist had fondly cherished in his precocious little brain, had to be abandoned. At the age of eleven the delicate child was called upon to do his part toward maintaining the family. He was engaged at sixpence a week, to paste labels on blacking bottles. He was poorly clothed, ill fed, forced to live in the cheapest place to be found, and to associate with the roughest kind of companions. This experience was so bitter and galling to the sensitive boy, that years after, when he was a successful, happy man, he could not look back upon it without tears in his eyes. Owing to a rupture between his employer and the elder Mr. Dickens, Charles was removed from this place and sent to school. At fifteen, however, he had to seek work again. This time he was employed in an attorney's office at Gray's Inn.

It was impossible, of course, for this ambitious boy to realize that he was receiving an education in the dirty streets, the warehouses, the tenements, and the prisons. But, for his peculiar bent of mind, these furnished far richer stores of learning than either school or college could have given. He had marvelous powers of observation. He noted everything, from the saucy street waif to the sorrowful prison child, from the poor little drudge to the brutal schoolmaster, and transplanted them from life to fiction, in such characters as Sam Weller, Little Dorrit, the Marchioness, Mr. Squeers, and a hundred others.

While in the attorney's office, Dickens began to study shorthand, in order to become a reporter. This was the beginning of his success. His reports were accurate and racy, even though they happened to be written in the pouring rain, in a shaking stage coach, or by the light of a lantern. They were also promptly handed in at the office, despite the fact that the stages sometimes broke down and left their passengers to plod on foot through the miry roads leading into London. These reports and newspaper articles soon attracted attention, and Dickens received an offer for a series of humorous sketches, which grew into the famous *Pickwick Papers*, and earned £20,000 for the astonished publishers. He was able to make his own terms for his future novels. Fame came to him almost at a bound. He was loved and toasted in England and America before he reached the age of thirty. When, late in life, he made lecture tours through his own country, Scotland, or America, they were like triumphal marches.

In his prime Dickens was an energetic, high-spirited, fun-loving man. He made a charming host, and was

DICKENS'S HOME, GAD'S HILL

never happier than when engineering theatrical entertainments at his delightful home, Gad's Hill. He was esteemed by all the literary men of London, and idolized by his children and friends. His strong personality was communicated to his audiences and his readers, so that his death in 1870 was felt as a personal loss throughout the English-speaking world.

Works. — *Pickwick Papers* (1836–1837), Dickens's first long story, is one of his best. Mr. Pickwick, with his genial nature, simple philosophy, and droll adventures, and Sam Weller, with his ready wit, his acute observations, and almost limitless resources, are amusing from start to finish. The book is brimful of its author's high spirits. It has no closely knit plot, only a succession of comical incidents, but these possess such a human touch and such kindly, good-natured fun, that they smooth out the reader's wrinkles and tend to keep his heart young.

Oliver Twist (1837–1838) is a powerful story, differing widely from *Pickwick Papers*. While the earlier work is delightful chiefly for its humor, *Oliver Twist* is strong in its pictures of passion and crime. Bill Sykes the murderer, Fagan the Jew, who teaches the boys deftness of hand in stealing, and poor Nancy, are drawn with such realistic power that they seem to be still actually living in some of the London alleys which Dickens frequently visited. There are some improbable features about the plot and some over-wrought sentimental scenes in the story, but the novel keeps the reader keenly interested, and it contains passages which make a powerful appeal to human emotion.

With the prodigality of a fertile genius, Dickens presented his expectant and enthusiastic public with a new novel on an average of once a year for fourteen years, and, even after that, his productivity did not fall off materially. The best and most representative of these works are *Nicholas Nickleby* (1838–1839), *Barnaby Rudge* (1841), *Martin Chuzzlewit* (1843–1844), *Dombey and Son* (1846–1848), *David Copperfield* (1849–1850), and *A Tale of Two Cities* (1859).

Of these *David Copperfield* is the masterpiece. David's early home, Miss Trotwood's rustic abode, and the old fishing village of Yarmouth, are never-to-be-forgotten scenes. The characters in the book are among the most human in the novels of Dickens. Chief among this interesting company are loyal, constant Mr. Peggotty, dear Aunt Betsey Trotwood, the inimitable Mr. Micawber, and, above all, little David, into whom his creator breathed the breath of his own childish life. Dickens always seemed to understand children. His child characters are natural and true. Most of them are sad, for no one realized more than Dickens the universal repression of childish impulses, and the frightful suffering it entailed. He laid bare to many readers for the first time the sorrows, fears, and struggles of the child world. Fuller knowledge of this world developed broader sympathy with it, and his writings helped to secure for children better treatment in the school and the workshop. With boys and girls, he is the most popular of the great Victorian novelists. Thackeray's children once naïvely asked him why he did not write like Dickens. Thackeray was sufficiently generous to recommend for children the unsullied pages of Dickens.

General Characteristics. — Charles Dickens and Walter Scott are probably the best-loved authors in England. Their works offer sound and healthy entertainment to a people almost too heavily burdened with problems of existence. Dickens widens the sympathies of people by taking the gay world with him into the slums of London, and exhibiting the misery and despair of those vice-haunted districts. He is a powerful portrayer of the poor and degraded classes of society. In this way, he is also an ethical force. While he points out, in a general way, the sufferings of poverty and crime, he does not, like George Eliot, probe deeply into the social evils and complex problems of modern life. His social creed is thus formulated by Dowden : " Banish from earth some few monsters of selfishness, malignity, and hypocrisy, set to rights a few obvious imperfections in the machinery of society, inspire all men with a cheery benevolence, and everything will go well with this excellent world of ours."

All classes of society are ready to join with Dickens in his hearty laughter. His infectious humor is the most remarkable quality of his works, but it is not of a kind to be quoted in short passages. The whole scene of Mr. Pickwick's trial is pervaded by irresistible mirth, and nearly all the caricatures are conceived in the light of a joke. Little David Copperfield, even in his saddest moments, sees things in a distorted childish way, very quaint and funny. This quality of humor is due to the peculiar, exuberant, and fantastic imagination of Dickens. He deals with real facts of life, but, like Alice in Wonderland, he sees them upside down and inside out.

Dickens is a master of caricature. The heroes and heroines of his books are usually colorless and lifeless, but certain characters, possessing some exaggerated mannerism, live forever in the memory. No one forgets the squalid gentility and vapid eloquence of the good-hearted Micawber, or the energetic figure of Miss Betsey Trotwood, with her cry of "Janet! Donkeys!" or Uriah Heep with the long fingers and clammy hands, or Sarah Gamp with her visionary confidant, or dozens of other characters with certain eccentricities of dress, speech, walk, or mind.

Closely allied to the fund of humor in Dickens is the feeling for the pathetic. *The Christmas Carol* contains a most exquisite blending of humor and pathos. David

Copperfield's childish griefs and little Paul Dombey's death are related with a touching pathos. But Dickens's efforts to be pathetic sometimes lead to a display of weak sentimentalism. We feel that he is laboring to be impressive in describing the death of little Nell in *The Old Curiosity Shop*, and that he might have added to the pathos of the scene, had he rested content with a few simple touches of nature. The death of Dora in *David Copperfield* is almost ludicrous, coming as it does in conjunction with that of her lap-dog.

Dickens is not a master in the artistic construction of his plots. The majority of his readers do not, however, notice this failing because he keeps them in such a delightful state of interest and suspense by the sprightliness with which he tells a story.

Dickens was a very rapid writer, and his English is consequently often careless in structure and in grammar. He was not a man of books, and so he never acquired that half-unconscious knowledge of fine phrasing which comes to the careful student of literature. The style of Dickens is clear and graphic, but it can lay slight claims to elegance or literary finish.

WILLIAM MAKEPEACE THACKERAY, 1811-1863

Life. — Though nearly a year older than Dickens, Thackeray made his way to popularity much more slowly. These two men, who became friends and generous rivals, were very different in character and disposition. Instead of possessing the self-confidence, energy, and industry which brought Dickens fame in his twenties, Thackeray had to contend with a somewhat shy and vacillating temperament, extreme modesty, and with a constitutional aversion to work.

W. M. Thackeray

Born in Calcutta in 1811, he was sent to England to be educated. He passed through Charter House and went one year to Cambridge. He was remembered by his school friends for his skill in caricature sketching. He hoped to make painting a profession and went to Paris to study, but he never attained correctness in drawing, and when he offered to illustrate the works of Dickens, the offer was declined. Thackeray certainly added to the charm of his own writings by his droll and delightful illustrations.

When Thackeray came of age in 1832, he inherited a

small fortune, which he soon lost in an Indian bank and in newspaper investments. He was then forced to overcome his idle, procrastinating habits. He became a literary hack, and contributed humorous articles to such magazines as *Fraser* and *Punch*. While his pen was causing mirth and laughter in England, his heart was torn by suffering. His wife, whom he had married in 1837, became insane. He nursed her patiently with the vain hope that she could recover, but he finally abandoned hope and put her in the care of a conscientious attendant. His home was consequently lonely, and the club was his only recourse. Here, his broad shoulders and kindly face

From an unpublished original.

ONE OF THACKERAY'S DRAWINGS

were always greeted with pleasure, for his affable manners and his sparkling humor, which concealed an aching heart, made him a charming companion.

It is pleasant to know that the later years of his life were happier. They were cheered by the presence of his daughters, and were free from financial worries. He had the satisfaction of knowing that, through the sales of his books and the returns from his lectures, he had recovered his lost fortune.

Novels. — *Vanity Fair* (1847–1848) is Thackeray's masterpiece. For the lifelikeness of its characters, it is one of the most remarkable creations in fiction. Thackeray called this work " A Novel without a Hero." He might have added "and without a heroine," for neither clever Becky Sharp nor beautiful Amelia Sedley satisfies the requirements for a heroine. No perfect characters appear in the book, but it is enlivened with an abundance of genuine human nature. Few people go through life without meeting a George Osborne, a Mrs. Bute Crawley, or a Mrs. Sedley. Even a penurious, ridiculous, old Sir Pitt Crawley is sometimes seen. The greatest stroke of genius in the book, however, is the masterly portrayal of the artful, scheming Becky Sharp, who alternately commands respect for her shrewdness and repels by her moral depravity.

In *Vanity Fair* certain classes of society are satirized. Their intrigues, frivolities, and caprices are mercilessly dealt with. Thackeray probes almost every weakness, vanity, and ambition which leads humanity to strive for a place in society, to long for a bow from a lord, and to stint in private in order to shine in public. He uncovers the great social farce of life, which is acted with such solemn gravity by the snobs, the hypocrites, and the other superficial *dramatis personæ*. Amid these satirized frivolities there appear occasional touches of true pathos and deep human tragedy, which are strangely effective in their unsympathetic surroundings.

Thackeray gives in *Henry Esmond* (1852) an enduring picture of high life in the eighteenth century. This work is one of the great historical novels in our language. The time of Queen Anne is reconstructed with remarkable skill. The social etiquette, the ideals of honor, the life and spirit of that bygone day, reappear with a powerful vividness. Thackeray even went so far as to disguise his own natural, graceful style, and to imitate eighteenth century prose. *Henry Esmond* is a dangerous rival of *Vanity Fair*. The earlier work has a freshness of humor and a spontaneity of manner which are not so apparent in *Henry Esmond*. On the other hand, *Esmond* has a superior plot and possesses a true hero.

In *The Newcomes* (1854–1855), Thackeray exhibits again his incisive power of delineating character. This book would continue to live if for nothing except the simple-hearted, courtly Colonel Newcome. Few scenes in English fiction are more affecting than those connected with his death. The accompanying lines will show what a simple pathos Thackeray could command : —

"At the usual evening hour the chapel bell began to toll, and Thomas Newcome's hands outside the bed feebly beat time, — and just as the last bell struck, a peculiar sweet smile shone over his face, and he lifted up his head a little, and quickly said, '*Adsum*,' — and fell back. It was the word we used at school when names were called ; and, lo! he whose heart was as that of a little child had answered to his name, and stood in the presence of his Maker!"

The History of Pendennis (1849) and *The Virginians* (1857–1859) are both popular novels and take rank inferior only to the author's three greatest works. *The Virginians* is a sequel to *Esmond*, and carries the Castlewood family through adventures in the New World.

Essays. — Thackeray will live in English literature as an essayist as well as a novelist. *The English Humorists of the Eighteenth Century* (1853) and *The Four Georges* (1860)

are among the most delightful essays of the age. The
author of *Henry Esmond* knew Swift, Addison, Fielding,
and Smollett almost as one knows the mental peculiarities
of an intimate friend. In *The English Humorists of the
Eighteenth Century*, Thackeray writes of their conversations, foibles, and strong points of character, in a most
easy and entertaining way. There is a constant charm
about his manner, which, without effort or display of
learning, brings the authors vividly before the reader.
In addition to this presentation of character, the essays
contain appreciative literary criticism. The essence of the
humor in these eighteenth century writers is distilled in its
purest, most delicate flavor, by this nineteenth century
member of their brotherhood.

The Four Georges deals with England's crowned heads
in a satiric vein, which caused much comment among
Thackeray's contemporaries. The satire is, however,
mild and subdued, never venomous. For example, he
says in the essay on George III. : —

"King George's household was a model of an English gentleman's
household. It was early; it was kindly; it was charitable; it was
frugal; it was orderly; it must have been stupid to a degree which I
shudder now to contemplate. No wonder all the princes ran away from
the lap of that dreary domestic virtue. It always rose, rode, dined, at
stated intervals. Day after day was the same. At the same hour at
night the King kissed his daughters' jolly cheeks; the Princesses kissed
their mother's hand; and Madame Thielke brought the royal nightcap."

General Characteristics. — Dickens and Thackeray have
left graphic pictures of a large portion of contemporary
London life. Dickens presents in striking caricatures the
vagabonds, the outcasts, and the merchants, and Thackeray portrays the suave, polite leisure class and its dependents.

Thackeray is an uncompromising realist and a satirist. He insisted upon picturing life as he believed that it existed in London society, and, to his satiric eye, that life was composed chiefly of the small vanities, the little passions, and the petty quarrels of commonplace people, whose main objects were money and title. He could conceive noble men and women, as is proved by Esmond, Lady Castlewood, and Colonel Newcome, but such characters are as rare in Thackeray as he believed they were in real life. The following passage upon mankind's fickleness is a good specimen of his satiric vein in dealing with human weaknesses : —

"There are no better satires than letters. Take a bundle of your dear friend's letters of ten years back — your dear friend whom you hate now. Look at a pile of your sister's ! How you clung to each other until you quarreled about the twenty-pound legacy ! . . . Vows, love promises, confidence, gratitude, —how queerly they read after a while ! . . . The best ink for Vanity Fair use would be one that faded utterly in a couple of days, and left the paper clean and blank, so that you might write on it to somebody else."

The phases of life which he describes have had no more subtle interpreter. He does not label his characters with external marks, but enters into communion with their souls. His analytic method of laying bare their motives and actions is strictly modern. His great master Fielding would have been baffled by such a complex personality as Becky Sharp. Amid the throng of Thackeray's men and women, there are but few who are not genuine flesh and blood.

The art of describing the pathetic is unfailing in Thackeray. He never jars upon the most sensitive feelings nor wearies them by too long a treatment. With a few simple but powerful expressions he succeeds in arousing intense emotions of pity or sorrow. He has been called a cynic, but wrongly, for no man can be a cynic who shows Thackeray's tenderness in the treatment of pathos.

Thackeray is master of a graceful, simple prose style. In its ease and purity, it most resembles that of Swift, Addison, or Goldsmith. Thackeray writes as a cultured, ideal, old gentleman may be imagined to talk to the young people, while he sits in his comfortable armchair in a corner by the fireplace. The charm of freshness, quaintness, and colloquial familiarity is seldom absent from the delightfully natural pages of Thackeray.

GEORGE ELIOT, 1819-1880

Life. — Mary Ann Evans, known to her family as Marian and to her readers as George Eliot, was born in 1819, at South Farm, in Arbury, Warwickshire, about twenty-two miles north of Stratford-on-Avon. A few months later,

GEORGE ELIOT'S BIRTHPLACE

the family moved to a spacious ivy-covered farmhouse at Griff, some two miles east, where the future novelist lived until she was twenty-two.

She was a thoughtful, precocious child. She lived largely within herself, passed much time in reverie, and pondered upon deep problems. She easily outstripped her school-mates in all mental accomplishments, and, from the first, gave evidence of a clear, strong intellect.

The death of her mother and the marriage of a sister left the entire care of the house and dairy to Marian before she was seventeen years old. Her labors were quite heavy for the next six years. At the end of that time, she and her father moved to Foleshill, near Coventry, where she had ample leisure to pursue her studies and music. At Foleshill, she came under the influence of free-thinking friends and became an agnostic, which she remained through the rest of her life. This home was again broken up in 1849 by the death of her father. Through the advice of friends she sought com-fort in travel on the continent.

Upon her return, she settled in London as assistant editor of the *Westminster Review*. By this time she had become familiar with five languages, had translated abstruse metaphysical books from the German into Eng-lish, and had so thoroughly equipped her naturally strong intellect that she was sought after in London by such men as Herbert Spencer and George Henry Lewes. A deep attachment sprang up between Mr. Lewes and Miss Evans, and they formed an alliance which lasted until his death.

George Eliot's early literary labors were mainly critical and scientific, being governed by the circle in which she moved. When she came under the influence of Mr. Lewes,

she was induced to attempt creative work. Her novels, published under the pen name of George Eliot, quickly became popular. Despite this success, it is doubtful whether she would have possessed sufficient self-reliance to continue her work without Mr. Lewes's constant encouragement and protecting love, which shielded her from contact with publishers and from a knowledge of harsh criticisms.

Their companionship was so congenial that her friends were astonished when she formed another attachment after his death in 1878, and married Mr. Cross. Her husband said that her affectionate nature required some deep love to which to cling. She had never been very robust, and, during her later years, she was extremely frail. She died in 1880.

Works. — George Eliot was fast approaching forty when she found the branch of literature in which she was to achieve fame. Her first volume of stories, *Scenes of Clerical Life* (1858), showed decisively that she was master of fiction writing. Three novels followed rapidly, *Adam Bede* (1859), *The Mill on the Floss* (1860), and *Silas Marner* (1861). Her mind was stored with memories of the Midland counties, where her young life was spent, and these four books present with a powerful realism this rich rural district and its quaint inhabitants, all of whom seem flushed with the warmth of real life.

Adam Bede is the freshest, healthiest, and most delightful of her books. Aside from its one painful interlude, this story leaves upon the memory a charming picture of peace and contentment, with its clearly drawn and interesting characters, its ideal dairy, the fertile stretches of meadow lands, the squire's birthday party, the harvest supper, and the sweet Methodist woman preaching on the green.

The Mill on the Floss also gives a fine picture of village life. This novel is one of George Eliot's most earnest productions. She exhibits one side of her own intense, brooding girlhood, in the passionate heroine, Maggie Tulliver. There is in this tragic story a wonderfully subtle revelation of a young nature which is morbid, ambitious, quick of intellect, and strong of will, and which has no hand firm enough to serve as guide.

Silas Marner, artistically considered, is George Eliot's

masterpiece. In addition to the ruddy glow of life in the characters, there is an idyllic beauty about the pastoral setting, and a poetic, half-mystic charm about the weaver's manner of connecting his gold with his bright-haired Eppie. The slight plot is well planned and rounded, and the narrative is remarkable for ease and simplicity.

Romola (1863) is a much bolder flight. It is an attempt to present Florence of the fifteenth century, to contrast Savonarola's ardent Christianity with the Medicis and the Greek love for beauty, and to show the influence of the time upon two widely different characters, Romola and Tito Melema. This novel is the greatest intellectual achievement of its author, but it has not the warmth of life, the vitality, and vigor of her English stories. Though no pains is spared to delineate Romola, Tito, and the inspiring monk, Savonarola, yet they do not possess the genuineness and reality that are felt in her Warwickshire characters.

Middlemarch (1871–1872) and *Daniel Deronda* (1876) mark the decline of George Eliot's powers. She still possessed the ability to handle dialogue, to analyze subtle, complex characters, and to attain a philosophical grasp of the problems of existence. Her weakening powers are shown in the length of tedious passages, in an undue prominence of ethical purpose, in the more studied and, on the whole, duller characters, and in the prolixity of style.

George Eliot's poetry does not bear comparison with her prose. *The Spanish Gypsy* (1868) is her most ambitious poem, and it contains some fine dramatic passages. Her most beautiful poem is the hymn beginning: —

> "Oh, may I join the choir invisible
> Of those immortal dead who live again
> In minds made better by their presence!"

There is a strain of noble thought and lofty feeling in her poems, and she rises easily to the necessary passion and fervor of verse, but her expression is hampered by the metrical form.

General Characteristics. — George Eliot is more strictly modern in spirit than either of the other two great contemporary novelists. This spirit is exhibited chiefly in her ethical purpose, her scientific sympathies, and her minute dissection of character.

Her writings manifest her desire to benefit human beings by convincing them that nature's laws are inexorable, and that an infraction of the moral law will be punished as surely as disobedience to physical laws. She strives to arouse people to a knowledge of hereditary influences, and to show how every deed brings its own results and works, directly or indirectly, toward the salvation or ruin of the doer. And she throws her whole strength into an attempt to prove that joy is to be found only in strict attendance upon duty and in self-renunciation. In order to carry home these serious lessons of life, she deals with powerful human tragedies, which impart a somberness of tone to all her novels. In her early works, she treats these problems with artistic beauty, but in her later ones she often forgets the artist in the moralist, and uses a character to preach a sermon.

The analytical tendency is pronounced in George Eliot. Her works exhibit an exhaustive study of the feelings, the thoughts, the dreams, and purposes of the characters. They become known more through description than through action.

A striking characteristic of her men and women is their power to grow. They do not appear ready made and finished at the beginning of a story, but, like real human beings amid the struggles of life, her characters change for the better or the worse. Tito Melema is an example of her skill in evolving character. At the outset, he is a beautiful Greek boy with a keen zest for pleasure. In order to escape pain, he forsakes a faithful friend, and lets his little sweetheart continue to believe that she is married to him. He enters political life, and, through his love for personal happiness, becomes involved in base intrigues. The consequences of his deeds entangle him finally in such a net of lies that he is forced to betray "every trust that was reposed in him, that he might keep himself safe."

George Eliot occasionally brightens the seriousness of her works with humor. Her pages are not permeated with joyousness, as Dickens's are, nor do they ripple with quiet amusement, like Thackeray's, but she puts witty and aphoristic sayings into the conversations of the characters. The scene at the "Rainbow" inn is bristling with mother wit. Mr. Macey observes:—

"'There's allays two 'pinions; there's the 'pinion a man has of himsen, and there's the 'pinion other folks have on him. There'd be two 'pinions about a cracked bell if the bell could hear itself.'"[1]

Great precision and scholarlike correctness mark the style of George Eliot. Her vocabulary, though large, is too full of abstract and scientific terms to permit of great flexibility and idiomatic purity of English. She is master of powerful figures of speech, original, epigrammatic turns of expression, and, sometimes, of a stirring eloquence.

ROBERT BROWNING, 1812–1889

Life.— The two most eminent poets of the Victorian age are Browning and Tennyson. Their long and peace-

[1] *Silas Marner*, Chap. VI.

Robert Browning,

ful lives are in marked contrast to the short and troubled careers of Byron, Shelley, and Keats.

Robert Browning's life was uneventful but happy. He inherited a magnificent physique and constitution from his father, who never knew a day's illness. With such health, Robert Browning felt a keen relish for physical existence and a robust joyousness in all kinds of activity. Late in life he wrote, in the poem *At the Mermaid:* —

> "Have you found your life distasteful?
> My life did, and does, smack sweet.

> I find earth not gray but rosy,
> Heaven not grim but fair of hue.
> Do I stoop? I pluck a posy.
> Do I stand and stare? All's blue."

Again, in *Saul*, he burst forth with the lines : —

> " How good is man's life, the mere living ! how fit to employ
> All the heart and the soul and the senses forever in joy."

These lines, vibrant with life and joy, could not have been written by a man of failing vitality or physical weakness.

Robert Browning was born in 1812 at Camberwell, whose slopes overlook the smoky chimneys of London. In this beautiful suburb he spent his early years in the companionship of a brother and a sister. A highly gifted father and a musical mother assisted intelligently in the development of their children. Browning's education was conducted mainly under his father's eye. The boy attended neither a large school nor a college. After he had passed from the hands of tutors, he spent some time in travel, and was wont to call Italy his university. Although his training was received in an irregular way, his scholarship cannot be doubted by the student of his poetry.

Upon reading the poems of Shelley and Keats, the boy's soul drank in the fancy and melody of these masters of song, and he yearned to become a great poet. His father had little faith in these boyish dreams, but he wisely refrained from interfering with his son's ambitions.

From this time, Browning's life was devoted to literature. His works met with little success, but he never lost faith in his power, and he continued to grow and develop along his own lines. Finally, in 1855, he published *Men and Women* and won an enthusiastic, if not a wide, audience.

In 1846 he married the poet Elizabeth Barrett, whose

reputation was then greater than his own. During the fifteen years of happy married life that followed, Browning and his wife lived in Italy, where the balmy air infused fresh life into the fragile form of Mrs. Browning. She has given expression to the deep love and joy of these years in her most beautiful work, the *Sonnets from the Portuguese*. Her death in 1861 was a shock from which her husband never fully recovered. There is a deeper note to the writings which followed this one great sorrow of his life.

BROWNING'S HOME IN VENICE, PALAZZO REZZONICO

His genial nature and the constantly increasing fame which he enjoyed during his later years caused him to be the center of much of London's social life. These years were spent with his sister or his famous son, Robert

Barrett Browning. In December, 1889, the poet lay upon his death bed in Venice, in a beautiful room, which Robert Barrett had frescoed. Turning to his son, the poet asked if any word had come concerning his last book. A telegram, expressing the enthusiastic reception given to *Asolando*, was shown him. " How gratifying," he murmured. In a few moments he was dead, and both Italy and England were in mourning.

. **Dramatic Monologues.** — Browning was a poet of great productivity. From the publication of *Pauline* in 1833 to *Asolando* in 1889, there were only short pauses between the appearances of his works. Unlike Tennyson, Browning could not stop to revise and recast them, but he constantly sought expression, in narratives, dramas, lyrics, and monologues, for new thoughts and feelings.

The study of the human soul held an unfailing charm for Browning. He analyzes with marked keenness and subtlety the experiences of the soul, its sickening failures and its eager strivings amid complex, puzzling conditions. In nearly all of his poems, whether narrative, lyric, or dramatic, the chief interest centers about some "incidents in the development of a soul."

The poetic form which he found best adapted to "the development of a soul" was the dramatic monologue. Requiring but one speaker, this form permits all the force to be concentrated upon his emotions, character, and growth. Browning is one of the greatest masters of the dramatic monologue. Most of his best monologues are to be found in the volumes known as *Dramatic Lyrics* (1842), *Dramatic Romances and Lyrics* (1845), *Men and Women* (1855), *Dramatis Personæ* (1864).

My Last Duchess, *Andrea del Sarto*, and *The Bishop Orders His Tomb at St. Praxed's Church* are three strong representative monologues. The speaker in *My Last Duchess* is the widowed Duke, who is describing the portrait of his lost wife. In his blind conceit, he is utterly unconscious that he is exhibiting clearly his own coldly selfish nature and his wife's sweet, sunny disposition. The chief power of the poem lies in the astonishing ease with which he is made to reveal his own character.

The interest in *Andrea del Sarto* is in the mental conflict of this "faultless painter." He wishes, on the one hand, to please his wife with popular pictures, and yet he yearns for higher ideals of his art. He says: —

> " Ah, but a man's reach should exceed his grasp,
>   Or what's a heaven for ? "

As he sits in the twilight, holding his wife's hand, and talking in a half-musing way, it is readily seen that his love for this beautiful but soulless woman has caused many of his failures and sorrows in the past, and will continue to arouse conflicts of soul in the future.

In the poem entitled *The Bishop Orders His Tomb at St. Praxed's Church*, Browning shows a keen insight into a luxurious, sensuous, vain nature. Even in the hour of death, the Bishop takes delight in reviewing his worldly successes, and in the thought that his tomb will be richer than his rival's, and will have a purer Latin inscription.

The beautiful song of David in the poem entitled *Saul* shows a wonderful sympathy with the old Hebrew prophecies. *Cleon* expresses the views of an early Greek upon the teachings of Christ and St. Paul. *The Soliloquy of a Spanish Cloister* describes the development of a coarse, jealous nature in monastic life. *Abt Vogler*, one of Browning's noblest poems, voices the exquisite raptures of a musician's soul. And that remarkable, grotesque, vulgarly humorous poem, *Caliban upon Setebos*, transcends human fields altogether, and displays the brutelike, Satanic theology of a fiend.

In these monologues, Browning interprets characters of varying faiths, nationalities, stations, and historic periods. He shows a wide range of knowledge and sympathy. One character, however, which he rarely presents, is the simple, commonplace man or woman. Browning excels in the portrayal of unusual, intricate, and difficult characters, that have complicated problems to face, weaknesses to overcome, or lofty ambitions to attain.

The Ring and the Book. — Browning's most masterly study of the human soul is *The Ring and the Book* (1868–1869), which is a long poem made up of a series of monologues. The tragic story is briefly told in the first and last books. In each of the ten remaining books, some one speaker or class expresses views of the incidents, and ten different versions of the tragedy are thus given. This was a bold and wholly unique plan, but it offered peculiar opportunities to such a subtle analyst as Browning.

The subject of the story is an innocent girl, Pompilia, who, under the protection of a noble priest, flees from her brutal husband and seeks the home of her foster parents. Her husband wrathfully pursues her and kills both her and her parents. While this is but the barest outline, yet the story in its complete form is very simple; and, as is usual with Browning, the chief stress is laid upon the character portrayal.

The four important characters — Guido, the husband; Caponsacchi, the priest; Pompilia, the girl-wife; and the Pope — stand out in strong relief. The greatest development of character is seen in Guido, who starts with a defiant, insulting spirit of certain victory, but gradually becomes more subdued and abject, when he finds that he is to be killed, and he finally shrieks in agony for the help of his victim, Pompilia. In Caponsacchi there is the inward questioning of the right and the wrong. He is a strongly drawn character, full of passion and noble desires. Pompilia is one of Browning's sweetest and purest women. She has an intuitive knowledge of the right. The Pope, with his calm, wise judgment and his lofty philosophy, is probably the greatest product of Browning's intellect.

The books containing the monologues of these characters take first place among Browning's writings and occupy a high position in the century's work. They have a striking originality, intensity, vigor, and imaginative richness. The remaining books are incomparably inferior, and are marked at times by mere acuteness of reason and thoroughness of legal knowledge.

A Dramatic Poet. — Although Browning's genius is strongly dramatic, his best work is not found in the field of the drama. *Strafford* (1837), *A Blot on the 'Scutcheon* (1843), and *Colombe's Birthday* (1843) have been staged successfully, but they cannot be called great acting plays. The action is slight, the characters are complex, the soliloquies are lengthy, and the climaxes are too often wholly dependent upon emotional intensity and not upon great or exciting deeds. The strongest interest of the dramas lies in their psychological subtlety, and this is more enjoyable in the study than in the theater.

Browning's dramatic power is well exhibited in poems like *In a Balcony* or *Pippa Passes*, where powerful individual scenes are presented without all the accompanying details of a complete drama. The great force of such scenes lies in his manner of treating moments of severe trial. He selects such a moment, focuses his whole genius

THE VICTORIAN AGE

upon it, as upon life's pivotal center, and makes the deed committed then stand forth as an explanation of all the past emotions and as a prophecy of all future acts.

Pippa Passes is one of Browning's most artistic presentations of such dramatic scenes. The little silk weaver, Pippa, rises on the morning of her one holiday in the year, with the intention of enjoying in fancy the pleasures "of the Happiest Four in our Asolo," not knowing, in her innocence, of their misery and guilt. She wanders from house to house, singing her pure, significant refrains, and, in each case, her songs arrest the attention of the hearer at a critical moment. She thus becomes unconsciously a means of salvation. The first scene is the most intense. She approaches the home of the lovers, Sebald and Ottima, after the murder of Ottima's husband, when they are triumphant in sin. As Sebald begins to reflect on the murder, there comes this song of Pippa's, like the knocking at the gate in Macbeth, to loose the floodgates of remorse : —

> "The year's at the spring
> And day's at the morn ;
> Morning's at seven ;
> The hillside's dew-pearled ;
> The lark's on the wing ;
> The snail's on the thorn :
> God's in his heaven —
> All's right with the world ! "

His Optimistic Philosophy. — It has been seen that the Victorian age, as presented by Matthew Arnold, was a period of doubt and negation. Browning would not be overcome and swept off the firm shore of faith by this enormous tidal wave of doubt. He recognized fully the difficulties of religious faith in an age just awakening to scientific inquiry, and yet he retained a strong, fearless trust in God and immortality.

Browning's reason demanded this belief. In this earthly life, he saw the evil overcome the good, and beheld injustice, defeat, and despair follow the noblest efforts. If there exists no compensation for these things, he says that life is a cheat, the moral nature a lie, and God a fiend. But when this present life is looked upon as a place of training for a purer life, when defeat is a discipline for ennobling the soul, when evil is an enemy to test the strength of man's might, and death is the last battle, which passes man on to his immortal heritage, then this life on earth is a reasonable, holy thing, and all the suffering and sin are divinely sent.

There is no hesitancy in this philosophy of Browning. With it, he does not fear to face all the problems and mysteries of existence. Such a philosophy of faith makes life wholly intelligible to him, and gives him a trust in God which is gloriously, exultingly firm. No other poet strikes such a resonant, hopeful note as he. His *Rabbi Ben Ezra* is more a song of triumphant faith than anything written since the Puritan days: —

> " Earth changes, but thy soul and God stand sure :
> What entered into thee,
> *That* was, is, and shall be :
> Time's wheel runs back or stops : Potter and clay endure."

General Characteristics. — Browning is a poet of striking originality and impelling force. His writings are the spontaneous outpourings of a rich, full nature, whose main fabric is intellect, but intellect illumined with the glittering light of spiritual hopefulness and flushed with the glow of deep human passion.

The subject of his greatest poetry is the human soul. While he possesses a large portion of dramatic suggestiveness, he nevertheless does not excel in setting off character against character in movement and speech, but rather in a minute, penetrating analysis, by which he insinuates himself into the thoughts and sensations of his characters, and views life through their eyes.

He is a pronounced realist. His verse deals not only with the beautiful and the romantic, but also with the prosaic and the ugly, if they furnish true pictures for the panorama of real life. The unconventionality and realism of his poetic art will be made manifest by merely reading through the titles of his numerous works.

Browning did not write to amuse and entertain, but to stimulate thought and to "sting" the conscience to activity. The meaning of his verse was, therefore, the matter of paramount importance, far overshadowing the form of expression. In the haste and carelessness with which he wrote many of his difficult abstruse poems, he laid himself open to the charge of obscurity.

His style has a strikingly individual stamp, which is marked far more by strength than by beauty. The bare and rugged style of his verse is often made profoundly impressive by its strenuous earnestness, its burning intensity, which seems to necessitate the broken lines and halting, interrupted rhythm. The following utterance of Caponsacchi, as he stands before his judges, will show the intensity and ruggedness of Browning's blank verse : —

> " Sirs, how should I lie quiet in my grave
> Unless you suffer me wring, drop by drop,
> My brain dry, make a riddance of the drench
> Of minutes with a memory in each ? "

His lines are often harsh and dissonant. Even in

the noble poem *Rabbi Ben Ezra,* this jolting line appears : —

" Irks care the crop-full bird?   Frets doubt the maw-crammed beast?"

And in *Sordello,* Browning writes : —

> " The Troubadour who sung
>   Hundreds of songs, forgot, its trick his tongue,
>   Its craft his brain."

No careful artist tolerates such ugly, rasping inversions.

In spite of these inharmonious tendencies in Browning, his poetry at times can sing with a lovely lyric lightness, such as is heard in these lines : —

> " Oh, to be in England
>   Now that April's there,
>   And whoever wakes in England
>   Sees, some morning, unaware,
>   That the lowest boughs and the brushwood sheaf
>   Round the elm-tree bole are in tiny leaf,
>   While the chaffinch sings on the orchard bough
>   In England — now!"[1]

Or his verse can swell and fall with a billowlike rhythm like that of *Saul* or of these lines in *Abt Vogler:* —

" There shall never be one lost good !   What was, shall live as before ;
    The evil is null, is nought, is silence implying sound ;
    What was good shall be good, with, for evil, so much good more ;
    On the earth the broken arcs ; in the heaven, a perfect round."

While, therefore, Browning's poetry is often harsh, faulty, and obscure, at times his melodies can be rhythmically simple and beautiful.   He is one of the subtlest analysts of the human mind, the most original and impassioned poet of his age, and one of the most hopeful, inspiring, and uplifting teachers of modern times.

[1] *Home Thoughts from Abroad.*

ALFRED TENNYSON, 1809-1892

Life. — Alfred Tennyson was born in Somersby, Lincolnshire, in 1809. He was the fourth child of the cultured rector of Somersby, and grew up with seven brothers
and four sisters amid a romantic world of the past. The
children knew far more about knights, giants, and princesses
than about the busy world a few miles distant.

When Alfred was seven years old, he went to his grandmother's in order to attend the Louth Grammar School,
which, to his dying day, he remembered with hatred be

cause of the stern, flogging master. At the age of eleven the boy returned home, and, under his father's tutelage, prepared for college. The future poet entered Trinity College, Cambridge, in 1828, but did not remain long enough to take a degree.

After his father's death in 1831, Alfred Tennyson continued to live for six years with his mother and sisters in the quiet little village where he was born. They then moved to a place in Epping Forest, where they spent three years. Tennyson resided at various places in England from that time until 1853, when he moved to Farringford, on the Isle of Wight.

TENNYSON'S BIRTHPLACE[1]

His life was consecrated to poetry, and his time was passed either in the study of nature or among his books. During these years existence was saddened for him by the death of his noblest and dearest friend, Arthur Henry

[1] " The silent woody places
　　By the home that gave me birth."

Hallam. Another cause of sorrow to Tennyson was the enforced breaking of his engagement to Miss Emily Sellwood on account of an insufficient income. It was not until thirteen years after he had first become engaged, that he felt able to offer Miss Sellwood a home. They were married in 1850, the same year in which he published *In Memoriam* and became poet laureate. By this time Tennyson was almost universally accorded first place among living poets. His popularity far exceeded that which Browning enjoyed. Unlike Browning, however, Tennyson had an extremely retiring nature, and he shunned the lionizing of London society and the gaze of sightseers.

Tennyson's most famous days are associated with two homes. Farringford on the northwestern part of the Isle of Wight was his residence for the greater part of each year from 1853 until his death. Here in his " ivied home among the pine trees," he looked with loving eyes on the "beautiful blue hyacinths, orchises, primroses, daisies, marsh marigolds, and cuckoo flowers," and magnificent trees. The song of the birds, the beauty of the fields, and the ever-changing face of the sea ministered to his different moods. In 1868 he built near Haslemere in Surrey a new residence, which he called Aldworth. In 1884 he was raised to the peerage with the title of Baron of Aldworth and Farringford. He died in 1892, at the age of eighty-three, and was buried in Westminster Abbey beside Robert Browning.

Poetic Apprenticeship. — Some poets, like Coleridge, attain the summit of their development at the age of twenty-five, but Tennyson does not belong to that class. Before he was thirty, he had written many poems distinguished for their lightness of touch and beauty of expression, but they lack depth. His verse was at this time in keeping with the spirit of the age, which felt no strong impulse in any direction.

We find him in his early poems writing of "Airy, fairy Lilian" and "sweet, pale Margaret," and asking : —

> "Who would be
> A mermaid fair
> Singing alone?"[1]

Some of these early lyrics have, however, such rare fancy, melody, and beauty, that they continue to give exquisite pleasure. The following lines from *The Sea-Fairies* show these qualities : —

> "And the rainbow lives in the curve of the sand;
> Hither, come hither and see;
> And the rainbow hangs on the poising wave,
> And sweet is the color of cove and cave
> And sweet shall your welcome be."

The majority of those poems in his 1833 volume, that are such favorites to-day, were unsparingly revised and changed for the better before they were again issued in the form in which we now have them.

The death of Hallam set Tennyson to musing on deeper themes. This event and the adverse comments of the critics on his earlier verse were among the influences which caused him to publish nothing for the next nine years. His son and biographer says that the poet during this period "profited by friendly and unfriendly criticism, and in silence, obscurity, and solitude, perfected his art. . . . Hundreds of lines were, as he expressed it, 'blown up the chimney with his pipe smoke, or were written down and thrown into the fire, as not being then perfect enough.'

[1] *The Mermaid.*

The Brook in later years was actually rescued from the waste-paper heap."

Volumes of 1842. — In 1842, at the age of thirty-three, he published two volumes, one of which contained many of his former poems vastly improved, while the other was filled with new material. In these volumes were such favorites as the richly ornamented lyric *The Palace of Art*, the gem called, from its first line, *Break, break, break,* the tender English idyls *Dora* and *The Gardiner's Daughter*, the stately specimens of blank verse entitled *Ulysses* and *Morte d'Arthur*, the passionate couplets of *Locksley Hall*, and *The Two Voices*.

These poems show that Tennyson had gained rare mastery over his art. They abound in passages which give exquisite pleasure because of the beauty of the picture or the felicity of the expression.

It would be too much to say that these poems are as remarkable for their depth of thought as for their beauty, but they show increasing power to grasp reality, and growing capacity for thought. For instance, these two lines from *Locksley Hall* —

" Love took up the harp of Life, and smote on all the chords with might ;
   Smote the chord of Self, that, trembling, pass'd in music out of sight,"

unfold a great moral truth. The more we reflect upon it, the deeper and the more beautiful does the significance of the thought appear.

A friend, wishing to secure a pension for Tennyson, read *Ulysses* to Sir Robert Peel. When that prime minister heard such lines as these : —

" I am a part of all that I have met ;
     Yet all experience is an arch wherethro'

> Gleams that untravel'd world, whose margin fades
> Forever and forever when I move.
> How dull it is to pause, to make an end,
> To rust unburnish'd, not to shine in use !
> As tho' to breathe were life,"

he gave Tennyson a yearly pension of £200.

The Princess and Maud. — Tennyson had hitherto produced only short poems, but his next three efforts, *The Princess* (1847), *In Memoriam* (1850), and *Maud* (1855) are of considerable length. *The Princess* and *Maud* may be grouped together because the short lyrics which they contain are the best parts of both poems.

The Princess : A Medley, as Tennyson rightly termed it, contains 3223 lines of blank verse. The poem tells in a half-humorous way the story of a Princess who broke off her engagement to a Prince, founded a college for women, and determined to devote her life to making them equal to men. The poem abounds in exquisite melody and glorious imagery, but nothing original is contributed to the solution of the woman question. The finest parts of the poem are the songs beginning : " Sweet and low," "The splendor falls on castle walls," " Tears, idle tears." " O, Swallow, Swallow, flying, flying South," and " Ask me no more."

Maud, a lyrical monodrama, paints the emotions of a lover who passes from morbid gloom to ecstasy. Then in a moment of anger he murders Maud's brother. Despair, insanity, and recovery follow, but he sees Maud's face no more. While the poem as a whole is not a masterpiece, yet it contains lyrics which justify Tennyson's classing it among his finest works. Note the beauty of these lines:—

> " And the woodbine spices are wafted abroad,
> And the musk of the rose is blown.

> " For a breeze of morning moves,
>   And the planet of Love is on high,
>   Beginning to faint in the light that she loves,
>   On a bed of daffodil sky.
>
> · · · · · ·
>
> " From the meadow your walks have left so sweet,
>   That whenever a March wind sighs,
>   He sets the jewel-print of your feet
>   In violets blue as your eyes."

Tennyson was fond of reading from *Maud*. His son, referring to the following stanza, says that his father's eyes " would suddenly flash as he looked up and spoke these words, the passion in his voice deepening in the last words of the stanza " :—

> " She is coming, my own, my sweet;
>   Were it ever so airy a tread,
>   My heart would hear her and beat,
>   Were it earth in an earthy bed;
>   My dust would hear her and beat,
>   Had I lain for a century dead;
>   Would start and tremble under her feet,
>   And blossom in purple and red."

In Memoriam. — One of the most profound experiences of Tennyson's life was the loss of Arthur Hallam. It brought the poet face to face with the vital questions of existence, and called forth the masterpiece of his genius, *In Memoriam* (1850). He did not originally intend publishing the short lyrics which he wrote from time to time to express his grief, but, in 1850, he collected them and published them as one long poem, made up of 725 four-line stanzas.

This work is one of the three great elegiacs of a literature which stands first in elegiac poetry. *Lycidas* has more of a massive, commanding power than *In Memoriam*, and *Adonais* rises at times to poetic heights which Tennyson could not reach, but neither *Lycidas* nor *Adonais* equals *In Memoriam* in expressions of a passionate living grief. Every shadow cast over the human heart by bereavement is traced, from the shadow of despair which mantles all when death is first met, through the softening of grief, when the mourner can say : —

> " Peace ; come away : the song of woe
>   Is after all an earthly song," [1]

to the final victory when the heart, feeling that its sorrows have purified it and widened its sympathy for other sufferers, can sing : —

> " Regret is dead, but love is more
>   Than in the summers that are flown,
>   For I myself with these have grown
>   To something greater than before." [2]

In dealing with this subject, Tennyson necessarily touched upon immortality. Sometimes he felt a " spectral doubt " that he should never more meet the dead. His reason told him that he could know nothing, that he was only

> " An infant crying in the night :
>   An infant crying for the light :
>   And with no language but a cry," [3]

and that he had no proof of immortality. But to Tennyson, cold intellect was not the final judge, as it was to Arnold. Tennyson turned to his feelings to hear the last word upon eternity, and they cried out : —

> " That life shall live forevermore." [4]

His heart

> " Stood up and answered 'I have felt,' " [5]

[1] LVII.   [2] CXXXII.   [3] LIV.   [4] XXXIV.   [5] CXXIV.

and he trusted it and defied the cold skepticism of the reason, and put his faith in

> "One God, one law, one element,
> And one far-off divine event
> To which the whole creation moves."[1]

With this hopeful assurance closes this poem, than which Tennyson wrote nothing nobler or more beautiful.

The Idylls of the King. — One of Tennyson's most ambitious poems is the *Idylls of the King* (1858–1886). It has for its subject the greatest of all the British heroes of romance, King Arthur, and the Knights of the Round Table. Tennyson took the characters and stories mainly as they are found in Malory's *Morte d'Arthur*. Into these he put his nineteenth century ideals of beauty, love, and morality, and ennobled the old tales of chivalry into revelations of spiritual truth.

King Arthur is more than the mighty warrior of the early stories; he is the impersonation of that spiritual power which can subdue the lower nature of man. The city, Camelot, in which he reigns, is the city of high ideals, which is indestructible, for Camelot was

> ". . . built
> To music, therefore never built at all,
> And therefore built forever."[2]

Arthur's kingdom is a delightful fairyland. The scenery is magnificent, and it seems to suggest heroic deeds for its counterpart. The characters are ideal. Lancelot is the knight of knights, unequaled in deeds of prowess, except by the King. Gareth is the embodiment of youth, Galahad of purity, Elaine of innocence, Enid of patient love, but these knights and ladies seem at times almost as far re-

---

[1] *In Memoriam*, CXXXII.   [2] *Idylls of the King: Gareth and Lynette.*

moved from actual life as the characters in Spenser's *Faerie Queene*. While the *dramatis personæ* of the *Idylls of the King* could not exist in a real world, there is wonderful harmony between them and their imaginary setting. When sin creeps into this beautiful realm, the order is disrupted, and King Arthur is borne away on a "dusky barge" by the mystic Queens, and he passes

"To the island-valley of Avilion," [1]

where he will be "King among the dead." The knight who watches the receding barge hears

"As from beyond the limit of the world,
Like the last echo born of a great cry,
Sounds, as if some fair city were one voice
Around a king returning from his wars." [1]

Arthur's spiritual rule has failed on earth, but this rule is welcomed in another land. This is the solace held out by the author.

The poem is of the nature of an epic. Amid a confusing mass of details, there is a thread of unity. The blank verse is noble and harmonious, highly polished in every line, exquisite in individual phrases, and extremely happy in the choice of single words.

Later Poetry. — In much of his later poetry, Tennyson paid more attention to the thought than to the form of its expression. The second *Locksley Hall* has more depth of thought than the first, but the form of the verse in the later poem is less pleasing. He could show, however, when he chose, that he still possessed his old artistic power. The lyric *Crossing the Bar*, one of the last things

[1] *The Passing of Arthur.*

that he wrote, stands in the front rank of his poems for artistic finish and for beauty.

As he grew older, he labored to produce poetry that would come in closer touch with life. *The Northern Farmer* and *The Northern Cobbler* are two poems in which Tennyson escaped from himself and looked at life from the point of view of his characters. He displays here a rich vein of humor. The drunken cobbler determined to reform, and, scorning to win a victory in the absence of his enemy, placed a quart bottle of gin in the window before himself. Anticipating the question why he chose a quart, the cobbler says : —

> " Wouldn't a pint a' sarved as well as a quart? Naw doubt:
> But I liked a bigger feller to fight wi' an' fowt it out."

This desire to draw closer to life and to portray it in action led Tennyson to attempt dramatic composition, and, at the age of sixty-six, he wrote his first play, *Queen Mary*. This was followed by several others, but for nine years he failed to achieve much success in this field, until he produced *Becket* in 1885. This play presents a strong character in Archbishop Becket, but Tennyson was too self-absorbed, the circle of his sympathies was too narrow, and he secluded himself too much from his fellow-men to make a great dramatist.

Poetry of Nature. — It is well to note the different points of view from which Tennyson and Wordsworth regarded nature. The elder poet communed with a spiritual presence in nature, and worshiped the mystic soul of sky, mountain glen, and humble flower. The beauty of the external face of nature appealed strongly to Tennyson. He loved pictorial effects, and he sought in Nature and her phenomena subjects for his poetic canvas. A great artist could paint pictures corresponding to these stanzas from *The Palace of Art :* —

> " One show'd an iron coast and angry waves.
>   You seem'd to hear them climb and fall
>   And roar rock-thwarted under bellowing caves,
>   Beneath the windy wall.
>
> " And one, a full-fed river winding slow
>   By herds upon an endless plain,
>   The ragged rims of thunder brooding low,
>   With shadow streaks of rain."

He often turned to Nature because her sensuous charms delighted his eye or ear. For this reason he calls our attention to

> " The little speedwell's darling blue,
>   Deep tulips dash'd with fiery dew,
>   Laburnums, dropping-wells of fire." [1]

He observed flowers and trees with something of a scientist's accuracy. He knew their colors, habitats, times of blossoming, and multiform changes through which they passed. This intellectual apprehension of natural objects enabled him to point out pleasing and instructive analogies between them and his human characters. Of a young man who made a thoughtless slip, but who had in him the elements of manhood, Tennyson says : —

> " He has a solid base of temperament;
>   But as the water lily starts and slides
>   Upon the level in little puffs of wind,
>   Tho' anchor'd to the bottom, such is he." [2]

His keen observation and acuteness of intellect enabled him to detect a likeness between the rushing water in the brook and the arms of a hero : —

[1] *In Memoriam*, LXXXIII.   [2] *The Princess*, Canto IV.

> ". . . arms on which the standing muscle sloped,
> As slopes a wild brook o'er a little stone,
> Running too vehemently to break upon it." [1]

In short, his poetry of nature is remarkable for careful observation, pictorial effects, sensuous beauty, and for tracing resemblances between her manifestations and certain qualities in his human characters.

An Exponent of the Age. — His poetry is deeply tinged with the new scientific philosophy. The evolution hypothesis affected him powerfully. *In Memoriam* calls man to

> "Move upward, working out the beast."

In the original *Locksley Hall* he was inspired by the prophecies of science for the future, and he

> "Saw the Vision of the world, and all the wonder that would be."

As he realized the birthright which past evolution had bequeathed to man, he exclaimed : —

> "I the heir of all the ages, in the foremost files of time." [2]

The student will find that *Locksley Hall Sixty Years After* (1886), written when Tennyson was seventy-seven years old, gives expression to many of the disappointments of the age : —

> "Evolution ever climbing after some ideal good,
> And Reversion ever dragging Evolution in the mud."

In the earlier *Locksley Hall* Tennyson would not, as in the later, have placed a question mark after these lines : —

> "All diseases quench'd by Science, no man halt, or deaf, or blind;
> Stronger ever born of weaker, lustier body, larger mind?"

---

[1] *Idylls of the King: Geraint and Enid.*   [2] *Locksley Hall.*

In his social ideals, and in the narrowness of his social sympathies, he was least in accord with the spirit of the nineteenth century. The struggles of the French toward freedom seemed to him nothing but

> " The red fool-fury of the Seine." [1]

It is, however, a mistake to say that he was not affected by the social movements of his time. High place is given to the hero who

> " Strove for sixty widow'd years to help his homelier brother men,
>   Served the poor, and built the cottage, raised the school, and drain'd the fen." [2]

In its groping after truth, his poetry is instinct with the ethical spirit of the age, with its sense of struggle for better things. Tennyson rightly describes himself as singing

> " To one clear harp in divers tones,
>   That men may rise on stepping stones
>   Of their dead selves to higher things." [3]

Such sentiments as this not only show the ethical spirit in the progress of the century, but they have also helped to mold this spirit. Readers of Tennyson have felt a fresh incentive to rise through failure "to higher things."

General Characteristics. — Like the early eighteenth century poets, Tennyson took especial pains with the form of his verse. He ranks high for artistic ability displayed in the selection of words, in the elaboration of figures, in securing pictorial effects, and in the metrical structure of his verse. As a metrical artist, he is outranked by few English poets. His shifting accents, bewitching melodies, and combinations of sound which echo the sense, are a

---

[1] *In Memoriam*, CXXVII.   [2] *Locksley Hall*.   [3] *In Memoriam*, I.

source of constant delight to an appreciative ear. We may instance such lines as,

> " The moan of doves in immemorial elms,
>   And murmuring of innumerable bees."[1]

When the thought demands abruptness and strength, we find those qualities in his verse : —

> "Flash brand, fall battle ax upon helm,
>   Fall battle ax, and flash brand!   Let the King reign."[2]

Tennyson is something more than a mere verbal artist or an elegant metrist. He can express noble sentiment. After reading these lines from *The Passing of Arthur*, let the student ask himself if they do not show a dignity of thought and a sublimity of feeling which are lacking in Pope's work : —

> " More things are wrought by prayer
> Than this world dreams of   Wherefore, let thy voice
> Rise like a fountain for me night and day.
> For what are men better than sheep or goats
> That nourish a blind life within the brain,
> If, knowing God, they lift not hands of prayer
> Both for themselves and those who call them friend?
> For so the whole round earth is every way
> Bound by gold chains about the feet of God."

Tennyson is further unlike the poets of the early eighteenth century in his desire to solve the problems of life and to find rest for troubled souls. In his fondness for nature, he shows no kinship with the school of Pope. Tennyson's nature poetry is distinguished for accuracy of observation, for pictorial effects, for appeals to the love of sensuous beauty, and often for subtle comparisons between natural objects and man.

[1] *The Princess*, Canto VII.　　　[2] *The Coming of Arthur*.

It is useless to deny that Tennyson has marked limitations. The spiritual interpretation of nature in Wordsworth, the rush and sweep of Byron and Shelley, the spontaneous flashes of Nature's fire in Burns, the imperious force and subtle revelations of character in Browning, are wanting in Tennyson. He has not the highest type of creative imagination. He often delights to throw into new forms the thoughts of the old classical writers. He is frequently conventional. He has no new message for his age, and he is more often its mouthpiece than its leader. His sympathies are not sufficiently wide for him to feel deep interest in the various social movements of the time.

But his excellences are of a high order. Future historians of English literature will turn to him for the most complete poetic exposition of the thought of the Victorian age, with its scientific spirit, its unrest, and feeling of world pain. Aside from his historical significance, he will continue to hold no mean place in English poetic literature for a rare combination of depth, simplicity, and beauty, in his chosen field of lyric and idyllic poetry.

SUMMARY

The literature of the Victorian age shows in a marked degree the influence of science. No preceding age can point to a body of scientific writers like Darwin, Tyndall, Huxley, and Herbert Spencer. Evolution introduced the idea of orderly development in every phase of life. All conceptions of human progress, of the growth of the individual and of society, underwent a change. Men no longer thought it possible for society to experience a sudden, radical change, such as was hoped for from the French Revolution. Evolution set men to considering all the problems of existence, here and hereafter, from a new point of view. The greater part of the literature is permeated with a new ethical and social spirit, with a sense of the responsibilities of life, and with a desire to aid human progress. The tendency to analysis and dissection is strongly marked.

In describing the prose of the Victorian age, we have considered seven great writers: Macaulay, the brilliant essayist and historian of the material advancement of England; Carlyle, the admirer of the heroic power of great men, and the champion of the spiritual interpretation of life in both philosophy and history; Ruskin, the apostle of the beautiful and of more ideal relations in social life; Arnold, the great analytical critic; Dickens, the novelist of the lower classes, who is noted for his humor, optimism, power of drawing caricatures, and of charming the masses; Thackeray, whose novels are not surpassed in keen, satiric analysis of the upper classes of society; and George Eliot, whose realistic stories of middle-class life are marked by high ethical ideals, by a recognition of the laws of heredity and development in the growth of character, and by agnosticism regarding ultimate human destiny.

In poetry, the age is best represented by three men: by Arnold, who voices the feeling of doubt and unrest; by Browning, who, by his optimistic philosophy, leads to impregnable heights of faith, who analyzes emotions and notes the development of souls as they struggle against opposition from within and without until they reach moments of supreme victory or defeat; by Tennyson, whose careful art mirrors in beautiful verse much of the thought of the age, the influence of science, the unrest, the desire to know the problems of the future as well as to steal occasional glances at beauty for its own sake.

As we stand on the threshold of the twentieth century, we can see that the Victorian age has struggled to find some unitary principle which would reconcile the apparent contradictions between government and the rights of man, duty and inclination, good and evil, life and death. The age has passed the problem unsolved to the twentieth century, but it would be a mistake to say that the preponderating tone in Victorian literature evidences lack of faith in a beneficent solution. Although Tennyson may say : —

> " My will is bondsman to the dark;
> I sit within a helmless bark," [1]

yet he hears at the end a clear call in the language of faith, a tongue that has since the earliest times been very intelligible to the Anglo-Saxon ; and in the beautiful lyric, *Crossing the Bar*, he shows that he awaits a Pilot to direct his helmless bark. The faith of even the coming centuries may be strengthened as they catch the echoes of Browning's refrain : —

> " God's in his heaven —
> All's right with the world." [2]

CONCLUSION

We have traced the major points in the development of a great literature. As we stop at the threshold of the twentieth century, we may pause and for a moment listen to the notes of a younger singer. Let us ask ourselves whether they indicate a peculiar enduring element in the

[1] *In Memoriam*, IV.　　　[2] *Pippa Passes*, Part I.

songs of the Anglo-Saxon race.   In answering this question, it will benefit each one to formulate clearly what he considers the elements of durability in poetry.

> " Yet do the songsmiths
> Quit not their forges ;
> Still on life's anvil
> Forge they the rhyme.
>
> "Lo, with the ancient
> Roots of man's nature
> Twines the eternal
> Passion of song.
>
> " Ever Love fans it,
> Ever Life feeds it,
> Time cannot age it ;
> Death cannot slay.
> .   .   .   .   .
> " God on his throne is
> Eldest of poets :
> Unto his measures
> Moveth the whole."

REQUIRED READINGS FOR CHAPTER X

HISTORICAL

Gardiner,[1] pp. 914–972 ; Underwood-Guest, pp. 557–592 ; Coman and Kendall's *History of England*, pp. 434–494 ; Bright's *History of England*, Period IV. ; Guerber, pp. 320–338 ; Oman's *England in the Nineteenth Century ;* Traill, VI., 111–690.

LITERARY

Macaulay. — Read either the *Essay on Milton* or the *Essay on Addison* (*Eclectic English Classics*) or the selections in Craik, V., 419–433. Read *History of England*, Chap. IX., or Craik, V., 436–441.
What are some of the qualities that cause Macaulay's writings to

---

[1] For full titles, see list at end of Chap. I.

outstrip in popularity other works of a similar nature? What qualities in his style may be commended to young writers? What are his special defects? Contrast his narrative style in Chap. IX. of the *History* with Carlyle's.in *The French Revolution*, Vol. I., Book V., Chap. VI.

Carlyle. — Read the *Essay on Robert Burns* (*Eclectic English Classics*) ; *Sartor Resartus,* Book III., Chap. VI. ; *The French Revolution*, Vol. I., Book V., Chap. VI. Selections may be found in Craik, V., 381–389.

What marked difference in manner of treatment is shown in Macaulay's *Milton* or *Addison* and Carlyle's *Burns?* What was Carlyle's philosophy? What was his message to the age? Point out differences between the humor of Carlyle, of Shakespeare, and of Ben Jonson. What are the striking peculiarities of Carlyle's style?

Ruskin. — In Vol. I., Part II., of *Modern Painters*, read the first part of Chap. I. of Sec. III., Chap. I. of Sec. IV., and Chap. I. of Sec. V., and note Ruskin's surprising accuracy of knowledge in dealing with aspects of the natural world. *Stones of Venice*, Vol. III., Chap. IV., states Ruskin's theory of art and its close relation to morality. Excellent selections from the various works of Ruskin will be found in *An Introduction to the Writings of John Ruskin*, by Vida D. Scudder (Sibley and Ducker's *Students' Series of English Classics*, 259 pp., 50 cents).

How do Ruskin's descriptions rank with those of other English prose writers? What are the marked qualities of his style? Compare his style with that of Macaulay and Carlyle. What is Ruskin's message to the age? Is his philosophy in accord with Macaulay's?

Arnold. — Read *Dover Beach, Memorial Verses, Stanzas in Memory of the Author of "Obermann"* (Crowell's *Students' Edition*).

Is Arnold the poet of exuberant fancy or of reflection? How does his poetry show one phase of nineteenth century thought?

Read in Craik, V., 705–721, the selections from the *Essays in Criticism, Culture and Anarchy*, and *The Study of Celtic Literature*, or Arnold's *Introduction* to Ward's *English Poets*, Vol. I., pp. xvii.–xlvii.

Is Arnold's attitude in criticism that of the controversialist or the calm seeker after truth? Contrast his style of criticism with Ruskin's. What are the main advantages in a prose style like Arnold's?

Dickens. — Read in Craik, V., " Mr. Pickwick on the Ice," 577–583, and " Christmas at the Cratchits'," 587–590. The first works of Dickens to be read are *Pickwick Papers*, *A Christmas Carol*, and *David Copperfield.*

Is there a well-developed plot in *David Copperfield?* Are the characters natural or overdrawn ? Would you like them for friends ? Is the early life of the hero more strongly presented than his later life ? Select a passage of mingled pathos and humor.

Thackeray. — Read *Henry Esmond* and *The English Humorists*. In Craik, V., 567–572, there are two fairly good specimens from these works.

Contrast the manner of treatment in Thackeray's historical novel, *Henry Esmond,* and in Scott's historical romance, *Ivanhoe.* Thackeray says : " The best humor is that which contains most humanity — that which is flavored throughout with tenderness and kindness." Would this serve as a definition of Thackeray's own style of humor? State definitely how he differs from Dickens in portraying character. Of all the prose authors thus far read, whose style merits most commendation from most points of view?

George Eliot. — Read *Silas Marner* (*Eclectic English Classics*), and selections in Craik, V., 671–677.

In what does the chief strength of *Silas Marner* consist, — in the plot, the characters, or the descriptions? Does the ethical purpose of this novel grow naturally out of the story? Is the inner life or only the outward appearance of the characters revealed? Wherein do they show growth?

Browning. — Read *Rabbi Ben Ezra, Abt Vogler, Home Thoughts from Abroad, Prospice,* which will be found in French's *Selections from Browning* (A. Lovell and Co.).

Define Browning's creed as found in *Rabbi Ben Ezra.* Do these poems exhibit any metrical skill? Compare *Prospice* with Tennyson's *Crossing the Bar.* What qualities in Browning entitle him to be ranked as a great poet?

Tennyson. — Read *The Poet, The Palace of Art, Ulysses, Maud,* XVIII. and XXII., *In Memoriam,* XLI., LIV.–LVII., and CXXXI., *Crossing the Bar,* and, from *The Idylls of the King,* read " The Passing of Arthur " (Palgrave's edition of Tennyson's *Lyrical Poems*).

In *The Palace of Art,* study carefully the stanzas from XIV. to XXIII., which are illustrative of Tennyson's characteristic style of description. Compare *Locksley Hall* with *Locksley Hall Sixty Years After,* and note the difference in thought and metrical form. Does the later poem show a gain over the earlier? Compare Tennyson's nature poetry with that of Keats and Wordsworth. To what is chiefly due the pleasure in reading Tennyson's poetry : to the imagery, form, meter, thought? What idea of his faith do you gain from *In Memoriam* and *The Passing of Arthur ?* In what is Tennyson the poetic exponent of the age?

WORKS FOR CONSULTATION AND FURTHER STUDY

(OPTIONAL)

McCarthy's *History of Our Own Times*.
Walker's *The Age of Tennyson* and *The Greater Victorian Poets*.
Frederic Harrison's *Early Victorian Literature*.
Saintsbury's *A History of Nineteenth Century Literature*.
Oliphant's *The Victorian Age of English Literature*.
Morley's *Literature in the Age of Victoria*.
Craik's *English Prose Selections*, Vol. V., pp. 373–771.
Gosse's *Modern English Literature*, pp. 334–385.
Scudder's *Social Ideals in English Letters*, pp. 114–318.
Stedman's *Victorian Poets*.
Victorian Literature in Dowden's *Transcripts and Studies*.
The Scientific Movement and Literature, Mr. Tennyson and Mr. Browning, and *George Eliot* in Dowden's *Studies in Literature*.

Symonds's *Elizabethan and Victorian Literature* in *Fortnightly Review*, Vol. 51, or *Living Age*, Vol. 180.

Myers's *Modern Poets and the Meaning of Life* in *Nineteenth Century*, Vol. 33.

Bagehot's *Literary Studies*. (Thackeray, Dickens, Macaulay, Tennyson, and Browning.)

Bayne's *Lessons from My Masters*. (Carlyle, Tennyson, and Ruskin.)

Zapp's *Three Great Teachers of Our Time*. (Carlyle, Tennyson, and Ruskin.)

Hutton's *Essays, Theological and Literary*. (Browning, Arnold, and Tennyson.)

Hutton's *Modern Guides of English Thought in Matters of Faith*. (Carlyle, Arnold, and George Eliot.)

Cooke's *Poets and Problems*. (Ruskin, Browning, and Tennyson.)

Masson's *British Novelists and Their Styles*. (Thackeray and Dickens.)

Anne Thackeray Ritchie's *Records of Tennyson, Ruskin, and Browning*.

Minto's *Manual of English Prose Literature*. (Macaulay and Carlyle.)
Trevelyan's *Life and Letters of Macaulay*.
Morrison's *Life of Macaulay*.
Froude's *Thomas Carlyle*.
Garnett's *Life of Carlyle*.

Nichol's *Life of Carlyle*.

Collingwood's *The Life and Works of John Ruskin*.

Mather's *John Ruskin: His Life and Teachings*.

Ruskin's *Præterita: Scenes of My Past Life*.

Waldstein's *The Work of John Ruskin: Its Influence upon Modern Thought and Life*.

Scudder's *An Introduction to the Writings of John Ruskin*.

Saintsbury's *Matthew Arnold*.

Introduction to Gates's *Prose Selections from Matthew Arnold*.

Arnold's *Letters*, edited by Russell.

Swinburne's *Essays and Studies*. (Matthew Arnold.)

Foster's *The Life of Charles Dickens*.

Ward's *Life of Dickens*.

Marzials's *Life of Dickens*.

Trollope's *Life of Thackeray*.

Merivale and Marzials's *Life of Thackeray*.

Cross's *George Eliot's Life, as Related in Her Letters and Journal*.

Oscar Browning's *Life of George Eliot*.

Cooke's *George Eliot: A Critical Study of Her Life, Writings, and Philosophy*.

Blind's *George Eliot*.

Brown's *The Ethics of George Eliot's Works*.

Sharp's *Life of Browning*.

Orr's *Life and Letters of Browning*.

Orr's *A Handbook to the Works of Robert Browning*.

Symon's *Introduction to the Study of Browning*.

Corson's *An Introduction to the Study of Robert Browning's Poetry*.

Berdoe's *Browning's Message to His Times*.

Berdoe's *The Browning Cyclopedia*.

Alfred, Lord Tennyson, A Memoir, by his son.

Waugh's *Alfred, Lord Tennyson: A Study of His Life and Work*.

Ainger's *Tennyson*, in the *Dictionary of National Biography*. (The best short life.)

Brooke's *Tennyson: His Art and Relation to Modern Life*.

Van Dyke's *The Poetry of Tennyson*.

Luce's *Handbook to the Works of Alfred, Lord Tennyson*.

APPENDIX

SUPPLEMENTARY LIST OF MINOR AUTHORS AND THEIR CHIEF WORKS

1400-1558

John Lydgate (1370?–1451?) : *Falls of Princes.* Thomas Occleve (1370?–1450?) : *Mother of God; Governail of Princes.* James I. of Scotland (1394–1437) : *The King's Quair.* Sir John Fortescue (1394?–1476?) : *Difference between an Absolute and Limited Monarchy. The Paston Letters* (1422–1509). Stephen Hawes (d. 1523?) : *Pastime of Pleasure.* John Skelton (1460?– 1529) : *Bowge of Court; Philip Sparrow.* Alex. Barclay (1475?– 1552) : *Ship of Fools.* Sir Thomas More (1478–1535) : *Utopia; History of Edward V. and Richard III.* Hugh Latimer (1485?– 1555) : *Sermon on the Ploughers.* Sir David Lindsay (1490– 1555) : *Satire of the Three Estates.*

1558-1603

Prose Writers. — Roger Ascham (1515–1568) : *The Scholemaster.* Raphael Holinshed (d. 1580?) : *Chronicles of England, Scotland, and Ireland.* John Stow (1525?–1605) : *Survey of London.* Sir Thomas North (1535?–1601?) : *Translation of Plutarch's Lives.* Richard Hakluyt (1552?–1616) : *Voyages.* George Puttenham (d. 1590?) : *Art of English Poesie.* Stephen Gosson (1555–1624) : *The School of Abuse.*

Poets and Dramatists. — George Gascoigne (1525?–1577) : *The Steele Glas.* John Lyly (1554?–1606) : *Alexander and Campaspe* (prose. For his *Euphues*, see p. 117). Thomas Kyd (1557?– 1595?) : *The Spanish Tragedy.* Thomas Lodge (1558?–1625) : *Phillis* (for his novel, see p. 276). William Warner (1558?–1609) :

Albion's England. George Peele (1558?–1597?) : *David and Bethsabe.* George Chapman (1559?–1634) : *Translation of Homer.* Robert Greene (1560?–1592) : *The Honourable History of Friar Bacon and Friar Bungay.* Thomas Dekker (1570?–1641?) : *Old Fortunatus.* John Donne (1573–1631) : *Poems.* Cyril Tourneur (1575?–1626) : *The Revenger's Tragedy.* Thomas Heywood (d. 1650?) : *A Woman Killed with Kindness.* John Marston (1575?–1634) : *Antonio and Mellida.*

1603-1660

Prose Writers. — Robert Burton (1577–1640) : *The Anatomy of Melancholy.* Sir Thomas Browne (1605–1682) : *Religio Medici ; Urn Burial.* Richard Baxter (1615–1691) : *The Saints' Everlasting Rest.* John Evelyn (1620–1706) : *Diary* (begins 1641, ends 1697).

Poets and Dramatists. — Thomas Middleton (1570?–1627) : *The Changeling.* Phineas Fletcher (1582–1650?) : *The Purple Island.* Philip Massinger (1583–1640) : *A New Way to Pay Old Debts.* William Drummond (1585–1649) : *Sonnets ; The Cypresse Grove* (prose). Giles Fletcher (1588?–1623) : *Christ's Victory and Triumph.* George Wither (1588–1667) : *Juvenilia.* George Herbert (1593–1633) : *The Temple.* James Shirley (1596–1666) : *The Traitor.* Sir William Davenant (1606–1668) : *Gondibert.* Edmund Waller (1606–1687) : *Poems ; Song* — " Go, lovely Rose." Richard Crashaw (1613?–1649?) : *Steps to the Temple ; The Delights of the Muses.* Sir John Denham (1615–1669) : *Cooper's Hill.* Abraham Cowley (1618–1667) : *Anacreontiques.* Andrew Marvell (1621–1678) : *The Garden.*

1660-1700

Prose Writers. — Sir William Temple (1628–1699) : *Essays.* Isaac Barrow (1630–1677) : *Sermons.* John Tillotson (1630–1694) : *Sermons.* Samuel Pepys (1633–1703) : *Diary* (1660 to 1669). Robert South (1634–1716) : *Sermons.* Aphra Behn (1640–1689) : *Oroonoko.* Jeremy Collier (1650–1726) : *Short View of*

the Immorality and Profaneness of the Stage. Richard Bentley
(1662–1742) : *Epistles of Phalaris.*

Dramatists of the Restoration. — George Etherege (1635?–
1691?) : *The Man of Mode.* William Wycherley (1640–1715) :
The Plain Dealer. Thomas Shadwell (1642?–1692) : *Epsom
Wells.* Thomas Otway (1652–1685) : *Venice Preserved.* John
Vanbrugh (1666?–1726) : *The Confederacy.* William Congreve
(1670–1729) : *Love for Love.* Colley Cibber (1671–1757) :
The Careless Husband. George Farquhar (1678–1707) : *The
Beaux' Stratagem.*

1700-1740

Prose Writers. — Gilbert Burnet (1643–1715) : *History of My
Own Time.* Francis Atterbury (1662–1732) : *Sermons.* John
Arbuthnot (1667–1735) ; *The History of John Bull.* Lord
Bolingbroke (1678–1751) : *Letter to Sir William Windham.*
Bishop Berkeley (1685–1753) : *Alciphron or the Minute Philoso-
pher.* Lady Mary Wortley Montagu (1689–1762) : *Letters.*
Bishop Butler (1692–1752) : *Analogy of Natural and Revealed
Religion.* William Warburton (1698–1779) : *The Divine Legation
of Moses.*

Poets. — Matthew Prior (1664–1721) : *Shorter Poems.* Isaac
Watts (1674–1748) : *Psalms and Hymns.* Thomas Parnell (1679–
1718) : *The Night-Piece on Death ; The Hermit.* John Gay
(1685–1732) : *Fables; Beggar's Opera.* Allan Ramsay (1686–
1758) : *The Gentle Shepherd.*

1740-1780

Prose Writers. — Gilbert White (1720–1793) : *Natural His-
tory of Selborne.* William Robertson (1721–1793) : *History of
the Reign of Charles V.* Adam Smith (1723–1790) : *Wealth of
Nations.* Sir Joshua Reynolds (1723–1792) : *Discourses on
Painting.* Thomas Warton (1728–1790) : *History of English
Poetry.* Sir Philip Francis (1740–1818) : *Letters of Junius.*
Richard Brinsley Sheridan (1751–1816) : *The Rivals; The School
for Scandal.* Fanny Burney (1752–1840) : *Evelina.*

Poets. — Edward Young (1681–1765) : *Night Thoughts*. Charles
Wesley (1708–1788) : *Hymns*. Mark Akenside (1721–1770) :
Pleasures of Imagination. James Beattie (1735–1803) : *The
Minstrel*. Robert Fergusson (1750–1774) : *Braid Claith; Ode
to the Gowdspink*. Thomas Chatterton (1752–1770) : *Rowley
Poems*.

1780-1837

Philosophers. — William Paley (1743–1805) : *Natural Theol-
ogy*. Jeremy Bentham (1748–1832) : *Principles of Morals and
Legislation*. William Godwin (1756–1836) : *Inquiry concerning
Political Justice*. Thomas Robert Malthus (1766–1834) : *Essay
on the Principle of Population*. David Ricardo (1772–1823) :
Principles of Political Economy. James Mill (1773–1836) :
Analysis of the Human Mind.

Historians. — John Lingard (1771–1851) : *History of England*.
Henry Hallam (1777–1859) : *Constitutional History of England*.
Sir William Napier (1785–1860) : *History of the Peninsular War*.

Essayists. — William Cobbett (1762–1835) : *Rural Rides in
England*. Sydney Smith (1771–1845) : *Letters of Peter Plymley*.
Francis Jeffrey (1773–1850) : *Essays*. William Hazlitt (1778–
1830) : *Lectures on the English Poets*. Leigh Hunt (1784–1859) :
Essays. John Wilson (1785–1854) : *Noctes Ambrosianæ*. John
Gibson Lockhart (1794–1854) : *Life of Sir Walter Scott*.

Novelists and Dramatists. — William Beckford (1759–1844) :
Vathek. Ann Radcliffe (1764–1822) : *The Mysteries of Udolpho*.
Maria Edgeworth (1767–1849) : *Castle Rackrent*. Jane Porter
(1776–1850) : *Scottish Chiefs*. James Sheridan Knowles (1784–
1862) : *The Hunchback; The Love Chase*. Thomas Love Peacock (1785–1866) : *Nightmare Abbey*. Mary Russell Mitford
(1787–1855) : *Our Village*.

Poets. — George Crabbe (1754–1832) : *The Borough*. William
Blake (1757–1827) : *Poetical Sketches; Songs of Innocence*.
Joanna Baillie (1762–1851) : *Poems*. James Hogg (1770–1835) :
Queen's Wake. Thomas Campbell (1777–1844) : *The Pleasures
of Hope*. Thomas Moore (1779–1852) : *Irish Melodies; Lalla*

Rookh. Ebenezer Elliott (1781–1849) : *Corn-Law Rhymes.*
Bryan W. Procter (1787–1874) : *English Songs.* John Keble
(1792–1866) : *The Christian Year.* Felicia Hemans (1793–
1835) : *Songs of the Affections.* Thomas Hood (1799–1845) :
The Song of the Shirt; The Bridge of Sighs. Winthrop Praed
(1802–1839) : *The Season ; The Letter of Advice.* Thomas Bed-
does (1803–1849) : *Lyrics* from *Death's Jest Book* and from *The
Bride's Tragedy.*

1837 -

Philosophers and Scientists. — Sir William Hamilton (1788–
1856) : *Lectures on Metaphysics and Logic.* Michael Faraday
(1791–1867) : *Experimental Researches.* Sir Charles Lyell (1797–
1875) : *Principles of Geology; Antiquity of Man.* John Henry
Newman (1801–1890) : *Apologia pro Vita Sua.* John Stuart Mill
(1806–1873) : *System of Logic; Utilitarianism.* George Henry
Lewes (1817–1878) : *A Biographical History of Philosophy;
Problems of Life and Mind.* Sir Henry Maine (1822–1888) :
Ancient Law ; Village Communities. George J. Romanes (1848–
1894) : *Mental Evolution in Animals and Man.*

Historians. — Henry Hart Milman (1791–1868) : *History of
Latin Christianity down to the Death of Pope Nicholas V.* George
Grote (1794–1871) : *History of Greece.* James Anthony Froude
(1818–1894) : *History of England from the Fall of Wolsey to the
Defeat of the Spanish Armada.* Henry Thomas Buckle (1821–
1862) : *History of Civilization.* Edward Augustus Freeman (1823–
1892) : *The History of the Norman Conquest.* William Stubbs
(1825–   ) : *The Constitutional History of England in its Origin
and Development.* Samuel Rawson Gardiner (1829–   ) : *History of England from the Accession of James I. to the Outbreak of
Civil War,* 1603–1642 ; *History of the Great Civil War,* 1642–
1649; *History of the Commonwealth and the Protectorate,* 1649–
1660. John Richard Green (1837–1883) : *A Short History of the
English People.* William Edward Hartpole Lecky (1838–   ) :
History of England in the Eighteenth Century.

Critics and Essayists — Walter Bagehot (1826–1877) : *Physics* *and Politics.* Leslie Stephen (1832–) : *Hours in a Library.* Algernon Charles Swinburne (1837–) : *Essays and Studies; Miscellanies.* Walter Pater (1839–1894) : *Studies in the History of the Renaissance; Marius the Epicurean.* John Addington Symonds (1840–1893) : *The History of the Renaissance in Italy.*

Novelists. — Edward Bulwer, Lord Lytton (1803–1873) : *Last Days of Pompeii.* Charles Lever (1806–1872) : *Charles O'Malley.* Elizabeth C. Gaskell (1810–1865) : *Cranford.* Charles Reade (1814–1884) : *The Cloister and the Hearth.* Anthony Trollope (1815–1882) : *Last Chronicle of Barset.* Charlotte Brontë (1816–1855) : *Jane Eyre.* Charles Kingsley (1819–1875) : *Hypatia; Westward ho!* Wilkie Collins (1824–1889) : *The Moonstone.* Richard D. Blackmore (1825–1900) : *Lorna Doone.* Dinah Maria Craik (1826–1887) : *John Halifax, Gentleman.* George Meredith (1828–) : *Diana of the Crossways; The Egoist; The Ordeal of Richard Feverel.* Thomas Hardy (1840–) : *Far from the Madding Crowd.* William Black (1841–1898) : *A Daughter of Heth.* Robert Louis Stevenson (1850–1894) : *David Balfour.* Mrs. Humphry Ward (1851–) : *Robert Elsmere.* Hall Caine (1853–) : *The Manxman.* Rudyard Kipling (1865–) : *Jungle Books.*

Poets. — Elizabeth Barrett Browning (1809–1861) : *Sonnets from the Portuguese.* Edward Fitzgerald (1809–1883) : *Rubaiyat of Omar Khayyam* (translation). Arthur Hugh Clough (1819–1861) : *Qua Cursum Ventus; Easter Day, Naples.* Dante Gabriel Rossetti (1828–1882) : *The King's Tragedy; The Blessed Damozel; Sonnets.* Christina Rossetti (1830–1894) : *The Goblin Market; Time Flies.* Jean Ingelow (1830–1897) : *Divided; The High Tide on the Coast of Lincolnshire.* Edwin Arnold (1832–) : *The Light of Asia.* William Morris (1834–1896) : *The Earthly Paradise.* Alfred Austin (1835–) : *Lyrics.* Algernon Charles Swinburne (1837–) : *Atalanta in Calydon; The Garden of Proserpine.* William Watson (1858–) : *Wordsworth's Grave and Other Poems; England my Mother.* Rudyard Kipling (1865–) : *The Seven Seas; The Recessional.*

INDEX

Diacritic marks.—VOWELS : ā in lāte, ă in făt, â in câre, ä in fär, a̤ in fa̤ll ; ē in mē, ĕ in mĕt, ȩ in vȩil, ẽ in tẽrm, ê in thêre ; ī in fīne, ĭ in tĭn, ï in polïce ; ō in nōte, ŏ ɪn nŏt ō in fôr, ǫ in wǫlf ; ū in tūne, ŭ in nŭt, ṳ in rṳde, ʉ in fʉll ; ȳ in hȳmn. CONSONANTS : ç in çent, e in ean ; ġ in ġem, g̃ in g̃et ; s̤ in has̤ ; t͟h in wit͟h.